Valentin SEROV

Valentin Serov. Self-portrait. 1885

Valentin SEROV

Paintings

Graphic Works

Stage Designs

HARRY N. ABRAMS, INC., PUBLISHERS, NEW YORK

AURORA ART PUBLISHERS, LENINGRAD

Selection by
DMITRY SARABYANOV and GRIGORY ARBUZOV

Introduction by
DMITRY SARABYANOV

Catalogue and Biographical Outline by
GRIGORY ARBUZOV

Designed by
IRINA PTAKHOVA

Library of Congress Catalogue Card Number: 80-68475
International Standard Book Number: 0-8109-1605-3

Created by Aurora Art Publishers,
Leningrad, for joint publication of Aurora
and Harry N. Abrams, Inc., New York

Printed and bound in Austria

CONTENTS

To assess the creative endeavor of a major artist is to ask what makes him great, what is his main contribution to art. The answers to that question may vary widely. Some artists discover new facets of life, facets previously inaccessible to art. Others develop an entirely new approach to the painting of their time and blaze a trail to new painterly techniques. Still others consummate a whole trend in the evolution of art. Valentin Alexandrovich Serov, who stands apart in the Russian painting of the late nineteenth and early twentieth centuries, was all three — a great reformer, a pace-setter and an artist who linked two important periods in Russian painting.

Serov began his career in the 1880s, when the realist artists of the Society for Circulating Art Exhibitions were at the pinnacle of their success. His first officially exhibited pictures, *Girl with Peaches* and *Girl in the Sunlight*, were done in 1887–88. Several years earlier his teacher Ilya Repin, an active member of the Society, had displayed his *Religious Procession in Kursk Province*, followed by the canvases *They Did Not Expect Him* and *Ivan the Terrible and His Son Ivan*. The foremost Russian history painter of the time, Vasily Surikov, completed his most outstanding creation, *The Boyarina Morozova*, in the same year that Serov produced his *Girl with Peaches*.

When, on the other hand, the artist was doing his last masterpieces, *The Rape of Europa* and *Odysseus and Nausicaä*, Russian art was striving not to recreate real-life scenes, but to paraphrase life, seeing in the artistic image a self-sustained artistic reality. It was now concerned not so much with analyzing the relationship between man and society as with finding a new symbolism, a new mythology and poetry to reflect the modern world.

This transition to a new set of creative principles that were to become the cornerstone of twentieth-century art spanned the end of the nineteenth and the dawn of the twentieth century, and Serov was fated to be the artist who carried that transition through. It can even be said that the road traveled by Russian art in the course of twenty-five years—from the late 1880s to the early 1910s—was the road from *Girl with Peaches* to the *Portrait of Ida Rubinstein*.

Without violating any of his teachers' traditions, the young artist initiated a new method which was to evolve further in the work of most of the artists of his generation. On that road he was sometimes overtaken and even outstripped by others. When this happened, Serov would size up those who had forged ahead, evaluating them soberly, often skeptically. But the skepticism would pass, and he would feel obliged to take up his brush again to keep from falling behind the times. Serov did not want to stand in anyone's way; he was deeply conscious of his duty to Russian painting, to his school, his teachers and his pupils. He spurned the privileges usually accorded to a *maître*. He was no *maître*, he was a toiler; in fact, to a certain degree he was even a pupil. It was by dint of great effort that he lived up to his role as a leader. Serov was an artist who honed his extraordinary talent on the whetstone of prodigious industry.

Serov was not alone in his search for new trends in art. His life was marked by a long-standing friendship with Mikhail Vrubel, Konstantin Korovin, Alexander Benois, and other artists from the World of Art group. With many of them he shared common creative interests. This is especially true of Vrubel, with whom the artist was closely associated in his youth. The two studied together and together dreamed of steering new courses in art. Their aspirations, however, did not entirely coincide. Vrubel broke with the traditions of the Itinerants and made an abrupt and unhesitating turn in another direction — to symbolism, to a new style of painting, thereby dooming himself to temporary isolation. Vrubel developed rapidly, changing to another manner with the resolve of a genius, a true revolutionary in art. Serov, on the other hand, proceeded cautiously, weighing every step along the difficult road ahead before finally combining the old with the new.

Konstantin Korovin was a close friend of Serov's in the 1880s and 1890s, and at the beginning of the twentieth century he became his colleague on the staff of the Moscow School of Painting, Sculpture and Architecture. To the end of his days, though, Korovin never once stepped beyond the principles that he and Serov had evolved together. This was not the case with Serov, who outgrew these principles and went on to new discoveries.

The very juxtaposition of the three names, Vrubel, Serov and Korovin—artists who, though bound by ties of friendship, were so unlike in their creative aspirations—reveals the complexity of Russia's art scene at the turn of the century. Their various paths of development do not sufficiently reflect all the diversity of trends or personalities involved. Serov's teacher Repin, after achieving unqualified success in the 1880s, attained new heights in the early 1900s with his huge group portrait of *The State Council in Formal Session* and a series of brilliant studies for it. In the 1890s landscape painting reached its zenith in the works of the Itinerants, with Isaac Levitan summing up its evolution, as it were, and at the same time opening new horizons in the art of painting. This was also a time when new trends and groups began to crop up which either coexisted or replaced one another; the World of Art, for example, was followed by the Blue Rose group and later by the Jack of Diamonds group. All these activities chronologically coincided with the creative endeavor of Serov.

It was a versatile endeavor in that its various component parts shared an affinity with one trend or another. Those of the Moscow painters who began their move towards Impressionism back in the 1880s admired above all his early sunlit canvases, his rural landscapes of the 1890s, his ability to see the poetic side of unpretentious, everyday phenomena and to perceive beauty in the commonplace.

At times Serov's art closely resembled that of another group of Moscow painters, nicknamed the junior Itinerants. Continuing in the realist traditions of the 1870s and 1880s, these artists, each in his own way, diversified their painting either by turning to modern themes and heroes, as did Nikolai Kasatkin and Sergei Korovin, or by perfecting their painting techniques. Sergei Ivanov, for instance, lent expressiveness to his images through laconic composition, precise draftsmanship and subtle color gradations. Abram Arkhipov integrated genre and landscape painting into contemplative, lyrical compositions: his peasant scenes are devoid of conflict or human collisions, reflecting the beauty of everyday life — a beauty perceived by the artist where others had never even sought it. It is this quality that particularly impressed Serov.

Other facets of Serov's art link him with other lines of development in the Russian painting of those years. In the late 1890s Repin's pupils in the St. Petersburg Academy of Arts, particularly Boris Kustodiev and Philip Maliavin, emulated their teacher, and they cultivated a free painterly manner and a sweeping, resolute brushstroke that set the stage for the decorative trend in early twentieth-century painting. This was the style seemingly adopted by the Serov of the 1890s and early 1900s, who enriched it with his own striking individuality.

Serov joined the World of Art group when it was created, in the late 1890s, and soon gained undisputed authority among its members. What united them all was a predilection for style, monumental scope and consummate craftsmanship.

Serov's art was an organic blend of tradition and innovation. That is why those who cherished the traditions of nineteenth-century Russian painting were gratified by his deeply realistic, at times almost Repinesque, approach to portraiture. As for the innovators, they accepted him as one of their own because he constantly sought that which had yet to be achieved. These two facets of Serov's work do not, however, indicate any eclecticism on his part. He was a versatile artist because he stood at the intersection of differing trends, because at that decisive turning-point in the evolution of art he did not forget the heritage of the past, but tried to utilize that heritage, to lend it new life and give it a new interpretation. It is precisely this addressing himself "to all" that made Serov the leader of an art trend, a scrupulous guardian of the interests of true art; and an artist who championed the new without discarding the old, thus easing the way for others. In this lies the secret of the role played by Serov as leader of the Moscow school of painting. Among his pupils at the Moscow Art School were such dissimilar masters as Kuzma Petrov-Vodkin, Nikolai Ulyanov, Pavel Kuznetsov, Martiros Saryan, Ilya Mashkov, Mikhail Larionov and Konstantin Yuon. Each could profit by Serov's experience, his wise advice, his example and his characteristic awareness of an artist's lofty mission.

Serov was immersed in an artistic environment from childhood. He was born in 1865 into the family of a famous Russian composer and music critic. His mother was also a composer and a pianist. Sharing the democratic ideals of the revolutionary writers of the 1860s, Chernyshevsky and Dobroliubov, she worked hard to popularize musical culture among the masses.

Until 1871, when his father died, the Serovs' apartment in St. Petersburg was a popular meeting place for famous painters and sculptors — Nikolai Gay, Mark Antokolsky, and Ilya Repin. These contacts continued abroad too.

Serov began to draw and to take drawing lessons at a very early age — first in Munich, where the family went after his father's death, then in Paris, where on Antokolsky's advice he was "delivered into the hands" of Repin, who not only taught, but also befriended his young colleague. Repin was in France at the time on a postgraduate assignment from the St. Petersburg Academy of Arts, and Serov began attending his studio. Repin made the boy draw from gypsum models and paint in color from nature.

On the family's return to Russia in 1875, these studies with Repin were broken off. They were renewed after a few years, in 1878, when Repin settled in Moscow, and became especially serious and systematic. Several sketches have survived which show how the teacher strove to foster in his pupil a painter's spontaneous perception of nature by training his hand and eye to capture on canvas various objects differing in form, texture or color. Repin did not attempt to mold Serov's talent with a system of forcible rules. Serov simply worked side by side with Repin; he would often sit near his teacher and watch him paint. At times they worked on one and the same model. Repin was doing several large compositions at the time, and Serov assisted him in those ventures. He drew the barn that can be seen in the background of Repin's *Send-off for a Recruit*, painted an oil portrait of the famous hunchback, one of Repin's favorite models and the central figure in his *Religious Procession in Kursk Province*. Finally, in 1880, Serov accompanied his teacher to Zaporozhye to gather material for the *Zaporozhye Cossacks* and together with Repin did many pencil sketches of typical local scenes.

Soon, however, their joint work came to an end. Repin concluded that he had nothing more to offer to the young Serov and decided to send him on to the St. Petersburg Academy, to Pavel Chistiakov. The latter, in the opinion of many contemporaries, was the only man in the Academy capable of teaching a novice the basic principles of art.

Serov enrolled in the Academy in 1880. This was for him the beginning of an eventful existence: studies in the Academy, painting together with Vrubel and Derviz, his fellow-pupils from Chistiakov's class, in a jointly rented studio, and discussing art and its mission during evenings spent at the house of his maternal aunt, Adelaida Simonovich, an educationist and advocate of kindergartens in Russia; with her daughters Serov maintained a long-standing friendship.

Chistiakov was a brilliant and systematic interpreter and teacher of the laws of form in painting and drawing. He tried to show his pupils how the three-dimensional world can be transformed on a two-dimensional piece of canvas into an artistic phenomenon. He instilled in Serov the strict, demanding and loving attitude to professional skill that was to become the bedrock of Serov's art.

The young student worked tirelessly. He painted nude models, his friends, scenes of nature — in a word, everything that surrounded him. He devoted much effort to the perfection of his drawing, combining the strict, constructive system of draftsmanship taught by Chistiakov with the pictorial quality of Repin's graphic works. Serov's self-portrait of 1885 was an attempt to create an artistic image through the expressiveness of line and hatching. The barely designated figure, the white background and the dense shading around the head conspire to focus the viewer's attention on the face. The meaningful expression in the eyes, where one reads a far from youthful self-discipline, a deep concentration, estrangement and withdrawal into himself, but above all the power of a unique mind and a somewhat precocious spiritual maturity, reflects not only the young Serov's inner world but also his awareness of what it means to be a creative artist.

The rigid formality that prevailed in the Academy was alien to Serov, and the only consideration that kept him from resigning was his faith in Chistiakov. He was extremely critical of the established system of teaching. In a letter to his fiancée (1885) he wrote: "I am very happy to be able to disregard their medals (you have no idea how pernicious are all these stratagems, all this chasing after medals). I can work on my own in any way I please, entrusting myself only to Repin and Chistiakov."*

The first flowering of Serov's talent relates to the 1880s. Such an early rise to the top is almost unparalleled in the history of art. The two works that brought Serov into the limelight, *Girl with Peaches* and *Girl in the Sunlight*, were done when he had barely turned twenty. The master later spoke of them with special affection and, according to Igor Grabar,** considered these early canvases unexcelled by any of his subsequent works. This was, of course, an exaggeration, but one has to admit that Serov's *Girls* were imbued with an absolutely unique quality, one that the artist never captured again. The period when Serov was carefree and happy, searching for and painting "only the joys of life," did not last long. These were Serov's words, and in recent times they have come to be used to define an entire school of Russian, and especially Moscow, painting. The early Korovin was a typical representative of this school; in the 1880s a joyful perception of nature came to characterize the art of Levitan; a tender lyricism marks the early paintings of Arkhipov and Alexei Stepanov, also of the Moscow school. All these artists sought to divorce their art from preconceived notions, from an analytical approach to life. Lyricism was becoming the main tendency in Moscow painting, and Serov with his program of the "joys of life" was its most consistent spokesman.

---

* See: *Serov's Correspondence,* 1937, p. 81 (for full information on sources quoted in the text see pp. 380–383).
** See: Grabar, *Serov,* 1914, p. 76.

Of course, the common objectives pursued by the new generation of artists cannot alone explain the creation of Serov's early masterpieces. An exceptional sequence of events had to occur for them to have been produced at all. Serov left the Academy, and this filled him with an exhilarating sense of freedom from all manner of rules and regulations. He went abroad, and there saw for himself the unfading beauty of the Old Masters, forever succumbing to their irresistible influence. His absorption with the painting of the great Dutchmen, Spaniards and Italians bred in Serov a desire to portray the beauty of man and express a love of life. At the same time the young artist began paying more and more attention to the problem of skill, to the "high craftsmanship" that characterized the Old Masters. Venice, with its divine architecture and fairy-tale canals, simply went to Serov's head. He felt himself at the height of his powers. He was surrounded by friends and loved ones. Finally, he had recently, in 1885, done an inconspicuous little study in Odessa entitled *Bullocks*: the harmony achieved in the color scheme of that piece filled him with satisfaction and led him to understand what an artist should aspire to.

Also conducive to the young artist's joyful mood was the environment he moved in, the friends he associated with and the creative atmosphere that prevailed in Abramtsevo, the country estate of Savva Mamontov, the famous patron of the arts. This remarkable house in the picturesque Moscow countryside was where many innovations in late nineteenth-century art were conceived. Serov had stayed here with the Mamontov family for long periods as a child: it was an ideal place for bringing his outstanding talents into play. Amateur theatricals were a favorite pastime in Abramtsevo, and Serov himself played a variety of roles. Under the benevolent guidance of his elders—Repin, Victor Vasnetsov, Vasily Polenov—and the beneficial influence of communion with his coevals—Vrubel, Korovin, Mikhail Nesterov—the young Serov's gift for painting blossomed and matured. It was here also that he came to love the central Russian landscape, the rural scene, the homely peasant horses and the plain peasant faces.

Another haven of refuge for the young artist was Domotkanovo inTver province, the country estate of Vladimir Derviz, an Academy friend who had married one of Serov's cousins, Nadezhda Simonovich. Serov spent many happy days here, lulled by the unhurried rhythm of rural life, inhaling the musty smells of autumn and admiring its even gray hues.

The joyful mood engendered in Serov by Abramtsevo and Domotkanovo helped the artist create his most significant early pieces. Almost all of Serov's works of this period, from the studies of the mid-1880s to the three masterpieces, the two *Girls* and *Overgrown Pond*, painted at about the same time in Domotkanovo, are imbued with the same feeling. Serov immerses himself, as it were, in the world's beauty, his colors are saturated with light and air, soaked by the sun and radiating joy. He contemplates this beauty with quiet admiration. Each picture is long in the making; he has his models pose for long hours, yet what is revealed on canvas is the very first impression of what he sees.

The model for *Girl with Peaches* was Mamontov's twelve-year-old daughter Vera, who sat for the artist in Abramtsevo, for *Girl in the Sunlight* — the artist's cousin Masha Simonovich in Domotkanovo. The two girls turned out to resemble one another, but most of the "blame" for that must go to Serov himself who wanted above all to see in them the beauty of youth. He sought in these pictures a gentle, contemplative expressiveness. He did not intend the portraits to provoke thoughts on the contradictions and complexities of life. "Only the joys of life." And it is this that sets Serov apart from his predecessors and his teachers. Repin's portrait of Modest Moussorgsky, done six years before *Girl with Peaches*, is also suffused with light, but here this only serves to render with the utmost veracity the aspect and condition of the composer going through a terminal illness. Behind the fleeting moment of human existence captured by the artist there looms a world choked by insoluble problems, a world whose only promise to man is suffering and perdition. With Serov, though, light, air, joy and youth are beautiful *per se*;

they are the ultimate purpose of the creative act, and it is in this above all that the novelty of Serov's approach and the originality of his artistic concept manifest themselves.

The *Girls* were painted from living persons, yet Serov did not refer to the paintings as portraits or give them the names of the models. This was hardly accidental, because the decisive factor was not the uniqueness of the image, not the individuality of the sitter, but Serov's overall program. In addition, these were not portraits in the customary meaning of the word. Serov's models are inseparable from their environment. One girl merges into a single entity with the old house and the garden visible through the windows, the other has settled down, as if for good, in the shade of a tree in a sleepy corner of an old, unkempt park. Neither can be imagined in other surroundings, because then we would have different pictures carrying different messages.

In *Girl with Peaches*, one actually senses a momentary stillness, a pregnant calm, after which the young creature will erupt into motion and transform the whole interior by mixing up the objects. Movement in the composition is stressed by a receding tabletop and a foreshortened figure. Serov offsets this movement with the pink triangle of the blouse and the free symmetry of the objects scattered around the room, seemingly at random but actually deliberately arranged.

A different motif is chosen for *Girl in the Sunlight*. The girl abides in a state of complete rest, with no intention of interrupting it. There is a stillness throughout, a repose, a fusion of the human being with the sun, the air, the environment. Whereas in *Girl with Peaches* the artist achieves the effect of balanced movement with the help of various compositional devices, here the opposite is true: he seeks to resolve the theme by harmoniously contrasting the motionless figure in the foreground against a backdrop that creates the impression of a spatial "breakthrough." In both cases Serov transcends the "study," and though he paints from nature he never loses sight of the finished picture existing in his mind's eye. This is where he differs from his constant companion Korovin, and in this lies his potential for further change.

There is every indication in both cases of a penchant for impressionism. Serov did not perceive the environment as a backdrop, as an accompaniment to the main theme. He was interested in every physical object that came into view and in every inch of the painted canvas. With Serov, the surface of each object reflects the light of adjacent objects and absorbs the rays of the sun. Everything is built on subtle transitions — the gradations of the color values are almost imperceptible, the contours of the figures and objects begin to shift. Moreover, Serov discovers the beauty of color as such: the tender pink of the girl's blouse stands in magnificent contrast to the black bow; the deep blue of the skirt in *Girl in the Sunlight* does not seem subject to the influence of the sun and retains its integrity. Each pure color, though, finds its "echo" in other parts of the canvas, sustaining the unity of the work.

Speaking of Serov's impressionism, we must bear in mind that it differs essentially from that of the French. To begin with, in the period in question Serov knew very little about the French Impressionists. The French artist he liked most, sharing this preference with many of his colleagues, was the extremely popular Bastien-Lepage, whose manner was a far cry from true Impressionism. Nevertheless, the logic of Russian art's evolution, its interest in *plein-air* painting and the experience gained in the study of nature all conspired to lead Serov to impressionist painting. The successes achieved by Repin, Polenov and Surikov in their depictions of nature opened up new vistas before the younger artists. But for Serov in *Girls*, as for Korovin in *Chorus Girl* or Levitan in *Birch Grove*, it was not enough to emulate their elders. His was a resolute step toward a new system, a step that makes it possible to regard him, together with his contemporaries, as a founder of early Russian impressionism, a method distinguished for its modesty, restraint and a certain stylistic disparity. In Serov's pictures, the painting of the human face was as yet substantially different from that of the landscape or interior. In *Girl with Peaches*, Vera Mamontova's head is done in smooth tenuous strokes, form and color coinciding completely, whereas in the blouse and the bow they do not. Serov often uses large areas of pure color, particularly black, which the French Impressionists did their best to avoid. But perhaps the most distinctive feature of Serov's art, compared to French Impressionism, is his unfeigned interest in the inner life of the model, an interest that continued to be the proud prerogative of Russian art in the 1870s and 1880s despite the new tasks it had to face.

The *Girls*, the early landscape studies, *Overgrown Pond*, and a number of portraits of the late 1880s — all these early works are shot through and through with a joyous admiration for life, all are suffused with a youthful blitheness. This integrity, however, this colorful rejoicing soon came to an end. In later years, when the artist recollected it all, he painted such works as *Summer* or *Portrait of Maria Lvova* (incidentally, the same Masha Simonovich who sat for *Girl in the Sunlight*), both done in 1895. Echoes of the former wealth of colors are discernible in *Portrait of Konstantin Korovin* (1891). But on the whole Serov's palette becomes more and more monochromatic, with a predominance of gray hues. His impressionism grows less pronounced and then vanishes for good, giving way to stylistic searchings of a totally different kind.

The 1890s saw the emergence of Serov the portraitist, an artist of pungent characterizations, a master of the grand style, a sharp-eyed analyst, a connoisseur of human types. "Serov," recollects P. Neradovsky, "painted his portraits slowly, sometimes agonizingly."* "Each portrait is for me an illness," Serov once said. Indeed, almost every one of the artist's portraits betrays a colossal expenditure of spiritual powers. Taken as a whole, Serov's portraits of the 1890s and early 1900s reflect his stylistic quests, his philosophy, and an intricate combination of trends in which he was currently caught up.

The new Serov begins with portraits of actors and artists done in the early 1890s. He now professes new principles in the very approach to his task. He does not let himself be swamped by reality, does not proceed from a spontaneous perception of nature, rejects all fortuitous elements in the model's aspect, and avoids any haphazard combinations in the compositional and color arrangements of the picture. Serov evolves his own method of "computation," of construction, of well-thought-out organization. This concept of "rational art" accompanies him to the end, and not only accompanies, but increasingly obsesses him. The impression of freedom, artistry, of effortless ease that Serov's paintings often produce is actually the result of calculation. Beginning with the 1890s, the eye is subordinated to the mind, its target and its position are predetermined. These are the principles that underlie the works of Serov's mature and late periods.

Another important element of Serov's art, which first manifested itself in the early 1890s and stayed with him to the end, is the type of personality he chose for his ideal. Serov's models represent various estates, social groups and professions. Formal portraits alternate with intimate ones; at times the two join hands, as it were, to create something in between. On different occasions, elements of one or the other type of portrait are accentuated, depending on the model. But what emerges in the final analysis is one basic, underlying principle: in most cases Serov portrays the creative personality. To him it is the creative personality alone who can enjoy an inner freedom: the creative process permits him to express his will, and in it lies his beauty as a human being.

Serov always admired intrinsic artistry in man: he always looked for that quality in the sitter, seeking to buttress it with his own artistry which was projected on the image. The creative impulse of the artist thus organically coincided with the theme of the portrait. This harmony was enhanced by the calculated, purposeful character of Serov's own creative method.

---

* See: *Serov in the Reminiscences of His Contemporaries*, 1971, 2, p. 33.

In the portrait legacy of Serov's contemporaries or junior colleagues—Vrubel and Petrov-Vodkin, World of Art members Konstantin Somov and Leon Bakst, Kustodiev and Zinaida Serebriakova—the foremost and most fully implemented theme was the creative personalities of theater people.

Serov loved to paint dramatic actors and opera singers, people accustomed to attracting public attention by the very nature of their profession. The artistry of Serov's models, therefore, always reflects the audience's interest. They offer themselves to the spectator. The behavior of each is always conditioned by the ingrained habit of "living his part," by a reciprocal consideration for the viewer, reflected in the expression of the face, the turn of the body, the pose and gesture. All these familiar factors constitute what used to be called a mask in the theater of old. Serov was blessed with an ability to fuse that mask (for Serov's personages the term is, of course, metaphorical) with the inimitable realness of the individual, to blend the role with the performer.

A case in point is the 1890 portrait of the famous Italian singer Masini, then touring Russia with considerable success. Serov's interest was aroused by Masini's artistic appearance and by his free and easy public manner. The impression is that of a success-spoiled, capricious man pampered by public adulation. Serov subordinates his mode of expression to the character of the model, deliberately limiting the color scheme to black and gray tones and using a stroke that is freer and broader than usual.

Also dating to the beginning of the 1890s is the portrait of Francesco Tamagno, another Italian singer who captivated Moscow audiences at the time. Tamagno attracted Serov's attention by his compelling personality. He is not singing in Serov's portrait and has no make-up on, but the profession is always in him and with him. Everything about Tamagno betrays the artist in him: the uplifted head shows inspiration, a creative concentration, as it were; the throat—that singular repository and transmitter of a superbly rich, typically Italian voice—is deliberately bared to demonstrate the singer's powerful "instrument." There is a demonstrativeness in all of Serov's devices, just as there is in the sitter himself.

In the portrait of Masini, one must add to the demonstrative artistry the demonstrative behavior of this handsome minion of fortune, this idol of the fans. The chief characteristics of the model are laid bare and hyperbolized. Serov extracts a theme out of the model, then projects it back, as it were.

This same principle underlies the portrait of Konstantin Korovin, amazing for its unrestrained, temperamental, painterly sweep and the deliberate outspokenness of its characterization. A cursory look is enough to identify the model as a painter, and not only because of the studies hanging on the wall behind him and the open box of paints on the table. It is not just the details, but the overall conceptual tonality of the portrait that reveal his occupation. Equally eloquent are the posture of a man accustomed to paint, not to sit for a painting; the sharp, professional eyes that know how to seize and to hold; the bohemian negligence in dress; and, finally, the temperamental painterly manner, similar to that of Korovin himself, that boldly combines the gray of the wall with the blue of the clothes, the red upholstery of the sofa and the red and white stripes of the cushion. Everything in the composition speaks of an artist in love with life, immersed in an atmosphere of creative work. And this is exactly the way Korovin was — an artist of great talent, a carefree man who tripped lightly through life. The portraits of Korovin and Tamagno depict two inimitable, vivid characters in which, for all their dissimilarity, one discerns a kindred type, a brilliant, temperamental, richly endowed artist who gives freely, almost wastefully, of his inexhaustible powers. There is in their full-blooded characters a broad artistic dimension, the magnetism of men physically strong and spiritually sound. These two portraits well illustrate the dominant feature of Serov's method — the ability to subordinate a portraitist's means of expression to the most adequate reflection of the main, salient idea. Serov never depicts character "in general." He is interested in a specific facet of that character, the all-important facet that most tellingly reveals the aesthetic worth of the person portrayed. He uses all the pictorial possibilities of the portrait—pose, gesture, composition, color scheme, the painterly style itself—to bring out the aesthetic merit of the sitter in the most vivid fashion.

It is this purposeful approach that reflects Serov's uncanny ability to spotlight the model's very being, an ability that afterwards, in the late 1890s and early 1900s, gained in maturity and artistry. Spotlighting is the heart and soul of Serov's method in portraiture. His portraits are always imbued with a serious idea, always have a theme and an artistic objective which determines the handling of the human image and the choice of expressive means.

The merits of two other portraits of the first half of the 1890s—*Isaac Levitan* (1893) and *Nikolai Leskov* (1894)—lie not so much in the keenness of Serov's characterization as in his psychological approach to the model's inner world. On the surface, this seems a more traditional kind of portraiture: after all, it is modeled on Repin's. But Serov's principle of spotlighting is realized here, too. It is not the model's character that interests Serov, but his emotional state. Levitan is presented in a state of introspective meditation. His gaze is directed seemingly at the viewer, but actually past and beyond him. Posing, Levitan himself wittingly suggests the theme of self-contemplation: the portraitist enhances it by means of light and color and with the aid of accessories.

In the portrait of Leskov, it is the look in the writer's eyes that rivets our attention, the wary, troubled, tragic look of a man standing on the threshold of the grave. Serov unshrouds that gaze by dispensing with details, neutralizing the entire canvas with tranquil painting and allowing freedom of expression only to the eyes. The same principle was later used by Serov, with equal brilliance, in *Portrait of Sophia Lukomskaya*, one of his finest watercolors.

During the mid-1890s Serov becomes an extremely popular, one might even say fashionable, portraitist. He receives a number of commissions. He does portraits of members of high society and of the royal family, but his new "heroes" do not bring the artist satisfaction — he fails to find any lofty human qualities in them. It is rather the painterly aspect of the task that interests Serov. He evolves his own style in formal portraiture.

One of the most brilliant formal portraits of that period is indisputably that of Grand Duke Pavel Alexandrovich (1897). At the Paris World Fair of 1900, it was awarded the highest distinction — an honorary medal. This was the first official step towards Serov's international recognition, though he had often displayed his works abroad, and with a large measure of success. In the 1890s and 1900s he exhibited in Munich (Serov was a member of the Munich Secession), Berlin, Vienna and Venice. At the 1911 World Fair in Rome Serov, in the words of the eminent art critic Yakov Tugendhold, "placed face to face with modern Western masters, passed the test with flying colors." *

The portrait is impressive. The sunlight that streams down on the Grand Duke standing by a horse is, in effect, the core of the composition. The duke's countenance expresses no significant thoughts, but the horse is splendidly done, the figures of the man and the steed brilliantly deployed and cleverly silhouetted. Serov creates a decorative and rhythmic pattern of dabs and lines, yet there is no hint of formal abstraction in the portrait because, instead of veiling the utter inaneness of the situation, every device used serves to accentuate it.

Even more indicative of his decorative talents are Serov's portraits of Sophia Botkina (1899) and Zinaida Yusupova (1902). These are true portrait-pictures. Serov brings the furniture and other details into play. He puts the two exquisitely dressed society belles into drawing-rooms and seats both on sofas. The pet dogs are meant to symbolize the boring, tiresome lives the ladies lead. The silhouettes of the

---

* See: *Serov in the Reminiscences of his Contemporaries*, 1971, 2, p. 406.

corseted figures, the curved lines of the bentwood furniture, the colorful dresses and upholstery tend to distract attention from the models themselves. Serov pays them hardly any heed. His aim is not to draw up a "character account," nor does he as yet go for the deliberate grotesque, as will be the case in his late period. Serov feels a little sorry for Botkina, while his attitude to Yusupova is one of subtle irony. But on the whole, he is indifferent to them, though the viewer learns something about them from the portraits.

Serov's work at the turn of the century did not begin and end with the formal portrait. His real interest lay elsewhere; his searchings went in many directions.

In the *Portrait of Mara Oliv* (1895), which for Serov was not a commission but rather an experiment, he tackled a new, self-imposed problem. What stands out in the characterization of this young woman is a certain elusiveness, a changefulness in her emotional state. This "slipping away" is achieved with the aid of the surroundings and the lighting. Consciously dispensing with any *plein-air* effects, he adds a sparkle to her face, hands, dress and especially the necklace which comes out as the brightest part of the canvas.

In the following years Serov turns ever more often to the informal portrait, his interpretation of the image becomes warm and lyrical. He evinces a growing interest in manifestations of spiritual beauty and limits the list of models for his informal portraits to women, children and close friends. The medium changes too — he now draws mostly graphic portraits which, however, are not mere preparatory sketches, but works of artistic merit in their own right.

In Serov's world the subject of spiritual beauty in man was one of the most controversial. In the 1870s and 1880s Repin saw his ideal in real persons. Unlike his teacher, Serov looks for true beauty, a beauty inaccessible to an eye not endowed with artistic vision; he seeks to fathom human emotions, to divine the human drama involved. It is these aspirations that brought Serov's artistry into being, investing him with a penetrating insight into nuances and minor details and an abhorrence for the insipid "verisimilitude" that, in Serov's opinion, destroys art.

The new Serovian approach to the human being began to manifest itself in his turn-of-the-century intimate portraits, often done in pencil or watercolors. Most were intended not for clients but for himself, and thus were distinguished by a freer, unconstrained quality.

A case in point is the watercolor *Sasha Serov* (1897), which subtly and easily conveys the boy's mood: he is lost in meditation, utterly absorbed in his child's thoughts.

The triumph of Serov's psychological approach is the half-length watercolor *Portrait of Sophia Lukomskaya* (1900), at first sight a very modest painting.

Lukomskaya's gaze is directed at the viewer, and it is her eyes that mirror the quintessence of the image — the suppressed tragedy which she tries to conceal and which despite herself comes through in the sad, suffering eyes. Serov handles the main and only theme of the portrait unobtrusively and, with regard to the model, tactfully. He gives compelling, painterly expression to his concept by evolving a whole range of browns based on subtle tonal transitions. The most sonorous colors are those that model Lukomskaya's face, as if pouring all their energy into the hub of the composition and enticing the viewer's gaze to the woman's eyes.

In this period Serov painted two portraits whose "heroes" were children. These pictures likewise rank among the artist's significant achievements.

Depicted in the first of these, *The Children* (1899), are Serov's two sons on the veranda of his *dacha* near the Gulf of Finland. It is a real-life scene perceived by the artist with a seemingly casual eye. He "catches" the children at a moment when they are not even thinking of what their father is doing. One, resting his elbows on the wooden balustrade, is lost in contemplation of the boundless sea; the other, head turned, is looking moodily at the viewer. Serov was fascinated by the psychology of children, the spontaneous, often naive impulses of their souls, by their peculiar "unspoiled quality." He saw these as immutable human virtues, as worthy qualities capable of evoking joy and an awareness of beauty.

Serov's painterly manner had by this time acquired greater sweep and freedom, and this helped him to heighten the psychological delineation of the image. In this painting he unifies into a coloristic whole the white and blue of the clothes, the steel-gray sea and the grayish-blue sky.

The evolution of the artist's painterly manner, which is easily discernible when one compares his early works with the canvases of the late 1890s and early 1900s, was not characteristic of Serov alone. It was part and parcel of Russian painting's general transition from the elegant *plein-air* method of the end of the 1880s to the broad, sweeping stroke of Arkhipov, Korovin, and Maliavin in their later period and of Levitan in his last works. It is no coincidence that when Zorn, a Swedish painter of European renown, visited Moscow in 1897, he found that many Russian artists shared his views. This new style helped them resolve the problem of unity in the canvas and embark on the road to its calculated organization. But the principle of spontaneity in the handling of the image remained, and Serov made a special effort to sharpen his perception.

In *Mika Morozov* (1901), the gesture and posture of the boy are so fortunate that the emotions of the little protagonist can be read like an open book. The curiosity he is gripped by makes him sit up, crane his neck, and stiffen; he seems to be the very embodiment of a child's inquisitiveness. The modest painterly means used have by now become the salient quality of Serov's art. Its merits lie not in showiness or bright colors, but in an evanescent quality that only a great talent, only a keen and highly sensitive eye, can achieve. Serov's exquisite touch lends charm to a number of children's pencil portraits done at about the same time, for example that of *The Botkin Children* (1900). In this work, Serov tackled the same difficult problem as a year before when painting his sons — the creation of a double portrait with a similar compositional arrangement: one of the girls faces the viewer, the other is presented in profile. In addition to characterizing each individual *per se*, both works had the common purpose of demonstrating an intrinsic bond between the models, the bond of their emotional state, of childish concentration. This bond was stressed not only by a similarity in the faces, clothes and hairdos, but by the overall linear rhythm, the subtle artistry of the graphic technique, and the singular airiness of the drawing.

Graphic techniques now came to play an increasingly important role in Serov's work. Well aware of their specific character, he undertakes several projects, some quite complicated. In 1899 and 1900 he executed a series of lithograph portraits of some prominent art figures of the period, which was published in a separate edition. This series illustrates the new principles espoused by Serov in the treatment of the portrait image. Two of the lithographs deserve special mention — the portraits of the composer Alexander Glazunov and of the music critic Alfred Nurok (both 1899). Both are indicative of Serov's understanding approach to his models. It is as though a certain communion were established between the sitter and the artist. This is stressed even by the narrative element in both portraits. Glazunov has briefly set his work aside and, interrupting the train of his thoughts, looks up at the artist; Nurok is apparently portrayed in conversation with the artist. Such an approach permits us to perceive the model in time, in a process of physical movement that betrays his emotions and certain aspects of his character. The seemingly casual composition allows that character to be presented with penetrating insight.

The line in Serov's drawings becomes increasingly expressive; it acquires a supple and precise quality. Designating the boundaries between objects, his line at the same time builds volume and lends tangibility to mass. Serov's graphic workmanship now attains maturity. This applies not only to pencil drawing or lithography, but to watercolor as well. A good example of his technical mastery is the *Portrait of Sophia Lukomskaya*; another is the watercolor *Pushkin on a Park Bench* (1899). In the latter work, the artist struck upon perhaps the most difficult, but certainly the most effective, concept of creating not a schoolbook image, but a live, authentic Pushkin. The poet is depicted in an autumn park, seemingly listening to the sounds of sublime melodies not yet solidified into poetic images, responding to the music of nature with his soul. This is creative inspiration, incarnated with the utmost simplicity and a truly Pushkinesque nobleness. The park's landscape, done in light, free brushstrokes, is but a hint of its natural self: it seems out of focus, as though glimpsed from a passing train. And it is not the landscape that draws the poet's attention. He has risen above the commonplace and retreated into himself; his eyes are directed into the distance — they look, but they do not see. Serov here admirably conveys all the lucid harmony, the utter naturalness of Pushkin's inspiration.

The watercolor *Pushkin on a Park Bench* introduces us to Serov the landscapist. His landscapes of the 1880s signaled only the beginning of Serov's quests in this field. In the 1890s the artist enriched his landscapes with elements of genre painting, the result of his growing interest in the village motif. It is this Serov that his biographer, Igor Grabar, called "the peasant Serov."

Many Moscow artists of Serov's generation had become "peasants" by the late 1880s. Arkhipov, Ivanov, Nesterov, Riabushkin and Stepanov all began with the village theme, and with all these artists genre painting, in comparison with their predecessors', acquired a new quality. They painted small-size pictures, did not people their canvases with human crowds, avoided dramatic situations, and shunned hackneyed subjects. The same can be said of Serov. His rural scenes touch on the most unassuming, the most ordinary phenomena, but he fathoms these phenomena to the very marrow.

Serov portrayed the Russian village mostly in autumn, less frequently in winter. He favored the Russian landscape in all its simplicity and modesty: he loved gray, cloudy skies, the drab autumn hues of the fields and thickets, bare trees, tumbledown shacks and huts, wind-blown haystacks, ungroomed animals and sad, withdrawn people lost in thought. His motifs can hardly be called motifs; they contain nothing at all. Serov's friend Levitan painted unassuming landscapes too, but for all his modest approach his motifs were often beautiful and impressive: golden autumn, a moonlit night, the wide expanses of lakes and rivers. Serov never did anything of the kind.

The "peasant" Serov is typified by such works as *October in Domotkanovo* (1895), *In a Village. Peasant Woman in a Cart* (1896), *Peasant Woman with a Horse* (1898), and *Rinsing Clothes* (1901). *October* is strongly reminiscent of a study. True, this study is to a certain extent translated into pictorial form: there is a hint of diagonal lines intersecting in the center, on the right and left the composition is framed by figures of horses and sheep, in the middle is a shepherd boy. But these balancing devices are barely noticeable. The overriding impression is that you have before you a real-life scene that cannot be invented or composed. Everything in it bears the stamp of direct observation, of calm contemplation of nature. Each of the participants in the scene, whether boy or horse, lives apart from the others. None of them is aware that he is posing for a picture. The boy is doing his job — whittling a stick or fixing a whip, the horses are nibbling the yellow autumn grass. In the distance are wind-blown trees and barn roofs, a flight of crows or jackdaws taking off from the roofs, and endless gray expanses in which rural Russia leads its eternal, monotonous existence. However, the complex emotions evoked in the viewer by Serov's picture are not confined to melancholy and dejection. There is in it the wondrous, exalted feeling of something especially dear to the heart, something inseparable from one's very being. Serov did not invest this composition with social, accusatory overtones; he did not specially pick a poor village to express his sympathy for the peasant. The shepherd boy has no need for sympathy — he feels completely at home in his familiar environment. And yet Serov does borrow something from the tradition of the literary and pictorial landscape which characterized Russian culture since Pushkin's time and which, as a rule, contained some elements of criticism. In the nineteenth century, the Russian rural landscape was construed either as a cause for sympathy with the poor and denunciation of the rich, or as something infused with an inexpressible enchantment. Serov adhered to the latter view.

Peasant Woman in a Cart has much in common with *October*. It is difficult to imagine anything more succinct than this painting: a horse pulling a cart, a narrow stream beyond and a wood on the opposite bank. There is in this idleness, in this monotony a kind of fairy-tale bewitchment. The world gives way to an all-pervading stillness, in which even time itself is dissolved. Present in *Rinsing Clothes* are the same horse and the peasant women, bent over a brook slowly flowing through the thawing snow. Serov does not elevate the motif to "aesthetic heights" by choosing bright colors for the women's dresses: on the contrary, he enwraps everything in gray hues and gray silence.

True, sometimes Serov's winter landscapes look brisk and lively. All of a sudden a small gray horse pulling a sleigh darts into view from around a corner. In another picture, a panorama of trees, fences and moving sleighs unfolds from the upper window of a mansion. And in the pastel *Peasant Woman with a Horse*, a typical Russian beauty in a red kerchief flashes a white-toothed smile as she stands next to a shaggy horse with an uncombed mane. The reddish-brown patches on the white snow are in this picture more resonant than usual.

Even more resounding is the color scheme of the pastel *Colts at a Watering Place* (1904). Serov depicts an early spring evening at that moment in time when the sunny day gives way to a frosty dusk that brings the triumphant march of spring to a temporary halt. The thick, grainy snow is shot through with cold, lilac-blue shadows. Serov captures with the utmost precision the contrast between the warm light of the sun and the cold blue of twilight, so typical of early spring. The barns stand in the thickening dusk, with thawing snow on their roofs; the colts drinking from a trough are seen as mere silhouettes. One of them, as if yielding to the compelling call of spring, has interrupted his drinking and turned his head in the direction of the setting sun. The landscape is permeated by a feeling of vague anxiety, thus setting *Colts at a Watering Place* apart from other works by the "peasant" Serov.

This new conceptual approach led Serov to resort to new means of artistic expression. He assigns a special role to the silhouette and the color patch and makes full use of the contrasts produced by color juxtapositions. The pastel technique, delicate and refined, is admirably fitted to express the expectancy of spring that lends romantic overtones to the entire landscape. Serov here asserts the beauty of life in tones so emphatic that one suspects a deliberate attempt on his part to put his own solemn and exalted worship of the wonder of life against all its naturalistic, dreary and insipid copies.

Beginning with 1905 Serov does fewer and fewer landscapes. This is understandable. The image of the poor Russian village that he had come to love could hardly be considered appropriate in a period of revolutionary upheaval. The new intonations that first appeared in *Colts* rang even louder in a 1905 landscape entitled *Bathing a Horse*. It was executed not in the central regions of Russia, whose scenery well accorded with the former lyrical tendencies of Serov's landscape painting, but on the shore of the Gulf of Finland, where the artist often spent his summers. The level horizon of the boundless sea, the direct rays of the sun illuminating the sky, the water, the boy, and the horse as it stands etched in a clear-cut brown silhouette against the sea — everything in this canvas is subordinated to a feeling of buoyant optimism. As if filled with a fresh wind, this picture is built on new rhythmic principles that "liberate" space rather than enclose it in a definite compositional framework.

Between 1905 and 1910 the landscape as such ceased to figure in Serov's art. However, the approach to nature manifested in *Bathing a Horse* was carried over into the landscape backdrops of his pictures on historical or mythological themes.

The last of Serov's works to depict the reality of contemporary life and to have some relation to genre painting were devoted to the revolutionary events of 1905.

Serov took those events very close to heart. He drew inspiration from the people's strength that had finally erupted in a mighty revolutionary upsurge. When the tsar's troops began shooting at unarmed people in cold blood, Serov could not remain aloof. He raised his voice in protest both as an artist and as an honest citizen.

Tsarism's monstrous crime of January 9, 1905, shook Serov to the marrow. He had previously believed that it was the privilege of a "free" artist to have no political convictions, but on that day he suddenly understood all the dangers inherent in such a stand. In his famous address to the Academy of Arts, Serov, together with Polenov, voiced a political protest against reaction by demanding the resignation of Grand Duke Vladimir from the Academy: "The terrible events of January 9 have left a deep scar in our hearts. Some of us saw with our own eyes soldiers killing defenceless people in the streets of St. Petersburg, and the picture of that bloody horror will remain impressed in our memories for ever. We artists deeply deplore the fact that the supreme commander of the troops who shed the blood of their brothers is at the same time head of the Academy of Arts, whose prime function is to foster the concept of humanity and supreme ideals."*

The revolution did not catch Serov the artist unprepared. His graphic on-the-spot recordings of revolutionary events had their predecessors. *Horseless Peasant* (1899) and *Recruits* (1904), for example, carry a distinct social message. Serov speaks in them of an impoverished Russia, of the calamity represented for the peasant by service in the tsar's army or, worse still, by war. They bore the seeds of the revolutionary theme that in 1905–6 hallmarked the work of many Russian artists.

In the very first days of the revolution Serov contributed to the political magazine *Zhupel* (*The Bugaboo*) a tempera drawing entitled *Soldiers, Soldiers, Heroes Every One. . .* This piece is one of the most powerful accusatory works produced by Russian artists during the 1905 revolution. It is symptomatic that Serov presented the drawing to Maxim Gorky, with whom he had struck up a friendship in 1905 and whose influence he undoubtedly felt in those years of revolutionary upheaval. The drawing is at once a denunciation and a call for retribution. Serov depicts the ominous pause that precedes a bloody massacre of innocent people. The mock-heroic figures of the Cossacks are sketched in a deliberately grotesque manner. Stressing the "fighting" spirit in their appearance, Serov unmasks their inhumanity, cynicism, their moral turpitude. He enhances the denunciatory power of the drawing by underlining the utter helplessness of the crowd proceeding under a white flag. The slanting space of the alley, the dirty, trodden snow and the yellow blind walls together create an image of a dead city hostile to man. A motley crowd has just broken into the gloomy alley and, sighting the Cossacks, ground to a halt. It is the confrontation between these defenseless people with their pathetic white flag and the brave, dashing Cossacks that constitutes the tragic essence of the scene. The mocking words of the picture's title, taken from an old army song, ring like a slap in the face: "Soldiers, soldiers, heroes every one, where has all your glory gone?"

The cartoon *Prospects for the 1906 Harvest* depicts an idyllic landscape with a blue sky and a sun-warmed field but with sheaves of rifles instead of wheat. The image that springs to mind is that of a tormented, devastated Russia with burnt fields and whole villages driven into exile and hard labor.

A totally different impression is produced by the sketch *The Funeral of Bauman* (1905). Despite its unfinished state, the artist's concept is quite obvious. The long drawn-out mass of a thousand-legged,

* See: *Serov's Correspondence*, 1937, p. 302.

thousand-faced multitude moves slowly along the surface of the cardboard, giving the composition its horizontal elongation. The heavy, monolithic rhythm of that slow yet relentless procession is the leitmotif of the theme. Serving as a majestic accompaniment are the red patches of the banners, coffin and flags, their changing rhythm punctuating the solemn march with an exultant melody in red. The confident strength of the people is expressed by Serov in a highly emotional vein. It is embodied in the musical and rhythmic structure of the sketch. Like the poet Alexander Blok after him, Serov was enraptured by the romantic "music of the revolution." The very concept of the sketch incorporated the idea of the revolutionary march of history, and this left its imprint on Serov's later work. He returned to the theme later in a picture devoted to Peter the Great.

The revolution strengthened Serov's faith in man's creative potential, in the dignity and significance of man as an individual. This influenced the evolution of Serov's portraiture, which in the early 1900s and especially from 1905 to 1910 acquired a new dimension: the artist began increasingly to monumentalize his subjects.

It is interesting in this respect to compare the children's portraits discussed earlier. In *The Children*, the lightning glance of the artist impinges against the slowness and "apartness" of the boys. In *Mika Morozov*, on the other hand, or the lithograph portraits, the models are very active indeed, and this calls for a spatial environment that would allow the figure to continue, as it were, the movement already begun and consummate it in the viewer's imagination. The pictorial surface thus gradually expands, now capable of incorporating the figure with a whole system of objects, and uniting them into a balanced composition. Movement begins to consolidate and comes to a stop, but always at a point which permits the phenomenon to be raised to a formula, at a point which enables the artist to embrace the event in its entirety and monumentalize it.

Especially typical is the treatment of time and movement in the portraits of Mikhail Morozov (1902), Ilya Ostroukhov (1902), Maxim Gorky (1905), and several others. There is in them no fixation of the transient. The fleeting second is "intercepted" and brought to a long halt. The figures freeze in unexpected poses. In the portrait of Morozov, the solid, stocky man stands as if transfixed, his legs set apart and his sharp, piercing gaze directed at the viewer. But though the model has come to a standstill, everything else around him seems in motion. The pictorial surface of this canvas as yet reflects only a fragment of the spatial environment.

The portrait of Morozov is indicative of impressionistic painting's last attempts to express the natural and the fortuitous, to capture the environment. The sitter himself, however, begs for another approach. Serov underlines his importance by presenting the figure full-face and full-length, from a low viewpoint. All this led the artist to abandon his old system and turn to a new one.

Another landmark on the road to a new painterly and compositional system is Serov's portrait of the writer Maxim Gorky, which has an interesting history. In the spring of 1904 Serov went to Italy where he did a number of watercolors and drawings. The most noteworthy of these is a sepia depicting Michelangelo's renowned Madonna of the Medici Chapel in Florence. It is only logical that this image of great grief and moral power, heroic for its sheer immensity, attracted Serov's attention and later probably prompted the compositional arrangement of Gorky's portrait. Whereas in the early 1890s Serov was attracted by the full-blooded imagery of Titian, and in his late works, to use the artist's own words, he was "getting closer to Raphael," this time he was drawn to the heroic, impassioned art of Michelangelo in which Serov saw reflected his own understanding of the essence of man in those years. In the portrait of Gorky one senses an attempt on the part of the artist to evolve a modern idiom that would adequately express the heroic.

Maxim Gorky was for Serov one of the makers of the revolution, a tribune and a leader of the people. This new hero differed from the models the artist had portrayed all his life. Gorky's outer aspect was simpler, his gestures more resolute, his workman's appearance went hand in hand with an ingrained intellectuality and high culture.

The expressiveness of Gorky's portrait is based on the contrast between the dark silhouette of the figure and the light, spacious, sun-spotted background. This contrast makes for the sharp linear clarity needed by Serov to stress Gorky's character. The writer is seated on a stool, with legs crossed, his face turned toward an unseen interlocutor. The broad gesture of the right hand emphasizes with conviction and a peculiarly Gorkyesque weightiness the words he has just spoken. Serov always knew how to fill the gesture with meaningful content. In this canvas it expresses the sincerity of a straightforward man, who fervently believed in the justice of his cause, and the sociability of a public figure.

The pronounced turn of the figure is full of stately simplicity and confidence. It is a complex posture — the head and body are turned in opposite directions, the shoulders rather sharply foreshortened, the legs diagonally positioned. All these involved movements do not contradict each other, they merge into an integral whole, lending the image a suppressed energy and a somewhat emotional uplift.

Similar in concept to Gorky's portrait is another portrait of 1905 — a charcoal drawing depicting the singer Fiodor Shaliapin. The creative essence of the actor is revealed in all its scope and power. Shaliapin stands full height, with legs planted apart and torso in a sharp turn. His magnificent head is proudly raised, the left hand pressed to the lapel of his frock coat, the right casually inserted into a trouser pocket. Deliberately stressing the proportions of the actor's portly figure, Serov highlights the natural artistry of Shaliapin's graceful and uninhibited pose. His face reflects the agonizing creative joy that only a great artist is given to experience.

Another work that ranks among Serov's finest is the portrait of the famous Russian actress Maria Yermolova (1905). She stands in a stately pose, with proudly tilted head. Her expressive face, aglow with a subdued but inextinguishable flame, is modeled with painstaking care. There is a faraway look in her deepset hazel eyes, the nostrils are distended, the lips tightly shut. A barely perceptible shadow of tragedy enhances the inspired expressiveness of her face.

As always, in this portrait Serov captured the very essence of the great actress's personality, creating at the same time a certain abstract model of "heroic artistry" governed by accepted standards of ethic and spiritual beauty in man. This desire to present the great tragic actress, whose every role was a significant public event, as an ideal example of human beauty determined the entire idiom of the work. The laconic composition, the strict and restrained coloristic ambiance well accord with the artist's concept of the lofty and heroic. The colors of the portrait are restrained, never overstepping the boundaries of the dominant triad — gray, black and brown. The color scheme is enriched by subtle shades of violet that appear in varying degrees of intensity in the backdrop, the floor, and the dress. The frame of the mirror and the line on the wall form the rhythmic leitmotif of the composition, in which the central place is allotted to the sharply outlined figure.

It is no accident that Serov arrived at such a treatment of the image in 1905, at the crest of the revolutionary wave. It is also no accident that this was precisely the time when he turned to the formal portrait to incarnate the image of the creative personality. He had done formal portraits before, from the 1880s to the early 1900s, but those were commissioned works and their models did not, as a rule, arouse any great interest in the artist. Now, however, the formal portrait, by tradition a field ideally suited for the use of the grand style, had discovered, as it were, its veritable subject. The heroic essence of the image now found its adequate embodiment.

In its compositional objectives, in size and scope, the portrait of Yermolova shares a close affinity with the portrait of Morozov discussed above. The two works invite comparison: the narrow, vertically elongated canvases are nearly equal in height, with an almost identical correlation between figure and pictorial surface; both pictures are distinguished by modest color schemes and a predominance of gray tones. Yet for all that there is a demarcation line separating the two works. Yermolova's portrait belongs to another style. Not volume, but the color patch dominates here. There is no room for any chance elements: the figure is sharply outlined and separated from the background; it is enclosed in a network of straight lines forming a kind of frame.

By that time the stylistic principles underlying the portrait of Yermolova and other portraits of the same period had come to be used by Serov in all of his art. Many other Russian artists also adopted these principles, which had developed at the turn of the century in various national schools and were designated by different names (Art Nouveau in France and Belgium, Jugendstil in Germany, Sezessionstil in Austria, etc.). This style found its most obvious expression in architecture and interior decoration. Its characteristics included a new approach to the plane of the wall, designed to achieve a maximum decorative effect, an interest in the color patch on that plane, the fluid, undulating line, intricate ornamentation using flat patterns of writhing vegetable forms, and, finally, an aestheticizing of the architectural entity as a whole. The same features, with certain modifications, are evident in painting, graphic arts and sculpture. The new trend tried to achieve a synthesis of different arts. Serov was involved with some of the monumental ventures of his time: he tried his hand at mural painting and took an interest in stage design. It is, however, in his easel painting that the Art Nouveau style manifested itself most clearly. The color patch enclosed in an asymmetrical, serpentine contour; the use of the canvas's very texture for artistic effect; a turning-away from *plein-air* objective—in other words, from a realist interpretation of the environment; the intricate intertwining of both tense and flabby lines on the pictorial surface—all these aspects of Art Nouveau are present in many of Serov's works.

Any style demands of the artist a clarity of thought, a definite concept; it provides him with a model, a certain standard. To espouse a style is to aim for a generalized image, and this is what characterized Serov's searchings of the early 1900s. It was, moreover, compatible with the overall objective of Art Nouveau where reality is transformed, to a certain extent even deformed. It is a reality "remade." Serov's vision of a physical entity primarily as material for an artistic image and not as an actually existing object mirrors the general spirit of Art Nouveau.

Many of Serov's later portraits, while fitting into the frame of the new style by exemplifying its method of concentrated characterization, at the same time emulate the portrait of Yermolova in that they possess a lofty, often heroic, conceptual context. To these may be referred the pastel *Konstantin Stanislavsky* (1911), *Portrait of Polina Shcherbatova* (1911), a charcoal sketch on canvas left unfinished at the time of the artist's death, or *Portrait of Maria Akimova* (1908).

The latter work bears an outer resemblance to the portraits of Botkina and Yusupova. It is built on the principle of decorativeness: the accessories and background are very much like those used in Serov's formal portraits of the late 1890s and early 1900s. Expressed in the image of Akimova herself, however, is a far greater degree of the human element. There is an innate nobleness to be felt in the magnificently modeled head, the figure, the bearing and the gesture of the woman's hands.

Another work where the formal element plays a significant role is *Portrait of Henrietta Girshman* (1907). Serov's work on this painting makes an interesting story.

The first variant of the composition was done in charcoal over a gouache drawing. Originally the picture was conceived as another of Serov's traditional formal portraits, but then he decided to dispense with the showiness of that genre, designating the contours with laconic lines and forgoing all sumptuous accessories. In this new portrait he sought for elements of restraint, trustfulness and sobriety, which at that period graced a number of his female images.

Soon Serov altered the composition, putting the high society beauty into a boudoir where she is surrounded by numerous luxury items and knick-knacks vying with one another in splendor and elegance. Serov renders with superb skill the warm halflight of the refined interior, bringing out the yellow sheen of the Karelian birch furniture, the glittering surface of the mirror and the glimmer of the glass and metallic trinkets. Such "surroundings," more typical of Mme Girshman, served the artist as material for a sharper characterization of the model, as an illustration to at least part of her being.

Still, Serov did not express any definite idea in this portrait. The model's inner world reflects a certain duality, leaves something unsaid. This painting was a crossroads in Serov's development — from here he could proceed either to the creation of the ideal image or to the almost grotesque portrait, brilliant examples of which appeared at the end of his life.

Shortly before his death, Serov once again turned to the image of Mme Girshman in a pastel portrait of 1911, left unfinished. In it we find the restrained classical spirit, the completeness of an image endowed with ideal features that are so typical of Serov's last works.

"Any human face," Serov once said, "is so complex and so unique that you can always find in it traits worthy of portrayal, be they good or bad. For my part, each time I appraise a person's face I am inspired, you might even say carried away, not by his or her outer aspect, which is often trivial, but by the characterization it can be given on canvas. That is why I am accused of sometimes having my portraits look like caricatures."*

In his quest for the characteristic, Serov was not afraid to overemphasize, exaggerate, or hyperbolize. This frequently led to a deformation of face, body or object, but it was always a reflection of the model's essential being, of his or her distinctive traits which the artist sought to reveal in manifest and unambiguous terms.

The famous portrait of the dancer Ida Rubinstein (1911) bears no traces of "accusatory" overtones, yet the keenness of characterization attained is remarkable. Serov was spellbound by Rubinstein. Having seen her on the stage once, he visualized the highly expressive image she would make on canvas. Serov's new model was a performer of the stylized, refined, yet temperamental dance, and he created an expressive image, enhancing her sharp, uncommon features.

This is how Nina Simonovich-Yefimova, who witnessed Serov's work on the portrait in his studio, describes Ida Rubinstein: "An oval face, as if flawlessly delineated with a fortunate stroke of someone's light pen; a nose of noble shape. And a lovely face, mat and white, framed by a shock of black curls. A modern figure, but the face is out of some ancient epoch. From the India of legend. It is this authenticity that attracted Serov because it precluded all thoughts of the artificial, the spurious. Serov says she has the mouth of a 'wounded lioness'."**

Portrait of Ida Rubinstein can be said to conform to the new style in every way. The famous ballerina posed for Serov in the nude, and this obliged the artist to forestall any associations of the future portrait with reality. Serov did not depict Ida Rubinstein: he created an image out of the boundless possibilities presented by the model. In so doing he sought to combine the abstract with the real, which is typical of Art Nouveau as such and also typical of almost all of Serov's portraits. The curving lines of the contours are traced directly on the canvas. Only three hues are present in the color scheme—blue, green and

* See: Mamontov 1911, pp. 167—168.
** See: Simonovich-Yefimova 1964, pp. 116—117.

brown—without any gradations or combinations. Each color is isolated and local. The spatial environment is not designated, be it by color or compositional arrangement or perspective. She seems not seated, but sprawled, pressed to the canvas, which, together with the model's piquant and extravagant aspect, creates an impression of weakness and vulnerability.

Serov regarded Ida Rubinstein with admiration, though he did stress the characteristic aspect of her image at the expense of the ideal. In a number of other portraits, however, his treatment of the model borders on the grotesque. This tendency attained its peak in the very last years of his life and above all in *Portrait of Princess Orlova* (1911).

The ideally synchronized composition and color scheme of the portrait are, in the full sense of the word, classically perfect. The soft fur of the coat slipping off the woman's shoulders makes a handsome contrast with the nacreous turquoise of the iridescent dress, emphasizing its smooth mat texture and the tender velvet of the well-cared-for neck and hands twisting a pearl necklace. Serov subtly conveys the textural and pictorial diversity of the articles that surround Orlova—the Sèvres vase on the gilt table, the old pictures—never once lapsing into naturalistic copying. The spatial and rhythmic problems of the composition are brilliantly resolved — the woman is seated in a corner of a large room and this corner, rather than a flat wall, serves as her background, which produces the effect of a three-dimensional stage set. All the objects are rendered in a fragmentary way, enhancing the impression of size and splendor. This fragmentary presentation, however, is by no means equivalent to a contrived casualness in the composition. Each of the objects is fully attuned to the rhythmic beat of the portrait, each "lives" its own full-blooded life.

Serov greatly admired the archetypal wholeness, the lack of ambiguity in Orlova's character and being. Her well-groomed, "pedigreed" look, the magnificent nonchalance with which she wears her expensive attire, and her innate "stylishness" all provide ample material for Serov's craftsmanship. What we have before us, though, is not just a society belle, as is often the case in formal portraits. The woman's vivid personality allowed the artist to create a definite social type. The keen eye of a sober realist and the sure hand of a master have here found an artistic formula which calls for a sharply delineated figure, a fixed pose characteristic even in its casualness, a certain new standard similar to that which existed in eighteenth-century portraiture and was based on stabilized traditional forms. Serov seems to be working out his own iconographic basis for the portrait genre. Orlova's portrait is an eloquent case in point. The pose, arrived at after long experimentation and repeated changes, the furniture, the solid composition wherein fragments constitute a harmonious whole, the refined painterly manner — all these may well be regarded as a set of rules in the making of a formal portrait.

In Serov's late portraits the Russian variant of Art Nouveau was given its most brilliant implementation. It can even be said that the style ran itself out in the supreme perfection of Serov's art, which inevitably led Russian painting to explore new paths.

The evolution of Serov's portraiture was consistent and logical. As for his thematic compositions, which were discussed earlier when we spoke about the "peasant" Serov, genre paintings gradually gave way to historical canvases which, beginning with the early 1900s, came to be Serov's dominant interest. A contributing factor in the process was his association with the World of Art group: its members were on the whole proponents of history painting which in their endeavor acquired a special character, a character entirely new to Russian art.

Serov's transition from everyday themes to historical pictures began in the early 1900s. Much of that process hinged on the "demands of style" listed earlier on. A concrete phenomenon taken from real life —a phenomenon devoid of inner potential and lacking substance, interesting only as an object of direct and impartial observation—did not fit in with the Art Nouveau style. History presented better opportunities for a distraction from reality.

Serov's first history pieces, done as illustrations to N. Kutepov's book *Royal Hunting in Russia*, were still, by and large, reminiscent of genre painting. It is precisely this type of history painting that most appealed to the masters of the World of Art group. Immersed in romantic dreams of the past, they pleasured in the life-style of epochs gone by, but always with a hint of irony over their subject matter. Subtle stylists, consummate craftsmen who knew the beauty of well-balanced composition, exquisite linear rhythm and modestly decorative coloring, they evolved their own firm artistic principles. They sought to inject into this new vision elements of stylization. Aiming at a decorative flatness in their compositions, they almost never painted in oils, preferring to work with watercolors, gouache, tempera and pastels — media not particularly suited to the production of fully-modeled, three-dimensional forms.

In Serov's illustrations, all done in tempera—*Peter II and Princess Elizabeth Riding to Hounds*, *Catherine II Setting Out to Hunt with Falcons*, *Young Peter the Great Riding to Hounds* (1900 to 1902)— every World of Art principle is realized with superb skill. Serov is not interested in any significant historic event. He tries to capture the spirit and style of the epoch, ignoring its conflicts and upheavals, and this brings his works well within the range of the World of Art's concept of the history genre. There are no noteworthy happenings in his pictures. The aging Catherine, her head turned, smiles at her current favorite who is accompanying the empress on horseback. Peter guffaws at the sight of a boyar fallen off his mount. Elizabeth and Peter II observe with mild interest the wayfarers passing by. True, Serov does hint at conflict (the bedraggled wayfarers and the richly attired emperor and princess; the young Peter, shaking the dust of medieval Russia even in trivial matters; and the ludicrous figure of the boyar), but this all takes place in the background, as it were, and does not determine the character of the pictures whose prime purpose is a living recreation of the Petrine and Catherine epochs.

These pictures of Serov's are utterly convincing because they are true to life. In *Peter and Elizabeth* one actually senses the headlong, ground-blurring speed of the horses and borzois as they race past the standing commoners. In the distance, where the tail of the cavalcade can be made out near a church, a flock of frightened birds has taken wing: the humdrum world of the shabby Russian village in the background has been invaded by an alien force. It is there, in the background, with its peasant huts under a gray, cloudy sky and the familiar Serovian horses grazing, that Serov's genre and historical painting come into contact.

Serov's historical vision has a ring of authenticity about it. We recognize his eighteenth-century Russia from certain details created by the artist with a deep feel for history. Much of Serov's conviction stems from his filigree craftsmanship: each of his color dabs has intrinsic artistic merit, but this does not violate the artistic harmony of the whole, a harmony sustained throughout. His curving, interlaced lines constitute the typically Art-Nouveau rhythmic pattern and at the same time emphasize the movement dictated by the theme.

The illustrations to *Royal Hunting* were for Serov a passing episode. His historical painting achieved real depth and originality only after 1905, when with true Serovian conscientiousness he set out to explore the Petrine epoch, an epoch that saw the radical transformation of Russia, a great epoch torn by contradictions and in that respect an echo of the artist's own time. The Petrine epoch helped Serov to sum up his impressions of the historic events he had seen happen, to reflect in his art his thoughts on the destinies of Russia, which in 1905 had gone through a heroic and bloody revolution.

Serov saw Peter the Great as the embodiment of the historic need to transform Russia, as an incarnation of the creative revolutionary element in Russian life. Despotic and ruthless, but great and sublime in his reformative zeal, Peter led Russia along the only possible road, even if it was a very cruel one. The image of Peter the Great created by Serov is historically accurate in that it is a complex and contradictory figure which evokes both horror and admiration.

This new concept received its most vivid and complete implementation in the composition *Peter the Great* (1907), commissioned by Knebel to be published in a series of pictures for schoolchildren on themes from Russian history. The publisher wanted Serov to depict the tsar overseeing the construction of St. Petersburg — a subject that fascinated the artist. Serov's Peter is the most realistic Peter in Russian art. We see him striding along the bank of the Neva, impetuous, majestic, awesome, looking the way he really did: lanky, with long stiltlike legs and a small, arrogantly tilted head. The artist deliberately exaggerates those features of Peter's aspect that characterize him as both a fanatic and a genius who transformed Russia, as a man of great creative energy.

The grandeur of Peter's image fits naturally into the picture's monumental compositional arrangement. Peter dominates both men and nature, and this is underlined by an appropriate compositional device: his figure, seen somewhat from below, is sharply etched against a gray, overcast sky. All around him are the flat banks of the Neva, the inhospitable northern lands that have bowed to the will of a genius. The picture is not large in size, yet the typical Serovian procession motif is monumentally resolved. The entire scene is built on an explicit, clear-cut rhythm, on a headlong movement that unfolds parallel to the surface of the canvas. The picture reflects the tendency toward the "grand style," characteristic of many of Serov's portraits painted in the early 1900s, while preserving intact his spontaneous perception of nature.

Both these qualities now set Serov's work apart from the historical painting of the World of Art group. He puts forward a new, totally different set of problems. The scope of Serov's imagery, the sweep of his grasp of history, the very character of his historical thinking all tend to differ from, rather than resemble, those of the World of Art. Also an important contributing factor to this opposition is the principle of correlating history with the present day, a principle engendered by the artist's world outlook. Unlike the World of Art members, Serov does not idealize bygone epochs; to him, history continues in the present, and he looks for the connecting links.

Serov was so taken with the image of Peter the Great that he could not part with it to the end of his days. In his later years the artist undertook several thematic paintings—*Peter the Great in the Palace of Monplaisir, The Grand Eagle Cup*, and *Peter the Great at a Construction Site*—but none were brought to completion. Nonetheless, Serov's interest in the personality of Peter is symptomatic. He wanted to split the synthetic image of Peter arrived at in the tempera of 1907 into separate parts to show the Russian emperor in various hypostases. The fact that he failed is no less indicative of his artistic evolution: the artist's attempts to individualize both image and phenomenon ran contrary to the spirit of the times, which called increasingly for a generalized approach.

In his final period Serov's infatuation with history gave way to an interest in classical mythology. The genre in which he recreated the myths of antiquity cannot be called historical in the full sense of the word. Only Neo-Classical art of the eighteenth and early nineteenth centuries produced works on antique subjects that could be called historical: in those times mythology was perceived as actual history. For Serov, however, the mythological theme was enwrapped in a double conventionality — that of the myth itself and that of its historical background. True, he also strove to inject some of the reality of life into this double conventionality.

Antiquity was Serov's last attachment, and this has its explanation. The above-mentioned double conventionality gave an additional impetus to his stylistic quests. To this must be added his first-hand impressions of Greece, which he visited in 1907 together with Leon Bakst, a World of Art colleague who soon after painted the decorative panel *Terror Antiquus*.

Greece impressed Serov by the way it combined the exalted and the monumental with the real-life and ordinary. He scrutinized its landscape, at once ancient and modern, recognizing in every passing maiden a caryatid from the Erechtheum, finding in all an antiquity resurrected in the present day. This dedication to the theme of ancient Greece stemmed not only from Serov's deeply rooted love for the art of that country, but from the very logic of his own searchings of the 1900s for a broadly generalized imagery to extol the beauty of nature and man, for ways of imparting a monumental character to his art, of creating twentieth-century "classics."

This was a period that saw a revived interest in antiquity in various countries, only this time it was a matter of reading it from a new angle, of putting an end to the academic speculations it had long been associated with in European culture.

Antiquity had always been the most favored theme of the academic school. In its poorest variant, antiquity survived in late nineteenth-century art the worse for wear, deprived of its very soul. In the early 1900s the theoreticians of Symbolism devoted much of their writing to antiquity, seeing in it two main aspects — the Apollonian, i.e., the sublime, the ideal, the harmonious, and the Dionysian, or the turbulent, the uncontrolled, the spontaneous. Serov was drawn above all to the harmony of antiquity. He discerned in it the contours of the Golden Age that mankind had dreamed of from time immemorial.

Three themes were uppermost in Serov's mind — Odysseus and Nausicaä, the rape of Europa, and episodes from Ovid's *Metamorphoses*, particularly the transformation of Actaeon into a stag by an enraged Diana and the vengeance wreaked on Niobe by Diana and Apollo. Each of these subjects was implemented in sketches and variants in the last two years of the artist's life.

In *Odysseus and Nausicaä*, the changes concerned above all the landscape and the relative proportions of sky, sea and shore. The central part of the composition was resolved by the artist without difficulty — the slender figure of Nausicaä in a chariot drawn by mules with heads turned upward in a characteristic movement, behind the princess her retinue trudging along the sandy beach, with Odysseus a little further behind. Art historians have already pointed out that this procession motif and its formal handling originated in Serov's endeavor around 1905 and via *Peter the Great* of 1907 were brought into *Odysseus and Nausicaä*. There is, of course, a certain similarity, but the conceptual connotations of the processions, first in the sketch for *Funeral of Bauman*, then in a theme from Russian history and, lastly, in a Homeric theme, are far apart. In *Odysseus*, everything breathes serenity and harmonious integrity. Men and nature abide in wondrous accord. The procession is joyful yet solemn and stately. It unfolds almost parallel to the surface of the canvas, and the difference between the variants lies only in the distance separating the figures. In what concerns the overall color scheme, the format and the relative proportions of the composition's elements, the difference is substantial. In one variant Serov paints a high sky whose silvery hue is the picture's predominant coloristic element. The sea is covered with whitecaps that glitter in the sun, the human and animal figures seem to reflect the sunlight. The little figure of Nausicaä, dimly reminiscent of an archaic caryatid, is full of an unfeigned vitality and maidenly grace. The other variant resembles a decorative panel and seems more like a stage set than a genuine landscape with figures. This is only natural if we bear in mind that Serov did try his hand at stage design, his most significant work being the curtain for *Sheherazade*, produced by Serge Diaghilev's Ballets Russes in Paris in 1911.

In each of Serov's variants of mythological subjects, his prime concern was the correlation between the real and the conventional. The latter predominates in his sketches for the decoration of the Nosov house in Moscow, so much so that the painting is subordinated to the architectural composition. There is a strict symmetry in these sketches, and the composition of many scenes is reminiscent of heraldic devices.

It is in *The Rape of Europa*, a theme that occurs not only in Serov's paintings and drawings, but has a sculptural version too, that the problem of bringing together the conventional and the real was resolved in the most coherent fashion. In Serov's composition, both aspects are emphasized in equal measure. Zeus the bull looks at the fair Europa with lustful, almost human eyes. The maiden's pose is completely realistic. Not for nothing did Serov seek this pose in a live model, making numerous sketches of her until he finally hit upon a variant that blended into one the archaic and the real. The movement of the swimming bull is quite vigorous, but at the same time it is arrested by the turn of his head, the equilibrium of the two waves flanking the heads of Europa and Zeus, and the sprawling blotch of orange that blends smoothly with the blue of the sea. It is as though a live bull were swimming in an unreal sea. True, this sense of unreality is relative because for all their conventionality the waves do create a sensation of rhythmic and measured motion as they lift the bull and the maiden to the crest and then bring them down again. This combining of the imaginary with the real was something Serov always tried to achieve, whether in his portraits or drawings for Krylov's fables or illustrations on historic themes. But it is in the artist's last works dedicated to antique subjects that this became practically the central problem. The very character of mythology was partly responsible for this.

The myth is always a blend of the real and the imaginary, perhaps that is why the entire art of the late nineteenth and early twentieth centuries was so attracted to it. In fact, the question even arose of creating a new mythology. Serov turned in his works to already existing myths: he did not create any new ones but rather gave the old ones a new artistic interpretation. The same can be said of Vrubel, another great Russian artist of that period. Pan or the Swan Princess, the Demon or Faust — these are the protagonists of most of Vrubel's works. With Vrubel, the blend of the fantastic and the real is even more striking. He invents rather than illustrates. Serov is calmer and more sober. Nevertheless, in their approach to mythological motifs the two masters are basically similar.

On a par with Serov's late painting is his graphic art. From 1905 to 1910 it acquired an unusual stylistic purity. This is evident in the portraits of Yura Morozov (1905) and of the ballerina Tamara Karsavina (1909), and in his illustrations to Krylov's fables which he undertook with enthusiasm in his last period. As in all his works, Serov searches for the last and final truth, the ultimate reason for the existence of all living things. But there is more to it than that — these drawings speak of a consummate craftsmanship. The line in Serov's drawing grows ever more meaningful; it now expresses different aspects of reality, retaining at the same time its own rhythm and beauty. And it should be pointed out that Serov's craftsmanship and superb artistry are expressive of content too. In his portraiture, they are a necessary component of the image; in his mythology and history pieces, they are part and parcel of a style born of modern vision and the historico-artistic approach; in his drawings on whatever subject, they express the artist's difficult, hard-won power over the material — his unwavering artistic perseverance, which tends to impart a convincing, real-life aspect to the image. With Serov one always marvels at the way form, which seems to be an end in itself, turns out full of deep, inner meaning. Much of this is due to the firm principles of the style to which Serov always aspired and which, along with a number of contemporaries, he had actually created. It is characteristic that this style was given its fullest expression in his drawings and in the graphic skeleton of his paintings.

Style is a type of art. Often one and the same type embraces not only different temperaments, but varying human interests that do not fall under the dominion of any style. Sometimes two artists stretch out their hands to each other through long centuries. Rouault, the sufferer of the twentieth century, can on occasion bring the great Rembrandt to mind. The magnificent Ingres aspired to don the mantle of Raphael. Some are united by the kindness in their hearts, others by the ecstasy in their souls. Among his contemporaries Serov is one of the few whose work lies outside the category of style. There are in it both sympathy and enmity. He can be unusually kind and share the painful thoughts and feelings of his models. He can understand the spontaneous emotional impulse of a child and echo with all his heart the creative inspiration of an actor. Yet at the same time he can appraise with cold analytical eyes the paltry essence of a petty man or woman.

Serov is intolerant of human platitude, unjustified pretentiousness, crying stupidity, parasitic wealth and idleness. Whatever his feelings, though, the artist always translates them into an aesthetic category. He never turns a portrait into a caricature. He seeks artistic formulas. In equal measure he transforms the characters of Yermolova and Orlova, obliterating incidental qualities and revealing the core of each model's individuality. Emotions are irrelevant; what counts is the ability to "raise to a numerical power." Perhaps it is this sharp-eyed vision that sets Serov apart from Vrubel, Korovin, Benois or Dobuzhinsky, and evokes memories of such dissimilar artists as Holbein and Goya the portraitist.

The above comparisons do not, of course, embrace the overall merits of any artist or his role in the history of world art. It is difficult to compare the great masters of the past with the artists of our time. But in the context of the actual historical and artistic developments in Russia at the turn of the century, Serov is a figure that stands alone. He was a true teacher who gave Russian art a number of dissimilar and talented painters, an artist whose work paved the way for others. Above all, he was a great master who performed to perfection the role assigned to him by history — to lead Russian art into the twentieth century.

DMITRY SARABYANOV

Plates

1. Portrait of Pavel Chistiakov. 1881. Cat. No 58

2. M. Tognon Sleeping in a Chair. 1884. Cat. No 73

3. Horse. 1884. Cat. No 71

4. Portrait of Maria Mamontova as Amazon. 1884. Cat. No 70

5. Winter in Abramtsevo. The Church. Study. 1886. Cat. No 91

6. Bullocks. Study. 1885. Cat. No 77

7. After a Fire. 1880. Cat. No 45

8. The Betrothal of the Virgin Mary and St. Joseph. 1881. Cat. No 57

9. Portrait of Liudmila Mamontova. 1884. Cat. No 69

10. Portrait of Olga Trubnikova. 1885. Cat. No 81

11. Portrait of Olga Trubnikova. 1885. Cat. No 87

12. Portrait of Olga Trubnikova. 1885. Cat. No 88

13. Portrait of Maria Van Sandt. 1886. Cat. No 99

14. Amsterdam. View from a Hotel Window. Study. 1885. Cat. No 86

15. Piazza di San Marco in Venice. Study. 1887. Cat. No 118

16. Riva degli Schiavoni in Venice. Study. 1887. Cat. No 116

17. The Overgrown Pond. Domotkanovo. 1888. Cat. No 133

18. Portrait of Yekaterina Chokolova. 1887. Cat. No 120

19. Portrait of Nadezhda Derviz and Her Child. 1888—89. Cat. No 146

20. Portrait of Angelo Masini. 1890. Cat. No 168

21. Portrait of Sergei Chokolov. 1887. Cat. No 123

22. Autumn Evening. Domotkanovo. 1886. Cat. No 96

24. Self-portrait. 1887. Cat. No 128

25. Self-portrait. 1885. Cat. No 76

26. Portrait of Olga Serova. 1889–90. Cat. No 173

27. By the Window. Portrait of Olga Trubnikova. 1886. Cat. No 103

28, 29. Girl with Peaches. Portrait of Vera Mamontova. 1887. Cat. No 111

30. Portrait of Praskovya Mamontova. 1889. Cat. No 148

31. Open Window. Lilacs. Study. 1886. Cat. No 97

32. Winter in Abramtsevo. The Manor House. Study. 1886. Cat. No 90

33. An Old Bathhouse in Domotkanovo. 1888. Cat. No 137

34. Little Pond in Abramtsevo. Study. 1886. Cat. No 100

35. Portrait of Adelaida Simonovich. 1889. Cat. No 142

36, 37. Girl in the Sunlight. Portrait of Maria Simonovich. 1888. Cat. No 132

38. Portrait of Sophia Dragomirova. 1889. Cat. No 149

39. Portrait of Francesco Tamagno. 1891. Cat. No 186

40. A Tatar Village in the Crimea (A Crimean Yard). 1893. Cat. No 229

41, 42. Portrait of Konstantin Korovin. 1891. Cat. No 187

43. Portrait of Savva Mamontov. 1887. Cat. No 122

44. Portrait of Zinaida Moritz. 1892. Cat. No 197

45. Abraham's Servant Finds Isaac a Bride, Rebekah. 1894. Cat. No 241

46. After the Battle on the Field of Kulikovo. 1894. Cat. No 242

47. After the Battle on the Field of Kulikovo. 1894. Cat. No 266

48. Portrait of Nikolai Leskov. 1894. Cat. No 239

49. Portrait of Ivan Zabelin. 1892. Cat. No 198

50. The White Sea. 1894. Cat. No 247

51. In the Tundra. Reindeer Ride. 1896. Cat. No 296

52. The Pomors. 1894. Cat. No 260

53. Portrait of Isaac Levitan. 1893. Cat. No 225

54. Portrait of Mara Oliv. 1895. Cat. No 274

55. Portrait of Countess Musina-Pushkina. 1895. Cat. No 270

56. Portrait of Maria Lvova. 1895. Cat. No 273

57. Interior of the Assumption Cathedral, Moscow. 1896. Cat. No 282

58. The Coronation. 1896. Cat. No 281

59. Portrait of Grand Duke Pavel Alexandrovich. 1897. Cat. No 301

60. Portrait of Sergei Diaghilev. 1904. Cat. No 442

61. Portrait of Nikolai Rimsky-Korsakov. 1898. Cat. No 317

62. In Summer. Portrait of Olga Serova. 1895. Cat. No 267

63. Barns. 1904. Cat. No 450

64. Haystack. 1901. Cat. No 393

65. October in Domotkanovo. 1895. Cat. No 268

66. Horse Grazing. 1897. Cat. No 305

67. October. 1898. Cat. No 325

68. Peasant Woman with a Horse. 1899. Cat. No 339

69. In a Village. Peasant Woman with a Horse. 1898. Cat. No 310

70. Village. 1898. Cat. No 324

71. Herd. 1890s. Cat. No 367

72. In Winter. 1898. Cat. No 312

73. Rinsing Linen. Study. 1901. Cat. No 385

74. Peasant Woman in a Cart. 1896. Cat. No 280

75. Pushkin in the Country. 1899. Cat. No 344

76. Portrait of Alexander Pushkin. 1899. Cat. No 343

77. The Wolf in the Kennels. Drawing for Krylov's fable. 1896–98. Cat. No 658

78. Trishka's Caftan. Drawing for Krylov's fable. 1895–1911. Cat. No 674

79. The Peasant and the Robber. Drawing for Krylov's fable. 1895–1911. Cat. No 669

80. The Lion and the Wolf. Drawing for Krylov's fable. 1895–1911. Cat. No 663

81. The Pestilence. Drawing for Krylov's fable. 1896. Cat. No 672

82. The Wolf and the Shepherds. Drawing for Krylov's fable. 1898. Cat. No 655

83. The Pike. Drawing for Krylov's fable. 1895–1911. Cat. No 675

84. The Monkey and the Eyeglasses. Drawing for Krylov's fable. 1895–1911. Cat. No 668

85. An Aging Lion. Drawing for Krylov's fable. 1895–1911. Cat. No 666

86. The Quartet. Drawing for Krylov's fable. 1895–1911. Cat. No 661

87. The Wolf and the Crane. Drawing for Krylov's fable. 1895–1911. Cat. No 654

88. The Fox and the Grapes. Drawing for Krylov's fable. 1895–1911. Cat. No 667

89. The Daw in Peacock Feathers. Drawing for Krylov's fable. 1895–1911. Cat. No 657

90. The Crow and the Fox. Drawing for Krylov's fable. 1895–1911. Cat. No 659

91. Portrait of Alfred Nurok. 1899. Cat. No 347

92. Portrait of Alexander Glazunov. 1899. Cat. No 348

93. Portrait of Sergei Botkin. 1900–1. Cat. No 397

94. Sasha Serov. 1897. Cat. No 308

95, 96. The Children. Sasha and Yura Serov. 1899. Cat. No 331

97. Self-portrait. 1901. Cat. No 394

98. Portrait of Vasily Mathé. 1899. Cat. No 340

99. Mika Morozov. 1901. Cat. No 384

100. Misha Serov. 1902–3. Cat. No 427

101. Portrait of Sergei Botkin's Children. 1900. Cat. No 382

102. Portrait of Mikhail Morozov. 1902. Cat. No 405

103, 104. Portrait of Sophia Botkina. 1899. Cat. No 338

105. Nude. 1900. Cat. No 380

106. Model. 1905. Cat. No 463

107. Nude. 1910–11. Cat. No 637

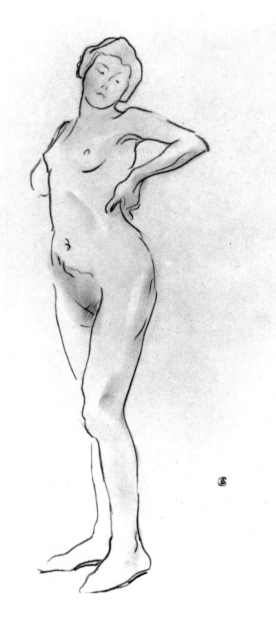

108. Nude. 1910–11. Cat. No 636

109. Nude. 1900. Cat. No 379

110. Portrait of Sophia Lukomskaya. 1900. Cat. No 383

111. Portrait of Ilya Repin. 1901. Cat. No 398

112. Portrait of Vera Ziloti. 1902. Cat. No 416

113. Portrait of Isaac Levitan. 1900. Cat. No 377

114. Portrait of Konstantin Pobedonostsev. 1902. Cat. No 418

115. Portrait of Piotr Semionov-Tien-Shansky. 1905. Cat. No 481

116. A Mill in Finland. 1902. Cat. No 408

117. A Finnish Yard. 1902. Cat. No 407

118, 119. Portrait of Zinaida Yusupova. 1900–2. Cat. No 403

120. Portrait of Nikolai Sumarokov-Elstone. 1903. Cat. No 423

121. Portrait of Felix Sumarokov-Elstone with a Dog. 1903. Cat. No 424

122. Terrace with a Balustrade. 1903. Cat. No 420

123, 124. Portrait of Felix Yusupov. 1903. Cat. No 425

125. Portrait of Ilya Ostroukhov. 1902. Cat. No 406

126. Portrait of Yevdokiya Loseva. 1903. Cat. No 422

127. Catherine II Driving Out. 1906. Cat. No 492

128. The Tsar's Borzois. 1900–1. Cat. No 395

129. Catherine II Setting Out to Hunt with Falcons. 1902. Cat. No 400

130. Peter II and Princess Elizabeth Riding to Hounds. 1900. Cat. No 368

131. Peter the Great Riding to Hounds. 1902. Cat. No 402

132. Portrait of Vladimir von Meck. 1901. Cat. No 396

133. Portrait of Cleopatra Obninskaya with a Hare. 1904. Cat. No 454

134. Colts at a Watering Place. Domotkanovo. 1904. Cat. No 446

135. Horses by the Seashore. 1905. Cat. No 462

136. Horses near a Pond. 1905. Cat. No 472

137. Bathing a Horse. 1905. Cat. No 461

138. Portrait of Fiodor Shaliapin. 1905. Cat. No 476

139. Iphigenia in Tauris. Sketch. 1893. Cat. No 230

140. Portrait of Konstantin Balmont. 1905. Cat. No 482

141, 142. Portrait of Maria Yermolova. 1905. Cat. No 466

143. Portrait of Glikeria Fedotova. 1905. Cat. No 465

144. Portrait of Alexander Turchaninov. 1906. Cat. No 493

145. Harvest. 1905–6. Cat. No 488

146. The Funeral of Bauman. 1905. Cat. No 468

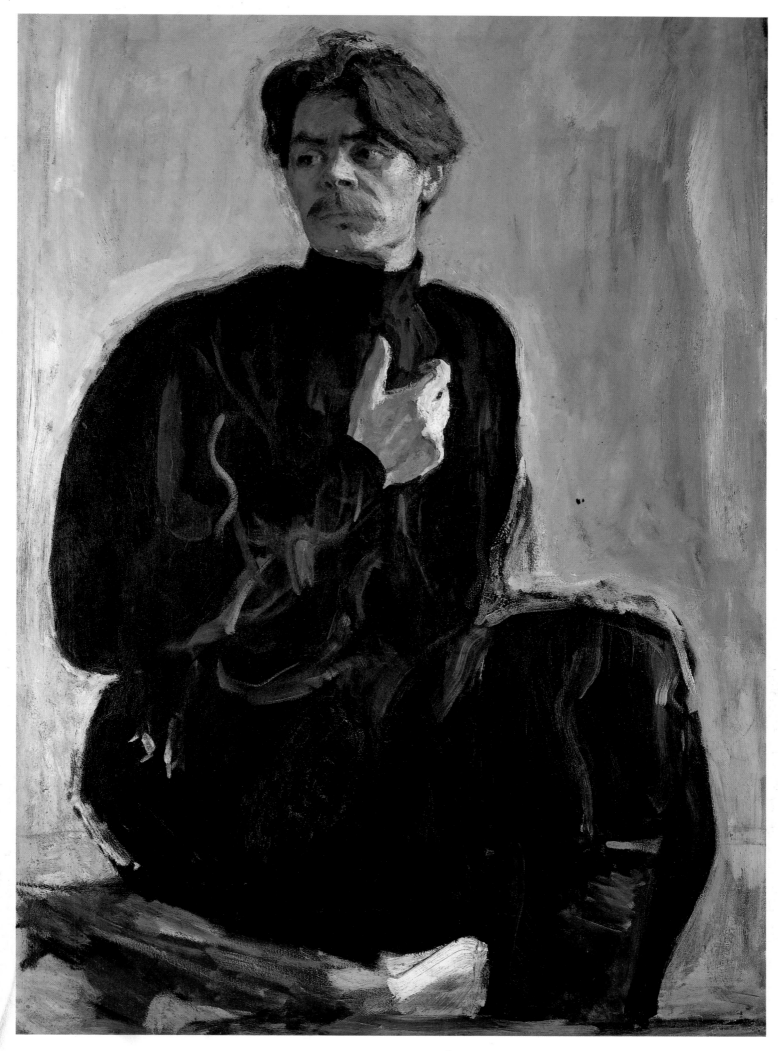

147, 148. Portrait of Maxim Gorky. 1905. Cat. No 467

149. "Soldiers, Soldiers, Heroes Every One . . ." 1905. Cat. No 469

150. The Year 1905. 1905. Cat. No 487

151. The Sumy Regiment. Sketch. 1905. Cat. No 486

152. The Year 1905. The Revolt Is Suppressed.
Caricature of Nicholas II. 1905. Cat. No 489

153. A Recruit. 1906. Cat. No 501

154. Pereyaslavl-Zalessky. Backyards. 1904–5. Cat. No 473

155. Wife Visits Her Husband
in Exile. 1904. Cat. No 448

156. Portrait of Vladimir Golitsyn. 1906. Cat. No 494

157. Portrait of Maria Botkina. 1905. Cat. No 480

158. Portrait of Henrietta Girshman. 1904. Cat. No 453

159, 160. Portrait of Henrietta Girshman. 1907. Cat. No 509

161. Portrait of Leonid Andreyev. 1907. Cat. No 522

162. Portrait of Leonid Andreyev. 1907. Cat. No 520

163. Peter the Great Riding.
1910–11. Cat. No 640

164. Peter the Great at a Construction Site. 1910–11. Cat. No 641

165. The Sporting Amusements of the Empress Anna Ioannovna. 1900s. Cat. No 567

166. Peter the Great. 1907. Cat. No 506

167. The Grand Eagle Cup. 1910. Cat. No 570

168. Peter the Great in the Palace of Monplaisir. 1910–11. Cat. No 578

169. Portrait of Mikhail Vrubel. 1907. Cat. No 523

170. Portrait of Nikolai Rimsky-Korsakov. 1908. Cat. No 542

171. Portrait of Yelizaveta Karzinkina. 1905. Cat. No 477

172. Portrait of Isabella Grünberg. 1910. Cat. No 606

173. Portrait of Anna Staal. 1910. Cat. No 580

174. Portrait of Nadezhda Lamanova. 1911. Cat. No 645

175. Portrait of Wanda Landowska. 1907. Cat. No 519

176. Portrait of Maria Akimova. 1908. Cat. No 534

177. Portrait of Nikolai Pozniakov. 1908. Cat. No 535

178. Portrait of Yelena Oliv. 1909. Cat. No 547

179. Portrait of the Kasyanov Children. 1907. Cat. No 518

180. Portrait of N. Z. Rappoport. 1908. Cat. No 543

181. Portrait of Ivan Moskvin. 1908. Cat. No 540

182. Portrait of Vasily Kachalov. 1908. Cat. No 539

183. Portrait of Konstantin Stanislavsky. 1908. Cat. No 541

184. Portrait of Tamara Karsavina. 1909. Cat. No 559

185. Portrait of Mikhail Fokine. 1909. Cat. No 562

186. Portrait of Vaslav Nijinsky. 1910. Cat. No 605

187. Portrait of Anna Pavlova. 1909. Cat. No 558

188, 189. Anna Pavlova in the Ballet *Sylphide*. 1909. Cat. No 550

190. Design of the curtain for the ballet *Sheherazade*.
1910. Cat. No 618

191. Design of the curtain for the ballet *Sheherazade.* 1910. Cat. No 623

192, 193. Portrait of Ida Rubinstein. 1910. Cat. No 582

194. Apollo and Diana Killing Niobe's Sons. 1911. Cat. No 650

195. Diana. 1911. Cat. No 653

196. Scenery design for the opera *Judith*. 1907. Cat. No 514

197. Scenery design for the opera *Judith*. 1907. Cat. No 510

198. Nausicaä. 1910. Cat. No 600

199. Odysseus and Nausicaä. 1910. Cat. No 574

200. Odysseus and Nausicaä. 1910. Cat. No 575

201. Odysseus and Nausicaä. 1910. Cat. No 573

202. The Rape of Europa. Sketch. 1910. Cat. No 616

203. The Rape of Europa. Sketch. 1909. Cat. No 563

204. Nude. 1910. Cat. No 615

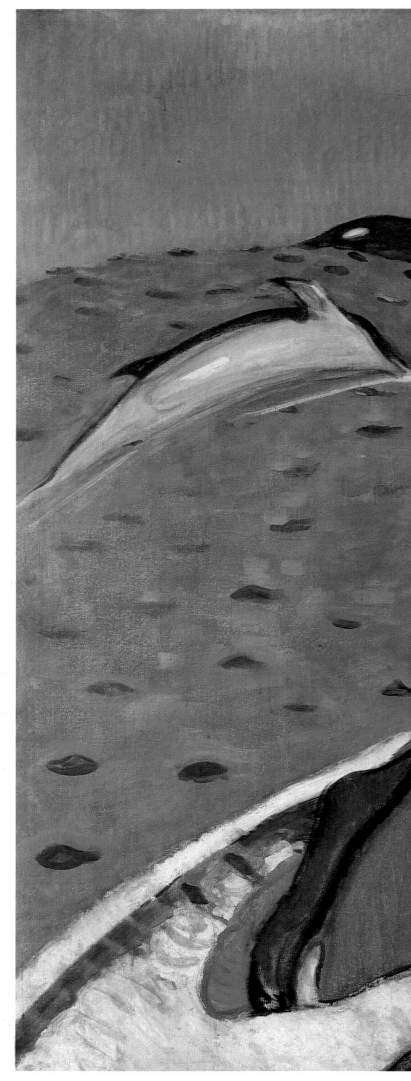

205. The Rape of Europa. 1910. Cat. No 589

206. The Rape of Europa. Terra-cotta. 1910. Cat. No 598

207. The Rape of Europa. Porcelain. 1915. Cat. No 599

208. Portrait of Vladimir Girshman. 1911. Cat. No 629

209. Portrait of Emmanuel Nobel. 1909. Cat. No 549

210. Portrait of Ivan Morozov. 1910. Cat. No 581

211. Portrait of Yelena Balina. 1911. Cat. No 630

212. Portrait of Alexei Morozov. 1909. Cat. No 556

213. Portrait of Olga Orlova. 1911. Cat. No 646

214, 215. Portrait of Olga Orlova. 1911. Cat. No 632

216. Portrait of Margarita Morozova. 1910. Cat. No 583

217. Portrait of Henrietta Girshman. 1911. Cat. No 644

218. Portrait of Polina Shcherbatova. 1911. Cat. No 647

Biographical Outline

Catalogue

List of Sources Cited
in the Catalogue

Index of Works Reproduced

Index of Museums

Biographical Outline

1865

7 January: born in St. Petersburg into the family of the composer and music critic Alexander Serov.

1869

Goes with his parents abroad. Visits Richard Wagner in Lucerne.

1871

20 January: his father dies in St. Petersburg. His mother, Valentina Serova, née Bergman, a pianist, later a composer and advocate of music for peasants, goes to Munich to continue her training. Serov is taken to Nikolskoye, the estate of the Drutsky-Sokolinsky family in Smolensk Province, where a commune in the spirit of the Populist ideals is established. His talent for drawing and painting becomes pronounced.

1872

Is taken to his mother in Munich after the commune in Nikolskoye disintegrated.

1873

Spends the summer with his mother at Mühltal near Munich. Becomes acquainted with the German etcher and engraver Karl Köpping and accompanies him on sketching tours. Autumn: returns to Munich, takes occasional drawing lessons from Köpping.

1874

October: Serov and his mother leave Munich and settle in Paris (Boulevard Clichy). Frequents the studio of Ilya Repin in Rue Véron, drawing from plaster casts and painting still lifes. At home, on his own, draws from imagination and from

Valentina Serova, the artist's mother

Alexander Serov, the artist's father

Valentin Serov as a child

Maria and Nadezhda Simonovich, the artist's
cousins, and Olga Trubnikova (right)

memory. Participates from time to time in the activities of
the Russian artistic colony in Paris. Meets the writer Ivan
Turgenev.

1875

Summer: Serov and his mother return to Russia and settle at
Abramtsevo, Savva Mamontov's estate near Moscow. The
Serovs become close friends of the Mamontov family, their
connection lasting throughout their lives. Autumn: the Serovs
leave for St. Petersburg. The young Serov studies at Mai's
boarding school on Vasilyevsky Island.

1876

Spring: moves with his mother to Kiev. Spends the summer at
the village of Akhtyrka, Kharkov Province, on the estate of
Doctor V. Nemchinov, his mother's common-law husband.
Prepares for high school.

1877

Spends the summer at Akhtyrka. Autumn: enters the second
form of the Kiev Gymnasium. Attends the drawing school of
Nikolai Murashko.

1878

Spends the summer at Akhtyrka. Autumn: moves from Kiev to
Moscow. Resumes systematic art training with Repin, who
settled at Khamovniki, a Moscow suburb. Studies in the third
form of the First Moscow Progymnasium.

1879

Spring: leaves the Progymnasium and settles at Repin's. Pre-
pares for the Academy of Arts. Summer: works at Abramtsevo
with Repin.
Autumn: accompanies Repin on his trip to St. Petersburg.
In the Hermitage, copies Rembrandt's *Portrait of an Old
Woman with Spectacles.*

1880

On New Year's day executes a drawing, *After a Fire,* from a
window of Repin's apartment at Khamovniki. Continues to
prepare for the Academy of Arts. Makes his first drawings from
a nude model, paints and draws still lifes.
May–July: accompanies Repin, who collects material for his
painting *The Zaporozhye Cossacks,* on his journey around the
Crimea, visiting Odessa, Chernigov, and Zaporozhye. Paints
studies, draws, executes independent compositions on subjects from the life of Zaporozhye Cossacks. Returns to Moscow via Kiev. Paints a study of a hunchback model, his last
work at Repin's studio in Khamovniki.
August: goes to St. Petersburg and takes entrance examina-
tions at the Academy of Arts (admitted as a "free attendant").
Meets Mikhail Vrubel. Joins the private studio of Professor
Chistiakov.

1881

March: draws a portrait of Chistiakov, showing a good knowl-
edge of the so-called "Chistiakov system."
Summer: works at Repin's *dacha* in Khotkov near Moscow
and at Abramtsevo.

Valentin Serov as a young man

Autumn: returns to St. Petersburg, works in academic classes and at Chistiakov's studio.

1882
Summer: sketches at Siabrintsy, Novgorod Province. Meets the writer Gleb Uspensky. August: returns to St. Petersburg. Is promoted from "free attendant" to "academist." Works at Chistiakov's studio. Friendship with Vrubel. Attends watercolor classes at the studio of Repin in Ekaterinhof Avenue.

1883
Attends academic classes. Early summer: passes science exams. Summer: sketches in the Crimea. Second half of June: together with his fellow student Vladimir Derviz makes a trip to the Caucasus. Autumn: continues his work in academic classes and at Chistiakov's studio. Together with Derviz joins Vrubel in the studio rented by him. Makes a watercolor from a model in a Renaissance setting.

1884
Summer: works in Siabrintsy, then at Abramtsevo. Simultaneously with Victor Vasnetsov, draws a portrait of the sculptor Mark Antokolsky, and estimates his sketch to be "better and more lifelike than Vasnetsov's." Autumn: returns to St. Petersburg, attends academic classes and Chistiakov's studio.

1885
Spring: works at Siabrintsy. Summer: travels abroad with his mother. At the Pinakothek in Munich, copies a portrait by Velázquez. In Belgium and Holland, studies paintings by the Flemish and Dutch Old Masters. 25 August—7 September: lives and works in Moscow and at Abramtsevo. Early Sep-

tember: returns to St. Petersburg and resumes academic studies, but in the latter half of the month leaves the Academy. Goes to Moscow, where he paints a commissioned portrait of the Italian singer Antonio d'Andrade. November: visits Odessa. Paints the study *Bullocks* on the estate of the artist Nikolai Kuznetsov. December: paints a portrait of Olga Trubnikova, his fiancée, in Odessa.

1886
2 January: the 5th Periodical Exhibition of the Moscow Society of Art Lovers, the first show in which Serov ever participated, opens in Moscow. Late winter — early spring: lives in Moscow. Attends classes at the Moscow School of Painting, Sculpture and Architecture. Early summer: stays at the village of Yedimonovo, Tver Province. Paints a portrait of Olga Trubnikova. Summer — autumn: stays at Domotkanovo, Derviz's estate in Tver Province. September: goes to St. Petersburg to confirm his retirement from the Academy. Returns to Domotkanovo. Paints the study *Autumn Evening. Domotkanovo.* Late October: returns to Moscow. Friendship with young artists — Ilya Ostroukhov, Mikhail Mamontov, and Nikolai Tretyakov. Works at the studio they rented in Lenivka Street. Early winter: sketches at Abramtsevo.

Valentin Serov (right) and his fellow students,
Mikhail Vrubel and Vladimir Derviz. 1883–84

Valentin Serov (standing left) and members of the Abramtsevo artistic circle. 1886

1887

Winter and spring: lives in Moscow. Before mid-March, visits Domotkanovo. At the studio in Lenivka Street, paints a decorative ceiling, *Phoebus Effulgent*, for Selezniov's country house. Paints a portrait of Savva Mamontov at the latter's studio in Sadovo-Spasskaya Street. May: together with Ostroukhov and the brothers Mikhail and Yury Mamontov makes a trip to Venice, Florence and Milan, visiting Vienna on the way. June — mid-July: works at Domotkanovo. Second half of July — September: lives at Abramtsevo. Paints a portrait of Vera Mamontova (*Girl with Peaches*). October: works in the Crimea, then goes for a short stay to Domotkanovo. November — early December: works in Yaroslavl on commissioned portraits, from time to time visits Abramtsevo. December: works in Moscow.

1888

Winter: lives in Moscow. Completes a portrait of Maria Yakunchikova (begun in 1886). Spring — mid-September: works at Domotkanovo. Summer: paints a portrait of Maria Simonovich (*Girl in the Sunlight*). End of summer: paints the landscape *The Overgrown Pond. Domotkanovo*. 17 September — 7 October: lives in Moscow. Collects material (photographs, engravings, etc.) for the portrait of his father, which he intends to finish for the jubilee performance of Serov's opera *Judith*. Late autumn — early winter: works in St. Petersburg. December: awarded first prize for the portrait of Vera Mamontova (*Girl with Peaches*) at the competition organized by the Moscow Society of Art Lovers. Shows his *Girl with Peaches*, *Girl in the Sunlight*, *The Overgrown Pond. Domotkanovo*, and a portrait of the composer Pavel Blaramberg at the 8th Periodical Exhibition of the Moscow Society of Art Lovers. Pavel Tretyakov buys the portrait of Maria Simonovich (*Girl in the Sunlight*) for his gallery.

1889

29 January: marries Olga Trubnikova in St. Petersburg. Settles at No 11, Mikhailovskaya Square. Works on the portrait of his father. Late April — early May: paints a commissioned portrait of the Reformist pastor Dalton. Copies *Portrait of the Pope Innocent X* by Velázquez in the Hermitage. August: works for a short time at Vvedenskoye near Zvenigorod. September: goes to Paris with his wife (via Berlin, Dresden, Nuremberg and Munich) to attend the World Exhibition. Early October: stays at Domotkanovo. Brief visit to St. Petersburg. End of the year: having left his wife at Domotkanovo, stays at the Mamontovs' in Sadovo-Spasskaya Street in Moscow. Friendship with Vrubel and Konstantin Korovin. Helps Vrubel to paint

Valentin Serov and Piotr Spiro,
a member of Mamontov's artistic circle

Valentin Serov. Late 1880s

stage sets for an amateur theatrical performance at Mamontov's house (with Konstantin Stanislavsky acting) and also plays a part in it.

1890

January — March: paints a portrait of the Italian singer Angelo Masini, commissioned by Savva Mamontov. February: his daughter Olga is born. 11 February — 20 March, St. Petersburg; 31 March — 22 April, Moscow: the 18th Exhibition of the Itinerant Society — the first Itinerants' exhibition to show works by Serov. Spring: together with Korovin paints a composition *Christ Walking upon the Water* for the parish church of the Tretyakov Factory in Kostroma and executes commissioned portraits there. Summer: paints portraits and landscapes at Domotkanovo. Autumn: moves with his family to Moscow for permanent residence. Settles in Maly Gnezdnikovsky Lane, in the house of Krummbügel. Probably in the same year, moves to a new apartment in Bolshoi Vorotnikovsky Lane. Awarded first prize for his portrait of Angelo Masini at the competition organized by the Moscow Society of Art Lovers; shows this portrait at the 10th Periodical Exhibition of the Society.

1891

Winter: paints a portrait of the Italian opera singer Francesco Tamagno. March: prepares illustrations for Lermontov's works. Spring: paints studies in Vladimir Province together with Korovin. Summer: works at Domotkanovo. Autumn: paints Korovin's portrait at the studio in Dolgorukovskaya (now Kaliayevskaya) Street, in the house of Chervenko.

1892

Winter: finishes the portrait of Zinaida Moritz, begun in 1891. May: paints a portrait of Sophia Tolstaya, the writer's wife, at Khamovniki. Meets Leo Tolstoy. Receives a commission from the nobility of Kharkov to paint *Alexander III with His Family*. Spends the summer traveling. Early June: visits Bolshiye Berezniaki, Simbirsk Province, where his mother established a free food kitchen during a famine and organized a peasant chorus. Paints a portrait of Derviz's daughter Liolia at Domotkanovo. Paints a portrait of Repin in St. Petersburg. Works on a portrait of the historian Ivan Zabelin in Moscow; paints *Coach from Moscow to Kuzminki*. Paints a portrait of Olga Tamara at Khimki. Autumn: works at Domotkanovo. Takes part in the 12th Periodical Exhibition of the Moscow Society of Art Lovers. End of the year: the artist Isaac Levitan sits for him at his studio. Serov's son Alexander is born.

1893

Winter: completes the portrait of Levitan. 15 February — 21 March, St. Petersburg; 29 March — 9 May, Moscow: shows his works at the 21st Exhibition of the Itinerant Society. Goes to St. Petersburg to carry out a commission. Summer: stays with his family at Kokoz in the Crimea; paints the studies *A Tatar Village in the Crimea (A Crimean Yard)*, *Tatar Women by the River*. *The Crimea*, and a portrait of Rosalia Lvova. Paints studies for the painting *Iphigenia in Tauris* in Yalta. On return works in Moscow and St. Petersburg. Contributes three oils to the 13th Periodical Exhibition of the Moscow Society of Art Lovers.

Valentin Serov (extreme right) at a party given by Savva Mamontov
(extreme left) in Abramtsevo. 1888

1894

Winter and spring: paints portraits of Liudmila Mamontova,
probably works on sketches for *After the Battle on the Field of
Kulikovo* and *Abraham's Servant Finds Isaac a Bride, Rebekah.* 8 March — 10 April, St. Petersburg; 18 April — 15 May,
Moscow: shows his works at the 22nd Exhibition of the Itinerant Society; is elected member of the Society. March — June:
brief visits to St. Petersburg to paint a portrait of the writer
Nikolai Leskov, commissioned by Pavel Tretyakov for his
gallery. June: goes to Kharkov and Borki to complete the work
commissioned by the Kharkov Assembly of the Nobility. Mid-
summer — late September: makes a trip to the North (to
Arkhangelsk and the Murman area) together with Korovin to
fulfill a commission of the Yaroslavl – Arkhangelsk Railway
Board. Probably in the same year, moves to Staropimenovsky
Lane, renting an apartment in the house of Princess
Kudasheva. His son George is born.

1895

First half of the year: works in Moscow. 17 February —
26 March, St. Petersburg; 3 April — 7 May, Moscow: shows
his works at the 23rd Exhibition of the Itinerant Society.
Spends the summer with his family at Domotkanovo, paints
portraits of his wife (*In Summer*) and Maria Lvova. Autumn:
paints *October in Domotkanovo.* End of the year: paints portraits of Mara Oliv, Varvara Musina-Pushkina, and V. Kapnist.
Takes part in the 15th Periodical Exhibition of the Moscow
Society of Art Lovers.

1896

January — May: works in Moscow. His son Mikhail is born.
Early February: makes a trip to St. Petersburg. 11 February —
17 March, St. Petersburg; 25 March — 21 May, Moscow:
shows his works at the 24th Exhibition of the Itinerant Society.
Spring: meets Alexander Benois. Exhibits for the first time at
the Munich Secession. Summer: works on the painting *The
River Nymph*, paints studies and makes drawings for Krylov's
fables at Domotkanovo. Autumn: paints *Peasant Woman in a
Cart* at Domotkanovo. Contributes to the 16th Periodical
Exhibition of the Moscow Society of Art Lovers.

1897

First half of the year: works in Moscow and St. Petersburg,
probably on portraits of Maria Morozova and Grand Duke
Pavel Alexandrovich. Meets Serge Diaghilev. 2 March —
6 April, St. Petersburg; 14 April — 11 May, Moscow: shows his
works at the 25th Exhibition of the Itinerant Society. Spends
the summer at Domotkanovo. Visits Munich, Berlin and Hamburg, sketching in zoological gardens. Begins teaching at the
Moscow School of Painting, Sculpture and Architecture. Contributes to the 17th Exhibition of the Moscow Society of Art
Lovers. Moves with his family to the house of the Dolgorukov
brothers in Volkhonka Street.

1898

January: takes part in the Exhibition of Russian and Finnish
Painters organized by Diaghilev in St. Petersburg. Winter:

Valentin Serov (left), Ilya Ostroukhov (at the piano), and Sergei, Mikhail and Yury Mamontov in Abramtsevo. 1888

works on the pastels *In a Village. Peasant Woman with a Horse, In Winter* and *From the Manor's Window.* End of winter: paints a portrait of the composer Nikolai Rimsky-Korsakov in St. Petersburg. 22 February — 29 March, St. Petersburg; 6 April — 10 May, Moscow: shows his works at the 26th Exhibition of the Itinerant Society. 23 March: at a general session of the Academy of Arts is given the title of Academician. 1 May — 1 June: contributes to the exhibition of works by Russian and Finnish painters held in Munich and then in Cologne, Düsseldorf and Berlin, showing *Portrait of Grand Duke Pavel Alexandrovich, Girl with Peaches* and *The Overgrown Pond. Domotkanovo.* Summer: stays on the Mologa River at Borisogleb; executes a watercolor portrait of Varvara Musina-Pushkina, engraves his illustration for *The Wolf and Shepherds* and paints a self-portrait. Is elected member of the Verein bildender Künstler (Munich Secession).

1899
January — February: shows his works at the 1st International Exhibition of Paintings Organized by the *Mir Iskusstva* Magazine in St. Petersburg. March: probably takes a trip to Munich. Displays his *Portrait of Mara Oliv* and *Peasant Woman with a Horse* at the Secession Exhibition. 17 March — 11 April, St. Petersburg; 19 April — 9 May, Moscow: contributes to the 27th Exhibition of the Itinerant Society, the last Itinerants' exhibition to show works by Serov. Early June: is

elected for a three-year term member of the Council of the Tretyakov Gallery, formed after the death of Pavel Tretyakov; remains in this position for the rest of his life, being continuously re-elected. Spends the summer at Terijoki near St. Petersburg. Friendship with Alexander Benois. Paints *The Children.* Second half of July: makes a tour of Denmark to collect material for the portrait of Alexander III. November: in Moscow, completes the portrait of Sophia Botkina begun in early September. Moves with his family to a new apartment in Malaya Dmitrovka Street.

1900
January — 21 March: works on portraits of Nicholas II and Grand Duke Mikhail Nikolayevich in St. Petersburg. 28 January — 26 February: contributes to the 2nd Exhibition of Paintings Organized by the *Mir Iskusstva* Magazine. A new artistic society, the World of Art, is established, with the managing committee of the next exhibition of the *Mir Iskusstva* Magazine including Benois, Diaghilev and Serov. Moves with his family to the Ulanovs' house in Bolshoi Znamensky Lane. Works on illustrations for the book *Royal Hunting in Russia.* June: begins work on a portrait of Zinaida Yusupova in St. Petersburg. August: participates in the Paris World Exhibition, and receives the highest award (Grande Médaille d'Honneur) for his *Portrait of Grand Duke Pavel Alexandrovich.* October: visits Paris to attend the World Exhibition.

1901

Winter: works in St. Petersburg and Moscow. Contributes to the 3rd Exhibition of Paintings Organized by the *Mir Iskusstva* Magazine in St. Petersburg. May: works in St. Petersburg. Spends the summer at his *dacha* at Ino, Finland. Late autumn and winter: paints landscapes at Domotkanovo. December: turns down a commission to paint the tsar's portrait.
28 December — 3 February 1902: participates in the 1st Exhibition of the Thirty-six Painters Society in Moscow.

1902

February: works on a portrait of Konstantin Pobedonostsev in St. Petersburg. Contributes to the 4th Exhibition of Paintings Organized by the *Mir Iskusstva* Magazine in St. Petersburg. Paints portraits of Mikhail Morozov and Ilya Ostroukhov in Moscow. Alexander Benois publishes *A History of Russian Painting in the 19th Century* with a few pages devoted to Serov. Summer: makes a trip to Bayreuth, Bavaria, together with his mother and the conductor Alexander Khessin to attend the performance of Wagner's operas; on his way visits Berlin and Leipzig. August: completes the portrait of Zinaida Yusupova in St. Petersburg. Autumn: lives at Ino, paints the canvas *A Finnish Yard* and the sketch *A Mill in Finland.* Completes work on the illustrations for the book *Royal Hunting in Russia.* Participates in the Exhibition Organized by the *Mir Iskusstva* Magazine in Moscow. Early December: meets (probably for the first time) the writer Maxim Gorky in Moscow.

Alexander and Olga, the artist's eldest children. Early 1890s

Valentin Serov painting the portrait of Isaac Levitan. 1893

1903

Works in Moscow, with occasional visits to St. Petersburg.
13 February — 23 March: contributes to the 5th Exhibition of
Paintings Organized by the *Mir Iskusstva* Magazine in
St. Petersburg. 21 April: is elected Professor, head of a studio
of the Higher Art School of the Academy of Arts at a session
of the Academy. 27 April: declines this post in a letter to the
Academy authorities. Summer: works at Ino. August — early
September: works on portraits of Felix Sumarokov-Elstone,
Felix Yusupov, and Nikolai Sumarokov-Elstone at Abramtsevo.
Portrait of Zinaida Yusupova and *A Peasant Yard* are shown
at the Berlin Secession International Exhibition. Early October:
Serov falls ill. 27 October: is elected Full Member of the
Imperial Academy of Arts at its general session. 25 November:
operated on at the hospital of Dr. Chegodayev.

1904

15 January: leaves the hospital. Begins to work on a portrait of
Henrietta Girshman (first version). February — March: visits
Domotkanovo where he works on his pastels *Colts at a
Watering-place. Domotkanovo, Road in Domotkanovo* and
Stable in Domotkanovo. April — May: tours Italy with his wife,
visiting Rome, Venice, Naples, Padua and Ravenna. Early
June: lives at Ino. Autumn: works at Belkino, the Obninsky
family estate near Moscow. November: works on Girshman's
portrait. Participates in the 2nd Exhibition of the Union of
Russian Artists.

1905

Paints a portrait of Maria Yermolova commissioned by the
Moscow Circle of Literature and Art. 9 January: becomes an
eye-witness of the massacre of a peaceful demonstration of
workers by tsarist troops in St. Petersburg. 18 February: sends
a letter, together with Vasily Polenov, to the Board of the
Academy of Arts, in which they accuse Grand Duke Vladimir,
President of the Academy, of being one of the organizers of
the massacre. 10 March: also in protest against it, puts in an
application of resignation from the Imperial Academy of Arts.
March — April: takes part in the Exhibition of Russian Portraits
arranged by Diaghilev at the Tauride Palace in St. Petersburg.
Summer: works on Korovin's estate on the Nerl (a tributary of
the Kliazma), at his *dacha* at Ino, and in St. Petersburg. July:
draws political caricatures for the newly established satirical
magazine *Zhupel.* From the end of August, lives in Moscow;
paints a portrait of the actress Glikeria Fedotova commissioned by the Moscow Circle of Literature and Art. September:
works on a portrait of Maxim Gorky. 4 December: begins a
portrait of Vladimir Golitsyn. Participates in a meeting of the
staff of the satirical magazine *Zhalo* at Maxim Gorky's apartment. Serov's drawing *Soldiers, Soldiers, Heroes Every
One . . .* published in the first issue of *Zhupel.*

1906

Beginning of the year: works in Moscow and St. Petersburg.
Completes the portrait of Vladimir Golitsyn. Paints a portrait of
Alexander Turchaninov. Begins another portrait of Henrietta
Girshman (at a dressing-table). 24 February — 26 March: participates in the World of Art Exhibition organized by Diaghilev
in St. Petersburg. Summer: lives at Ino. September: moves to
a new apartment in Golofteyev's house near the Church of

Our Saviour in Moscow. November: begins to work regularly
on Girshman's portrait. Participates in the Exhibition of Russian Art at the Salon d'Automne in Paris and in the Exhibition
of Russian Art in Berlin. Igor Grabar starts work on a monograph devoted to Serov. Serov's works shown at the
3rd Exhibition of the Union of Russian Artists in Moscow.

1907

Winter and spring: works on the portrait of Girshman in Moscow and completes it. Contributes to the 4th Exhibition of the
Union of Russian Artists in Moscow. May — June: together
with Leon Bakst, travels through Greece with the purpose
(according to Bakst) of "finding a modern manner of represen-
tation." Executes a great number of watercolors and sketches,
among them the first version of *The Rape of Europa.* End of
summer: works at Ino, probably paints a portrait of Leonid
Andreyev. Works on a double portrait of two famous actors,
Alexander Lensky and Alexander Yuzhin, commissioned by
the Moscow Circle of Literature and Art. Works on the painting
Peter the Great. October — December: works on stage
designs for Alexander Serov's opera *Judith.* His works shown
at the International Art Exhibition in Venice and at the 5th
Exhibition of the Union of Russian Artists in Moscow.

Valentin Serov by Ilya Repin. 1901

1908

Paints portraits of Maria Akimova, Nikolai Pozniakov, Yevdokia Morozova, Dmitry Stasov and Anna Benois in Moscow and St. Petersburg. Works on the composition *The Smart Moscow Cabman.* March: draws a portrait of Nikolai Rimsky-Korsakov for Diaghilev in St. Petersburg. July: moves to a new apartment in Kliukin's house in Vagankovsky Lane in Moscow, the artist's last home. Summer: lives at Ino. Autumn: draws portraits of the actors Konstantin Stanislavsky, Vasily Kachalov and Ivan Moskvin in Moscow. His works shown at the 5th Exhibition of the Union of Russian Artists in St. Petersburg and at the 6th Exhibition of the Union of Russian Artists in Moscow. His daughter Natalia is born.

1909

6 January: the Exhibition of Works by Russian Artists opens in the Vienna Secession, including paintings by Serov. 26 January: resigns his teaching job at the Moscow School of Painting. February: contributes to the Exhibition of Painting, Architecture, Sculpture and Graphics (the "Salon") in St. Petersburg. March: begins work on a portrait of Princess Orlova in St. Petersburg. Summer: lives at Ino, probably working on sketches for the composition *Odysseus and Nausicaä.* End of the year: stays in Paris with Ivan and Nina Yefimov, who rented a chapel in the Sacré-Cœur Monastery near the Boulevard des Invalides. Draws at the Colarossi school. His works shown at the 6th Exhibition of the Union of Russian Artists in St. Petersburg, at the 7th Exhibition of the Union of Russian Artists in Moscow, and at the 10th International Secession Exhibition in Munich.

1910

17 January — 7 February: his works shown at the Exhibition of Contemporary Russian Female Portraits organized by the *Apollon* magazine in St. Petersburg. Works on versions of *The Grand Eagle Cup, Peter the Great at a Construction Site,* and *The Rape of Europa* in Moscow. Late March — early April: works on commissioned portraits in St. Petersburg. Early May: makes a trip to Italy, visiting Rome, Siena, Orvieto and Genoa. Second half of May — July: lives in Paris with the Yefimovs. Works on a portrait of Ida Rubinstein. Attends the performances of the *Ballets Russes* (the Russian Seasons) at the Grand-Opéra in Paris. Meets French painters, Matisse among them. Late July — August: lives at Ino. Works on versions of *Odysseus and Nausicaä.* 31 July: is commissioned by the Italian Ministry of Popular Education to paint a self-portrait for the Uffizi Gallery in Florence. Second half of August — September: paints a double portrait of Oscar and Rosa Grusenberg in Sestroretsk. 22 September: publishes a letter in the newspaper *Rech* in connection with a discussion of Diaghilev's theatrical activities, much admired by Serov. Second half of October: lives in Paris. End of October — November: paints a portrait of Maria Zetlin in Biarritz. Travels to Madrid. Visits his son Anton in a sanatorium at Berck-sur-Mer. Early December: works in Paris. Contributes to the 7th Exhibition of the Union of Russian Artists in St. Petersburg.

1911

Early January: visits Domotkanovo. Participates in the first exhibition of the re-established World of Art Society in

Valentin Serov's Studio in Paris.
Etching by N. Simonovich-Yefimova

St. Petersburg. Second half of January — early February: works on the portrait of Princess Orlova and completes it. Works on curtain designs for the ballet *Sheherazade.* April: in Paris, with Ivan and Nina Yefimov, begins to paint the curtain for *Sheherazade.* 7 April — 4 May: together with his wife visits Rome to attend the International Art Exhibition, where his works are shown in a special room. Tours the vicinity of Rome in the company of the families of Alexander Benois, Igor Stravinsky and Tamara Karsavina. Returns to Paris. 11 June: completes the curtain for *Sheherazade.* First performances of *Sheherazade* with Serov's curtain at the Théâtre du Châtelet in Paris (between 11 and 17 June) and Covent Garden in London (7 July). End of June: leaves for London to attend the Russian Seasons. Returns from London by sea via Hamburg, Lubeck, Copenhagen and Abo. The Alexander III Museum in St. Petersburg acquires his *Portrait of Ida Rubinstein.* Lives at Ino from mid-July, with occasional visits to St. Petersburg. Works on drawings for Krylov's fables. Late August: works on the compositions *Peter the Great in the Palace of Monplaisir, Peter the Great at a Construction Site,* and on mural designs for Nosov's house in Moscow. Autumn: paints a portrait of the village teacher M. Shelamova at Domotkanovo. Late October — early November: meets Henri Matisse during the latter's visit to Moscow. 13 November: the 12th Lemercier Gallery Exhibition opens in St. Petersburg, including works by Serov. 20 November: the exhibition of the World of Art Society including works by Serov opens in Moscow. Works on portraits of Henrietta Girshman, Polina Shcherbatova, Nadezhda Lamanova and Konstantin Stanislavsky. 22 November: Serov dies in Moscow.

Catalogue

(See Note to the Catalogue on p. 379)

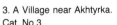

1. Blue Vase. Cat. No 1

2. At Akhtyrka. Wooden House.
Cat. No 2

3. A Village near Akhtyrka.
Cat. No 3

1875
PAINTINGS

1
Blue Vase. 1875
Oil on canvas. 40×28.3 cm
Present whereabouts unknown
Provenance: The Serov family collection,
Moscow
Exhibitions: 1914 (posthumous) St. Peters-
burg (No 1), Moscow (No 1); 1935 The
Tretyakov Gallery (No 1), The Russian
Museum (No 1, as *Vase with Brushes*)
References: Grabar, *Serov*, 1914, pp. 23,
281; Grabar, *Serov*, 1965, pp. 23 (de-
scribed incorrectly as housed at the
Tretyakov Gallery), 374

1878
DRAWINGS

2
At Akhtyrka. Wooden House. 1878
Black lead. 12×21 cm
Signed and dated, bottom right:
В. Съровъ 1878 (V. Serov, 1878)
The Russian Museum (since 1916).
Inv. No. P-3147
Provenance: I. Repin collection, Kuokkala
Exhibitions: 1935 The Tretyakov Gallery
(No 215, as *A House in the Province*),
The Russian Museum (No 216, under the
same title)
References: Grabar, *Serov*, 1965, p. 375

3
A Village near Akhtyrka. 1878
Black lead. 10.9×21.9 cm
Signed and dated, bottom right:
В. Съровъ 1878 года (V. Serov, 1878)
The Russian Museum (since 1916).
Inv. No P-3149
Provenance: I. Repin collection, Kuokkala
Exhibitions: 1935 The Tretyakov Gallery
(No 212), The Russian Museum (No 213,
as *In the Ukraine*)
References: Grabar, *Serov*, 1965, p. 375

1879
PAINTINGS

4
Head of a Man in a Fur Cap.
Study. ⟨1879⟩
Oil on canvas
Present whereabouts unknown
Provenance: O. Serova collection, Moscow
The same model sat at the time for Ilya
Repin.

References: Grabar, *Serov*, 1914, p. 28
(as *Head of a Peasant*?); Grabar, *Serov*,
1965, p. 379

5
Keg with a Pen. 1879
Oil on canvas. 42.5×28.8 cm
Signed and dated, bottom left: *В. Съровъ
1879* (V. Serov, 1879)
Present whereabouts unknown
Provenance: O. Serova collection, Mos-
cow; F. Podtynnikov collection, Moscow
Exhibitions: 1935 The Tretyakov Gallery
(No 3), The Russian Museum (No 3); 1946
Central House of Art Workers, Moscow
(No 56); 1952 Moscow (No 2, as *Khokhlo-
ma Keg with a Pen*)
Reproductions: Serova 1968, between
pp. 188 and 189 (as *Still Life*)
References: Grabar, *Serov*, 1914, p. 28
(as *Still Life. Patterned Keg*);
Grabar, *Serov*, 1965, pp. 36, 378
(as *Keg. Still Life*)

6

Forest. Abramtsevo. 1879
Oil on canvas. 45×31 cm
Signed and dated, bottom right:
В. Съровъ 79 (V. Serov, 1879). Inscribed
by the artist, bottom left: *Абрамцево*
(Abramtsevo)
The Russian Museum. Inv. No Ж-1924
References: Grabar, *Serov*, 1965, p. 380

7

Copper Basin. 1879
Present whereabouts unknown
Provenance: I. Repin collection, Kuokkala
(until 1930)
References: *Serov in the Reminiscences
of His Contemporaries*, 1971, 1, p. 35;
Grabar, *Serov*, 1965, p. 379

8

**Eagle over the Body of a Dead
Cossack.** 1879 (on the subject of the
Ukrainian ballad of *Three Brothers
Fleeing Azov*)
Oil on cardboard. 29.5×22.5 cm
Signed and dated, top left: *В. Съровъ
1879* (V. Serov, 1879)
The Russian Museum (since 1916).
Inv. No Ж-1916
Provenance: I. Repin collection, Kuokkala
Exhibitions: 1935 The Tretyakov Gallery
(No 201, without date), The Russian
Museum (No 6)
References: Grabar, *Serov*, 1965, pp. 379,
380

9

Glazed Jug. 〈1879〉
Oil on canvas
Signed and dated, bottom right:
В. Съровъ 1879 (V. Serov, 1879)
Private collection, Paris
Provenance: I. Repin collection, Kuokkala
(until 1930)
Reproductions: Serova 1968, between
pp. 188 and 189
References: *Serov in the Reminiscences
of His Contemporaries*, 1971, 1, p. 35;
Grabar, *Serov*, 1965, p. 379

10

Cup. 1879
Oil on canvas, mounted on cardboard.
19.8×29 cm
Signed and dated, bottom left:
В. С. 1879 г. (V. S., 1879)
Present whereabouts unknown
Provenance: O. Serova collection,
Moscow; E. Helzer collection, Moscow;
V. Dmitriyev collection, Moscow
Exhibitions: 1935 The Tretyakov Gallery
(No 4, as *Cup against a Blue Back-
ground*), The Russian Museum (No 4,
under the same title); 1952 Moscow (No 1,
as *White Cup with a Saucer on a Blue
Tablecloth*)
References: Grabar, *Serov*, 1914, p. 281
(as *Still Life. White Cup*); Grabar, *Serov*,
1965, pp. 36, 379

11

A Horse's Skull on Red Drapery.
1879
Oil on canvas. 33.7×28.2 cm
Signed and dated, bottom right:
В. Съровъ 1879 (V. Serov, 1879)
The Tretyakov Gallery. Inv. No 30269
Provenance: The Serov family collection,
Moscow

Exhibitions: 1935 The Tretyakov Gallery
(No 2), The Russian Museum (No 2); 1946
Central House of Art Workers, Moscow
(No 70)
Reproductions: Chistiakov 1953, between
pp. 368 and 369
References: Grabar, *Serov*, 1914, p. 281;
Grabar, *Serov*, 1965, pp. 36, 279

12

A Human Skull. 〈1879〉
Oil on canvas
The Athenaeum, Helsinki
Provenance: I. Repin collection, Kuokkala
References: *Serov in the Reminiscences
of His Contemporaries*, 1971, 1, p. 35;
Grabar, *Serov*, 1965, p. 379

13

Apples and Leaves. 1879
Oil on canvas, mounted on cardboard.
23.6×52 cm
Signed and dated, bottom left: *В. Съровъ
1879* (V. Serov, 1879)
Abramtsevo Museum, Moscow region.
Inv. No Ж-82
"This still life was set for Serov by Ilya
Repin (see No 21) late in the winter
of 1879. The still life so fascinated
Repin himself that he also painted it. A
comparison of Repin's still life, now in the
Russian Museum, with that of Serov
shows that in respect of color the latter is
not inferior to the former" (Grabar, *Serov*,
1965, p. 379). This commentary can in no
way clarify the dating of the canvas. Having just arrived in Moscow to study under
Repin at the end of 1878, Serov, then a
boy of fourteen, could hardly have painted

4. Keg with a Pen. Cat. No 5

a work so perfect that it can be compared
with Repin's. Most likely this still life was
painted during the summer of 1879, when
Serov was working with Repin in Abramtsevo. The fact that the setting of this still
life is early autumn rather than winter con-
firms its later dating.
Exhibitions: 1935 The Tretyakov Gallery
(No 48), The Russian Museum (No 5);
1952 Moscow (No 43)
Reproductions: Grabar, *Serov*, 1965, p. 39
References: Grabar, *Serov*, 1965,
pp. 40, 379

5. Forest. Abramtsevo.
Cat. No 6

6. Eagle over the Body of a
Dead Cossack. Cat. No 8

7. Apples and Leaves.
Cat. No 13

277

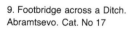
8. Village of Mutovki
in the Vicinity of Abramtsevo.
Cat. No 15

9. Footbridge across a Ditch.
Abramtsevo. Cat. No 17

DRAWINGS

14
Running Horse in Harness. ⟨1879⟩
Pencil. 11×17.2 cm
The Russian Museum (since 1919).
Inv. No P-3100
Provenance: V. Argutinsky-Dolgoruky
collection, St. Petersburg
Exhibitions: 1935 The Russian Museum
(No 249 — 2nd ed.)
References: Grabar, *Serov*, 1965, p. 378

15
**Village of Mutovki in the Vicinity of
Abramtsevo.** 1879
Graphite. 34.2×25.2 cm
Inscribed by the artist, bottom left:
Мутовки 28 Июля (Mutovki, 28 July).
Dated, bottom right: *1879 г.*
The Tretyakov Gallery (since 1936).
Inv. No 24193
Provenance: Yu. Danziger collection,
Moscow
Exhibitions: 1935 The Tretyakov Gallery
(No 235), The Russian Museum (No 243);
1965 The Tretyakov Gallery (p. 51), The
Russian Museum; / 1963 The Tretyakov
Gallery — Pencil Drawings, Watercolors,
Pastels, and Gouaches (p. 67)
Reproductions: Grabar, *Serov the Drafts-
man*, 1961; Grabar, *Serov*, 1965, p. 244
References: Grabar, *Serov*, 1965, be-
tween pp. 253 and 254, 378

16
**Village of Bykovo in the Vicinity
of Abramtsevo.** ⟨1879⟩
Graphite. 25×35 cm
Inscribed by the artist, bottom right:
Быково (Bykovo)
The Tretyakov Gallery (since 1914).
Inv. No 3613

Provenance: O. Serova collection, Moscow
Exhibitions: 1914 (posthumous) St. Peters-
burg (No 2), Moscow (No 3); 1935 The
Tretyakov Gallery (No 224), The Russian
Museum (No 231)
Reproductions: Grabar, *Serov*, 1914,
pp. 12, 243; Grabar, *Serov*, 1980, p. 242
References: Grabar, *Serov*, 1914, pp. 39,
40, 281; Grabar, *Serov*, 1965,
pp. 253, 378

17
**Footbridge across a Ditch.
Abramtsevo.** 1879
Graphite. 25.1×34.9 cm
Inscribed by the artist, bottom right: *Июля
26* (July 26); bottom left: *Абрамце[во]*
(Abramtsevo), and an impression of the
artist's signet: *ВС* (VS)
The Tretyakov Gallery (since 1935).
Inv. No 21247
Provenance: F. Afanasyev collection
Exhibitions: 1952 Moscow (No 42);
1958–59 The Tretyakov Gallery; 1959–60
The Russian Museum; 1965 The Tret-
yakov Gallery (pp. 51, 52), The Russian
Museum
Reproductions: Grabar, *Serov the Drafts-
man*, 1961; Grabar, *Serov*, 1965, p. 37
References: Grabar, *Serov*, 1965, pp. 39,
253, 377

18
**Portrait of Maria Yakovlevna
Simonovich.** 1879
Graphite. 34.4×25.4 cm
Signed and dated, bottom right:
В. Съровъ 1879 Петербургъ (V. Serov,
1879, Petersburg)
The Tretyakov Gallery (since 1938).
Inv. No 24339
Provenance: M. Simonovich collection,
Paris
Maria Yakovlevna Simonovich, Lvova by
marriage (1864–1955), Serov's cousin,
sculptor.
Exhibitions: 1952 Moscow (No 3);
1958–59 The Tretyakov Gallery; 1959
Museum of Russian Art, Kiev; 1959–60
The Russian Museum; 1965 The Tret-
yakov Gallery (p. 52), The Russian
Museum; / 1941 The Tretyakov Gallery —
Portrait Drawings: 18th to Early 20th Cen-
tury (No 117)

Reproductions: Serova 1968, between
pp. 104 and 105
References: Grabar, *Serov*, 1965, pp. 256,
345; Simonovich-Yefimova 1964, p. 73

19
**Portrait of Savva Ivanovich
Mamontov.** 1879
Graphite on paper, mounted on cardboard.
34.8×25.1 cm
Signed in pencil, bottom left: *В. Съровъ*
(V. Serov). Dated by the artist, bottom
right: *21-го Августа, 1879 года*
(21 August 1879)
The Russian Museum (since 1971).
Inv. No P-56234
Provenance: O. Serova collection,
Moscow; B. Popova collection, Paris
Savva Ivanovich Mamontov (1841–1918),
powerful businessman and devoted patron
of the arts.
Exhibitions: 1914 (posthumous) St. Peters-
burg (No 1a), Moscow (No 2); / 1978 The
Russian Museum — Drawings of the 18th
to Early 20th Century. New Acquisitions
Reproductions: Grabar, *Serov*, 1914, p. 9
References: Grabar, *Serov*, 1914, pp. 40,
181; Grabar, *Serov*, 1965, pp. 40, 253,
345; Liaskovskaya 1965, p. 56

20
**Portrait of Tatyana Anatolyevna
Mamontova.** 1879
Graphite. 35×25.2 cm
Dated on the reverse, bottom center:
1879 г.
The Tretyakov Gallery (since 1941).
Inv. No 26474
Provenance: T. Mamontova-Rachinskaya
collection; L. Mamontova collection
Tatyana Anatolyevna Mamontova,
Rachinskaya by marriage (1864–1920),
daughter of Anatoly Ivanovich Mamontov,
publisher and owner of a printing office
and a book shop in Moscow, and niece of
Savva Ivanovich Mamontov (see No 19).
Exhibitions: 1952 Moscow (No 46);
1958–59 The Tretyakov Gallery; 1959
Museum of Russian Art, Kiev; 1959–60
The Russian Museum; 1965 The Tret-
yakov Gallery (p. 51), The Russian
Museum; / 1941 The Tretyakov Gallery —
Portrait Drawings: 18th to Early 20th Cen-
tury (No 134)

References: Grabar, *Serov*, 1965, p. 345

21
Portrait of Ilya Yefimovich Repin. 1879
Pencil. 34×25 cm
Signed, bottom left: *В. Съровъ* (V. Serov).
Inscribed by the artist, bottom right: *1879-го Москва. 9-го октября* (1879, Moscow, 9 October)
Present whereabouts unknown
Provenance: O. Serova collection, Moscow (until 1914)
Ilya Yefimovich Repin (1844–1930), celebrated Russian artist.
Exhibitions: 1914 (posthumous) St. Petersburg (No 4), Moscow (No 7)
Reproductions: Grabar, *Serov*, 1914, p. 11
References: Grabar, *Serov*, 1914, pp. 40, 281; Grabar, *Serov*, 1965, pp. 256, 345

22
A Horse's Skull (Jaws). 1879
Graphite. 25.5×33.5 cm
Dated in ink, bottom left: *1879*; lower, signed and dated in pencil (half-obliterated): *В. Съровъ. 1879 г. Москва* (V. Serov, 1879, Moscow).
Inscribed by the artist, bottom right: *Москва* (Moscow)
The Tretyakov Gallery. Inv. No 28426
Provenance: The Serov family collection, Moscow
A preliminary sketch for *A Horse's Skull on Red Drapery* (see No 11).
Exhibitions: 1935 The Russian Museum (No 248)
Reproductions: Yaremich, *Serov: Drawings*, 1936
References: Grabar, *Serov*, 1965, p. 379

1880
PAINTINGS

23
Fair-haired Girl. Study. ⟨1880⟩
Oil on canvas
Present whereabouts unknown
Provenance: O. Serova collection, Moscow
References: Grabar, *Serov*, 1914, p. 281

24
In a Railroad Car. ⟨1880⟩
Oil on canvas, mounted on cardboard. 20×16 cm

Present whereabouts unknown
Provenance: O. Serova collection, Moscow; V. Idashkin collection, Moscow
References: Grabar, *Serov*, 1965, p. 384

25
Interior of a Church with Banners of the Zaporozhye Cossacks. Village of Pokrovskoye. Study. 1880
Oil on canvas. 40×28 cm
Inscribed, bottom left: *Покровское В. С. 1880 Iюнь* (Pokrovskoye, V. S., 1880, June)
Present whereabouts unknown
Provenance: A. Bogdanov collection, Moscow
Exhibitions: 1952 Moscow (No 6)
References: Grabar, *Serov*, 1965, p. 381

26
Head of a Tatar. Study. 1880
Oil on canvas
Present whereabouts unknown
Provenance: O. Serova collection, Moscow (until 1914)
Exhibitions: 1914 (posthumous) Moscow (No 22a — 2nd ed.)
References: Grabar, *Serov*, 1965, p. 381

27
Humpback. Study. ⟨1880⟩
Oil on canvas
Present whereabouts unknown
This model was painted at about the same time by Ilya Repin.
Provenance: O. Serova collection, Moscow; S. Bykhovsky collection, St. Petersburg
Exhibitions: 1914 (posthumous) St. Petersburg (No 10)
Reproductions: Grabar, *Serov*, 1914, p. 19
References: Grabar, *Serov*, 1914, pp. 45, 46, 282; Grabar, *Serov*, 1965, pp. 45, 46, 327; Leniashin 1980, p. 16

28
Farmyard with Peasant House and Barn in the Background. Village of Pokrovskoye. Study. 1880
Oil on canvas. 25.7×43 cm
Inscribed by the artist, bottom right: *Покровское* (Pokrovskoye). Dated, bottom left: *1880*
Present whereabouts unknown
Provenance: R. Preobrazhenskaya collection, Moscow
Exhibitions: 1914 (posthumous) Moscow (No 18a — 2nd ed.); 1952 Moscow (No 5)
References: Grabar, *Serov*, 1914, pp. 40, 282; Grabar, *Serov*, 1965, p. 383

29
Dead Hare on a Chair. ⟨1880⟩
Oil on canvas
Present whereabouts unknown
Provenance: O. Serova collection, Moscow
References: Grabar, *Serov*, 1914, p. 281; Grabar, *Serov*, 1965, pp. 43, 380

30
Coachman by a Tavern. Study. 1880
Oil on cardboard. 24×20 cm
At the bottom, Repin's authenticating inscription of 1880
Present whereabouts unknown
Provenance: E. Helzer and T. Helzer collection, Moscow
Exhibitions: 1935 The Tretyakov Gallery (No 6); 1952 Moscow (No 75)
References: Grabar, *Serov*, 1965, p. 381

31
Fox-skin Rug. ⟨1880⟩
Oil on canvas. 38.5×44.7 cm
Signed, bottom left: *Съровъ* (Serov)
Picture Gallery, Vologda. Inv. No Ж-224
Provenance: Museum of Local Lore, Vologda
References: Grabar, *Serov*, 1965, p. 384

32
Horse by a House. Study. ⟨1880⟩
Oil on canvas
Present whereabouts unknown
Provenance: E. Helzer collection, Moscow
References: Grabar, *Serov*, 1965, p. 382

33
Peasant Wearing an Armiak (Cloth Coat). Study. ⟨1880⟩
Oil on canvas. 68.5×52.5 cm
Signed, bottom left: *В. Съровъ* (V. Serov)
P. Krylov collection, Moscow

10. Portrait of Maria Yakovlevna Simonovich. Cat. No 18

11. Portrait of Savva Ivanovich Mamontov. Cat. No 19

12. Portrait of Tatyana Anatolyevna Mamontova. Cat. No 20

279

13. The Nenasytets Rapids
on the Dnieper. Study.
Cat. No 34

14. Portrait of Kolia Simonovich.
Cat. No 35

15. Portrait of Lialia Simonovich.
Cat. No 36

Provenance: O. Serova, Moscow
Exhibitions: 1952 Moscow (No 74)
References: Grabar, *Serov*, 1914, p. 282;
Grabar, *Serov*, 1965, p. 380

34
The Nenasytets Rapids on the Dnieper.
Study. 1880
Oil on canvas, mounted on cardboard.
28.5×45.6 cm
Signed, bottom right: *B.C.* (V.S.). Inscribed
by the artist, bottom left: *Ненасытецъ
1880 Іюль* (Nenasytets, 1880, July)
The Tretyakov Gallery. Inv. No 5716
Provenance: O. Serova collection, Mos-
cow; V. Vorobyov collection, Moscow
Exhibitions: 1935 The Tretyakov Gallery
(No 5), The Russian Museum (No 7); 1952
Moscow (No 7); 1958–59 The Tretyakov
Gallery; 1965 The Tretyakov Gallery
(p. 25), The Russian Museum
Reproductions: *Annual of the Institute of
the History of Arts*, 1952, p. 6
References: Grabar, *Serov*, 1914, pp. 40,
282; Grabar, *Serov*, 1965, pp. 44, 382

35
Portrait of Kolia Simonovich. ⟨1880⟩
Unfinished
Oil on canvas. 30.5×23 cm
The Russian Museum (since 1939).
Inv. No Ж-1735
Provenance: N. Simonovich collection,
Tver
Nikolai (Kolia) Yakovlevich Simonovich
(1869–1940), Serov's cousin.
Exhibitions: 1914 (posthumous) St. Peters-
burg (No 17, dated 1881), Moscow (No 19,
the same wrong date)
Reproductions: Simonovich-Yefimova
1964, p. 23; Leniashin 1980, p. 113
References: Grabar, *Serov*, 1914, p. 282;
Grabar, *Serov*, 1965, p. 327

36
Portrait of Lialia Simonovich. ⟨1880⟩
Oil on canvas. 31×26.5 cm
The Russian Museum (since 1937).
Inv. No Ж-1733
Provenance: V. Derviz collection, Moscow;
A. Derviz collection, Moscow
Adelaida (Lialia) Yakovlevna Simonovich
(1872–1945), Serov's cousin, was the wife
of the mathematician Valerian Dmitriyevich
Derviz, the younger brother of Vladimir
Derviz (see No 72). This portrait was
erroneously included in the catalogue

of Serov's works twice (Grabar, *Serov*,
1965, p. 327), the first time under the title
of *Nadezhda Yakovlevna Simonovich
(1876–1908) as a Child*.
In 1880 Nadezhda Simonovich, one of
Serov's elder cousins who later married
Vladimir Derviz, was no longer a child —
she was already fourteen years old (she
was born not in 1876, as indicated by the
compilers of the catalogue, but in 1866).
Serov never painted the portrait of
Nadezhda Simonovich as a child. The er-
ror stems from the wrong caption *N. Ya.
Simonovich* under the portrait of Adelai-
da Simonovich reproduced in Grabar's
book (Grabar, *Serov*, 1914, p. 21).
Exhibitions: 1914 (posthumous) St. Peters-
burg (No 12), Moscow (No 14); 1935 The
Tretyakov Gallery (No 7), The Russian
Museum (No 8); 1965 The Russian
Museum; / 1914–15 Moscow — Moscow
Artists in Aid of War Victims (No 493)
Reproductions: Grabar, *Serov*, 1914, p. 21
(as *Nadezhda Simonovich*); Leniashin
1980, p. 17
References: Grabar, *Serov*, 1914, pp. 54,
282; Grabar, *Serov*, 1965, pp. 53 (as
Nadezhda Simonovich), 327; *Serov in the
Reminiscences of His Contemporaries*,
1971, 2, p. 245; Leniashin 1980, p. 16

37
After a Fire. Study. ⟨1880⟩
Oil
Present whereabouts unknown
Provenance: I. Repin collection, Kuokkala

References: Grabar, *Serov*, 1914, p. 282;
Grabar, *Serov*, 1965, p. 380

DRAWINGS

38
**Valentina Semionovna Serova
at the Piano.** ⟨1880⟩
Pencil. 25.2×32.4 cm
The Russian Museum (since 1916).
Inv. No P-3187
Provenance: I. Repin collection, Kuokkala
Valentina Semionovna Serova, née Berg-
man (1846–1924), the artist's mother;
pianist, composer, important social and
musical figure.
Exhibitions: 1935 The Tretyakov Gallery
(No 724), The Russian Museum (No 364)
Reproductions: Serova 1968, pp. 16, 17
(dated to the early 1880s)
References: Grabar, *Serov*, 1965, p. 346

39
Icebreakers on the Moskva River. 1880
India ink and graphite. 23.5×33 cm
Inscribed and dated by the artist, bottom
left: *Зима 1880* (Winter, 1880)
The Tretyakov Gallery (since 1914).
Inv. No 5708
Provenance: O. Serova collection, Moscow
Variant of the similarly entitled drawing
housed in the Russian Museum
(Inv. No P-3079).
Exhibitions: 1914 (posthumous) St. Peters-
burg (No 6), Moscow (No 9); 1935 The
Tretyakov Gallery (No 241), The Russian
Museum (No 258)
Reproductions: Grabar, *Serov*, 1914,
p. 17; Grabar, *Serov*, 1980, p. 245
References: Grabar, *Serov*, 1914, pp. 43,
182 (as *Icebreaker*. Sepia from the 1880
sketchbook); Grabar, *Serov*, 1965,
pp. 259, 380; *Serov in the Reminiscences
of His Contemporaries*, 1971, 1, p. 34

40
**Zaporozhye Cossacks on Their Way
to the Sech.** ⟨1880⟩
Graphite. 23.3×31.5 cm
Signed, bottom right: *В. Съровъ* (V. Se-
rov). Inscribed by the artist, lower, on the
margins: *Запорожцы на пути в Съчь*
(Zaporozhye Cossacks on Their Way to
the Sech)
The Tretyakov Gallery (since 1927).
Inv. No 9868

Provenance: O. Loewenfeld collection, Moscow; Eckert collection, Moscow; State Museum Reserve, Moscow

The artist repeated this drawing in 1889 for the illustrated magazine *Niva* (F. Marx Publishing House, St. Petersburg, 1890, No 30) and also used it in the similarly entitled painting of 1889 now in a private collection in Moscow.
Exhibitions: 1935 The Tretyakov Gallery (No 239), The Russian Museum (No 256); 1958–59 The Tretyakov Gallery; 1959 Museum of Russian Art, Kiev; 1959–60 The Russian Museum; 1965 The Tretyakov Gallery (p. 52); The Russian Museum
Reproductions: Grabar, *Serov*, 1914, p. 16 (as *Zaporozhye Cossacks in the Steppe*)
References: Grabar, *Serov*, 1914, pp. 42, 282; Grabar, *Serov*, 1965, pp. 44, 383

41

Portrait of Valentina Semionovna Serova. ⟨1880⟩
Graphite. 32.8×23.5 cm
Inscribed by the artist, bottom right: *Питеръ* (Peter[sburg])
The Tretyakov Gallery (since 1914).
Inv. No 3615

Provenance: V. Serova collection, Moscow
A similar portrait is housed in the Russian Museum (see No 38).
Exhibitions: 1914 (posthumous) St. Petersburg (No 11), Moscow (No 13); 1935 The Tretyakov Gallery (No 237), The Russian Museum (No 254); 1958–59 The Tretyakov Gallery; 1959 Museum of Russian Art, Kiev; 1959–60 The Russian Museum; 1965 The Tretyakov Gallery (p. 53), The Russian Museum; / 1925 The Tretyakov Gallery — Women in Russian Painting (No 49); 1963 The Tretyakov Gallery — Pencil Drawings, Watercolors, Pastels, and Gouaches (p. 68)
Reproductions: Grabar, *Serov*, 1914, p. 20; Serova 1968, between pp. 16 and 17
References: Grabar, *Serov*, 1914, pp. 54, 282; Grabar, *Serov*, 1965, pp. 52, 263, 346

42

Portrait of Vera Alexeyevna Repina.
1879 — first half of 1880. Unfinished
Black pencil. 33.1×23.5 cm
The Tretyakov Gallery (since 1949).
Inv. No 28466

Vera Alexeyevna Repina, née Shevtsova (1855–1918), Ilya Repin's first wife (see No 21).
The model for this drawing was apparently Repin's portrait of his wife (1878), now in a private collection in Paris.
Exhibitions: 1958–59 The Tretyakov Gallery; 1965 The Tretyakov Gallery (p. 52), The Russian Museum
References: Grabar, *Serov*, 1965, p. 347

43

Portrait of Nikolai Yakovlevich Simonovich. 1880
Graphite. 33.2×23.5 cm
Inscribed by the artist, bottom right: *1880. Петербургъ* (1880, Petersburg); bottom center: *3*
The Tretyakov Gallery (since 1940).
Inv. No 25104
Provenance: O. Serova collection, Moscow
Nikolai Yakovlevich Simonovich — see No 35.
Exhibitions: 1914 (posthumous) St. Petersburg (No 14), Moscow (No 17); 1952 Moscow (No 76); / 1941 The Tretyakov Gallery — Portrait Drawings: 18th to Early 20th Century (No 118)
Reproductions: Grabar, *Serov*, 1914, p. 22
References: Grabar, *Serov*, 1914, pp. 54, 282; Grabar, *Serov*, 1965, pp. 263, 346; Liaskovskaya 1965, p. 56

44

The Schoolboy Potekhin. 1880
Graphite. 33.2×23.5 cm
Inscribed by the artist, bottom right: *Петербургъ 1880* (Petersburg, 1880); bottom center: *3*
The Tretyakov Gallery. Inv. No 9897
Provenance: M. Riabushinsky collection, Moscow
The portrait depicts the son of the playwright Alexei Potekhin (1829–1908).
Exhibitions: 1914 (posthumous) St. Petersburg (No 13), Moscow (No 15); 1935 The Tretyakov Gallery (No 243), The Russian Museum (No 260); 1952 Moscow (No 78)
Reproductions: Grabar, *Serov*, 1914, p. 22
References: Grabar, *Serov*, 1914, pp. 54, 282; Grabar, *Serov*, 1965, pp. 265, 346

16. Valentina Semionovna Serova at the Piano. Cat. No 38

17. Zaporozhye Cossacks on Their Way to the Sech. Cat. No 40

18. Portrait of Valentina Semionovna Serova. Cat. No 41

19. Portrait of Nikolai Yakovlevich Simonovich. Cat. No 43

20. Peasant House. Cat. No 47

21. Self-portrait. Cat. No 54

282

45 (Plate 7)
After a Fire. 1880
Graphite. 32.8×23.5 cm
Inscribed by the artist, bottom left: *1880 года Москва* (1880, Moscow).
The two last figures, 80, are written over 79
The Tretyakov Gallery (since 1914).
Inv. No 3614
Provenance: O. Serova collection, Moscow
Exhibitions: 1914 (posthumous) St. Petersburg (No 3a), Moscow (No 6); 1935 The Tretyakov Gallery (No 238), The Russian Museum (No 255); 1958–59 The Tretyakov Gallery; 1965 The Tretyakov Gallery (p. 52), The Russian Museum; / 1963 The Tretyakov Gallery — Pencil Drawings, Watercolors, Pastels, and Gouaches (p. 67)
Reproductions: Grabar, *Serov*, 1914, p. 13; Grabar, *Serov*, 1965, p. 41; *Drawings and Watercolors. Catalogue*, 1956
References: Grabar, *Serov*, 1914, pp. 40, 282; Grabar, *Serov*, 1965, pp. 43, 258, 380

46
Dead Hare on a Chair. 1880
Pencil
Signed and dated along the edge of the chair, bottom left: *Съровъ 1880* (Serov, 1880)
Present whereabouts unknown
Provenance: O. Serova collection (until 1914)
Exhibitions: 1914 (posthumous) St. Petersburg (No 15, as *Little Hare*), Moscow (No 18, under the same title)
Reproductions: Grabar, *Serov the Draftsman*, 1961
References: Grabar, *Serov*, 1914, p. 281 (as *Dead Hare on an Armchair*); Grabar, *Serov*, 1965, pp. 43, 258, 380

47
Peasant House. 1880
Graphite. 13.2×21 cm
Inscribed, bottom left: *1880 Привалъ В. Сър* (1880, resthouse, V. Ser[ov])
The Russian Museum (since 1916).
Inv. No P-3097
Provenance: I. Repin collection, Kuokkala
Exhibitions: 1935 The Tretyakov Gallery (No 247), The Russian Museum (No 264)
References: Grabar, *Serov*, 1965, p. 382

1881
PAINTINGS

48
Girl Wearing a Sarafan. Study. ⟨1881⟩
Oil on canvas. 35×25 cm
Signed, bottom right: *B.C.* (V.S.)
Present whereabouts unknown
Provenance: O. Serova collection, Moscow; N. Yermakov collection, St. Petersburg; The Russian Museum (until 1941)
Exhibitions: 1914 (posthumous) St. Petersburg (No 21); 1935 The Tretyakov Gallery (No 8), The Russian Museum (No 9)
References: Grabar, *Serov*, 1914, p. 282; Grabar, *Serov*, 1965, p. 327

49
Zaporozhye Cossacks in the Steppe.
Sketch. ⟨1881⟩
Oil
Present whereabouts unknown
Provenance: O. Serova collection, Moscow
There is no information concerning this sketch in art literature, except one reference made by Igor Grabar (Grabar, *Serov*, 1914, p. 282). In his later monograph on Serov (Grabar, *Serov*, 1965), there is no mention of it at all. Most likely the well-known painting of 1889, *Zaporozhye Cossacks in the Steppe*, was included in the lists of Serov's works twice — as the 1881 sketch and as the picture of 1889.
References: Grabar, *Serov*, 1914, p. 282

50
The Well. Study. ⟨1881⟩
Oil on canvas
Present whereabouts unknown
Provenance: O. Serova collection, Moscow
References: Grabar, *Serov*, 1914, p. 282; Grabar, *Serov*, 1965, p. 389

51
Crimean View. Study. ⟨1881⟩
Oil
Present whereabouts unknown
Exhibitions: 1914 (posthumous) Moscow
(No 22b — 2nd ed.)
References: Grabar, *Serov*, 1965, p. 388

52
Crimean View. Study. ⟨1881⟩
Oil
Present whereabouts unknown
Provenance: O. Serova collection, Moscow
Exhibitions: 1914 (posthumous) Moscow
(No 22c — 2nd ed.)
References: Grabar, *Serov*, 1965, p. 388

53
Portrait of Milusha Mamontova (?).
⟨1881⟩
Oil on canvas. 28.3×20.2 cm
Present whereabouts unknown
Provenance: V. Kalyanov collection, village
of Choboty, near Moscow
Liudmila (Milusha) Anatolyevna Mamontova, Muravyova by marriage (1874–1937),
was the daughter of Anatoly Ivanovich
Mamontov and niece of Savva Ivanovich
Mamontov (see Nos 19, 20).
Exhibitions: 1952 Moscow (No 63)
References: Grabar, *Serov*, 1965, p. 327

DRAWINGS

54
Self-portrait. 1881
Pencil. 31.4×23.8 cm
Signed, bottom right: *1881 Самъ
В. Съровъ* (1881, V. Serov himself). At the
bottom, inscription (partially effaced): *говорятъ что похожъ* (they say the portrait
is a good likeness)
The Russian Museum (since 1945).
Inv. No P-6555
Provenance: O. Serova collection, Moscow; N. Kharina collection, St. Petersburg;
A. Rabotnova collection, Moscow
Exhibitions: 1914 (posthumous) St. Petersburg (No 18); 1935 The Tretyakov Gallery
(No 256), The Russian Museum (No 281);
1965 The Russian Museum; / 1974 The
Russian Museum — Drawings by Russian
Artists: Late 19th and Early 20th Centuries
(p. 19, the data is given wrongly as 1885)
Reproductions: Grabar, *Serov*, 1914,
p. 26; Serova 1968, between pp. 112 and
113 (dated 1885; in the list of illustrations,
p. 292, the same wrong date and
erroneous whereabouts — The Tretyakov
Gallery)
References: Grabar, *Serov*, 1914, pp. 56,
282; Grabar, *Serov*, 1965, pp. 271, 347

55
**Zaporozhye Cossack with a
Stubborn Horse. Sketch.** ⟨1880–81⟩
India ink and pen. 22.1×17.3 cm
The artist's remark, bottom right:
пыль (dust)
The Russian Museum (since 1916).
Inv. No P-3092
Provenance: I. Repin collection, Kuokkala
Exhibitions: 1935 The Tretyakov Gallery
(No 248), The Russian Museum (No 267)
Reproductions: *Annual of the Institute of
the History of Arts*, 1952, p. 8; Grabar,
Serov, 1980, p. 49
References: Grabar, *Serov*, 1965, p. 383

56
**Portrait of Maria Yakovlevna
Simonovich.** 1881
Graphite and black chalk. 32.5×24.5 cm
Dated by the artist, bottom center:
1881 годъ
The Tretyakov Gallery (since 1938).
Inv. No 24338
Provenance: M. Lvova collection, Paris
Maria Yakovlevna Simonovich — see
No 18.
Exhibitions: 1965 The Tretyakov Gallery
(p. 54), The Russian Museum; / 1955 Moscow — Paintings by Pavel Chistiakov and
His Pupils (No 191, as *Head of a Girl*)
References: Grabar, *Serov*, 1965, p. 347

57 (Plate 8)
**The Betrothal of the Virgin Mary
and St. Joseph.** 1881
Black chalk. 21.9×17.7 cm
Signed and dated, bottom right: *BC
1881 г.* (VS, 1881)
Inscribed, top left: *Обручение Богородицы
съ Iосифомъ* (The Betrothal of the Virgin
and St. Joseph)
The Pushkin Museum of Fine Arts (Print
Room), Moscow (since 1924). Inv. No 984
Provenance: A. Kasyanov collection,
Moscow
Exhibitions: 1914 (posthumous) St. Petersburg (No 23a), Moscow (No 24); 1958–59
The Tretyakov Gallery; 1959 Museum of
Russian Art, Kiev; 1959–60 The Russian

Museum; 1965 The Tretyakov Gallery
(p. 53, as *The Betrothal of the Mother of
God and St. Joseph*)
Reproductions: Grabar, *Serov*, 1914, p. 25
References: Grabar, *Serov*, 1914, pp. 56,
282; Grabar, *Serov*, 1965, p. 384

58 (Plate 1)
**Portrait of Pavel Petrovich
Chistiakov.** 1881
Black chalk. 34×25.3 cm
Signed and dated, bottom right: *BC
31. Марта. 1881 г.* (V.S., 31 March, 1881)
The Tretyakov Gallery (since 1924).
Inv. No 7634
Pavel Petrovich Chistiakov (1832–1919),
history and portrait painter; teacher at the
Academy of Arts in St. Petersburg.
Provenance: The Tsvetkov Gallery,
Moscow
Exhibitions: 1958–59 The Tretyakov Gallery; 1959–60 The Russian Museum; 1965
The Tretyakov Gallery (p. 53), The Russian Museum; / 1955 Moscow — Paintings
by Pavel Chistiakov and His Pupils
(No 198)
Reproductions: Grabar, *Serov*, 1914,
p. 24; *Alexander and Valentin Serov*,
1914, between pp. 206 and 207;
Yaremich, *Serov: Drawings*, 1936; Grabar,
Serov, 1965, p. 47; *Drawings and Watercolors. Catalogue*, 1956; Chistiakov 1953
(frontispiece)
References: Grabar, *Serov*, 1914, pp. 55,
56, 282; Grabar, *Serov*, 1965, pp. 53, 271,
347

1882
PAINTINGS

59
Misha Simonovich. ⟨1882⟩
Oil on yellow cardboard. 16×12 cm
Inscribed by Nadezhda Simonovich on the
reverse: *Мишенька Симонович (ум.
4 лет 1882 г.) Жив[опись] Сърова 1882*
(Mishenka Simonovich, died at the age of
four in 1882. Painted by Serov, 1882)
A. Yefimov collection, Moscow (since
1959)
Provenance: I. Yefimov collection, Moscow
Mikhail (Misha, Mishenka) Yakovlevich
Simonovich (1878?–1882), Serov's cousin.

22. Zaporozhye Cossack with
a Stubborn Horse. Sketch.
Cat. No 55

23. Portrait of
Maria Yakovlevna Simonovich.
Cat. No 56

24. Portrait of Vera Alexeyevna
Repina. Cat. No 60

References: Grabar, *Serov*, 1965, p. 327;
Simonovich-Yefimova 1964, p. 24

60
**Portrait of Vera Alexeyevna
Repina.** ⟨1882⟩
Oil on canvas, mounted on cardboard.
29.5×26.4 cm
Signed, bottom right: *B.C.* (V.S.)
The Tretyakov Gallery (since 1917).
Inv. No 5715
Vera Alexeyevna Repina — see No 42.
Provenance: V. Vorobyov collection,
Moscow
Along with the traditional dating of the
portrait, 1882, an earlier date, 1881, is
given by Grabar in his monograph on
Serov (Grabar, *Serov*, 1965, pp. 53, 327).
Exhibitions: 1914 (posthumous) Moscow
(No 269); 1935 The Tretyakov Gallery
(No 9), The Russian Museum (No 10);
1958–59 The Tretyakov Gallery; 1965 The
Tretyakov Gallery (p. 25), The Russian
Museum; / 1955 Moscow — Paintings by
Pavel Chistiakov and His Pupils (No 305)
Reproductions: Serova 1968, between
pp. 188 and 189; Leniashin 1980, p. 20
References: Grabar, *Serov*, 1965, pp. 53,
327; Leniashin 1980, p. 19

1883
PAINTINGS

61
View of the Black Sea Coast.
Study. ⟨1883⟩
Oil on canvas
Present whereabouts unknown
Provenance: O. Serova collection, Moscow
References: Grabar, *Serov*, 1914, p. 282;
Grabar, *Serov*, 1965, p. 389

DRAWINGS

62 (Plate 23)
Self-portrait. ⟨1883⟩
Black chalk. 33×23 cm
The Russian Museum (since 1916).
Inv. No P-13405
Provenance: I. Repin collection, Kuokkala
This self-portrait was drawn jointly with
Ilya Repin.
Exhibitions: 1935 The Tretyakov Gallery
(No 264), The Russian Museum (No 292);
1965 The Russian Museum; / 1974 The
Russian Museum — Drawings by Russian
Artists: Late 19th and Early 20th Centuries
(p. 19, without date)
Reproductions: Grabar, *Serov the Drafts-
man*, 1961 (frontispiece); Lebedev, *Serov*,
1946 (No 1)
References: Grabar, *Serov*, 1965, p. 348

63
Self-portrait. ⟨1883⟩
Black lead. 34×26 cm
The Russian Museum (since 1912).
Inv. No P-3127
Exhibitions: 1935 The Tretyakov Gallery
(No 262), The Russian Museum (No 290)
Reproductions: *Tvorchestvo*, 1965,
No 1, p. 16
References: Grabar, *Serov*, 1965, p. 348

64
Tatar Woman. ⟨1883⟩
Pencil and watercolors. 25.2×16.9 cm
The Russian Museum (since 1912).

Inv. No P-3170
Exhibitions: 1935 The Tretyakov Gallery
(No 384, as *Peasant Woman Wearing a
Folk Head-dress*. 1890s), The Russian
Museum (No 446, under the same title)
Reproductions: *Serov: The Sun of Russia*,
1913
References: Grabar, *Serov*, 1965, p. 389

65
**Portrait of Mikhail Alexandrovich
Vrubel.** ⟨1883⟩
Pencil (?)
Present whereabouts unknown
Mikhail Alexandrovich Vrubel (1856–1910),
Russian painter.
Exhibitions: 1914 (posthumous) St. Peters-
burg (No 29)
Reproductions: Grabar, *Serov*, 1914, p. 29
References: Grabar, *Serov*, 1914, pp. 58,
59, 282 (described incorrectly as housed
in the Tretyakov Gallery); Grabar, *Serov*,
1965, pp. 274, 348

1884
PAINTINGS

66
Peasant on the Outskirts of a Village.
Sketch. ⟨1884⟩
Oil on canvas
Present whereabouts unknown
Provenance: O. Serova collection,
Moscow; E. Romanova collection,
St. Petersburg
Exhibitions: 1914 (posthumous) St. Peters-
burg (No 31)
References: Grabar, *Serov*, 1914, p. 283;
Grabar, *Serov*, 1965, p. 390

67
**Male Model Dressed
in a Renaissance-style Costume.**
Study. ⟨1883–84⟩
Oil on canvas

Present whereabouts unknown
Provenance: O. Serova collection, Mos-
cow; S. Bykhovsky collection, St. Peters-
burg
The study may have been painted in
watercolors and not in oils.
Exhibitions: 1914 (posthumous) St. Peters-
burg (No 26 — 2nd and 4th ed.)
References: Grabar, *Serov*, 1914, p. 282;
Grabar, *Serov*, 1965, p. 386

68
**Female Model in a Renaissance-style
Setting.** Study. ⟨1883–84⟩
Watercolors
Present whereabouts unknown
Provenance: O. Serova collection,
Moscow; S. Bykhovsky collection,
St. Petersburg
Exhibitions: 1914 (posthumous) St. Peters-
burg (No 25 — 2nd and 4th ed.)
References: Grabar, *Serov*, 1914, p. 282;
Grabar, *Serov*, 1965, pp. 273, 386 (de-
scribed incorrectly as oil)

69 (Plate 9)
**Portrait of Liudmila Anatolyevna
Mamontova.** ⟨1884⟩
Oil on canvas. 57×45 cm
Museum of History and Architecture,
Novgorod (since 1925). Inv. No 2612
Liudmila Anatolyevna Mamontova — see
No 53.
Provenance: M. Muravyov and
L. Muravyova collection, Novgorod; The
Russian Museum
Exhibitions: 1914 (posthumous) Moscow
(No 28); 1935 The Tretyakov Gallery
(No 10, dated 1882), The Russian
Museum (No 11); 1958–59 The Tretyakov
Gallery; 1965 The Tretyakov Gallery
(p. 25), The Russian Museum
Reproductions: Grabar, *Serov*, 1914,
p. 33; Grabar, *Serov*, 1965, p. 59
References: Grabar, *Serov*, 1914, pp. 64,
283; Grabar, *Serov*, 1965, pp. 57, 327

DRAWINGS

70 (Plate 4)
Portrait of Maria Fiodorovna Mamonto-va as Amazon. 1884
Graphite on paper, mounted on cardboard. 32.6×24.2 cm
Signed and dated, bottom left: *BC 1884* (VS, 1884). Inscribed, top right: *Машъ отъ Антона иначе В. Сърова* (To Masha from Anton, alias V. Serov)
M. Kupriyanov collection, Moscow
Maria Fiodorovna Mamontova, Yakun-chikova by marriage (1864–1952), Savva Mamontov's niece (see No 19); played an active part in the development of Russian handicraft industry.
Exhibitions: 1952 Moscow (No 51); 1958–59 The Tretyakov Gallery; 1965 The Tretyakov Gallery (p. 54); / 1949 The Pushkin Museum of Fine Arts, Moscow — Russian Graphic Art: 18th to Early 20th Century
Reproductions: Grabar, *Serov*, 1965, p. 51
References: Grabar, *Serov*, 1965, pp. 274, 349

71 (Plate 3)
Horse. 1884
Graphite. 34.2×43.8 cm
Signed, bottom left: *BC* (VS). Inscribed by the artist, bottom right: *Абрамцево, 1884* (Abramtsevo, 1884)
The Tretyakov Gallery. Inv. No 11316
Provenance: I. Ostroukhov collection, Moscow
Exhibitions: 1914 (posthumous) St. Peters-burg (No 33), Moscow (No 30); 1935 The Tretyakov Gallery (No 73), The Russian Museum (No 304); 1958–59 Museum of Russian Art, Kiev; 1959–60 The Russian Museum; 1965 The Tretyakov Gallery (p. 54), The Russian Museum; / 1955 Mos-cow — Paintings by Pavel Chistiakov and His Pupils (No 199); 1963 The Tretyakov Gallery — Pencil Drawings, Watercolors, Pastels, and Gouaches (p. 68)
Reproductions: Grabar, *Serov*, 1914, p. 34
References: Grabar, *Serov*, 1914, pp. 62, 283; Grabar, *Serov*, 1965, p. 390; Lias-kovskaya 1965, p. 56

72
Portrait of Vladimir Dmitriyevich Derviz. ⟨1884⟩
Sanguine and pressed charcoal. 34.5×25 cm
The Tretyakov Gallery. Inv. No 26536
Vladimir Dmitriyevich Derviz (1859–1937), an artist and a prominent Zemstvo official, was a close friend of Serov and the hus-band of his cousin, Nadezhda Yakovlevna Simonovich (see No 146).
References: Grabar, *Serov*, 1965, p. 349

73 (Plate 2)
M. Tognon Sleeping in a Chair. 1884
Graphite and pressed charcoal. 48×34 cm
Signed and dated in pencil, bottom right: *1884. Абрамцево Сьровъ* (1884. Abramtsevo, Serov)
Below this, an impression of the artist's signet: *BC* (VS).
The Tretyakov Gallery. Inv. No 9875
Yuly Pavlovich Tognon, French tutor of Savva Mamontov's children (see No 19).
Provenance: O. Loewenfeld collection, Moscow; Eckert collection, Moscow
Exhibitions: 1914 (posthumous) Moscow (No 33a); 1935 The Tretyakov Gallery

(No 271, as M. Troyon), The Russian Museum (No 302, as M. Tognon); / 1955 Moscow — Paintings by Pavel Chistiakov and His Pupils
Reproductions: Grabar, *Serov*, 1914, p. 35 (as *M. Troyon*)
References: Grabar, *Serov*, 1914, pp. 62, 283; Grabar, *Serov*, 1965, pp. 274, 349; Liaskovskaya 1965, p. 56; *Serov in the Reminiscences of His Contemporaries*, 1971, 1, p. 701

1880–1885
PAINTINGS

74
Male Model Seated on a Tiger Skin.
⟨1880–85⟩
Oil on canvas. 80×122 cm
Signed, top left: *Сьровъ* (Serov)
The Tretyakov Gallery. Inv. No 24785
References: Grabar, *Serov*, 1965, p. 388

75
Male Model with a Red Cloth.
⟨1880–85⟩
Oil on canvas. 123.5×61.5 cm
Signed, top right: *В. Сьровъ* (V. Serov)
Present whereabouts unknown
Provenance: S. Tushmalova collection, Leningrad
Exhibitions: 1935 The Russian Museum (No 46a — 2nd ed.)
References: Grabar, *Serov*, 1965, p. 388

1885
PAINTINGS

76 (Plate 25)
Self-portrait. ⟨1885⟩
Oil on canvas. 50×40 cm
The Serov family collection, Moscow
According to Grabar (Grabar, *Serov*, 1914, p. 284; 1965, p. 328), the picture was painted in Moscow in 1885. This dating seems to be better grounded than the dating 1889–90, suggested by some art historians.
Exhibitions: 1935 The Tretyakov Gallery (No 45), The Russian Museum; 1952 Mos-cow (No 107 — the date given wrongly as 1889–90); 1958–59 The Tretyakov Gal-lery; 1959 Museum of Russian Art, Kiev; 1959–60 The Russian Museum; 1965 The Tretyakov Gallery (p. 30, dated 1889–90), The Russian Museum; / 1951–52 Central House of Art Workers, Moscow — Rus-sian Painting: Second Half of the 19th and Early 20th Centuries (No 225, dated 1889–90); 1954 Central House of Art Workers, Moscow — Portraits of Promi-nent Personalities in Russian Art: 18th to 20th Century (No 230, dated 1889–90); 1976 The Tretyakov Gallery, 1977 The Russian Museum — Self-portraits in Rus-sian and Soviet Art (Painting and Graphic Arts)
Reproductions: Simonovich-Yefimova 1964 (frontispiece)
References: Grabar, *Serov*, 1914, p. 284; Grabar, *Serov*, 1965, p. 328

77 (Plate 6)
Bullocks. Study. ⟨1885⟩
Oil on canvas. 47.5×59.5 cm
Signed, bottom left: *BC* (VS)
The Tretyakov Gallery (since 1929).
Inv. No 11186

Provenance: I. Ostroukhov collection, Mos-cow; The Ostroukhov Museum of Icons and Painting, Moscow
Exhibitions: 1914 (posthumous) St. Peters-burg (No 42), Moscow (No 38); 1935 The Tretyakov Gallery (No 15), The Russian Museum (No 13); 1958–59 The Tretyakov Gallery; 1959–60 The Russian Museum; 1965 The Tretyakov Gallery (p. 25), The Russian Museum; / 1892 Moscow — 4th Exhibition of Sketches and Studies Organized by the Moscow Society of Art Lovers (No 340); 1898 St. Petersburg — Works by Russian and Finnish Artists (No 264); 1955 Moscow — Paintings by Pavel Chistiakov and His Pupils (No 268); 1957 Warsaw — Russian Painting: 14th to 20th Century (No 86)
Reproductions: *Mir Iskusstva*, 1900, No 1/2, p. 7 (as *Bulls*); *Apollon*, 1911, No 10, p. 89; Grabar, *Serov*, 1914, be-tween pp. 48 and 49
References: Grabar, *Serov*, 1914, pp. 68, 69, 284; Grabar, *Serov*, 1965, p. 328

26. Tatar Woman. Cat. No 64

78
St. George. ⟨1885⟩
Oil on canvas. 110.5×58.5 cm
Bottom right, an impression of the artist's signet: *BC* (VS)
Art Museum, Kirov (since 1924).
Inv. No 309
Provenance: V. Gardenin collection, Mos-cow; T. Gardenina collection, Moscow
Exhibitions: 1914 (posthumous) St. Peters-burg (No 41), Moscow (No 37); 1935 The Tretyakov Gallery (No 14), The Russian Museum (No 14)
Reproductions: Grabar, *Serov*, 1914, p. 41
References: Grabar, *Serov*, 1914, pp. 66, 284; Grabar, *Serov*, 1965, pp. 67, 391

79
Commissioned portrait of an unknown man (?). ⟨1885⟩
Present whereabouts unknown
References: Grabar, *Serov*, 1914, p. 284; Grabar, *Serov*, 1965, p. 328

80

Portrait of Antonio d'Andrade. ⟨1885⟩
Oil on canvas. 60.8×49.5 cm
Signed, bottom right: *В. Съровъ*
(V. Serov)
Art Museum, Sumy (since 1948).
Inv. No Ж-355
Provenance: N. Chelishchev collection,
Moscow; A. Prianishnikov collection,
St. Petersburg; P. Schucht collection,
Sumy
Antonio d'Andrade, real name di Andradi
(1854–1942), a Portuguese tenor, was a
member of the Italian company which per-
formed at Mamontov's Private Opera in
Moscow in the 1880s.
Exhibitions: 1914 (posthumous) St. Peters-
burg (No 47, dated 1886), Moscow
(No 43); 1959–60 The Russian Museum; /
1886–87 Moscow — 5th Periodical Exhibi-
tion of the Moscow Society of Art Lovers
(No 72); 1910 The Lemercier Gallery,
Moscow — Exhibition Sale of the
N. Chelishchev Collection of Paintings by
Russian Artists (No 173)
Reproductions: Grabar, *Serov*, 1914, p. 45
References: Grabar, *Serov*, 1914, pp. 69,
284 (dated 1886); Grabar, *Serov*, 1965,
pp. 68, 69, 328; *Serov's Correspondence*,
1968, p. 102

81 (Plate 10)

Portrait of Olga Fiodorovna Trubnikova.
⟨1885⟩. Unfinished
Oil on canvas. 88×71 cm
The Tretyakov Gallery. Inv. No 22467
Provenance: The Serov family collection,
Moscow
Olga Fiodorovna Trubnikova, Serova by
marriage (1865–1927), became the artist's
wife on January 29, 1889.
Exhibitions: 1935 The Tretyakov Gallery
(No 15), The Russian Museum (No 15);
1952 Moscow (No 83); / 1955 Moscow —
Paintings by Pavel Chistiakov and His
Pupils (No 307)
Reproductions: Grabar, *Serov*, 1914, p. 43
References: Grabar, *Serov*, 1914, p. 284;
Grabar, *Serov*, 1965, pp. 70–72

82

Portrait of Savva Ivanovich Mamontov.
⟨1885⟩
Oil on canvas. 62×58.2 cm
Art Museum, Tula (since 1965).
Inv. No 670-ж
Provenance: S. Mamontov collection, Moscow; T. Liubatovich collection, Moscow;
N. Kokorev collection, Moscow; Yu. Danziger collection, Moscow
Savva Ivanovich Mamontov — see No 19.
The portrait was dated by some art historians to 1891 (Sokolova, Vlasov 1959,
pp. 38, 81), by others to the late 1880s
(Grabar, *Serov*, 1965, p. 331). However,
neither dating is correct, as follows from
the quotation given below: "At the same
time (i.e. the time when Serov completed
his drawing *Savva Mamontov Translating
'Carmen'* dated 1885, August 29, now in
the Abramtsevo Museum, Inv. No P-271)
he painted the portrait of Savva Ivanovich
which was in the possession of the
Mamontov family" (Grabar, *Serov*, 1965,
p. 67). It should be added that this portrait
is closely related to the drawing both
thematically and stylistically, so that there
is every reason to believe that the former

was painted at the end of August or in
September 1885.
Exhibitions: 1935 The Russian Museum
(No 61, the date is given wrongly as
1891); 1946 Central House of Art Work-
ers, Moscow (No 19); 1952 Moscow
(No 114, date given wrongly as 1891);
1965 The Russian Museum; / 1913 (?)
The Stroganov Art School, Moscow —
Paintings from Private Collections
(No 211); 1946 Central House of Art
Workers, Moscow — Portraits by Russian
Artists: 18th to Early 20th Century,;
1951–52 Central House of Art Workers,
Moscow — Russian Painting of the 19th
and Early 20th Centuries (No 268)
Reproductions: Sokolova, Vlasov 1959,
p. 38; Grabar, *Serov*, 1965, p. 123
References: Grabar, *Serov*, 1965, p. 67

83

Portrait of a Youth. ⟨1885⟩
Oil on canvas. 78×63.2 cm
Signed, bottom left: *В. Съровъ* (V. Serov)
The Tretyakov Gallery. Inv. No 11195
Provenance: I. Ostroukhov collection,
Moscow
A copy of Velázquez's picture in the Alte
Pinakothek, Munich.
Exhibitions: 1935 The Tretyakov Gallery
(No 12), The Russian Museum (No 12); /
1889–90 Moscow — 9th Periodical Exhibi-
tion of the Moscow Society of Art Lovers
(No 131); 1955 Moscow — Paintings by
Pavel Chistiakov and His Pupils (No 306)
Reproductions: Sokolova, *Serov*, 1935,
p. 25
References: Grabar, *Serov*, 1914, p. 284;
Grabar, *Serov*, 1965, p. 390; Sokolova,
Serov, 1935, p. 23

84

Youth Leaning on a Chair. ⟨1885⟩
Present whereabouts unknown
Provenance: O. Serova collection, Moscow
References: Grabar, *Serov*, 1914, p. 284;
Grabar, *Serov*, 1965, p. 328

DRAWINGS
AND WATERCOLORS

85 (frontispiece)
Self-portrait. ⟨1885⟩
Black chalk and graphite. 34×25.5 cm
Bottom right, an impression of the artist's
signet: *BC* (VS)
The Tretyakov Gallery (since 1914).
Inv. No 3616
Exhibitions: 1935 The Tretyakov Gallery
(No 231), The Russian Museum (No 317);
1958–59 The Tretyakov Gallery; 1965 The
Tretyakov Gallery (pp. 54, 55), The Rus-
sian Museum; / 1963 The Tretyakov Gal-
lery — Pencil Drawings, Watercolors, Pas-
tels, and Gouaches (No 68)
Reproductions: *Apollon*, 1912, No 10, p. 7;
Grabar, *Serov*, 1914, p. 38; *Alexander and
Valentin Serov*, 1914, between pp. 156
and 157; Grabar, *Serov*, 1965, p. 251
References: Grabar, *Serov*, 1914, pp. 66,
284; Grabar, *Serov*, 1965, pp. 274, 349;
Liaskovskaya 1965, p. 57

86 (Plate 14)
Amsterdam. View from a Hotel Window.
Study. 1885
Watercolors. 21×28.8 cm (exposed area)
Signed and dated, bottom right: *Amster-
dam 1885 BC* (VS)
Present whereabouts unknown
Provenance: F. Schechtel collection,
Moscow; E. Helzer collection, Moscow
Exhibitions: 1914 (posthumous) St. Peters-
burg (No 40), Moscow (No 36); 1935 The
Tretyakov Gallery (No 288); 1952 Moscow
(No 81); 1958–59 The Tretyakov Gallery; /
1895 Moscow and 1896 St. Petersburg —
Exhibition of Watercolors, Pastels and
Drawings Organized by the Moscow Soci-
ety of Art Lovers (Nos 25, 98)
Reproductions: Grabar, *Serov*, 1914,
p. 37; *Khudozhnik*, 1965, No 1, p. 37
References: Grabar, *Serov*, 1914, pp. 66,
284; Grabar, *Serov*, 1965, pp. 67, 391;
Fiodorov-Davydov 1965, No 1, p. 37

87 (Plate 11)
Portrait of Olga Fiodorovna Trubnikova. ⟨1885⟩
Graphite. 15×15.5 cm
The Serov family collection, Moscow
Olga Fiodorovna Trubnikova — see No 81.
Exhibitions: 1914 (posthumous) Moscow (No 41a — 2nd ed.); 1935 The Tretyakov Gallery (No 282), The Russian Museum (No 318); 1946 Central House of Art Workers, Moscow (No 63); 1952 Moscow (No 85); 1958–59 The Tretyakov Gallery; 1959 Museum of Russian Art, Kiev; 1959–60 The Russian Museum; 1965 The Tretyakov Gallery (p. 55), The Russian Museum
Reproductions: Grabar, *Serov*, 1914, p. 42; Grabar, *Serov*, 1965, p. 56
References: Grabar, *Serov*, 1914, pp. 69, 284; Grabar, *Serov*, 1965, pp. 71, 349

88 (Plate 12)
Portrait of Olga Fiodorovna Trubnikova. ⟨1885⟩
Pencil. 14.5×8.5 cm
Inscribed by the artist, bottom right: *Одесса* (Odessa)
The Serov family collection, Moscow
Olga Fiodorovna Trubnikova — see No 81.
Exhibitions: 1952 Moscow (No 84); 1958–59 The Tretyakov Gallery; 1959 Museum of Russian Art, Kiev; 1959–60 The Russian Museum; 1965 The Tretyakov Gallery (p. 55), The Russian Museum
Reproductions: Grabar, *Serov*, 1914, p. 46
References: Grabar, *Serov*, 1914, pp. 69, 284; Grabar, *Serov*, 1965, pp. 71, 349

89
Savva Ivanovich Mamontov Translating *Carmen*. 1885
Pencil. 30×26.3 cm

Signed and dated, bottom right: *BC 1885. 29 Августа* (VS, 1885, 29 August).
Inscribed by the artist, bottom left: *Абрамцево Савва Ивановичъ сидѣлъ и переводилъ* (Abramtsevo. Savva Ivanovich was sitting and translating)
The Abramtsevo Museum, Moscow region. Inv. No P-271
Savva Ivanovich Mamontov — see No 19.
Exhibitions: 1935 The Tretyakov Gallery (No 289), The Russian Museum (No 325); 1952 Moscow (No 53)
Reproductions: Serova 1968, between pp. 200 and 201
References: Grabar, *Serov*, 1965, p. 349

1886
PAINTINGS

90 (Plate 32)
Winter in Abramtsevo. The Manor House. Study. 1886
Oil on panel. 37×29 cm
Signed and dated, bottom right: *BC 1886. Абрамцево* (VS, 1886, Abramtsevo)
P. Krylov collection, Moscow
Exhibitions: 1914 (posthumous) St. Petersburg (No 49), Moscow (No 45); 1952 Moscow (No 54); 1958–59 The Tretyakov Gallery; 1965 The Tretyakov Gallery (p. 26), The Russian Museum
Reproductions: Grabar, *Serov*, 1914, p. 55; Sokolova, Vlasov 1959, p. 25; Grabar, *Serov*, 1980, pl. 3
References: Grabar, *Serov*, 1914, pp. 70, 284; Grabar, *Serov*, 1965, pp. 77, 392; Fiodorov-Davydov 1965, No 1, p. 38

91 (Plate 5)
Winter in Abramtsevo. The Church. Study. ⟨1886⟩
Oil on canvas. 20×15.5 cm
Signed, bottom right: *BC* (VS)
The Tretyakov Gallery (since 1929).

Inv. No 11190
Provenance: I. Ostroukhov collection, Moscow
Exhibitions: 1914 (posthumous) St. Petersburg (No 49a), Moscow (No 46); 1935 The Tretyakov Gallery (No 19), The Russian Museum (No 22); 1952 Moscow (No 55); 1958–59 The Tretyakov Gallery; 1959 Museum of Russian Art, Kiev; 1959–60 The Russian Museum; 1965 The Tretyakov Gallery (p. 26), The Russian Museum; / 1955 Moscow — Paintings by Pavel Chistiakov and His Pupils (No 272)
Reproductions: *Apollon*, 1911, No 10, between pp. 8 and 9; Grabar, *Serov*, 1914, p. 54; *Khudozhnik*, 1965, No 1, p. 38; Grabar, *Serov*, 1980, pl. 4
References: Grabar, *Serov*, 1914, pp. 70, 284; Grabar, *Serov*, 1965, pp. 77, 392; Fiodorov-Davydov 1965, p. 38

28. Portrait of Savva Ivanovich Mamontov. Cat. No 82

92
Peasant Girl in a Pink Dress. 1886
Oil on canvas. 33×25.5 cm
Dated, bottom left: . . . *86*
Present whereabouts unknown
Provenance: I. Moskvin collection, Moscow; L. Moskvina collection, Moscow; P. Krylov collection, Moscow; A. Gordon collection, Moscow
The model for this portrait was a parlormaid of the Mamontovs' in Abramtsevo.
Exhibitions: 1935 The Tretyakov Gallery (No 22), The Russian Museum (No 24); 1946 Central House of Art Workers, Moscow; 1952 Moscow (No 57)
References: Grabar, *Serov*, 1965, p. 328

29. Savva Ivanovich Mamontov Translating *Carmen*. Cat. No 89

93
Farmyard. Study. 1886
Oil on canvas. 53.8×66.4 cm
Signed and dated, bottom right: *В. Сѣровъ 86* (V. Serov, 1886). Below, another (partially effaced) signature: *В. Сѣровъ 88 г.* (V. Serov, 1888)
The Tretyakov Gallery. Inv. No 5538
Provenance: V. Girshman collection, Moscow
Exhibitions: 1914 (posthumous) St. Petersburg (No 46), Moscow (No 42); 1935 The Tretyakov Gallery (No 16), The Russian Museum (No 17); 1952 Moscow (No 88); / 1955 Moscow — Paintings by Pavel Chistiakov and His Pupils (No 269)
Reproductions: Grabar, *Serov*, 1914, p. 50
References: Grabar, *Serov*, 1914, pp. 70,

30. Peasant Girl in a Pink
Dress. Cat. No 92

31. The Dog Pirate. Cat. No 102

284; Grabar, *Serov*, 1965, pp. 77, 391;
Simonovich-Yefimova 1964, pp. 26, 27

94
Cloudy Day. Study. ⟨1886⟩
Oil on canvas, mounted on cardboard.
19×31 cm
The Kustodiev Picture Gallery, Astrakhan
(since 1918). Inv. No Ж-99
Provenance: O. Serova collection, Mos-
cow; P. Dogadin collection, Astrakhan
Exhibitions: 1914 (posthumous) St. Peters-
burg (No 50), Moscow (No 47); 1965 The
Russian Museum
References: Grabar, *Serov*, 1965, p. 392

95
Oaks in Autumn. Study. 1886
Oil on mahogany. 19×24 cm
Signed and dated, bottom left: *В. Съровъ
1886 г.* (V. Serov, 1886)
Present whereabouts unknown
Provenance: A. Zhigalko collection, Mos-
cow; V. Dmitriyev collection, Moscow
Exhibitions: 1935 The Russian Museum
(No 21); 1952 Moscow (No 87, as *Early
Spring. Oaks*); / 1955 Central House of Art
Workers, Moscow — Landscape in Rus-
sian Painting: 19th and Early 20th Cen-
turies (No 297, under the same title)
References: Grabar, *Serov*, 1965,
pp. 77, 382

96 (Plate 22)
Autumn Evening. Domotkanovo. ⟨1886⟩
Oil on canvas. 54×71 cm
Signed, bottom right: *В. Съровъ*
(V. Serov)
The Tretyakov Gallery (since 1910).
Inv. No 1515
Provenance: The Morozov family collec-
tion, Moscow
Exhibitions: 1935 The Tretyakov Gallery
(No 17), The Russian Museum (No 18);

1958–59 The Tretyakov Gallery; 1965 The
Tretyakov Gallery (p. 26), The Russian
Museum; / 1890 Moscow — Exhibition of
Sketches and Studies Organized by the
Moscow Society of Art Lovers; 1898
St. Petersburg — Works by Russian and
Finnish Artists (No 262); 1900 Paris —
World Exhibition (p. 71, as *Autumn*); 1955
Moscow — Paintings by Pavel Chistiakov
and His Pupils (No 270)
Reproductions: *Mir Iskusstva*, 1900,
No 1/2, p. 8 (as *Autumn*); Grabar, *Serov*,
1914, p. 49; Grabar, *Serov*, 1965, p. 72
References: Grabar, *Serov*, 1914, pp. 70,
284 (as *Autumn. Study*); Grabar, *Serov*,
1965, p. 77 (described incorrectly as
painted in Abramtsevo), p. 392; Fiodorov-
Davydov 1965, No 1, pp. 37, 38

97 (Plate 31)
Open Window. Lilacs. Study. ⟨1886⟩
Oil on canvas. 49.4×39.7 cm
Art Museum, Minsk (since 1962).
Inv. No РГ-788
Provenance: I. Kraitor collection, Moscow;
A. Kraitor collection, Moscow
A study for the 1886 *Portrait of Olga Trub-
nikova*, now in the Tretyakov Gallery (see
No 103). Since the dating of the
portrait has been finally established as
1886, the study should also be dated 1886
and not 1887 (Grabar, *Serov*, 1965,
p. 395).
Olga Fiodorovna Trubnikova — see
No 81.
Exhibitions: 1952 Moscow (No 94);
1958–59 The Tretyakov Gallery; / 1953
Central House of Art Workers, Moscow —
Russian Painting: 18th and 19th Centuries
(No 256); 1961–62 Art Museum, Minsk —
Works of Russian Art From Private Collec-
tions (p. 25)
References: Grabar, *Serov*, 1914,
p. 285 (?); Grabar, *Serov*, 1965, p. 395

98
Horse. 1886
Oil on canvas. 85×85 cm
Signed and dated, bottom right:
В. Съровъ 86 (V. Serov, 1886)

Horse-Breeding Museum of the Timiriazev
Agricultural Academy, Moscow (since
1928). Inv. No 160
Provenance: N. Maliutin collection, Moscow; P. Cherkov collection; Ya. Butovich
collection, Tula province
The painting, commissioned by the stud-
farm owner N. Maliutin, depicts the gray
trotter Letuchy.
Exhibitions: 1935 The Tretyakov Gallery
(No 20); 1952 Moscow (No 86); / 1890–91
Moscow — 10th Periodical Exhibition of
the Moscow Society of Art Lovers (No 7)
References: *Serov in the Reminiscences
of His Contemporaries*, 1971, 1, p. 150; 2,
pp. 529–531; Grabar, *Serov*, 1914, p. 284;
Grabar, *Serov*, 1965, pp. 75, 392

99 (Plate 13)
**Portrait of Maria Yakovlevna
Van Sandt.** ⟨1886⟩
Oil on canvas. 65×55 cm
Art Museum, Kuibyshev (since 1927).
Inv. No Ж-17
Provenance: The Tsvetkov Gallery,
Moscow; The Tretyakov Gallery
Maria Van Sandt (1861–1919), famous
Swedish singer, performed in the opera
theaters of Paris, London and other
European cities. In the 1880s she sang in
Mamontov's Private Opera in Moscow.
Exhibitions: 1935 The Russian Museum
(No 16, dated 1885); 1958–59 The Tret-
yakov Gallery; 1965 The Russian Museum
Reproductions: Grabar, *Serov*, 1914,
p. 44; Grabar, *Serov*, 1965, p. 64
References: Grabar, *Serov*, 1914, pp. 69,
284; Grabar, *Serov*, 1965, pp. 73, 328

100 (Plate 34)
Little Pond in Abramtsevo.
Study. ⟨1886⟩
Oil on panel. 34.5×24.5 cm
The Tretyakov Gallery (since 1910).
Inv. No 1516
Provenance: M. Morozov collection,
Moscow
Exhibitions: 1935 The Tretyakov Gallery
(No 18, the size given wrongly as

20×15 cm), The Russian Museum
(No 19); 1952 Moscow (No 56); 1958–59
The Tretyakov Gallery; 1965 The Tret-
yakov Gallery (p. 26), The Russian
Museum; / 1955 Moscow — Paintings by
Pavel Chistiakov and His Pupils (No 271)
Reproductions: Grabar, *Serov*, 1914, p. 53
References: Grabar, *Serov*, 1914, pp. 70,
284; Grabar, *Serov*, 1965, pp. 77, 392;
Fiodorov-Davydov, 1965, No 1, p. 38

101
Lilacs on a Window Sill. Study. ⟨1886⟩
Oil on canvas
Present whereabouts unknown
Provenance: O. Serova collection, Moscow
It is quite possible that this is the same
work as No 97, erroneously included
in the list of Serov's works for a
second time (Grabar, *Serov*, 1965,
p. 395).
References: Grabar, *Serov*, 1914, p. 285;
Grabar, *Serov*, 1965, p. 395

102
The Dog Pirate. 1886
Oil on canvas. 50×40 cm
Signed and dated, bottom left: *BC 1886*
(VS, 1886)
The Penates: The Repin Memorial
Museum, Leningrad region (since 1963).
Inv. No П-850
Provenance: A. Kol collection, Leningrad;
N. Chernov collection, Leningrad
Exhibitions: 1914 (posthumous) St. Peters-
burg (No 51a); 1935 The Tretyakov Gal-
lery (No 20), The Russian Museum
(No 23)
Reproductions: Serova 1968, between
pp. 184 and 185
References: Grabar, *Serov*, 1965, p. 392

103 (Plate 27)
**By the Window. Portrait
of Olga Fiodorovna Trubnikova.** ⟨1886⟩.
Unfinished
Oil on canvas, mounted on cardboard.
74.5×56.3 cm
The Tretyakov Gallery. Inv. No 8910
Olga Fiodorovna Trubnikova — see
No 81.
Exhibitions: 1935 The Tretyakov Gallery
(No 27), The Russian Museum (No 29);
1952 Moscow (No 92); 1958–59 The
Tretyakov Gallery; 1965 The Tretyakov
Gallery (on p. 27 it is erroneously stated
that this portrait was displayed at the
21st Exhibition of the Itinerant Society,
1893, St. Petersburg — Moscow, No 138,
whereas in fact the exhibition included the
portrait of Olga Fiodorovna Tamara, 1892)
Reproductions: Simonovich-Yefimova
1964, p. 25

References: *Serov's Correspondence*,
1937, p. 111; Grabar, *Serov*, 1914, p. 285;
Grabar, *Serov*, 1965, pp. 77, 328;
Simonovich-Yefimova 1964, pp. 24–26

104
**By the Window. Portrait of
Olga Fiodorovna Trubnikova.**
Study. ⟨1886⟩
Oil on canvas. 97×71 cm (exposed area)
On the reverse, O. Serova's inscription er-
roneously dating the study to 1888
Present whereabouts unknown
Olga Fiodorovna Trubnikova — see No 81.
Provenance: I. Kraitor collection, Moscow;
D. Budinov collection, Moscow;
V. Gorenstein collection, Moscow
A study for the portrait is described under
No 103.
Exhibitions: 1952 Moscow (No 93)
References: Grabar, *Serov*, 1965, p. 328

105
**By the Window. Portrait of
Olga Fiodorovna Trubnikova.** ⟨1886⟩.
Unfinished
Oil on panel. 28.5×19.5 cm
The Tretyakov Gallery (since 1911).
Inv. No 1517
Olga Fiodorovna Trubnikova — see
No 81.
Igor Grabar erroneously dates the panel
to 1887.
Exhibitions: 1935 The Tretyakov Gallery
(No 26), The Russian Museum (No 28);
1952 Moscow (No 91); 1958–59 The
Tretyakov Gallery; 1965 The Tretyakov
Gallery (on p. 27 it is erroneously stated
that the painting was displayed at the
21st Exhibition of the Itinerant Society,
1893, St. Petersburg — Moscow, No 138,
whereas in fact the exhibition included the
portrait of Olga Fiodorovna Tamara, 1892)
References: Grabar, *Serov*, 1965, pp. 77,
328, 329

DRAWINGS
106
**Portrait of Konstantin Dmitriyevich
Artsibushev.** 1886
Pencil. 34.1×25.2 cm
Signed and dated in pencil, bottom right:
BC 1886. Абрамцево (VS, 1886, Abram-
tsevo)
The Russian Museum (since 1926).
Inv. No Р-3160
Provenance: O. Serova collection, Mos-
cow; Ruchko collection, Leningrad
Konstantin Dmitriyevich Artsibushev
(1849–1901), an engineer and Savva
Mamontov's partner in railway construction
(see No 19), was a noted art lover and
collector.
Exhibitions: 1914 (posthumous) St. Peters-
burg (No 48), Moscow (No 44); 1935 The
Tretyakov Gallery (No 292), The Russian
Museum (No 330)
Reproductions: Grabar, *Serov*, 1914, p. 51
References: Grabar, *Serov*, 1914, pp. 70,
284; Grabar, *Serov*, 1965, pp. 274, 349,
350

107
**Portrait of Savva Ivanovich
Mamontov.** 1886
Pencil. 33.5×25 cm
Dated, bottom right: *1886*
The Abramtsevo Museum, Moscow region
(since 1948). Inv. No Р-203

32. By the Window. Portrait of
Olga Fiodorovna Trubnikova.
Cat. No 105

33. Portrait of Konstantin
Dmitriyevich Artsibushev.
Cat. No 106

Savva Ivanovich Mamontov — see No 19.
Exhibitions: 1952 Moscow (No 58)
Reproductions: Serova 1968, between
pp. 200 and 201
References: Grabar, *Serov*, 1965, p. 350

108

The Artist Ilya Semionovich Ostroukhov at the Piano. 1886
Graphite. 27.8×23.2 cm
Signed, right: *BC* (VS). Below, the artist's
inscription: *И. О. Абрамцево 86*
(I. O., Abramtsevo, 1886); the figures are
partially cut off
The Tretyakov Gallery (since 1929).
Inv. No 15784
Provenance: O. Serova collection, Moscow
Ilya Semionovich Ostroukhov
(1858–1929), landscape painter and art
collector; took an active part in the artistic
life of Russia.
Exhibitions: 1935 The Tretyakov Gallery
(No 290), The Russian Museum (No 328);
1965 The Tretyakov Gallery (p. 55), The
Russian Museum; / 1941 The Tretyakov
Gallery — Portrait Drawings: 18th to Early
20th Century (No 121)
Reproductions: Serova 1968, between
pp. 200 and 201
References: Grabar, *Serov*, 1965, p. 350

34. The Artist Ilya Semionovich
Ostroukhov at the Piano.
Cat. No 108

1887
PAINTINGS

109

Vase of Lilacs. Study. ⟨1887⟩
Oil on canvas. 58.5×52.5 cm
Signed, bottom left: *BC* (VS)
Present whereabouts unknown
Provenance: T. Rachinskaya collection,
Moscow; E. Helzer and T. Helzer collec-
tion, Moscow
Exhibitions: 1914 (posthumous) Moscow
(No 55); 1935 The Tretyakov Gallery
(No 28); 1946 Central House of Art Work-
ers, Moscow (No 13); 1952 Moscow
(No 96); / 1892 Moscow — 4th Exhibition
of Sketches and Studies Organized by the
Moscow Society of Art Lovers (No 189);
1951–52 Central House of Art Workers,
Moscow — Russian Painting: Second Half
of the 19th and Early 20th Centuries
(No 233)

Reproductions: Grabar, *Serov*, 1965,
p. 75; Sokolova, Vlasov 1959, p. 27
References: Grabar, *Serov*, 1914, p. 284;
Grabar, *Serov*, 1965, p. 394

110

Moonrise. Study. ⟨1887⟩
Oil on panel. 19×24 cm
Private collection, Moscow
Provenance: I. Brodsky collection,
St. Petersburg — Leningrad; V. Petrov
collection, Leningrad
Exhibitions: 1914 (posthumous) St. Peters-
burg (No 56, as *Twilight*); 1935 The Tret-
yakov Gallery (No 29), The Russian
Museum (No 30); 1965 The Russian
Museum; / 1954 Leningrad — Paintings by
Russian Artists from Private Collections in
Leningrad: 18th to Early 20th Century
(p. 24)
References: Grabar, *Serov*, 1914, p. 284;
Grabar, *Serov*, 1965, p. 395

111 (Plates 28, 29)

**Girl with Peaches. Portrait of
Vera Savvishna Mamontova.** 1887
Oil on canvas. 91×85 cm
Signed and dated, bottom right: *Сѣровъ
87* (Serov, 1887)
The Tretyakov Gallery (since 1929).
Inv. No 13011
Provenance: S. Mamontov collection, Mos-
cow; E. Mamontova collection, Moscow;
S. Samarin collection, Moscow; A. Mamon-
tova collection, Abramtsevo; A. Mamontov
collection, Moscow
Vera Savvishna Mamontova, Samarina by
marriage (1875–1907), Savva Mamontov's
daughter (see No 19).
Exhibitions: 1914 (posthumous) St. Peters-
burg (No 58), Moscow (No 53); 1935 The
Tretyakov Gallery (No 25), The Russian
Museum (No 27); 1958–59 The Tretyakov
Gallery; 1965 The Tretyakov Gallery
(p. 28), The Russian Museum; / 1888–89
Moscow — 8th Periodical Exhibition of the
Moscow Society of Art Lovers (No 97);
1898 Munich, Cologne, Düsseldorf, Berlin
— Paintings by Russian and Finnish
Artists; 1900 Paris — World Exhibition
(p. 71); 1975 The Pushkin Museum of
Fine Arts, Moscow — European Portrait
Painting
Reproductions: *Mir Iskusstva*, 1900,
No 1/2, p. 17 (as *Portrait*); Grabar, *Serov*,
1914, between pp. 72 and 73; Grabar,
Serov, 1965, pp. 87, 88 (detail)
References: Grabar, *Serov*, 1914,
pp. 72–74, 284; Grabar, *Serov*, 1965,
pp. 85–89, 92–94, 96, 329; Sarabyanov,
Reforms by Valentin Serov, 1971,
pp. 9, 11

112

Wolf-skin Rug. Study. ⟨1887⟩
Oil on canvas. 26×34 cm
Museum of Fine Arts, Voronezh (since
1933). Inv. No 505
Provenance: N. Guchkov collection; State
Museum Reserve, Moscow; The Tretyakov
Gallery
Exhibitions: 1935 The Tretyakov Gallery
(No 49), The Russian Museum (No 48)
References: Grabar, *Serov*, 1965, p. 395

113

Summer Landscape. Study. ⟨1887⟩
Oil on canvas. 20×25 cm (approx.)
Present whereabouts unknown

Provenance: O. Serova collection, Moscow
Exhibitions: 1914 (posthumous) Moscow
(No 54, as *Study*)
References: Grabar, *Serov*, 1965, p. 395

114

Tatar on Horseback. Study. 1887
Present whereabouts unknown
References: Sakharova, *Polenov*, 1950,
p. 239; Grabar, *Serov*, 1965, p. 394

115

Lad on Horseback. Study. 1887
Oil on canvas
Signed and dated, bottom right: *BC 1887*
(VS, 1887)
Private collection, France
Provenance: N. Kuznetsov collection,
Odessa
References: Grabar, *Serov*, 1914, p. 285;
Grabar, *Serov*, 1965, p. 395; *Serov's Cor-
respondence*, 1937, p. 132

116 (Plate 16)

Riva degli Schiavoni in Venice.
Study. ⟨1887⟩
Oil on canvas. 22.5×31.5 cm
The Tretyakov Gallery (since 1929).
Inv. No 11192
Provenance: I. Ostroukhov collection, Mos-
cow; The Ostroukhov Museum of Icons
and Painting, Moscow
Exhibitions: 1914 (posthumous) St. Peters-
burg (No 57), Moscow (No 52); 1935 The
Tretyakov Gallery (No 24), The Russian
Museum (No 26); 1952 Moscow (No 97);
1958–59 The Tretyakov Gallery; 1959–60
The Russian Museum; 1965 The Tret-
yakov Gallery (p. 27), The Russian
Museum; / 1892 Moscow — 4th Exhibition
of Sketches and Studies Organized by the
Moscow Society of Art Lovers (No 196, as
Venice); 1898 St. Petersburg — Works by
Russian and Finnish Artists (No 265)
Reproductions: *Mir Iskusstva*, 1900,
No 1/2, p. 20; *Apollon*, 1912, No 10, be-
tween pp. 34 and 35 (as *Piazza di San
Marco in Venice*, watercolor); Grabar,
Serov, 1914, p. 63; Grabar, *Serov*, 1980,
pl. 6
References: Grabar, *Serov*, 1914, pp. 71,
284; Grabar, *Serov*, 1965, pp. 84, 394;
Fiodorov-Davydov 1965, No 1, p. 38

117

Red-haired Model. ⟨1886–87⟩
Oil on canvas
Present whereabouts unknown
References: *Serov's Correspondence*,
1937, p. 107; Grabar, *Serov*, 1965, p. 393

118 (Plate 15)

Piazza di San Marco in Venice.
Study. 1887
Oil on canvas. 22×31 cm
Signed and dated, bottom right:
B. Сѣровъ 87 (V. Serov, 1887)
The Tretyakov Gallery (since 1929).
Inv. No 11191
Provenance: I. Ostroukhov collection, Mos-
cow; The Ostroukhov Museum of Icons
and Painting, Moscow
Exhibitions: 1935 The Tretyakov Gallery
(No 23), The Russian Museum (No 25);
1952 Moscow (No 98); 1958–59 The
Tretyakov Gallery; 1965 The Tretyakov
Gallery (p. 27)
Reproductions: Grabar, *Serov*, 1965, p. 80
References: Grabar, *Serov*, 1914, p. 284;

Grabar, *Serov*, 1980, pl. 7; Fiodorov-Davydov 1965, No 1, p. 38

119
Portrait of Vsevolod Savvich Mamontov. Study. ⟨1887⟩
Oil on cardboard. 39.4×34.1 cm
Present whereabouts unknown
Provenance: A. Mamontova collection, Moscow; E. Mamontova collection, Moscow; A. Miasnikov collection, Moscow
Vsevolod Savvich Mamontov (1870–1951), son of Savva Mamontov (see No 19), President of the Board of the Moscow –Yaroslavl–Arkhangelsk Railway in the 1890s. In the last years of his life worked on the staff of the Abramtsevo Museum near Moscow.
Exhibitions: 1935 The Tretyakov Gallery (No 50), The Russian Museum (No 49); 1952 Moscow (No 61); 1958–59 The Tretyakov Gallery; 1965 The Tretyakov Gallery (p. 28), The Russian Museum; / 1951–52 Central House of Art Workers, Moscow — Russian Painting: Second Half of the 19th and Early 20th Centuries (No 224)
References: Grabar, *Serov*, 1965, p. 331; *Serov in the Reminiscences of His Contemporaries*, 1971, 1, p. 152

120 (Plate 18)
Portrait of Yekaterina Nikolayevna Chokolova. 1887
Oil on canvas. 91×73 cm
Signed and dated, bottom left: *В. Съровъ 1887 г.* (V. Serov, 1887)
O. Rybakova collection, Leningrad
Provenance: S. Chokolov collection, Yaroslavl; I. Rybakov collection, Leningrad
Yekaterina Nikolayevna Chokolova (1863–?), wife of the railway engineer Sergei Petrovich Chokolov (see No 123).
Exhibitions: 1935 The Tretyakov Gallery (No 30), The Russian Museum (31); 1952 Moscow (No 90); 1965 The Russian Museum; / 1915 Museum of Fine Arts, Moscow — Paintings by Russian Artists, Old and New (No 297, No 303 — 4th ed.); 1951 Leningrad — Paintings by Russian Artists from Private Collections in Leningrad: Second Half of the 19th Century (p. 16); 1954 Leningrad — Paintings by Russian Artists from Private Collections in Leningrad: 18th to Early 20th Century (p. 24)
Reproductions: Grabar, *Serov*, 1965, p. 90; Leniashin 1980, p. 93
References: Grabar, *Serov*, 1914, pp. 74, 285 (as one of the two commissioned portraits of anonymous persons in Yaroslavl); Grabar, *Serov*, 1965, pp. 93, 94, 96

121
Portrait of Praskovya Anatolyevna Mamontova. ⟨1887⟩
Oil on canvas. 59×46 cm
Present whereabouts unknown
Provenance: V. Winterfeld collection, St. Petersburg; P. Lezin (?) collection, Moscow; M. Monson collection, Stockholm
Praskovya Anatolyevna Mamontova, Rachinskaya by marriage (1873—1945), daughter of Anatoly Ivanovich Mamontov (see No 20).
Exhibitions: 1914 (posthumous) St. Petersburg (No 52), Moscow (No 49); 1914 Malmö (Sweden) — Baltic Art Exhibition (No 3218)

Reproductions: Grabar, *Serov*, 1914, p. 57 (dated 1886); Grabar, *Serov*, 1965, p. 95; Serova 1968, between pp. 200 and 201
References: Grabar, *Serov*, 1914, pp. 70, 284; Grabar, *Serov*, 1965, pp. 81, 329

122 (Plate 43)
Portrait of Savva Ivanovich Mamontov. 1887
Oil on canvas. 89×71.5 cm
On the reverse is the authenticating inscription by I. Ostroukhov (see No 108)
Picture Gallery, Odessa (since 1926).
Inv. No Ж-542
Provenance: S. Mamontov collection, Moscow; M. Braikevich collection, Odessa
The traditional dating of the portrait is based on Grabar's evidence that "it was painted in 1890 on Mamontov's commission and presented to the latter in compensation for the artist's stay in the Mamontov house" (Grabar, *Serov*, 1965, p. 331). Yet the erroneousness of this statement becomes particularly clear when compared with Serov's letter of January 5, 1887: "I am painting portraits — both on commission and at my own pleasure. The portrait of Savva Ivanovich, a serious one, was commissioned by him . . . I live with the Mamontovs and my position, if viewed offhandedly, is rather awkward. Am I a boarder? Not precisely, for I am just finishing a portrait of Savva Ivanovich, and this portrait will be a sort of compensation for my lodging, for I shall not charge him at all." (*Serov's Correspondence*, 1937, pp. 107, 108). There can be no doubt that Serov's words refer precisely to this portrait. When dating the portrait, we must also take into account the pencil sketches of 1886, particularly the sketch dated by the artist (Abramtsevo Museum, Inv. No P-203). The sketch is reproduced in Serova 1968, between pp. 200 and 201.
Exhibitions: 1914 (posthumous) St. Petersburg (No 84a), Moscow (No 75 — 1st ed., No 74 — 2nd ed.); 1935 The Tretyakov Gallery (No 61), The Russian Museum (No 59); / 1926 Odessa — Paintings from the Odessa Art Museum Reserve (No 120)
Reproductions: Grabar, *Serov*, 1914, p. 79
References: Grabar, *Serov*, 1914, pp. 98, 286; Grabar, *Serov*, 1965, pp. 80, 93, 121 (with incorrect information), 331; *Serov's Correspondence*, 1937, pp. 107, 108

123 (Plate 21)
Portrait of Sergei Petrovich Chokolov. 1887
Oil on canvas. 68×54 cm
Signed and dated, top left: *В. Съровъ 1887* (V. Serov, 1887)
The Russian Museum (since 1939).
Inv. No Ж-1923
Provenance: S. Chokolov collection, Yaroslavl; I. Rybakov collection, Leningrad; O. Rybakova collection, Leningrad
Sergei Petrovich Chokolov (1848–1921), railway engineer; worked on the Yaroslavl –Vologda Railway owned by Savva Mamontov (see No 19).
Exhibitions: 1935 The Tretyakov Gallery (No 31), The Russian Museum (No 32); 1965 The Tretyakov Gallery (p. 28), The Russian Museum; / 1915 Museum of Fine Arts, Moscow — Paintings by Russian Artists, Old and New (No 304, No 298 — 4th ed.)

Reproductions: Grabar, *Serov*, 1980, pl. 8
References: Grabar, *Serov*, 1914, pp. 74, 285 (as one of the two commissioned portraits of anonymous persons in Yaroslavl); Grabar, *Serov*, 1965, pp. 93, 94, 96

35. Portrait of Vsevolod Savvich Mamontov. Study. Cat. No 119

124
Portrait of Maria Vasilyevna Yakunchikova. Study. ⟨1887⟩. Unfinished
Oil on cardboard. 35.8×24 cm
The Polenov Memorial Museum, Tula region (since 1939). Inv. No 244
Maria Vasilyevna Yakunchikova, Weber by marriage (1870–1902), landscape painter and etcher.
References: Grabar, *Serov*, 1965, p. 329

125
Lilac (A Lilac Twig). Study. ⟨1887⟩
Oil on canvas. 28.5×23.5 cm
Top right, an impression of the artist's signet: *ВС* (VS)
The Kustodiyev Picture Gallery, Astrakhan (since 1918). Inv. No Ж-61
Provenance: P. Dogadin collection, Astrakhan
Exhibitions: 1914 (posthumous) Moscow (No 55); 1935 The Russian Museum (No 197); 1965 The Russian Museum
References: Grabar, *Serov*, 1965, p. 395

126
Lilac Bush. Study. ⟨1887⟩
Oil on canvas. 52×40 cm
Present whereabouts unknown
Provenance: The Serov family collection, Moscow
Exhibitions: 1952 Moscow (No 95)
References: Grabar, *Serov*, 1965, p. 394

127
Phoebus Effulgent. Ceiling painting. ⟨1887⟩
Oil on canvas. Diameter 325 cm (circular)
Art Museum, Tula (since 1946).
Inv. No 277-ж
Provenance: The Selezniov Estate, Tula province
Reproductions: *Literaturnaya Tula*, book 13, 1957, p. 343; *Iskusstvo*, 1958, No 3, p. 72
References: Grabar, *Serov*, 1914, pp. 70, 284 (as *Apollo*. A ceiling painting for the manor house on the Selezniov estate); Grabar, *Serov*, 1965, pp. 78–80 (diameter given wrongly as 290 cm), 394 (as *Helios*);

36. Self-portrait
(with a sketchbook).
Cat. No 129

37. St. Stephen's Cathedral
in Vienna. Cat. No 131

Nechayeva 1957, pp. 342—344; Gorin
1958, pp. 71—73

DRAWINGS

128 (Plate 24)
Self-portrait. ⟨1887⟩
Graphite. 33.5×24.3 cm
The Tretyakov Gallery (since 1914).
Inv. No 3617
Provenance: O. Serova collection, Moscow
Exhibitions: 1914 (posthumous) St. Peters-
burg (No 53), Moscow (No 50); 1935 The
Tretyakov Gallery (No 297), The Russian
Museum (No 336); 1958—59 The
Tretyakov Gallery; 1965 The Tretyakov
Gallery (pp. 55, 56), The Russian
Museum; / 1954 Central House of Art
Workers, Moscow — Portraits of Promi-
nent Personalities in Russian Art: 18th to
20th Century (No 229); 1955 Moscow —
Paintings by Pavel Chistiakov and His
Pupils (No 200)
Reproductions: Grabar, *Serov*, 1914,
p. 59; Grabar, *Serov*, 1965, pp. 32, 33
References: Grabar, *Serov*, 1914, p. 284;
Grabar, *Serov*, 1965, pp. 227, 351

38. The Overgrown Pond.
Cat. No 134

292

129
Self-portrait (with a sketchbook). ⟨1887⟩
Graphite. 24.3×15.8 cm. Signed, bottom
right: *BC* (VS)
The Tretyakov Gallery (since 1929).

Inv. No 11517
Provenance: I. Ostroukhov collection, Mos-
cow; The Ostroukhov Museum of Icons
and Painting, Moscow
Exhibitions: 1935 The Tretyakov Gallery
(No 244, dated 1880), The Russian
Museum (No 261, the same wrong date);
1952 Moscow (No 77, the same wrong
date); 1958—59 The Tretyakov Gallery;
1965 The Tretyakov Gallery (p. 56), The
Russian Museum; / 1941 The Tretyakov
Gallery — Portrait Drawings: 18th to Early
20th Century (No 119, date 1885); 1963
The Tretyakov Gallery — Pencil Drawings,
Watercolors, Pastels, and Gouaches
(p. 69)
Reproductions: Serova 1968, between
pp. 80 and 81
References: Grabar, *Serov*, 1965, p. 351

130
**Portrait of Yelizaveta Grigoryevna
Mamontova.** 1887
Graphite and pressed charcoal.
46×33.6 cm
Signed and dated in pencil, right: *1887
Абрамцево В. Сѣровъ* (1887, Abram-
tsevo, V. Serov; the name is half-obliter-
ated)
The Tretyakov Gallery (since 1929).
Inv. No 11800
Provenance: I. Ostroukhov collection, Mos-
cow; The Ostroukhov Museum of Icons
and Painting, Moscow
Yelizaveta Grigoryevna Mamontova, née
Sapozhnikova (1847—1908), wife of Savva
Mamontov (see No 19).
Exhibitions: 1935 The Tretyakov Gallery
(No 274), The Russian Museum (No 335);
1958—59 The Tretyakov Gallery; 1959—60
The Russian Museum; 1965 The
Tretyakov Gallery (p. 55), The Russian
Museum; / 1941 The Tretyakov Gallery —
Portrait Drawings: 18th to Early 20th Cen-
tury (No 124, date given wrongly as
1907); 1955 Moscow — Paintings by
Pavel Chistiakov and His Pupils (p. 71,
incorrectly described as done in Abram-
tsevo, 1884); 1963 The Tretyakov Gallery
— Pencil Drawings, Watercolors, Pastels,
and Gouaches (p. 68)
Reproductions: *Drawings and Watercolors.
Catalogue*, 1956; Serova 1968, between
pp. 80 and 81
References: Grabar, *Serov*, 1965, pp. 277,
350, 351; Liaskovskaya 1965, pp. 56, 57,
60

131
St. Stephen's Cathedral in Vienna.
⟨1887⟩
Pencil drawing on primed canvas.
32×24 cm
The Russian Museum (since 1960).
Inv. No P-53343
Provenance: The Serov family collection,
Moscow
This is a drawing for a study which was
never painted. In the 1965 catalogue
(Grabar, *Serov*, 1965, p. 450) it is listed as
an undated work under the title *A Gothic
Cathedral* (sketch). The subject and date
of the drawing are suggested on the basis
of Ilya Ostroukhov's memoirs.
Exhibitions: 1952 Moscow (No 379)
References: Grabar, *Serov*, 1965, p. 450;
*Serov in the Reminiscences of His Con-
temporaries*, 1971, 1, pp. 244—248

1888
PAINTINGS

132 (Plates 36, 37)
**Girl in the Sunlight. Portrait
of Maria Yakovlevna Simonovich.**
⟨1888⟩
Oil on canvas. 89.5×71 cm
The Tretyakov Gallery (since 1888).
Inv. No 1518
Maria Yakovlevna Simonovich — see
No 18.
Exhibitions: 1935 The Tretyakov Gallery
(No 32), The Russian Museum (No 33);
1958—59 The Tretyakov Gallery; 1965 The
Tretyakov Gallery (p. 28), The Russian
Museum; / 1888—89 Moscow —
8th Periodical Exhibition of the Moscow
Society of Art Lovers (No 71, as *Study of
a Girl*); 1923 The Tretyakov Gallery —
Exhibition Commemorating the 25th Anniversary of P. Tretyakov's Death (No 74)
Reproductions: *Mir Iskusstva*, 1900,
No 1/2, p. 10 (as *Portrait*); Benois 1902,
p. 233; Grabar, *Serov*, 1914, between
pp. 80 and 81; Grabar, *Serov*, 1965,
pp. 97, 99 (detail)
References: Grabar, *Serov*, 1914,
pp. 74—80, 186; Simonovich-Yefimova
1964, pp. 30—32; Grabar, *Serov*, 1965,
pp. 98—102, 329; Sarabyanov, *Reforms by
Valentin Serov*, 1971, pp. 9, 11; *Serov in
the Reminiscences of His Contemporaries*,
1971, 2, pp. 250—252; Fiodorov-Davydov
1960, No 3, pp. 36—40

133 (Plate 17)
The Overgrown Pond. Domotkanovo.
1888
Oil on canvas. 70.5×89.2 cm
Signed and dated, top right: *Съровъ 88*
(Serov, 1888)
The Tretyakov Gallery (since 1917).
Inv. No 5343
Provenance: V. Yakunchikov collection,
Moscow; M. Yakunchikova collection,
Moscow
Exhibitions: 1914 (posthumous) St. Peters-
burg (No 63), Moscow (No 60); 1935 The
Tretyakov Gallery (No 35), The Russian
Museum (No 34); 1958–59 The Tretyakov
Gallery; 1965 The Tretyakov Gallery
(pp. 28, 29), The Russian Museum; /
1888–89 Moscow — 8th Periodical Exhibi-
tion of the Moscow Society of Art Lovers
(No 76, as *Twilight*); 1896 Nizhni-Nov-
gorod — All-Russia Exhibition (No 386);
1898 St. Petersburg (No 267), Munich,
Cologne, Düsseldorf, Berlin — Paintings
by Russian and Finnish Artists; 1900 Paris
— World Exhibition (p. 61)
Reproductions: *Mir Iskusstva*, 1900,
No 1/2, p. 18; Grabar, *Serov*, 1914,
between pp. 64 and 65; Grabar, *Serov*,
1965, p. 83; *Khudozhnik*, 1965, No 1,
p. 41
References: Grabar, *Serov*, 1914, pp. 80,
82, 286; Grabar, *Serov*, 1965, pp. 101,
396; Fiodorov-Davydov 1965, No 1, p. 40

134
The Overgrown Pond. ⟨1888⟩
Oil on canvas. 21×25 cm
Signed, bottom right: *B. C.* (V. S.)
Picture Gallery, Tiumen (since 1960).
Inv. No Ж-401
Provenance: M. Semionov collection
A study for *The Overgrown Pond. Domot-
kanovo*, now in the Tretyakov Gallery
(see No 133).
Exhibitions: 1959–60 The Russian
Museum
References: Grabar, *Serov*, 1965, p. 396

135
**Portrait of Pavel Ivanovich
Blaramberg.** 1888
Oil on canvas. 59×49 cm
Signed and dated, top left: *B. Съровъ
1888* (V. Serov, 1888)
The Tretyakov Gallery (since 1935).
Inv. No 15702
Provenance: A. Wrangel collection, Mos-
cow; E. Wrangel collection, Moscow

Pavel Ivanovich Blaramberg (1841–1907),
composer and writer, a close friend of the
Serov family.
Exhibitions: 1935 The Tretyakov Gallery
(No 35), The Russian Museum (No 35);
1958–59 The Tretyakov Gallery; 1965 The
Tretyakov Gallery (p. 29), The Russian
Museum; / 1888–89 Moscow —
8th Periodical Exhibition of the Moscow
Society of Art Lovers (No 93)
Reproductions: Grabar, *Serov*, 1980,
pl. 13
References: Grabar, *Serov*, 1914, pp. 83,
286; Grabar, *Serov*, 1965, pp. 101, 329

136
**Portrait of Maria Fiodorovna
Yakunchikova.** 1888
Oil on canvas
Signed and dated, top left: *B. Съровъ
1888* (Serov, 1888)
Art Museum, Malmö (Sweden)
Provenance: M. Yakunchikova collection,
Moscow; private collection
Maria Fiodorovna Yakunchikova —
see No 70.
This portrait was begun in 1885.
Exhibitions: 1914 (posthumous) St. Peters-
burg (No 60), Moscow (No 57); / 1889–90
Moscow — 9th Periodical Exhibition of the
Moscow Society of Art Lovers (No 76, as
Portrait of Mrs. M. F. Ya.)
Reproductions: Grabar, *Serov*, 1914, p. 65

References: Grabar, *Serov*, 1914, pp. 74,
285 (erroneously mentioned that the portrait was begun in 1886); Grabar, *Serov*,
1965, pp. 96, 329, 330

137 (Plate 33)
An Old Bathhouse in Domotkanovo.
1888
Oil on canvas. 76.5×60.8 cm
Signed and dated, bottom left: *B. Съровъ
88* (V. Serov, 1888)
The Russian Museum (since 1933).
Inv. No 4312
Provenance: N. Guchkov collection, Mos-
cow
Exhibitions: 1914 (posthumous) St. Peters-
burg (No 61), Moscow (No 58); 1935 The
Tretyakov Gallery (No 199, as *Landscape
with a Hut*), The Russian Museum (No 37,
under the same title); 1965 The Russian
Museum (under the same title)
References: Grabar, *Serov*, 1914, p. 285;
Grabar, *Serov*, 1965, pp. 101, 396

1889
PAINTINGS

138
**Vasilyev II, an Actor
of the Alexandrinsky Theatre.** Study
for the 1889 portrait of Alexander
Nikolayevich Serov. ⟨1889⟩

Present whereabouts unknown
Provenance: I. Repin collection, Kuokkala
Alexander Nikolayevich Serov —
see No 143.
References: Grabar, *Serov*, 1914, p. 286;
Grabar, *Serov*, 1965, p. 330

139
**Zaporozhye Cossack in a Red Caftan
on Horseback.** ⟨1889⟩
Oil on canvas. 35×29 cm
Present whereabouts unknown
Provenance: V. Derviz collection, Moscow;
I. Yefimov collection, Moscow
Exhibitions: 1935 The Tretyakov Gallery
(No 43), The Russian Museum (No 43)
References: Grabar, *Serov*, 1914, p. 286;
Grabar, *Serov*, 1965, p. 396

140
Zaporozhye Cossacks in the Steppe.
⟨1889⟩
Oil on canvas. 40×60 cm
Present whereabouts unknown
Provenance: O. Serova collection, Moscow; V. Khenkin collection, Moscow;
A. Miasnikov collection, Moscow
Exhibitions: 1946 Central House of Art
Workers, Moscow; 1965 The Russian
Museum; 1953 Central House of Art Workers, Moscow — Russian Painting: 18th
and 19th Centuries (No 251)
References: Grabar, *Serov*, 1914, p. 286
(as *Zaporozhye Cossacks Riding*); Grabar,
Serov, 1965, p. 397

41. Portrait of
Alexander Nikolayevich Serov.
Cat. No 144

141
Horses in a Stable. Study. 1889
Oil on canvas. 22.2×31.2 cm
Signed and dated, bottom left: *В. Съровъ
89 г. Сябринцы* (V. Serov, 1889,
Siabrintsy)
Present whereabouts unknown
Provenance: V. Dmitriyev collection, Moscow
References: Grabar, *Serov*, 1965, p. 399

142 (Plate 35)
**Portrait of Adelaida Yakovlevna
Simonovich.** ⟨1889⟩
Oil on canvas. 87×69 cm
The Russian Museum. Inv. No Ж-8480
Provenance: A. Derviz collection, Moscow;
G. Derviz collection, Moscow
Adelaida Yakovlevna Simonovich —
see No 36.
Exhibitions: 1935 The Tretyakov Gallery
(No 42), The Russian Museum (No 42);
1959–60 The Russian Museum; 1965
The Russian Museum; / 1975 The Russian
Museum — Russian Portrait Painting: Late
19th and Early 20th Centuries (No 186)
Reproductions: Simonovich-Yefimova
1964, between pp. 40 and 41
References: Simonovich-Yefimova 1964,
pp. 34, 36; *Serov in the Reminiscences of
His Contemporaries*, 1971, 2, p. 246

143
**Portrait of Alexander Nikolayevich
Serov.** ⟨1889⟩
Oil on canvas. 102×77 cm
Art Gallery, Perm (since 1946).
Inv. No Ж-810
Provenance: N. Kokarev collection, Moscow; A. Mosolov collection, Moscow
First version of the portrait (see No 144).
Alexander Nikolayevich Serov
(1820–1871), the artist's father, renowned
Russian composer and musical critic.
Exhibitions: 1914 (posthumous) Moscow
(No 61a); 1935 The Tretyakov Gallery
(No 38)
References: Grabar, *Serov*, 1965,
pp. 108, 330

144
**Portrait of Alexander Nikolayevich
Serov.** 1889
Oil on canvas. 197×125 cm
Signed and dated, left:
В. Съровъ 89. (V. Serov, 1889)
The Russian Museum (since 1912).
Inv. No Ж-4286
Provenance: I. Ostroukhov collection,
Moscow
Alexander Nikolayevich Serov —
see No 143.
Exhibitions: 1935 The Tretyakov Gallery
(No 37), The Russian Museum (No 38);
1965 The Tretyakov Gallery (p. 29); / 1890
St. Petersburg, Moscow, Kharkov, Kiev —
18th Exhibition of the Itinerant Society
(No 99); 1896 Nizhni-Novgorod — All-Russia Exhibition (No 389)
Reproductions: *Apollon*, 1912, No 10,
between pp. 24 and 25; Grabar, *Serov*,
1914, p. 73; *Alexander and Valentin
Serov*, 1914, between pp. 2 and 3; Serova
1968, between pp. 176 and 177;
Grabar, *Serov*, 1980, pl. 16
References: Grabar, *Serov*, 1914, pp. 84,
90, 286; Grabar, *Serov*, 1965, pp. 108,
109, 330

145
**Portrait of Maria Grigoryevna
Grünberg.** 1889
Oil on canvas. 52.5×43 cm
Signed and dated, top left: *В. Съровъ 89.
Спб.* (V. Serov, 1889, St. Petersburg)
Present whereabouts unknown
Provenance: M. Grünberg collection,
St. Petersburg; I. Grünberg-Kamenetskaya
collection, Moscow
Maria Grigoryevna Grünberg (1853–1924),
wife of Yuly Osipovich Grünberg, office
manager of the *Niva* magazine.
Exhibitions: 1935 The Tretyakov Gallery
(No 41), The Russian Museum (No 41);
1946 Central House of Art Workers, Moscow (No 16); 1952 Moscow (No 101)
References: Grabar, *Serov*, 1914, p. 286;
Grabar, *Serov*, 1965, pp. 114, 330

146 (Plate 19)
**Portrait of Nadezhda Yakovlevna Derviz
and Her Child.** 1888–89
Oil on metal plate. 142×71 cm
The Tretyakov Gallery (since 1935).
Inv. No 24365
Provenance: V. Derviz collection, Moscow
(Zagorsk?)
Nadezhda Yakovlevna Derviz, née
Simonovich (1866–1908), Serov's cousin.
Exhibitions: 1914 (posthumous) St. Petersburg (No 62), Moscow (No 59); 1935 The
Tretyakov Gallery (No 36), The Russian
Museum (No 36); 1958–59 The Tretyakov
Gallery; 1965 The Tretyakov Gallery
(p. 20); / 1914 Malmö (Sweden) — Baltic
Art Exhibition (No 3217); 1924 New York
— Russian Art (No 680)
Reproductions: Grabar, *Serov*, 1914, p. 67
References: Grabar, *Serov*, 1914, pp. 80,
285, 286

147
Portrait of the Reverend Dalton. 1889
Oil on canvas. 149×100 cm (top rounded)
Signed and dated, bottom left: *V. Seroff 89*
Museum of History and Architecture, Novgorod (since 1930). Inv. No 1923
Provenance: Reformed Church on Bolshaya Morskaya Street, St. Petersburg;
The Russian Museum
Exhibitions: 1914 (posthumous) St. Petersburg (No 67); 1935 The Tretyakov Gallery
(No 40), The Russian Museum (No 40)
Reproductions: Sokolova, *Serov*, 1935,
p. 26
References: Grabar, *Serov*, 1914, p. 286;
Grabar, *Serov*, 1965, pp. 113, 330

148 (Plate 30)
**Portrait of Praskovya Anatolyevna
Mamontova.** 1889
Oil on canvas. 65×45 cm
Signed and dated, bottom right:
89. В. Съровъ (1889, V. Serov)
M. Sokolov collection, Moscow
Provenance: M. Mamontova collection,
Moscow; V. Pavlov collection, Leningrad;
N. Sokolov collection, Moscow
Praskovya Anatolyevna Mamontova —
see No 121.
Exhibitions: 1952 Moscow (No 102);
1958–59 The Tretyakov Gallery; 1965 The
Tretyakov Gallery (p. 29); / 1890–91 Moscow — 2nd Exhibition of Sketches and
Studies Organized by the Moscow Society
of Art Lovers (No 72, as *Study of a Girl*.
M. Mamontova collection?); 1951 Leningrad — Paintings by Russian Artists from

42. Portrait of the Reverend
Dalton. Cat. No 147

154
Road in Abramtsevo. Study. ⟨1880s⟩
Oil on canvas, mounted on cardboard.
28.2×32.2 cm
The Polenov Memorial Museum, Tula
region (since 1939). Inv. No 245
References: Grabar, *Serov*, 1965, p. 402
(as *Summer Landscape in Abramtsevo*)

155
Cossack in the Steppe. Study. ⟨1880s⟩
Oil on cardboard. 35.5×29.3 cm
Museum of Russian Art, Kiev (since
1945). Inv. No Ж-225
Provenance: V. Derviz collection, Moscow;
I. Yefimov collection, Moscow; E. Derviz
collection, Moscow
References: Grabar, *Serov*, 1965, p. 400

156
Male Model. ⟨1880s⟩
Oil on canvas. 75×69.3 cm
Present whereabouts unknown
Exhibitions: 1935 The Russian Museum
(No 46)
References: Grabar, *Serov*, 1965, p. 398

157
Male Model. ⟨1880s⟩
Oil on canvas. 123×58 cm
Signed, top right: *В. Съровъ* (V. Serov)
The Brodsky Art Museum, Berdiansk.
Inv. No Ж-46
References: Grabar, *Serov*, 1965, p. 398

158
Portrait of Olga Fiodorovna Serova.
⟨Late 1880s⟩
Oil on canvas. 28×25 cm

43. Self-portrait. Cat. No 150

44. Cossack in the Steppe.
Study. Cat. No 155

Private Collections in Leningrad: Second
Half of the 19th Century (p. 16)
Reproductions: Zotov, *Serov*, 1964, pl. 8;
Grabar, *Serov*, 1980, pl. 17
References: Grabar, *Serov*, 1965, p. 330;
*Serov in the Reminiscences of His Con-
temporaries*, 1971, 1, p. 152

149 (Plate 38)
**Portrait of Sophia Mikhailovna
Dragomirova.** ⟨1889⟩
Oil on canvas. 71×57 cm
Picture Gallery, Kazan (since 1927).
Inv. No Ж-101
Provenance: S. Dragomirova-Lukomskaya
collection, St. Petersburg; Z. Ratkova-
Rozhnova collection, St. Petersburg
Sophia Mikhailovna Dragomirova, Lukom-
skaya by marriage (1871–1953), daughter
of Mikhail Ivanovich Dragomirov
(1830–1905), general and military
theoretician.
Exhibitions: 1914 (posthumous) St. Peters-
burg (No 69), Moscow (No 61); 1935 The
Tretyakov Gallery (No 39), The Russian
Museum (No 39); 1958–59 The Tretyakov
Gallery; 1959 Museum of Russian Art,
Kiev; 1959–60 The Russian Museum
Reproductions: Grabar, *Serov*, 1914,
p. 77; Grabar, *Serov*, 1965, p. 115
References: Grabar, *Serov*, 1914, pp. 90,
91, 286; Grabar, *Serov*, 1965, pp. 117,
118, 330

1880s
PAINTINGS

150
Self-portrait. ⟨1880s⟩
Oil on canvas. 29.5×23 cm
N. Sokolov collection, Moscow

Provenance: N. Krymov collection, Moscow
The dating of the picture to the early
1880s (Grabar, *Serov*, 1965, p. 327)
seems hardly convincing. On stylistic and
iconographic grounds it may be dated to
the mid-1880s.
Exhibitions: 1965 The Russian Museum
Reproductions: Grabar, *Serov*, 1965, p. 66
(dated to the early 1880s); Sarabyanov,
Serov, 1974, pl. 1
References: Grabar, *Serov*, 1965, p. 327
(dated to the early 1880s)

151
The Wind. ⟨1880s⟩
Oil
Present whereabouts unknown
Provenance: N. Gordov collection
Exhibitions: 1914 (posthumous) St. Peters-
burg (No 71 — 2nd and 4th ed.)
References: Grabar, *Serov*, 1965, p. 401

152
Head of an Old Man. Study. ⟨1880s⟩
Oil on canvas
Present whereabouts unknown
Provenance: P. Gurevich collection,
St. Petersburg
Exhibitions: 1914 (posthumous) St. Peters-
burg (No 70 — 2nd and 4th ed.)
References: Grabar, *Serov*, 1914, p. 286;
Grabar, *Serov*, 1965, p. 399

153
House in Abramtsevo. Summer.
Study. ⟨1880s⟩
Oil on panel. 17.7×11 cm
The Tretyakov Gallery. Inv. No 17333
Exhibitions: 1935 The Tretyakov Gallery
(No 51), The Russian Museum (No 50)
References: Grabar, *Serov*, 1965, p. 399

45. Portrait of Olga Fiodorovna
Serova. Cat. No 158

The Serov family collection, Moscow
Olga Fiodorovna Serova — see No 81.
Exhibitions: 1935 The Tretyakov Gallery
(No 46), The Russian Museum (No 47);
1946 Central House of Art Workers, Mos-
cow (No 61); 1952 Moscow (No 104);
1958–59 The Tretyakov Gallery; 1959
Museum of Russian Art, Kiev; 1959–60

The Russian Museum; 1965 The
Tretyakov Gallery (p. 30), The Russian
Museum; / 1951–52 Central House of Art
Workers, Moscow — Russian Painting:
Second Half of the 19th and Early
20th Centuries (No 222a)
Reproductions: Grabar, *Serov*, 1965, p. 76
References: Grabar, *Serov*, 1965, pp. 330,
331

159
Pond. ⟨1880s⟩
Oil on canvas. 49.5×63 cm
Art Museum, Omsk (since 1927).
Inv. No Ж-343
Provenance: V. Musina-Pushkina collec-
tion, St. Petersburg; The Russian Museum
Exhibitions: 1914 (posthumous) Moscow;
1958–59 The Tretyakov Gallery; 1959–60
The Russian Museum
Reproductions: *Art Museum, Omsk*, 1980

160
Barn. Study. ⟨1880s⟩
Oil on canvas. 66×97 cm (approx.)
Present whereabouts unknown
Provenance: O. Serova collection, Moscow

Exhibitions: 1914 (posthumous) St. Petersburg (No 72), Moscow (No 62)
References: Grabar, *Serov*, 1965, p. 399

161
Saddled Dapple-gray Horse.
Study. ⟨1880s⟩
Oil on cardboard. 18.5×26.2 cm
V. Petrov collection, Leningrad
Provenance: Yu. Danziger collection,
Moscow
Exhibitions: 1946 Central House of Art
Workers, Moscow (No 25); 1952 Moscow
(No 369)
References: Grabar, *Serov*, 1965, p. 402

162
**Terrace in Vvedenskoye,
near Zvenigorod.** Study. ⟨1880s⟩
Oil on cardboard. 54×64 cm
Present whereabouts unknown
Provenance: Barkov collection, Moscow;
B. Chernogubov collection, Moscow;
V. Chernogubova collection, Moscow
Exhibitions: 1935 The Russian Museum
(No 196); 1952 Moscow (No 105)
References: Grabar, *Serov*, 1965, p. 399

WATERCOLORS

163
The Novodevichy Monastery.
Study. ⟨1880s⟩
Watercolors and white on cardboard.
42.5×59.6 cm
Signed, bottom right: *BC* (VS)
The Russian Museum. Inv. No P-3221
Provenance: G. Bloch collection,
Leningrad
Exhibitions: 1935 The Russian Museum
(No 754a); 1965 The Russian Museum
References: Grabar, *Serov*, 1965, p. 400

46. The Novodevichy
Monastery. Study.
Cat. No 163

1890
PAINTINGS

164
Head of an Old Man. Study. ⟨1890⟩
Oil on canvas. 23×17 cm
Present whereabouts unknown
Provenance: E. Helzer collection, Moscow
Exhibitions: 1935 The Tretyakov Gallery
(No 47, dated to the 1880s)
References: Grabar, *Serov*, 1965, p. 403

165
Road in Domotkanovo. ⟨1890⟩
Oil on canvas
Present whereabouts unknown
Provenance: V. Derviz collection, Domot-
kanovo, Tver province
The present landscape is possibly the
study which appears under the same title
on the list of Serov's works of 1892.
Exhibitions: 1914 (posthumous) St. Peters-
burg (No 78), Moscow (No 68)
References: Grabar, *Serov*, 1914, p. 286
(canvas missing in the description);
Grabar, *Serov*, 1965, p. 403

166
Fir Trees. 1890
Oil on canvas. 101.5×66 cm
Signed and dated, bottom left: *В. Съровъ
90* (V. Serov, 1890)
Art Museum, Kharkov. Inv. No 160-Ж-ру
Provenance: S. Morozov collection, Mos-
cow; A. Liapunov collection, Moscow
Exhibitions: 1914 (posthumous) St. Peters-

47. Landscape with Horses
(Rural Landscape). Cat. No 167

burg (No 76), Moscow (No 67); 1935 The
Tretyakov Gallery (No 55, as *Northern
Landscape*); 1958–59 The Tretyakov Gallery; / 1900 St. Petersburg — 2nd Exhibition of Paintings Organized by the *Mir
Iskusstva* Magazine (No 178, as *Pine-tree*)
Reproductions: Grabar, *Serov*, 1914,
p. 81; Grabar, *Serov*, 1965, p. 116
References: Grabar, *Serov*, 1914, pp. 104,
286; Grabar, *Serov*, 1965, pp. 122, 402,
403

167
Landscape with Horses
(Rural Landscape). ⟨1890⟩
Oil on canvas. 50×64.5 cm
The Brodsky Memorial Museum,
Leningrad. Inv. No Ж-124
Provenance: I. Brodsky collection,
Leningrad
Exhibitions: 1935 The Tretyakov Gallery
(No 58, as *Landscape. Autumn*), The Rus-
sian Museum (No 55, under the same title)
References: Grabar, *Serov*, 1965, p. 402

168 (Plate 20)
Portrait of Angelo Masini. ⟨1890⟩
Oil on canvas. 89×70 cm
Signed, top right: *В. Сѣровъ*
(V. Serov)

The Tretyakov Gallery (since 1939).
Inv. No 24787
Provenance: S. Mamontov collection,
Moscow; I. Baranov collection, Moscow
Angelo Masini (1845–1926), celebrated
Italian tenor, frequently sang in the opera
houses of Moscow and St. Petersburg.
Exhibitions: 1914 (posthumous) St. Peters-
burg (No 75), Moscow (No 66); 1935 The
Tretyakov Gallery (No 56); 1952 Moscow
(No 109); 1958–59 The Tretyakov Gallery;
1959–60 The Russian Museum; 1965 The
Tretyakov Gallery (p. 30), The Russian
Museum; / 1890–91 Moscow —
10th Periodical Exhibition of the Moscow
Society of Art Lovers (No 25); 1964 Malmö
(Sweden), Bucharest — Russian Pre-
revolutionary and Soviet Art
Reproductions: Grabar, *Serov*, 1914,
p. 78; *Apollon*, 1914, No 6/7, between pp.
14 and 15; Grabar, *Serov*, 1965, p. 119
References: Grabar, *Serov*, 1914, pp. 96,
97, 286; Grabar, *Serov*, 1965, pp. 120,
121, 331; Kopschitzer, *Mamontov*, 1972,
pp. 114, 115

169
Portrait of the Manager's Wife
of a Kostroma Factory. 1890
Oil on canvas. 89×71.5 cm

Signed and dated, top left: *В. Сѣровъ 90*
(V. Serov, 1890)
Art Gallery, Yerevan (since 1926).
Inv. No Ж-356
In the inventory of the Art Gallery the
picture is listed as *Portrait of an Unknown
Woman.*
Exhibitions: 1935 The Tretyakov Gallery
(No 95, as *Portrait of Mrs. X*), The Russian
Museum (No 88, under the same title)
References: Grabar, *Serov*, 1965, pp. 122,
315, 331

170
Portrait of Vasily Alexandrovich
Schmidt. 1890
Oil on canvas. 85.2×70.5 cm
Signed, top right: *В. Сѣровъ 90*
(V. Serov, 1890)
The Nesterov Art Museum, Ufa (since
1927). Inv. No Ж-301
Provenance: The Yaroslavl Railway
Station, Moscow; The Tretyakov Gallery
Vasily Alexandrovich Schmidt, engineer,
honorary trustee of the Dallwig Railway
School.
Exhibitions: 1935 The Tretyakov Gallery
(No 57), The Russian Museum (No 54)
References: Grabar, *Serov*, 1965, p. 331

171
Portrait of Nadezhda Yakovlevna
Derviz. ⟨1890⟩
Oil on canvas. 43×29 cm
M. Favorskaya collection, Moscow
Provenance: V. Derviz collection, Zagorsk;
E. and M. Derviz collection, Moscow
Nadezhda Yakovlevna Derviz — see
No 146.
The portrait is dated either 1890 (Grabar,
Serov, 1914, p. 286) or 1888 (Grabar,
Serov, 1965, p. 329). The latter dating
contradicts the information contained in
Simonovich-Yefimova's book (Simonovich-
Yefimova 1964, p. 61) and is apparently
incorrect.
Exhibitions: 1935 The Tretyakov Gallery
(No 53), The Russian Museum (No 52);
1946 Central House of Art Workers, Mos-
cow (No 27); 1952 Moscow (No 111);
1965 The Tretyakov Gallery (p. 31); /
1914–15 Moscow — Moscow Artists in Aid
of War Victims (No 500)

48. Portrait of the Manager's
Wife of a Kostroma Factory.
Cat. No 169

49. Fir Trees. Cat. No 166

297

50. Portrait of
Vasily Alexandrovich Schmidt.
Cat. No 170

51. Portrait of
Nadezhda Yakovlevna Derviz.
Cat. No 171

Reproductions: Simonovich-Yefimova
1964, p. 65; Grabar, *Serov*, 1965, p. 103
(dated 1888)
References: Simonovich-Yefimova 1964,
p. 61; Grabar, *Serov*, 1914, p. 286;
Grabar, *Serov*, 1965, p. 329 (dated 1888)

172
Portrait of a Woman (O. Pavlova?).
1890
Oil on canvas. 59×49 cm
Signed and dated, bottom right:
В. Съровъ 1890 (V. Serov, 1890)
Present where abouts unknown
Provenance: V. Andreyevskaya collection,
Moscow; A. Gordon collection, Moscow;
D. Sezeman collection, Moscow
Exhibitions: 1914 (posthumous) St. Peters-
burg (No 77); 1946 Central House of Art
Workers, Moscow (No 2); 1952 Moscow
(No 112); 1958–59 The Tretyakov Gallery;
1965 The Tretyakov Gallery (p. 30)
References: Grabar, *Serov*, 1914, p. 286
(as *O. K. Pavlova*. Oil. Unfinished portrait);
Grabar, *Serov*, 1965, p. 336 (as *Portrait of
a Woman* [O. Pavlova?]. 1890s)

173 (Plate 26)
Portrait of Olga Fiodorovna Serova.
〈1889–90〉
Oil on canvas. 32×28.5 cm
The Serov family collection, Moscow
Olga Fiodorovna Serova — see No 81.
Exhibitions: 1935 The Tretyakov Gallery
(No 44), The Russian Museum (No 44);
1946 Central House of Art Workers, Mos-
cow (No 62); 1952 Moscow (No 108);
1958–59 The Tretyakov Gallery; 1959
Museum of Russian Art, Kiev; 1959–60
The Russian Museum; 1965 The
Tretyakov Gallery (pp. 29, 30), The Rus-
sian Museum; / 1951–52 Central House of
Art Workers, Moscow — Russian Painting:
Second Half of the 19th and Early
20th Centuries (No 226)
Reproductions: Grabar, *Serov*, 1965,
p. 112
References: Grabar, *Serov*, 1965, p. 330

174
**Portrait of Praskovya Dmitriyevna
Antipova.** 1890
Oil on canvas. 89.2×71.3 cm

Signed and dated, top left: *В. Съровъ 90*
(V. Serov, 1890)
Art Museum, Yaroslavl (since 1920).
Inv. No Ж-120
Provenance: P. Antipova collection,
Yaroslavl
Praskovya Dmitriyevna Antipova, headmis-
tress of a girls' school in Yaroslavl.
Exhibitions: 1935 The Tretyakov Gallery
(No 54), The Russian Museum (No 53);
1958–59 The Tretyakov Gallery
References: Grabar, *Serov*, 1914, p. 286;
Grabar, *Serov*, 1965, pp. 124, 331

175
**Portrait of Vladimir Dmitriyevich
Derviz.** 〈1890〉
Oil on canvas. 40×32 cm
M. Favorskaya collection, Moscow
Provenance: V. Derviz collection, Zagorsk;
E. and M. Derviz collection, Moscow
Vladimir Dmitriyevich Derviz — see No 72.
This portrait was painted as a pendant to
the *Portrait of Nadezhda Yakovlevna Der-
viz* (see No 171).
Exhibitions: 1935 The Tretyakov Gallery
(No 52), The Russian Museum (No 51);
1946 Central House of Art Workers, Mos-
cow (No 26); 1952 Moscow (No 110);
1965 The Tretyakov Gallery (p. 31), The
Russian Museum; / 1914–15 Moscow —
Moscow Artists in Aid of War Victims
(No 496)
Reproductions: Simonovich-Yefimova
1964, p. 66; Grabar, *Serov*, 1965, p. 106
(dated 1888)
References: Grabar, *Serov*, 1914, p. 286;
Grabar, *Serov*, 1965, p. 329 (dated 1888);
Simonovich-Yefimova 1964, p. 61

176
A Street in a Provincial Town.
Sketch. 〈1890〉
Oil
Present whereabouts unknown

Provenance: O. Serova collection,
Moscow; S. Kapnist collection
Exhibitions: 1914 (posthumous) St. Peters-
burg (No 64 — 2nd ed., dated 1889)
References: Grabar, *Serov*, 1914, p. 286;
Grabar, *Serov*, 1965, p. 402

177
Christ Walking upon the Water. 〈1890〉
Oil on canvas. 550×700 cm
The Russian Museum (since 1970).
Inv. No Ж-8602
Provenance: Picture Gallery, Kostroma
This large composition was painted by
Konstantin Korovin (see No 180), and only
the figures in it were executed by Serov. It
hung in the parish church of the Tretyakov
Factory in Kostroma.
References: Grabar, *Serov*, 1914, pp. 100,
102, 104, 286; Grabar, *Serov*, 1965,
pp. 122, 402

178
Christ Walking upon the Water. 〈1890〉
Oil on canvas. 55×72 cm
Present whereabouts unknown
Provenance: A. Gordon collection,
Moscow; V. Dmitriyev collection, Moscow
A sketch for the picture painted together
with Konstantin Korovin (see No 177).
References: Grabar, *Serov*, 1965,
pp. 122, 402

1891
PAINTINGS

179
**Boyaryshnia (a boyar's unmarried
daughter).** Study. 〈1891〉
Oil on canvas. 60.8×41.5 cm
At the bottom is an authenticating inscription in brush by Konstantin Korovin, apparently made later and erroneously dating
the study to 1895.

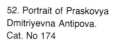

52. Portrait of Praskovya
Dmitriyevna Antipova.
Cat. No 174

References: Grabar, *Serov*, 1914, p. 286
(as *A Church*); Grabar, *Serov*, 1965,
pp. 126, 127 (as *A Church*), 403

182
Little Bridge. Study. ⟨1891⟩
Oil on canvas
Present whereabouts unknown
References: Grabar, *Serov*, 1914, p. 286;
Grabar, *Serov*, 1965, pp. 126, 127, 404

183
At a Dam by a Mill. ⟨1891⟩
Oil on canvas. 55×85 cm (approx.)
Signed, bottom right: *Съровъ* (Serov)
Present whereabouts unknown
Provenance: O. Serova collection, Moscow
In the catalogue of Serov's works (Grabar,
Serov, 1965, p. 404) this canvas was
listed twice, first as *The Mill* (1891) and
then under the title *At a Dam by a Mill*.
Exhibitions: 1914 (posthumous) St. Peters-
burg (No 68 — 2nd. ed. and 4th ed., as
The Dam. 1889), Moscow (not included in
the catalogue)
References: Grabar, *Serov*, 1914, p. 286
(as *The Mill*); Grabar, *Serov*, 1965,
pp. 126 (under the same title), 404; *Serov
in the Reminiscences of His Contemporaries*, 1971, 2, p. 535

Present whereabouts unknown
Provenance: V. Beloruchev collection,
Moscow; Z. Gudtsova collection, Moscow
References: Grabar, *Serov*, 1965,
pp. 127, 404

180
Konstantin Korovin Painting
en plein air. ⟨1891⟩
Oil on canvas. 46×62 cm
Present whereabouts unknown
Provenance: O. Serova collection, Mos-
cow; E. Helzer and T. Helzer collection,
Moscow
Konstantin Alexeyevich Korovin
(1861–1939), painter, stage-set designer,
one of the most brilliant representatives of
Impressionism in Russian painting, was a
close friend of Serov.
Exhibitions: 1914 (posthumous) Moscow
(No 73 — 1st ed., No 72 — 2nd ed.); 1946
Central House of Art Workers, Moscow
(No 12); 1952 Moscow (No 251, wrongly
dated to the 1900s); 1958–59 The Tret-
yakov Gallery; / 1954 Central House of Art
Workers, Moscow — Portraits of Promi-
nent Personalities in Russian Art: 18th to
20th Century (No 165, the same wrong
dating)
References: Grabar, *Serov*, 1914, p. 286;
Grabar, *Serov*, 1965, p. 331

181
Summer Landscape with a Church.
Study. 1891
Oil on canvas. 53.5×71 cm
Signed and dated, bottom right: *Съровъ
91* (Serov, 1891)

Present whereabouts unknown
Provenance: O. Serova collection, Moscow; V. (R.) Krotte collection, St. Petersburg; F. Podtynnikov collection, Moscow
Exhibitions: 1914 (posthumous) St. Petersburg (No 83); 1935 The Tretyakov Gallery
(No 62), The Russian Museum (No 60);
1946 Central House of Art Workers, Moscow (No 55); 1952 Moscow (No 116); /
1947 Central House of Art Workers, Moscow — Landscape in Russian Painting:
Second Half of the 19th Century (No 105);
1951–52 Central House of Art Workers,
Moscow — Russian Painting: Second Half
of the 19th and Early 20th Centuries
(No 227)

184
**Portrait of Yelena Petrovna
Konchalovskaya.** 1891
Oil on canvas. 62×58.5 cm
Signed and dated, top left: *Съровъ 91*
(Serov, 1891)
The Russian Museum. Inv. No Ж-6650
Provenance: Ye. Konchalovskaya collec-
tion, Moscow; M. Yasinovskaya collection,
Leningrad
Yelena Petrovna Konchalovskaya,
Yasinovskaya by marriage (1872–1935),
daughter of Piotr Petrovich Konchalovsky
(see No 185) and sister of the artist
Piotr Konchalovsky.
Exhibitions: 1965 The Russian Museum; /
1954 Leningrad — Paintings by Russian
Artists from Private Collections in Lenin-
grad: 18th to Early 20th Century (p. 36);
1959 Leningrad — Russian Portrait Paint-

53. Portrait of
Vladimir Dmitriyevich Derviz.
Cat. No 175

54. Portrait of Yelena Petrovna
Konchalovskaya. Cat. No 184

299

55. Portrait of Piotr Petrovich
Konchalovsky. Cat. No 185

56. The Demon and Tamara.
Illustration for Lermontov's
poem *The Demon*. Cat. No 188

57. Princess Mary and Pechorin.
Illustration for Lermontov's story
A Hero of Our Times.
Cat. No 189

ing: 18th to Early 20th Century (p. 34)
Reproductions: Leniashin 1980, p. 234
References: Grabar, *Serov*, 1965, p. 332

185
**Portrait of Piotr Petrovich
Konchalovsky.** ⟨1891⟩
Oil on canvas. 69×64 cm
Signed and dated, bottom right: *Съровъ
1891 г.* (Serov, 1891)
Picture Gallery, Sverdlovsk (since 1959).
Inv. No Ж-1014
Provenance: M. Konchalovsky collection,
Moscow; T. Konchalovskaya-Bakunina
collection, Moscow
Piotr Petrovich Konchalovsky (Kanchalov-
sky, 1838–1904), book publisher and
translator of European classics.
Exhibitions: 1935 Moscow (No 63), The
Russian Museum (No 61); 1946 Central
House of Art Workers, Moscow (No 45);
1952 Moscow (No 115); 1958–59 The Tret-
yakov Gallery; / 1915 The Lemercier Gal-
lery, Moscow — In Aid of War Victims and
Refugees: Paintings and Sculptures by
Russian Artists (No 250, No 306 —
2nd ed.)
Reproductions: Grabar, *Serov*, 1914,
p. 85; Grabar, *Serov*, 1965, p. 120
References: Grabar, *Serov*, 1914, pp. 108,
286; Grabar, *Serov*, 1965, pp. 124, 331

186 (Plate 39)
Portrait of Francesco Tamagno. ⟨1891⟩
Oil on canvas. 78.3×69.2 cm
Signed and dated, left: *Съровъ 93*
(Serov, 1893)
The Tretyakov Gallery (since 1917).
Inv. No 5589
Provenance: V. Girshman collection,
Moscow
Francesco Tamagno (1851–1905), cele-
brated Italian tenor. Serov painted his por-
trait in the winter of 1890–91 and signed it
two years later, in 1893.
Exhibitions: 1914 (posthumous) St. Peters-
burg (No 82), Moscow (No 72 — 1st ed.,
No 71 — 2nd ed.); 1935 The Tretyakov
Gallery (No 59), The Russian Museum
(No 73); 1958–59 The Tretyakov Gallery;
1965 The Tretyakov Gallery (p. 33),
The Russian Museum; / 1891–92
Moscow — 11th Periodical Exhibition of
the Moscow Society of Art Lovers (No 45);
1896 Nizhni-Novgorod — All-Russia
Exhibition (No 388); 1898 St. Petersburg
— 26th Exhibition of the Itinerant
Society (No 110); 1906 Paris — Russian
Art (No 521); 1911 Rome — International
Art Exhibition (No 399); 1959 London —
Works of Art by Russian and Soviet Artists
(No 73); 1960 Paris — Russian and
Soviet Painting (No 53); 1975 The Russian
Museum — Russian Portrait Painting:
Late 19th and Early 20th Centuries
(No 188)
Reproductions: Grabar, *Serov*, 1914,
p. 87; Grabar, *Serov*, 1965, p. 125 (dated
1890/91–93)
References: Grabar, *Serov*, 1914, pp. 108,
109, 286; Grabar, *Serov*, 1965, pp. 77,
124, 126, 332; Sarabyanov, *Reforms by
Valentin Serov*, 1971, pp. 13, 21; *Serov in
the Reminiscences of His Contemporaries*,
1971, 1, pp. 279–282

187 (Plates 41, 42)
**Portrait of Konstantin Alexeyevich
Korovin.** ⟨1891⟩
Oil on canvas. 11.2×89 cm
The Tretyakov Gallery. Inv. No 8633
Konstantin Alexeyevich Korovin — see
No 180.
Provenance: I. Morozov collection, Mos-
cow; Museum of Modern Western Art,
Moscow

Exhibitions: 1914 (posthumous) Moscow
(No 69); 1935 The Tretyakov Gallery
(No 60), The Russian Museum (No 57);
1958–59 The Tretyakov Gallery; 1959–60
The Russian Museum; 1965 The
Tretyakov Gallery (p. 31), The Russian
Museum; / 1902 St. Petersburg, Moscow
— 4th Exhibition Organized by the *Mir Is-
kusstva* Magazine (Nos 174, 209); 1906
Paris, Berlin — Russian Art (Nos 520,
431); 1907 Venice — 7th International Art
Exhibition (No 45); 1975 The Russian
Museum — Russian Portrait Painting:
Late 19th and Early 20th Centuries
(No 187)
Reproductions: *Mir Iskusstva*, 1902,
Nos 1–6, p. 295; Grabar, *Serov*, 1914,
between pp. 96 and 97; Grabar, *Serov*,
1965, pp. 130 (detail), 131
References: Grabar, *Serov*, 1914, pp. 109,
110, 286; Grabar, *Serov*, 1965, pp. 127,
132, 331; Sarabyanov, *Reforms by Valen-
tin Serov*, 1971, pp. 13, 21; Leniashin
1980, pp. 80, 82

WATERCOLORS
188
The Demon and Tamara.
Illustration for Mikhail Lermontov's poem
The Demon. 1891
Black watercolor and white on cardboard.
60×56 cm
Signed and dated, bottom right:
В. Съровъ 91 (V. Serov, 1891)
The Tretyakov Gallery (since 1907).
Inv. No 5626
Provenance: M. Riabushinsky collection,
Moscow
Exhibitions: 1914 (posthumous) St. Peters-
burg (No 79), Moscow (No 70); 1935 The
Tretyakov Gallery (No 321), The Russian
Museum (No 378); 1965 The Tretyakov
Gallery (p. 56), The Russian Museum; /
1907 Moscow — Exhibition of the Moscow
Society of Art Lovers; 1939–40 Museum of
Literature, Moscow — Works of Art De-
voted to Lermontov from Moscow
Museums (p. 108)
Reproductions: Lermontov 1891, 2,
between pp. 10 and 11; Grabar, *Serov*,
1914, p. 83; *Apollon*, 1914, No 6/7,
between pp. 20 and 21
References: Grabar, *Serov*, 1914, pp. 108,
286; Grabar, *Serov*, 1965, pp. 283, 403

189

Princess Mary and Pechorin.
Illustration for Mikhail Lermontov's
story *A Hero of Our Times.* 1891
Black watercolor and white
on cardboard. 45.5×60.5 cm
Signed and dated, bottom right:
В. Съровъ 91 (V. Serov, 1891)
The Tretyakov Gallery (since 1923).
Inv. No 4987
Provenance: A. Golikov collection, Mos-
cow; State Museum Reserve, Moscow
Exhibitions: 1935 The Tretyakov Gallery
(No 323), The Russian Museum (No 380);
1952 Moscow (No 117); 1959 Museum of
Russian Art, Kiev; 1959–60 The Russian
Museum; 1965 The Tretyakov Gallery
(p. 56), The Russian Museum; / Moscow
— Exhibition Sale of the A. Golikov collec-
tion (No 422); 1939–40 Museum of Litera-
ture, Moscow — Works of Art Devoted to
Lermontov from Moscow Museums
(p. 108); 1963 The Tretyakov Gallery —
Pencil Drawings, Watercolors, Pastels,
and Gouaches (p. 69)
Reproductions: Lermontov 1891, 2,
between pp. 180 and 181
References: Grabar, *Serov*, 1965,
pp. 283, 403

1892
PAINTINGS

190

Road in Domotkanovo.
Study. 〈1892〉
Oil on panel. 33.2×40 cm
Signed, bottom left: *Съровъ* (Serov)
Inscribed on the back of the panel:
*Писалъ В. А. Съровъ въ с. Домотканово
Тверской губ. 1888–1892 г.* (Painted by
V. A. Serov in the village of Domotkanovo,
Tver province, 1888–92)
Art Museum, Ulyanovsk (since 1920).
Inv. No 410
It may well be that *Road in Domotkanovo*
(1890) and the present study are in fact
the same work. In earlier catalogues such
a title occurs only once (among the works
of 1890), with oil missing in the description
of the medium (Grabar, *Serov*, 1914,
p. 286).

58. Coach from Moscow
to Kuzminki. Cat. No 194

59. Road in Domotkanovo.
Study. Cat. No 190

Exhibitions: 1935 The Tretyakov Gallery
(No 74), The Russian Museum (No 70)
References: Grabar, *Serov*, 1965, p. 404
(see also p. 403 — *Road in Domotkanovo.*
1890)

191

**Male Figure in the Hall
of the Assembly of the Nobility
in Kharkov.** Study. 〈1892〉
Oil on canvas. 60×44.2 cm
V. Petrov collection, Leningrad (since
1955)
Provenance: The Serov family collection,
Moscow
A study for the group portrait entitled *Alex-
ander III with His Family* (1892–94) — see
No 232.
References: Grabar, *Serov*, 1965,
p. 404

192

**Male Figure in the Hall
of the Assembly of the Nobility
in Kharkov.** 〈1892〉
Oil on canvas. 53.5×43.3 cm
Present whereabouts unknown
Provenance: V. Dmitriyev collection,
Moscow

A study for the group portrait *Alexander III
with His Family* (1892–94) — see No 232.
References: Grabar, *Serov*, 1965,
p. 404

193

Liolia Derviz. 1892
Oil on canvas. 68×45 cm (exposed area)
Signed and dated, top right: *В. Съровъ 92*
(V. Serov, 1892)
The Tretyakov Gallery (since 1961).
Inv. No П-32750
Provenance: V. Derviz collection, Zagorsk;
M. and Ye. Derviz collection, Moscow
Yelena (Liolia) Vladimirovna Derviz
(1889–?), daughter of Vladimir and
Nadezhda Derviz (see Nos 72 and 146).
Exhibitions: 1935 The Tretyakov Gallery
(No 73), The Russian Museum (No 69a);
1946 Central House of Art Workers, Mos-
cow (No 28); 1952 Moscow (No 122);
1958–59 The Tretyakov Gallery; 1965 The
Tretyakov Gallery (p. 32), The Russian
Museum; / 1914–15 Moscow — Moscow
Artists in Aid of War Victims (No 502);
1962 The Tretyakov Gallery — Russian
Pre-revolutionary Art: New Acquisitions
(p. 21)

60. Liolia Derviz. Cat. No 193

Reproductions: Simonovich-Yefimova 1964, p. 44; Grabar, *Serov*, 1965, p. 129
References: Grabar, *Serov*, 1914, p. 287; Grabar, *Serov*, 1965, p. 332; Simonovich-Yefimova 1964, p. 43

194
Coach from Moscow to Kuzminki.
⟨1892⟩
Oil on canvas. 58×83.5 cm
Signed, bottom left: *Съровъ* (Serov)
The Russian Museum (since 1927).
Inv. No Ж-4301
Provenance: M. Riabushinsky collection, Moscow
Exhibitions: 1914 (posthumous) St. Petersburg (No 88), Moscow (No 78 — 1st ed., No 77 — 2nd ed.); 1935 The Tretyakov Gallery (No 67), The Russian Museum (No 65); 1965 The Tretyakov Gallery (p. 32), The Russian Museum
Reproductions: Grabar, *Serov*, 1914, p. 90; Grabar, *Serov*, 1965, p. 128
References: Grabar, *Serov*, 1914, pp. 112, 116, 287; Grabar, *Serov*, 1965, pp. 132, 404

195
Horse. Study. ⟨1892⟩
Oil on panel. 17×10.3 cm
Inscribed, top right: *Любезному Сергъю отъ автора* (To dear Sergei from the author)
The Tretyakov Gallery (since 1929).
Inv. No 11235
Provenance: I. Ostroukhov collection, Moscow; The Ostroukhov Museum of Icons and Painting, Moscow
Exhibitions: 1935 The Tretyakov Gallery (No 65), The Russian Museum (No 64); 1965 The Tretyakov Gallery (p. 31)
References: Grabar, *Serov*, 1965, p. 404

196
Autumn. Domotkanovo. 1892
Oil on canvas. 60.4×105.3 cm
Signed and dated, bottom right: *Съровъ 92* (Serov, 1892)
Art Museum, Ivanovo (since 1930).
Inv. No Ж-115
Provenance: V. Girshman collection, Moscow; The Tretyakov Gallery
Exhibitions: 1914 (posthumous) St. Petersburg (No 91), Moscow (No 81 — 1st ed., No 80 — 2nd ed.); 1935 The Tretyakov Gallery (No 66), The Russian Museum (No 66); 1958–59 The Tretyakov Gallery; 1959–60 The Russian Museum
Reproductions: Grabar, *Serov*, 1914, p. 92; Grabar, *Serov*, 1965, p. 128
References: Grabar, *Serov*, 1914, p. 287; Grabar, *Serov*, 1965, pp. 132, 404; Fiodorov-Davydov 1965, No 2, p. 35

197 (Plate 44)
Portrait of Zinaida Vasilyevna Moritz. 1892
Oil on canvas. 81×83 cm
Signed and dated, bottom right: *Съровъ 92* (Serov, 1892)
Art Museum, Ivanovo (since 1930).
Inv. No Ж-116
Provenance: Z. Grey collection, Moscow; The Tretyakov Gallery
Zinaida Vasilyevna Moritz, née Yakunchikova (1864–1929).
Exhibitions: 1935 The Tretyakov Gallery (No 69), The Russian Museum (No 67); 1958–59 The Tretyakov Gallery; 1959 Museum of Russian Art, Kiev; 1959–60 The Russian Museum; 1965 The

Tretyakov Gallery (p. 32); / 1892–93 Moscow — 12th Periodical Exhibition of the Moscow Society of Art Lovers (No 21, as *Portrait of Mrs. Z. V. M.*); 1895 St. Petersburg — 23rd Exhibition of the Itinerant Society (No 100, as *Portrait of Mrs. Z. V. G.*)
Reproductions: Grabar, *Serov*, 1914, p. 86; Grabar, *Serov*, 1980, pl. 21
References: Grabar, *Serov*, 1914, pp. 110 (erroneous mention of the picture being displayed the following year at the Exhibi-

tion of the Itinerant Society), 112, 286 (erroneously included in the list of Serov's works of 1891); Grabar, *Serov*, 1965, pp. 132 (described incorrectly as displayed in 1893 at the exhibition of the Itinerant Society), 332

198 (Plate 49)
Portrait of Ivan Yegorovich Zabelin. 1892
Oil on canvas. 80×67 cm
Signed and dated, top right: *В. Съровъ 92* (Serov, 1892)
History Museum, Moscow. Inv. No 2882
Ivan Yegorovich Zabelin (1820–1908), historian and archaeologist, one of the founders and directors of the History Museum in Moscow.
Exhibitions: 1935 The Tretyakov Gallery (No 72), The Russian Museum (No 69); 1952 Moscow (No 119); 1958–59 The Tretyakov Gallery; 1959 Museum of Russian Art, Kiev; 1959–60 The Russian Museum; 1965 The Tretyakov Gallery (p. 32); / 1893–94 Moscow — 13th Periodical Exhibition of the Moscow Society of Art Lovers (No 10)
Reproductions: Grabar, *Serov*, 1914, p. 95
References: Grabar, *Serov*, 1914, pp. 116, 117, 287; Grabar, *Serov*, 1965, pp. 132, 332

199
Portrait of Olga Fiodorovna Tamara. 1892
Oil on canvas. 149.6×98.6 cm
Signed and dated, bottom left: *В. Съровъ 92* (V. Serov, 1892)
Art Museum, Minsk (since 1962).

201
Portrait of Ilya Yefimovich Repin. 1892
Oil on canvas. 66.4×53.3 cm
Signed and dated, top left: *В. Съровъ 92*
(V. Serov, 1892)
The Tretyakov Gallery (since 1925).
Inv. No 6264
Provenance: The Tsvetkov Gallery,
Moscow
Ilya Yefimovich Repin — see No 21.
Exhibitions: 1935 The Tretyakov Gallery
(No 64), The Russian Museum (No 62);
1952 Moscow (No 120); 1958–59 The Tretyakov Gallery; 1965 The Tretyakov Gallery (p. 31), The Russian Museum
Reproductions: Grabar, *Serov*, 1914, p. 93
References: Grabar, *Serov*, 1914, pp. 116,
287; Grabar, *Serov*, 1965, pp. 132, 332

202
Kholstomer (The Story of a Horse).
⟨1892⟩
Oil on canvas, mounted on cardboard.
22.2×34.3 cm
The Tretyakov Gallery (since 1929).
Inv. No 11187
Provenance: I. Ostroukhov collection, Moscow; The Ostroukhov Museum of Icons
and Painting, Moscow
Exhibitions: 1935 The Tretyakov Gallery
(No 66), The Russian Museum (No 64a);
1952 Moscow (No 123); 1958–59 The Tretyakov Gallery; 1959 Museum of Russian

63. Portrait of
Sophia Andreyevna Tolstaya.
Cat. No 200

Inv. No Ж-789
Provenance: O. Tamara collection, Moscow; M. Yakunchikova collection, Moscow;
E. Helzer and T. Helzer collection,
Moscow
Olga Fiodorovna Tamara, née Mamontova
(1870–1952), niece of Savva Mamontov
(see No 19), opera singer.
Exhibitions: 1914 (posthumous) St. Petersburg (No 89), Moscow (No 79 — 1st ed.,
No 78 — 2nd ed.); 1935 The Tretyakov
Gallery (No 71); 1952 Moscow (No 121); /
1893 Moscow, St. Petersburg — 21st Exhibition of the Itinerant Society (No 138);
1961–62 Art Museum, Minsk — Works of
Russian Art from Private Collections
Reproductions: Grabar, *Serov*, 1914, p. 91
References: Grabar, *Serov*, 1914, pp. 116,
287; Grabar, *Serov*, 1965, pp. 132, 332

200
Portrait of Sophia Andreyevna
Tolstaya. 1892
Oil on canvas. 112×92 cm
Signed and dated, bottom right: *92.*
В. Съровъ (1892, V. Serov)
The Tolstoy Memorial Museum, Yasnaya
Poliana. Inv. No 1086
Provenance: S. Tolstaya collection, Yasnaya Poliana
Sophia Andreyevna Tolstaya, née Bers
(1844–1919), wife of Leo Tolstoy.
Exhibitions: 1914 (posthumous) St. Petersburg (No 85), Moscow (No 76 — 1st ed.,
No 75 — 2nd ed.); 1935 The Tretyakov
Gallery (No 70), The Russian Museum
(No 68); 1958–59 The Tretyakov Gallery; /
1894 St. Petersburg, Moscow — 22nd Exhibition of the Itinerant Society (No 159)
Reproductions: Ernst, *Serov*, 1922,
between pp. 16 and 17
References: Grabar, *Serov*, 1914, pp. 112,
286; Grabar, *Serov*, 1965, pp. 132, 332;

64. Portrait of Ilya Yefimovich
Repin. Cat. No 201

303

65. Kholstomer (The Story of
a Horse). Cat. No 202

Art, Kiev; 1959–60 The Russian Museum;
1965 The Tretyakov Gallery (p. 32), The
Russian Museum; / 1898 St. Petersburg —
Works by Russian and Finnish Artists
References: Grabar, *Serov*, 1914, p. 287;
Grabar, *Serov*, 1965, p. 404

1893
PAINTINGS

203
Grand Princess Olga Alexandrovna.
1893
Oil on canvas. 60×49 cm
Signed and dated, bottom right:
Съровъ 93 (Serov, 1893)
The Russian Museum, Leningrad (since
1924). Inv. No Ж-1918
Provenance: Empress Maria Fiodorovna
collection, St. Petersburg
A study for the group portrait *Alexander III
with His Family* (1892–94) — see No 232.
Exhibitions: 1914 (posthumous) St. Peters-
burg (No 94c — 3rd and 4th ed.), Moscow
(No 86 — 1st ed., No 85 — 2nd ed.)
Reproductions: Ernst, *Serov*, 1922, be-
tween pp. 16 and 17; Leniashin 1980,
p. 81
References: Grabar, *Serov*, 1914, p. 287;
Grabar, *Serov*, 1965, p. 332

204
Grand Princess Xenia Alexandrovna.
1893
Oil on canvas. 63×39 cm
Signed and dated, bottom right:
В. Съровъ 93 (V. Serov, 1893)
Art and History Museum, Pskov (since
1930). Inv. No 798/129
Provenance: Empress Maria Fiodorovna
collection, St. Petersburg; The Russian
Museum
A study for the group portrait *Alexander III
with His Family* (1892–94) — see No 232.
Exhibitions: 1914 (posthumous) St. Peters-
burg (No 94b — 3rd and 4th ed.), Moscow
(No 85 — 1st ed., No 84 — 2nd ed.)
Reproductions: Ernst, *Serov*, 1922, be-
tween pp. 16 and 17 (wrongly called
Empress Maria Fiodorovna)
References: Grabar, *Serov*, 1914, p. 287;
Grabar, *Serov*, 1965, p. 333

205
Grand Duke Mikhail Alexandrovich.
1893
Oil on canvas. 65×54 cm
Signed and dated, bottom right:

Съровъ 93 (Serov, 1893)
The Russian Museum (since 1924).
Inv. No Ж-1917
Provenance: Empress Maria Fiodorovna
collection, St. Petersburg
A study for the group portrait *Alexander III
with His Family* (1892–94) — see No 232.
Exhibitions: 1914 (posthumous) St. Peters-
burg (No 94a — 3rd and 4th ed.), Moscow
(No 84 — 1st ed., No 83 — 2nd ed.)
References: Grabar, *Serov*, 1914, p. 287;
Grabar, *Serov*, 1965, p. 332

206
**Vladimir Dmitriyevich Derviz on a
Bench in Domotkanovo.**
Study. ⟨1892–93⟩
Oil on cardboard. 23.3×17.8 cm
Bottom right, an impression of the artist's
signet: *BC* (VS)
The Tretyakov Gallery (since 1960).
Inv. No П-32751
Provenance: V. Derviz collection, Zagorsk;
E. Derviz collection, Moscow
Vladimir Dmitriyevich Derviz — see No 72.
Exhibitions: 1914 (posthumous) St. Peters-
burg (No 86, as *A Walk in Domotkanovo*),
Moscow (No 77 — 1st ed., under the
same title; No 76 — 2nd ed., under the
same title); 1935 The Russian Museum
(No 194, as *In a Park*, not dated); 1946
Central House of Art Workers, Moscow

(No 29); 1952 Moscow (No 124); 1958–59
The Tretyakov Gallery; 1959 Museum of
Russian Art, Kiev; 1959–60 The Russian
Museum; 1965 The Tretyakov Gallery
(p. 34); / 1962 The Tretyakov Gallery —
Russian Pre-revolutionary Art: New
Acquisitions (p. 21)
Reproductions: *Iskusstvo*, 1934, No 6,
p. 120 (as *Landscape in Domotkanovo*);
Simonovich-Yefimova 1964, p. 71 (the
date is given wrongly as 1899); Grabar,
Serov, 1965, p. 259 (dated 1892–93)
References: Grabar, *Serov*, 1965, pp. 332
(dated 1892–93), 416; Simonovich-
Yefimova 1964, p. 70

207
A House in the Crimea. ⟨1893⟩
Oil
Present whereabouts unknown
Provenance: O. Serova collection, Mos-
cow; S. Feleisen collection
Exhibitions: 1914 (posthumous) St. Peters-
burg (No 87 — 3rd and 4th ed.)
References: Grabar, *Serov*, 1965, p. 405

208
A House in the Crimea. Study. ⟨1893⟩
Oil on cardboard. 24.2×19.8 cm
Present whereabouts unknown
Provenance: A. Koludarov collection,
Moscow
Probably a replica of No 207.
Exhibitions: 1952 Moscow (No 126); /
1955
Central House of Art Workers, Moscow —
Landscape in Russian Painting: 19th and
Early 20th Centuries (No 296)
References: Grabar, *Serov*, 1914, p. 287;
Grabar, *Serov*, 1965, p. 405

209
Iphigenia in Tauris. ⟨1893⟩
Unfinished
Oil on canvas. 94×134 cm
Art Gallery, Kazan (since 1930).
Inv. No Ж-102
Provenance: O. Serova collection, Mos-
cow; A. Korovin collection, St. Petersburg;
The Russian Museum
Exhibitions: 1935 The Tretyakov Gallery
(No 80), The Russian Museum (No 75)
Reproductions: *Apollon*, 1917, No 2/3,
between pp. VIII and IX

66. Vladimir Dmitriyevich Derviz
on a Bench in Domotkanovo.
Study. Cat. No 206

304

References: Grabar, *Serov*, 1914, p. 287;
Grabar, *Serov*, 1965, p. 405; Fiodorov-
Davydov 1965, No 2, p. 34

Sketches and studies for
Iphigenia in Tauris. 1893
(Nos 210–214)

210
Iphigenia in Tauris. Sketch. ⟨1893⟩
Oil on cardboard. 28.5×39.5 cm
Signed, bottom right: *BC* (VS)
The Brodsky Memorial Museum,
Leningrad. Inv. No Ж-126
Provenance: I. Brodsky collection,
Leningrad
References: Grabar, *Serov*, 1965, p. 405

211
Seashore. 1893
Oil on canvas. 28.2×45.5 cm
Signed and dated, bottom left:
Съровъ 1893 (Serov, 1893)
Museum of Local Lore, Vladimir.
Inv. No $\frac{Ж-352}{В-3222}$
Exhibitions: 1958–59 The Tretyakov
Gallery; 1965 The Tretyakov Gallery
(pp. 33, 34)

212
Seashore. ⟨1893⟩
Oil on canvas. 25×28.5 cm
History Museum, Moscow. Inv. No 5506
Provenance: P. Shchukin collection,
Moscow
Exhibitions: 1958–59 The Tretyakov Gal-
lery; 1965 The Tretyakov Gallery (p. 34)

213
Seashore. The Crimea. ⟨1893⟩
Oil on canvas. 23.1×32.6 cm
History Museum, Moscow.
Inv. No И1 $\frac{5567}{23376щ}$
Provenance: P. Shchukin collection,
Moscow
Exhibitions: 1952 Moscow (No 128)
References: Grabar, *Serov*, 1965, p. 405

214
**Seashore with a Standing Female
Figure. The Crimea.** ⟨1893⟩
Oil on canvas. 19×28.5 cm
History Museum, Moscow.
Inv. No И1 $\frac{5566}{23374щ}$
Provenance: P. Shchukin collection,
Moscow

Exhibitions: 1952 Moscow (No 129)
References: Grabar, *Serov*, 1965, p. 405

67. Crimean Study. Cat. No 217

215
The Crimea. ⟨1893⟩
Oil on canvas
Present whereabouts unknown
Provenance: Basnin collection
References: Grabar, *Serov*, 1914, p. 287;
Grabar, *Serov*, 1965, p. 406

216
A Crimean Yard. Study. ⟨1893⟩
Oil on canvas, mounted on cardboard.
39.7×31.2 cm
Art Museum, Minsk (since 1957).
Inv. No РЖ-135
Provenance: A. Zhigalko collection,
Moscow
Exhibitions: 1952 Moscow (No 127)
References: Grabar, *Serov*, 1965, p. 405

68. Iphigenia in Tauris. Sketch.
Cat. No 210

217
Crimean Study. ⟨1893⟩
Oil on canvas, mounted on cardboard.
14.4×22.7 cm
V. Petrov collection, Leningrad
References: Grabar, *Serov*, 1965, p. 405

218
Crimean Study. ⟨1893⟩
Oil on panel. 18×28 cm
Present whereabouts unknown
References: Grabar, *Serov*, 1965, p. 405

219
**Crimean Study.
View of the Mountains.** ⟨1893⟩
Oil. Study of a small size (along the hori-
zontal axis)
Present whereabouts unknown
Exhibitions: 1914 (posthumous) Moscow
(No 85)
References: Grabar, *Serov*, 1965, p. 405

220
The Mill. Study. ⟨1893⟩
Oil on canvas
Present whereabouts unknown
Provenance: O. Serova collection, Mos-
cow; V. Kravtsov collection, St. Petersburg
Exhibitions: 1914 (posthumous) St. Peters-
burg (No 65 — 3rd and 4th ed., dated
1889?)
References: Grabar, *Serov*, 1965, p. 406

69. Seashore with a Standing
Female Figure. The Crimea.
Cat. No 214

221
The Sea. ⟨1893⟩
Oil
Present whereabouts unknown
Provenance: V. Derviz collection, Moscow
Exhibitions: 1914 (posthumous) St. Peters-
burg (No 90), Moscow (No 80 — 1st ed.,
No 79 — 2nd ed.)
References: Grabar, *Serov*, 1965, p. 405

222

**Portrait of an Unknown Woman
(Kononovich?).** 1893
Oil on canvas. 70.5×57.5 cm
Signed and dated, top right: *Съровъ 93 г.*
(Serov, 1893)
Picture Gallery, Odessa (since 1926).
Inv. No Ж-548
Provenance: P. Delarov collection,
St. Petersburg; M. Braikevich collection,
Odessa
The portrait probably depicts a certain
Mrs. Kononovich.
Exhibitions: 1935 The Tretyakov Gallery
(No 78); / 1914 St. Petersburg — Paintings
and Drawings by Russian Artists from the
Delarov Collection (No 83); 1926 Art
Museum, Odessa — Paintings from the
Odessa Art Museum Reserve (No 112, as
Portrait of a Woman)
References: Grabar, *Serov*, 1914, p. 287;
Grabar, *Serov*, 1965, p. 333

223

Portrait of Rosalia Lvova. 1893
Oil on canvas. 64×45 cm
Signed and dated, top left: *Съровъ 93*
(Serov, 1893)
Art Museum, Ashkhabad. Inv. No КП-1288
Rosalia Solomonovna Lvova, mother-in-
law of Maria Lvova, née Simonovich (see
No 18).
Provenance: V. Lazaris collection, Odessa;
The Tretyakov Gallery
Exhibitions: 1935 The Tretyakov Gallery
(No 81), The Russian Museum (No 76);
1958–59 The Tretyakov Gallery; 1959
Museum of Russian Art, Kiev; 1959–60
The Russian Museum; 1965 The Tretyak-
ov Gallery (p. 33), The Russian Museum
Reproductions: Grabar, *Serov*, 1914, p. 97
References: Grabar, *Serov*, 1914, pp. 117,
287; Grabar, *Serov*, 1965, pp. 133, 333

224

Portrait of T. Voitkevich. 1893
Oil on canvas
Signed and dated, top right: *Съровъ 93 г.*
(Serov, 1893)
Present whereabouts unknown
Provenance: T. Voitkevich collection,
Moscow
Exhibitions: 1893–94 Moscow —
13th Periodical Exhibition of the Moscow
Society of Art Lovers (No 59, as *Portrait of
T.S.V.*)
References: Grabar, *Serov*, 1914, p. 287;
Grabar, *Serov*, 1965, p. 333 (described in-
correctly as housed in the Picture Gallery,
Odessa)

225 (Plate 53)

Portait of Isaac Ilyich Levitan. 1893
Oil on canvas. 82×86 cm
Signed and dated, bottom right:
Съровъ 93 (Serov, 1893)
The Tretyakov Gallery (since 1894).
Inv. No 1520
Isaac Ilyich Levitan (1860–1900), major
representative of Russian lyrical landscape
painting in the late nineteenth century.
Exhibitions: 1935 The Tretyakov Gallery
(No 75), The Russian Museum (No 71);
1958–59 The Tretyakov Gallery; 1959
Museum of Russian Art, Kiev; 1959–60
The Russian Museum; 1965 The
Tretyakov Gallery (p. 33), The Russian
Museum; / 1893 St. Petersburg, Moscow,
Kiev — 21st Exhibition of the Itinerant
Society (No 137); 1923 The Tretyakov

Gallery — Exhibition Commemorating the
25th Anniversary of P. Tretyakov's Death
(No 49); 1939 The Russian Museum —
Paintings by Levitan
Reproductions: Benois 1902, p. 227;
Grabar, *Serov*, 1914, p. 94; Grabar, *Serov*,
1965, p. 133
References: Grabar, *Serov*, 1914, pp. 117,
287; Grabar, *Serov*, 1980, pl. 22

226

Lioness. ⟨1893⟩
Oil on panel. 18×42 cm
Signed, bottom right: *ВС* (VS)
The Brodsky Memorial Museum,
Leningrad. Inv. No Ж-129
References: Grabar, *Serov*, 1965, p. 406
(as *Sphynx-lioness Drinking Water from
the River*)

227

Tatar Woman. Study. ⟨1893⟩
Oil on canvas. 18.5×15 cm
History Museum, Moscow.
Inv. No И1$\frac{5564}{23372щ}$
Provenance: P. Shchukin collection, Mos-
cow
Exhibitions: 1952 Moscow (No 132)
References: Grabar, *Serov*, 1965, p. 405

228

Tatar Women by the River. The Crimea.
Study. 1893
Oil on canvas. 54×72 cm
Signed and dated, bottom left: *Съровъ 93*
(Serov, 1893)
P. Nortsov collection, Moscow
Provenance: A. Zhigalko collection, Mos-
cow
Exhibitions: 1935 The Tretyakov Gallery
(No 79), The Russian Museum (No 74);
1952 Moscow (No 125, as *Crimean
Landscape*)
Reproductions: Zotov, *Serov*, 1964, pl. 12
(as *Tatar Women*)
References: *Serov in the Reminiscences

of His Contemporaries, 1971, 1, p. 209;
Grabar, *Serov*, 1914, pp. 118, 287 (as
Two Tatar Women. Study); Grabar, *Serov*,
1965, p. 405; Zotov, *Serov*, 1964, p. 16

229 (Plate 40)

**A Tatar Village in the Crimea
(A Crimean Yard).** 1893
Oil on canvas. 53×53 cm
Signed and dated, bottom right:
Съровъ 93 (Serov, 1893)
The Tretyakov Gallery (since 1895).
Inv. No 1521
Exhibitions: 1935 The Tretyakov Gallery
(No 76), The Russian Museum (No 72);
1958–59 The Tretyakov Gallery; 1965 The
Tretyakov Gallery (p. 33); / 1893–94 Mos-
cow — 13th Periodical Exhibition of the
Moscow Society of Art Lovers (No 91);
1894 St. Petersburg (?), Moscow —
22nd Exhibition of the Itinerant Society
(No 160, as *In the Crimea*); 1895
St. Petersburg — 23rd Exhibition of the
Itinerant Society (No 101)

Reproductions: Grabar, *Serov*, 1914,
p. 96; Grabar, *Serov*, 1965, p. 134
References: *Serov in the Reminiscences
of His Contemporaries*, 1971, 1, p. 207;
Grabar, *Serov*, 1914, pp. 118, 287;
Grabar, *Serov*, 1965, pp. 133, 134, 405;
Fiodorov-Davydov 1965, No 1, p. 40,
No 2, p. 34

72. Tatar Women by the River.
The Crimea. Study. Cat. No 228

WATERCOLORS
AND GOUACHES

230 (Plate 139)
Iphigenia in Tauris. Sketch. ⟨1893⟩
Watercolors, white and graphite on gray
paper. 20.5×30.7 cm
Bottom right, an impression of the artist's
signet: *BC* (VS)
The Tretyakov Gallery (since 1922).
Inv. No 4914
Provenance: State Museum Reserve,
Moscow
Exhibitions: 1935 The Tretyakov Gallery
(No 327), The Russian Museum (No 385);
1958–59 The Tretyakov Gallery; 1965 The
Tretyakov Gallery (p. 56); / 1954 The
Tretyakov Gallery — Sketches and
Studies by Russian Artists from the Tret-
yakov Gallery Reserve: 18th to Early
20th Century (p. 54); 1963 The Tret-
yakov Gallery — Pencil Drawings, Water-
colors, Pastels, and Gouaches (p. 69)
Reproductions: Grabar, *Serov*, 1980,
pl. 24
References: Grabar, *Serov*, 1965, p. 405

231
Iphigenia in Tauris. ⟨1893⟩
Gouache. 39×69 cm (top rounded)
Present whereabouts unknown
Provenance: Ya. Ettinger collection, Mos-
cow; R. Viktorova collection, Moscow;
N. Shmeliov collection, Moscow
References: Grabar, *Serov*, 1965, p. 406

73. Crimean Horse. Study.
Cat. No 234

1894
PAINTINGS

232
Alexander III with His Family.
⟨1892–94⟩
Oil on canvas. 388×297 cm
Present whereabouts unknown
Provenance: Hall of the Assembly of the
Nobility, Kharkov; Art Museum, Kharkov
(until 1941)
Alexander III (1845–1894), Emperor of
Russia (1881–94).
Reproductions: Grabar, *Serov*, 1914,
pp. 88, 89 (detail)
References: Grabar, *Serov*, 1914, pp. 112,
287; Grabar, *Serov*, 1965, p. 333; *Serov in
the Reminiscences of His Contemporaries*,
1971, 1, pp. 146, 208, 209; Leniashin
1980, pp. 24, 26

233
Alexander III. ⟨1894⟩
Present whereabouts unknown
A repetition of the figure in the group
portrait (No 232).
References: Grabar, *Serov*, 1965, p. 333

234
Crimean Horse. Study. 1894
Oil on canvas. 27×36 cm

Signed and dated, bottom left: *Съровъ 94*
(Serov, 1894)
Art Museum, Kuibyshev (since 1926).
Inv. No Ж-18
Exhibitions: 1965 The Russian Museum
References: Grabar, *Serov*, 1965, p. 406

235
Landscape Sketch. ⟨1894⟩
Oil on canvas
Present whereabouts unknown
Provenance: L. Muravyova collection,
Novgorod
References: Grabar, *Serov*, 1914, p. 287;
Grabar, *Serov*, 1965, p. 406

236
**Portrait of Liudmila Anatolyevna
Mamontova.** 1894
Pastel
Signed, bottom right: *Съровъ 94*
(Serov, 1894)
Present whereabouts unknown
Provenance: A. Mamontov collection,
Moscow; V. Winterfeld collection,
St. Petersburg
Liudmila Anatolyevna Mamontova — see
No 53.
Exhibitions: 1914 (posthumous) St. Peters-

burg (No 95), Moscow (No 88 — 1st ed.,
No 87 — 2nd ed.); / 1894–95 Moscow —
14th Periodical Exhibition of the Moscow
Society of Art Lovers (No 21, as *Portrait of
L. Muravyova*)
Reproductions: Grabar, *Serov*, 1914, p. 99
References: Grabar, *Serov*, 1914, pp. 118,
287; Grabar, *Serov*, 1965, pp. 134, 333

237
**Portrait of Liudmila Anatolyevna
Mamontova.** 1894. Not extant
Oil on canvas
Signed and dated, bottom right: *Съровъ
94* (Serov, 1894)
Provenance: A. Mamontov collection, Mos-
cow; L. Mamontova-Muravyova collection,
Novgorod
Liudmila Anatolyevna Mamontova — see
No 53.
Exhibitions: 1914 (posthumous) Moscow
(No 87 — 1st ed., No 86 — 2nd ed.); /
1896 St. Petersburg, Moscow —
24th Exhibition of the Itinerant Society
(No 136)
Reproductions: Grabar, *Serov*, 1914,
p. 101; Grabar, *Serov*, 1965, p. 136
References: Grabar, *Serov*, 1914, pp. 118,
287; Grabar, *Serov*, 1965, pp. 134, 333

74. Portrait of Liudmila
Anatolyevna Mamontova. Study.
Cat. No 238

The Tretyakov Gallery. Inv. No 1522
Nikolai Semionovich Leskov (N. Stebnits-
ky, 1831–1895), renowned Russian writer.
Exhibitions: 1935 The Tretyakov Gallery
(No 72), The Russian Museum (No 77);
1958–59 The Tretyakov Gallery; 1959–60
The Russian Museum; 1965 The Tret-
yakov Gallery (p. 34), The Russian
Museum; / 1895 St. Petersburg, Moscow
— 23rd Exhibition of the Itinerant Society
(No 99); 1955 Sweden — Works by
Foreign Artists; 1959 London — Works by
Russian and Soviet Artists (No 75)
Reproductions: Grabar, *Serov*, 1914,
p. 98; Grabar, *Serov*, 1965, p. 137
References: Benois 1902, p. 234; Grabar,
Serov, 1914, pp. 118, 387; Grabar, *Serov*,
1965, pp. 134, 333; Leskov 1954, pp. 464,
465, 664, 665

238
Portrait of Liudmila Anatolyevna
Mamontova. Study. ⟨1894⟩. Unfinished
Oil on canvas. 60×48 cm
N. Sokolov collection, Moscow
Provenance: L. Mamontova-Muravyova
collection, Novgorod; E. Helzer collection,
Moscow
Liudmila Anatolyevna Mamontova — see
No 53.
Exhibitions: 1914 (posthumous) Moscow
(No 88 — 2nd ed.); 1952 Moscow
(No 143)
NOTE: One of Mamontova's portraits was
displayed at the exhibition of paintings by
Russian and Finnish artists held in
St. Petersburg in 1898 (No 259).
Reproductions: Grabar, *Serov*, 1980,
pl. 26
References: Grabar, *Serov*, 1914, p. 287;
Grabar, *Serov*, 1965, p. 333

239 (Plate 48)
Portrait of Nikolai Semionovich Leskov.
1894
Oil on canvas. 64×53 cm
Signed and dated, top right: *Съровъ 94*
(Serov, 1894)

240
Abraham's Servant Finds Isaac a Bride,
Rebekah. ⟨1894⟩
Oil on canvas. 103×143 cm
The Russian Museum (since 1912).
Inv. No Ж-4287
Exhibitions: 1935 The Tretyakov Gallery
(No 87), The Russian Museum (No 80);
1965 The Russian Museum
Reproductions: *Apollon*, 1912, No 10, be-
tween pp. 32 and 33; Grabar, *Serov*, 1914,
p. 103; Dmitriyev, *Serov*, 1917, pl. 4
References: Grabar, *Serov*, 1914, pp. 118,
119, 287; Grabar, *Serov*, 1965, pp. 134,
135, 406

241 (Plate 45)
Abraham's Servant Finds Isaac a Bride,
Rebekah. ⟨1894⟩
Oil on panel. 23.5×33 cm
Inscribed and signed in pencil by the
artist, top right: *Слуга Авраама
находитъ невъсту Исааку Съровъ 1/3
величины картины* (Abraham's Servant
Finds Isaac a Bride. Serov. 1/3 of the size
of the picture)
The Tretyakov Gallery. Inv. No 5776
Provenance: S. Kusevitsky collection,
Moscow

A sketch for the 1894 picture, now in the
Russian Museum (see No 240).
Exhibitions: 1935 The Tretyakov Gallery
(No 88), The Russian Museum (No 81);
1952 Moscow (No 45); 1954 The
Tretyakov Gallery — Sketches and
Studies by Russian Artists from the Tret-
yakov Gallery Reserve: 18th to Early
20th Century (p. 50)
References: Grabar, *Serov*, 1965, p. 406

Sketches for the panels
*After the Battle on the Field
of Kulikovo* commissioned by
the History Museum in Moscow
(Nos 242–245)

242 (Plate 46)
**After the Battle on the Field
of Kulikovo.** ⟨1894⟩
Oil on canvas. 56.5×112.5 cm
(top rounded)
M. Kupriyanov collection, Moscow
Provenance: O. Serova collection, Moscow; A. Danziger collection, Moscow
Exhibitions: 1914 (posthumous) St. Petersburg (No 96), Moscow (No 89); / 1957
Central House of Art Workers, Moscow —
Works of Russian Art from Private Collections: Late 19th and Early 20th Century
(p. 13)
References: Grabar, *Serov*, 1914, pp. 119,
120, 287; Grabar, *Serov*, 1965, pp. 135,
138, 408

243
**After the Battle on the Field
of Kulikovo.** ⟨1894⟩
Oil on canvas. 72×90 cm (top rounded);
painted area, 41×92 cm
The Tretyakov Gallery (since 1930).
Inv. No 22004
Provenance: History Museum, Moscow
Exhibitions: 1914 (posthumous) St. Peters-
burg (No 97), Moscow (No 90); 1935 The
Tretyakov Gallery (No 89), The Russian
Museum (No 83a); 1952 Moscow
(No 136); 1958–59 The Tretyakov Gallery;
1959 Museum of Russian Art, Kiev;
1959–60 The Russian Museum; 1965 The
Tretyakov Gallery (p. 35), The Russian
Museum; / 1954 The Tretyakov Gallery —
Sketches and Studies by Russian Artists
from the Tretyakov Gallery Reserve: 18th
to Early 20th Century (p. 50)
References: Grabar, *Serov*, 1914, p. 287;
Grabar, *Serov*, 1965, p. 408

244
**After the Battle on the Field
of Kulikovo.** ⟨1894⟩
Oil on canvas
Present whereabouts unknown
Provenance: O. Serova collection, Moscow
Exhibitions: 1914 (posthumous) St. Peters-
burg (No 98), Moscow (No 90); / 1914 Mal-
mö (Sweden) — Baltic Art Exhibition
(No 3223); 1924 New York — Russian Art
References: Grabar, *Serov*, 1965, p. 408

245
**After the Battle on the Field
of Kulikovo.** ⟨1894⟩
Oil on cardboard. 21.5×46.5 cm (top
rounded)
Present whereabouts unknown
Provenance: I. Kaplun collection, Moscow;
N. Salzman collection, Moscow

75. Abraham's Servant
Finds Isaac a Bride, Rebekah.
Cat. No 240

Exhibitions: 1935 The Tretyakov Gallery
(No 89), The Russian Museum (No 82);
1952 Moscow (No 137)
References: Grabar, *Serov*, 1965, p. 408

Sketches made during a trip to the North (Nos 246–265)

246
Arkhangelsk. ⟨1894⟩
Oil on panel. 24×23 cm
Art Museum, Voronezh (since 1926).
Inv. No 16
Exhibitions: 1965 The Russian Museum
References: Grabar, *Serov*, 1965, p. 407

247 (Plate 50)
The White Sea. ⟨1894⟩
Oil on cardboard. 14.2×26 cm
The Tretyakov Gallery (since 1938).
Inv. No 24583
Exhibitions: 1952 Moscow (No 141);
1965 The Tretyakov Gallery (p. 34),
The Russian Museum
References: Grabar, *Serov*, 1965, p. 407;
Fiodorov-Davydov 1965, No 2, p. 35 (as
The Sea)

248
In Lapland. A Reindeer. ⟨1894⟩
Present whereabouts unknown
Provenance: Collection of the Prince-
Regent Luitpold of Bavaria, Munich
Exhibitions: 1894–95 Moscow —
14th Periodical Exhibition of the Moscow
Society of Art Lovers (No 48, as *A Rein-
deer*); 1896 Munich, Sezession — Interna-
tional Art Exhibition (No 349, as *Ein
lappländisches Dorf*)
Reproductions: Catalogue, 1894, pl. 26 (as
In Lapland); Lvov 1895 (between pp. 196
and 197, as *A Lapp Village at Pozarek*);
Grabar, *Serov*, 1914, p. 100 (as *A Rein-
deer*); Radlov, *Serov*, 1914
References: Grabar, *Serov*, 1914, pp. 124,
287; Grabar, *Serov*, 1965, p. 407

249
Head of a Reindeer. ⟨1894⟩
Present whereabouts unknown
Exhibitions: 1898 St. Petersburg — Works
by Russian and Finnish Artists (No 263)
References: Grabar, *Serov*, 1965, p. 408

250
**A Monk from the Solovetsky Monas-
tery.** ⟨1894⟩
Oil on cardboard. 23×32 cm
Signed, top left: *BC (VS)*
Present whereabouts unknown
Provenance: O. Loewenfeld collection,
Moscow
Exhibitions: 1935 The Tretyakov Gallery
(No 86), The Russian Museum (No 79)
Reproductions: Lvov 1895, between pp. 76
and 77
References: Grabar, *Serov*, 1914, p. 287
(as *A Lapp in a Boat*); Grabar, *Serov*,
1965, p. 407

251
The Sea. Murman Coast. ⟨1894⟩
Oil on panel. 9×22 cm
Present whereabouts unknown
Provenance: A. Beniakov collection, Mos-
cow; E. Krushinskaya collection, Moscow
Exhibitions: 1952 Moscow (No 139); 1965
The Russian Museum
References: Grabar, *Serov*, 1965, p. 407

252
Murman Coast. 1894
Oil on panel. 16×22 cm
Inscribed on the back of the panel:
В. А. Съровъ. Бухта Трифона

Печенскаго. 1894 (V. A. Serov, Bay of
St. Tryphon of Pechenga, 1894)
The Tretyakov Gallery (since 1929).
Inv. No 11193
Provenance: I. Ostroukhov collection, Mos-
cow; The Ostroukhov Museum of Icons
and Painting, Moscow
Exhibitions: 1935 The Tretyakov Gallery
(No 84), The Russian Museum (No 78);
1952 Moscow (No 140); 1958–59 The Tre-
tyakov Gallery; 1965 The Tretyakov Gal-
lery (p. 35), The Russian Museum
References: Grabar, *Serov*, 1914, p. 287;
Grabar, *Serov*, 1965, p. 407

253
**In the North. The Town of Vardø
in Norway.** 1894
Oil on paper, mounted on cardboard.
22×37.5 cm (22×34 cm)
Inscribed by the artist, bottom right: *Var-
de 94*
The Savitsky Picture Gallery, Penza.
Inv. No 223
Exhibitions: 1965 The Russian Museum
Reproductions: Lvov 1895, between
pp. 204 and 205
References: Grabar, *Serov*, 1965, p. 407

254
The Norwegian Sea. ⟨1894⟩
Present whereabouts unknown
Provenance: S. Chokolov collection,
Moscow

76. After the Battle
on the Field of Kulikovo.
Cat. No 243

77. A Monk from the Solovetsky
Monastery. Cat. No 250

78. Murman Coast. Cat. No 252

259
Seacoast Boats. Arkhangelsk. ⟨1894⟩
Oil
Present whereabouts unknown
Reproductions: Lvov 1895, between pp. 40
and 41
References: Grabar, *Serov*, 1965, p. 407

260 (Plate 52)
The Pomors.* ⟨1894⟩
Oil on panel. 33×23.3 cm
The Tretyakov Gallery (since 1920).
Inv. No 4688
Provenance: A. Bakhrushin collection,
Moscow; State Museum Reserve, Moscow
Exhibitions: 1935 The Tretyakov Gallery
(No 82), The Russian Museum (No 77);
1958–59 The Tretyakov Gallery; 1965 The
Tretyakov Gallery (p. 34), The Russian
Museum; / 1894–95 Moscow —
14th Periodical Exhibition of the Moscow
Society of Art Lovers; 1954 The
Tretyakov Gallery — Sketches and
Studies by Russian Artists from the Tret-
yakov Gallery Reserve: 18th to Early
20th Century (p. 50)
Reproductions: Grabar, *Serov*, 1965,
p. 135
References: Fiodorov-Davydov 1965,
No 2, p. 35; Grabar, *Serov*, 1980, pl. 27

261
After the Ice-drift. ⟨1894⟩
Oil on cardboard. 12.2×19 cm
M. Kupriyanov collection, Moscow
References: Grabar, *Serov*, 1965, p. 407

262
Fishing Pier. ⟨1894⟩
Present whereabouts unknown
Provenance: S. Chokolov collection,
Moscow
Exhibitions: 1915 Museum of Fine Arts,
Moscow — Paintings by Russian Artists,
Old and New (No 306, No 300 — 4th ed.)
References: Grabar, *Serov*, 1965, p. 407;
Fiodorov-Davydov 1965, No 2, p. 35
(as *Pier*)

263
The Northern Dvina. 1894
Oil on panel. 9.5×22 cm
Signed and dated, bottom right:
Съровъ 94 (Serov, 1894)
Art Museum, Ivanovo (since 1929).
Inv. No Ж-230
Provenance: N. Chelishchev collection,
Moscow; K. Kolesnikova collection,
Moscow
Exhibitions: 1935 The Tretyakov Gallery
(No 85), The Russian Museum (No 78a);
1958–59 The Tretyakov Gallery; 1959–60
The Russian Museum; / 1910 The Lemer-
cier Gallery, Moscow — Exhibition Sale of
the N. Chelishchev Collection of Paintings
by Russian Artists (No 72)
References: Grabar, *Serov*, 1965,
pp. 406, 407

264
Northern Landscape. ⟨1894⟩
Oil
Present whereabouts unknown
Provenance: A. Lipnitskaya collection,
Moscow
References: Grabar, *Serov*, 1965, p. 407

Exhibitions: 1915 Museum of Fine Arts,
Moscow — Paintings by Russian Artists,
Old and New (No 305, No 299 — 4th ed.)
References: Grabar, *Serov*, 1965, p. 407

255
Lake on the Murman Coast. ⟨1894⟩
Oil on cardboard. 19×31.5 cm
On the back is the authenticating inscrip-
tion by I. Ostroukhov and another by
S. Mamontov: *Озеро св. Трифона на
Мурманскомъ берегу. В. Сърова*
(St. Tryphon Lake on the Murman Coast
by V. Serov)
Present whereabouts unknown
Provenance: N. Kokarev collection, Mos-
cow; E. Helzer and T. Helzer collection,
Moscow
Exhibitions: 1935 The Tretyakov Gallery
(No 119); 1952 Moscow (No 138)
References: Grabar, *Serov*, 1965, p. 407

256
Sailing Vessels by the Pier. ⟨1894⟩
Oil on cardboard. 21×31.5 cm
Present whereabouts unknown
Provenance: A. Zhigalko collection, Mos-
cow; Ya. Ettinger collection, Moscow;
R. Viktorova collection, Moscow
Exhibitions: 1935 The Tretyakov Gallery
(No 90), The Russian Museum (No 83, as

Long Boats); 1955 Central House of Art
Workers, Moscow — Landscape in Rus-
sian Painting: 19th and Early 20th Cen-
turies (No 298)
Reproductions: Grabar, *Serov*, 1980, pl. 28
References: Grabar, *Serov*, 1965, p. 407

257
The Bay of Pechenga. ⟨1894⟩
Oil on panel. 9.4×14.7 cm
Museum of Russian Art, Kiev (since
1946). Inv. No Ж-523
References: Grabar, *Serov*, 1965, p. 407

258
Seacoast Vessels in Arkhangelsk.
⟨1894⟩
Oil on panel. 23×32 cm (exposed area)
Signed, bottom left: *Съровъ* (Serov)
Present whereabouts unknown
Provenance: A. Golikov collection, Mos-
cow; Ya. Ettinger collection, Moscow;
R. Viktorova collection, Moscow
Exhibitions: 1914 (posthumous) Moscow
(No 82a, No 81a — 2nd ed., as
*Solambola**)
Reproductions: Grabar, *Serov*, 1980, pl. 29
References: Grabar, *Serov*, 1965, p. 407

_____

* An island near Arkhangelsk.

_____

* Inhabitants of the seacoast in the Russian North.

265

A Street in Trøms, Norway. ⟨1894⟩
Oil
Present whereabouts unknown
Reproductions: Lvov 1895, between
pp. 208 and 209
References: Grabar, *Serov*, 1965, p. 407
NOTE: At the 14th Periodical Exhibition
of the Moscow Society of Art Lovers
(1894–95) Serov displayed a number of
sketches painted during his trip to the
North. These included *Seashore in Nor-
mandy, A Street in Trøms, The Murman
Coast, Fishermen's Camp on Lake Mur-
man, Among the Lapps, The Norwegian
Sea, The Fishing Pier in Arkhangelsk* and
The Pechenga. Probably some of these
sketches are identical with the works listed
in our catalogue under Nos 246–265 (see
Catalogue, 1894, Nos a–з).

GOUACHES

266 (Plate 47)
**After the Battle on the Field
of Kulikovo.** ⟨1894⟩
Gouache, partly varnished, on cardboard.
15.5×32.5 cm (top rounded)
The Russian Museum (since 1928).
Inv. No P-6550
Provenance: Zh. Rumanova collection,
Leningrad
Exhibitions: 1914 (posthumous) St. Peters-
burg (No 99), Moscow (No 92); 1935 The
Tretyakov Gallery (No 334), The Russian
Museum (No 392)
References: Grabar, *Serov*, 1965, p. 408

1895
PAINTINGS

267 (Plate 62)
**In Summer. Portrait of Olga Fiodorovna
Serova.** ⟨1895⟩
Oil on canvas. 73.5×93.8 cm
Signed, bottom right: *Съровъ* (Serov)
The Tretyakov Gallery (since 1898).
Inv. No 1523
Olga Fiodorovna Serova — see No 81.

81. The Northern Dvina.
Cat. No 263

Exhibitions: 1935 The Tretyakov Gallery
(No 2); The Russian Museum (No 85);
1958—59 The Tretyakov Gallery; 1965
The Tretyakov Gallery (p. 35), The Rus-
sian Museum; / 1896 St. Petersburg, Khar-
kov, Moscow — 24th Exhibition of the
Itinerant Society (No 135); 1896 Nizhni-
Novgorod — All-Russia Exhibition
(No 384); 1897 Stockholm — Art and Indus-
try; 1964 Malmö (Sweden), Bucharest—
Russian Pre-revolutionary and Soviet Art
Reproductions: *Mir Iskusstva,* 1900,
No 1/2, p. 6 (as *Portrait*); Grabar, *Serov,*
1914, p. 104; Grabar, *Serov,* 1965, p. 139
References: Benois 1902, p. 234; Grabar,
Serov, 1914, pp. 128, 287 (as *Summer*);
Grabar, *Serov,* 1965, pp. 143, 334;
Simonovich-Yefimova 1964, p. 43;
Fiodorov-Davydov 1965, No 2, pp. 34, 35

268 (Plate 65)
October in Domotkanovo. ⟨1895⟩
Oil on canvas. 48.5×70.7 cm
Signed, bottom left: *Съровъ* (Serov)
The Tretyakov Gallery (since 1907).
Inv. No 1524
Provenance: V. von Meck collection,
Moscow
Exhibitions: 1935 The Tretyakov Gallery
(No 93), The Russian Museum (No 86);
1958–59 The Tretyakov Gallery; 1959–60
The Russian Museum; 1965 The
Tretyakov Gallery (pp. 35, 36), The Rus-

sian Museum; / 1896 St. Petersburg, Moscow, Kharkov — 24th Exhibition of the Itinerant Society (No 138, as *Stubble*); 1896
Munich, Sezession — International Art Exhibition; 1896 Nizhni-Novgorod — All-Russia Exhibition (No 385, as *Stubble*);
1900 Paris — World Exhibition (p. 71)
Reproductions: *Mir Iskusstva,* 1900,
No 1/2, p. 11 (as *Landscape*); Benois
1902, p. 235; Grabar, *Serov,* 1914, p. 105;
Grabar, *Serov,* 1965, p. 191
References: Benois 1902, p. 235; Grabar,
Serov, 1914, pp. 128, 287; Grabar, *Serov,*
1965, pp. 143, 200, 408; Fiodorov-Davydov 1965, No 2, pp. 35, 37, 38

269
**Portrait of Alexei Ivanovich
Abrikosov.** ⟨1895⟩. Unfinished
Oil on canvas. 100×84 cm
History Museum, Moscow. Inv. No 1334
Alexei Ivanovich Abrikosov (1824–1904),
founder and owner of a confectionery in
Moscow.
Exhibitions: 1952 Moscow (No 144)
References: Grabar, *Serov,* 1965, p. 334;
*Serov in the Reminiscences of His Con-
temporaries,* 1971, 1, p. 146

270 (Plate 55)
**Portrait of Countess
Varvara Vasilyevna Musina-Pushkina.**
1895
Pastel on paper, mounted on canvas.
70×55 cm
Signed and dated, bottom right:
Съровъ 95 (Serov, 1895)
The Russian Museum (since 1978).
Inv. No Ж-9745
Provenance: V. Musina-Pushkina collec-
tion, St. Petersburg
Exhibitions: 1914 (posthumous) St. Peters-
burg (No 102), Moscow (No 95)
Reproductions: Grabar, *Serov,* 1914,
p. 106; Leniashin 1980, p. 32
References: Grabar, *Serov,* 1914, pp. 128,
287; Grabar, *Serov,* 1965, pp. 143, 334;
Leniashin 1980, p. 33

271
**Portrait of Countess
Varvara Nikolayevna Kapnist.** 1895
Pastel on canvas. 56×52 cm
Signed and dated, top right: *Съровъ 95*
(Serov, 1895)
The Russian Museum (since 1978).
Inv. No Ж-9746
Provenance: V. Musina-Pushkina collec-
tion, St. Petersburg
Exhibitions: 1914 (posthumous) St. Peters-
burg (No 103), Moscow (No 96)
Reproductions: Grabar, *Serov,* 1914,
p. 102

82. Portrait of Countess
Varvara Nikolayevna Kapnist.
Cat. No 271

83. Illustration for the *Tale of the She-bear* by Pushkin. Cat. No 279

References: Grabar, *Serov*, 1914, pp. 128, 287 (described incorrectly as an oil painting); Grabar, *Serov*, 1965, pp. 143, 334

272
Portrait of Dmitry Grigoryevich Derviz. ⟨1895⟩
Oil on canvas
Present whereabouts unknown
Provenance: V. Derviz collection, Moscow
Dmitry Grigoryevich Derviz (1829–1916), member of the State Council; father of the artist Vladimir Derviz (see No 72).
Exhibitions: 1914–15 Moscow — Moscow Artists in Aid of War Victims (No 492)
References: Grabar, *Serov*, 1914, p. 287; Grabar, *Serov*, 1965, p. 334

273 (Plate 56)
Portrait of Maria Yakovlevna Lvova. 1895
Oil on canvas. 87×58 cm
Signed and dated, bottom right: *Съровъ 95* (Serov, 1895)
A. Lvov collection, Paris (since 1956)
Provenance: S. and M. Lvov collection, Paris
Maria Yakovlevna Lvova — see No 18.
Exhibitions: 1914 (posthumous) St. Petersburg (No 104a — 3rd and 4th ed.), Moscow (No 97); / 1895–96 Moscow — 15th Periodical Exhibition of the Moscow Society of Art Lovers (No 33, as *Portrait of Mrs. M. Ya. L.*); 1896 St. Petersburg — 24th Exhibition of the Itinerant Society (No 136, under the same title); 1896 Munich (?), Sezession — International Art Exhibition
Reproductions: Grabar, *Serov*, 1914, between pp. 112 and 113; Leniashin 1980, p. 31
References: Grabar, *Serov*, 1914, pp. 128, 187; Grabar, *Serov*, 1965, pp. 143, 149, 333, 334; Simonovich-Yefimova 1964, pp. 72, 73

274 (Plate 54)
Portrait of Mara Konstantinovna Oliv. ⟨1895⟩
Oil on canvas. 88×68.5 cm
The Russian Museum (since 1904).
Inv. No Ж-4284
Provenance: Yu. Mamontov collection
Mara Konstantinovna Oliv (1870–1963), Savva Mamontov's distant relative.
Exhibitions: 1935 The Tretyakov Gallery (No 94), The Russian Museum (No 87); 1958–59 The Tretyakov Gallery; 1959 Museum of Russian Art, Kiev; 1959–60 The Russian Museum; 1965 The Tretyakov Gallery (p. 36), The Russian Museum; / 1899 Munich, Sezession — International Art Exhibition (p. 25, No 209, as *Portrait*); 1899 St. Petersburg — 1st International Exhibition of Paintings Organized by the *Mir Iskusstva* Magazine (No 266, as *Portrait of Mrs. M.*); 1959 Leningrad — Russian Portrait Painting: 18th to Early 20th Century (p. 34); 1972 Moscow, Leningrad, Kiev, Minsk — Portrait Paintings by the Itinerants
Reproductions: *Offizieller Katalog der Internationalen Kunstausstellung des Vereins bildender Künstler „Sezession", Munich, 1899 (pl. 26); Mir Iskusstva, 1899, No 6, p. 102; Grabar, *Serov*, 1914, between pp. 104 and 105; Grabar, *Serov*, 1965, pp. 144, 145 (detail)

References: Grabar, *Serov*, 1914, pp. 104, 287; Grabar, *Serov*, 1965, pp. 140, 142, 143, 333

275
Portrait of an Unknown Woman. 1895
Pastel on paper, mounted on canvas.
38×43 cm
Signed and dated, top left: *Съровъ 95* (Serov, 1895)
Art Museum, Omsk (since 1927).
Inv. No Ж-562
Provenance: English Club, Moscow; State Museum Reserve, Moscow
Reproductions: *Art Museum, Omsk*, 1980
References: Grabar, *Serov*, 1965, p. 352

276
Portrait of Sergei Mikhailovich Tretyakov. 1895
Oil on canvas. 102×84 cm
Signed and dated, top right: *Съровъ 95* (Serov, 1895)
The Tretyakov Gallery. Inv. No 1525
Sergei Mikhailovich Tretyakov (1834–1892), merchant and collector of Western European paintings of the nineteenth century; younger brother of Pavel Mikhailovich Tretyakov (1832–1898), the founder of the Tretyakov Gallery. The portrait was painted from a photograph, on a commission of the Tretyakov Gallery.
Exhibitions: 1935 The Tretyakov Gallery (No 91), The Russian Museum (No 84); 1954 Central House of Art Workers, Moscow — Portraits of Prominent Personalities in Russian Art: 18th to 20th Century (No 266)
Reproductions: *History of Russia*, VI, between pp. 144 and 145
References: Grabar, *Serov*, 1914, p. 287; Grabar, *Serov*, 1965, p. 334

DRAWINGS

277
Bare Feet. ⟨1895⟩
Pencil. 22.8×29.2 cm
Bottom right, an impression of the artist's signet: *BC* (VS)
The Brodsky Memorial Museum, Leningrad. Inv. No Г-289
A preliminary drawing for the painting *October in Domotkanovo* (see No 268).

Exhibitions: 1935 The Tretyakov Gallery (No 338),The Russian Museum (No 394)
References: Grabar, *Serov*, 1965, p. 408

278
Sketch of a Horse. ⟨1895⟩
Present whereabouts unknown
A preliminary drawing for the painting *October in Domotkanovo* (see No 268).
Provenance: O. Serova collection, Moscow
Reproductions: Yaremich, *Serov: Drawings*, 1936 (pl. 25, as *Sketch of a Horse* for the painting *October*. 1895)

279
Illustration for the *Tale of the She-bear* by Pushkin. 1895
India ink, pen and brush. 26×39.8 cm
Signed in pen, bottom right: *Съровъ 95* (Serov, 1895)
The Russian Museum (since 1925).
Inv. No P-3215
Provenance: Museum of the Academy of Arts, Petrograd
The drawing was previously described incorrectly as an illustration for Krylov's fable *Hare on the Run*.
Exhibitions: 1914 (posthumous) St. Petersburg (No 345/6, as *Hare on the Run*); 1935 The Tretyakov Gallery (No 337), The Russian Museum (No 948, as *Hare on the Run*); 1958–59 The Tretyakov Gallery (without catalogue, as *The Pestilence*); 1965 The Russian Museum
Reproductions: *Children's Leisure*, 1899, No 5, p. 90; Dmitriyev, *Serov*, 1917 (as *Hare on the Run*, described incorrectly as a pencil drawing); Grabar, *Serov*, 1965, p. 287; Gorlov 1951, pl. 56 (as *Hare on the Run*)
References: *Pushkin and His Time*, 1962, pp. 436–441; Grabar, *Serov*, 1965, pp. 411, 412

1896
PAINTINGS

280 (Plate 74)
Peasant Woman in a Cart. ⟨1896⟩
Oil on canvas. 48×70 cm
Signed and dated by the artist, bottom right, for a 1899 exhibition: *99. Съровъ* (1899, Serov)
The Russian Museum (since 1927).
Inv. No Ж-4302

Provenance: M. Riabushinsky collection, Moscow

Exhibitions: 1914 (posthumous) St. Petersburg (No 108), Moscow (No 101); 1935 The Tretyakov Gallery (No 111, dated 1899), The Russian Museum (No 104, the same wrong dating); 1958–59 The Tretyakov Gallery; 1965 The Tretyakov Gallery (pp. 37, 38, dated 1899), The Russian Museum; / 1900 St. Petersburg — 2nd Exhibition of Paintings Organized by the *Mir Iskusstva* Magazine (No 176); 1901–2 Moscow — Thirty-six Painters (No 155); 1911 Rome — International Art Exhibition (No 401, as *Una contadina*); 1924 The Tretyakov Gallery (Rogozhsko-Simonovsky Branch) — The Peasant in Russian Painting (No 115)

Reproductions: *Mir Iskusstva*, 1900, No 1/2, p. 22; Grabar, *Serov*, 1914, p. 107; Grabar, *Serov*, 1965, p. 194

References: Grabar, *Serov*, 1914, pp. 128, 130; Grabar, *Serov*, 1965, pp. 192, 196, 410; Fiodorov-Davydov 1965, No 2, p. 38 (dated 1899)

281 (Plate 58)
The Coronation. The Anointing of Nicholas II in the Assumption Cathedral, Moscow. 1896
Oil on canvas. 43×64 cm
Signed and dated, bottom right:
Съровъ 96 (Serov, 1896)
The Tretyakov Gallery (since 1929).
Inv. No 11187
Provenance: I. Ostroukhov collection, Moscow; The Ostroukhov Museum of Icons and Painting, Moscow
Nicholas II (1868–1918), the last tsar of Russia (1894–17).
Exhibitions: 1914 (posthumous) St. Petersburg (No 106), Moscow (No 99); 1935 The Tretyakov Gallery (No 96, as *The Ceremonial Anointing*), The Russian Museum (No 89, *The Anointing in the Assumption Cathedral*); 1965 The Russian Museum; / 1902 Moscow — Exhibition of Paintings Organized by the *Mir Iskusstva* Magazine (No 211)
Reproductions: Grabar, *Serov*, 1914, between pp. 120 and 121 (as *The Coronation of Emperor Nicholas II. Sketch*)
References: Grabar, *Serov*, 1914, pp. 128, 288; Grabar, *Serov*, 1965, pp. 180, 408

Studies for the painting
The Coronation. The Anointing of Nicholas II in the Assumption Cathedral, Moscow.
1896 (Nos 282–284)

282 (Plate 57)
Interior of the Assumption Cathedral, Moscow. ⟨1896⟩
Oil on canvas. 53.7×71.7 cm
Art Museum, Minsk (since 1963).
Inv. No Рж-137
Provenance: A. Karzinkin collection, Moscow; A. Liapunov collection, Moscow; G. Afonin collection, Moscow; G. Yerozolimsky collection, Moscow; E. Helzer and T. Helzer collection, Moscow
Exhibitions: 1946 Central House of Art Workers, Moscow (No 43); 1952 Moscow (No 146)
References: Grabar, *Serov*, 1914, pp. 128, 288 (as *Study for the Coronation?*); Grabar, *Serov*, 1965, pp. 180, 409

283
Sakkos. ⟨1896⟩
Oil on mahogany. 15×9.3 cm
The Tretyakov Gallery (since 1953).
Inv. No Ж-7
References: Grabar, *Serov*, 1965, p. 410

284
The Holy Gates. ⟨1896⟩
Oil on mahogany. 15×9.3 cm
The Tretyakov Gallery (since 1953).
Inv. No Ж-8
References: Grabar, *Serov*, 1965, p. 410

285
Portrait of Countess E. Musina-Pushkina. ⟨1896⟩
Oil on canvas
Present whereabouts unknown
Provenance: V. Musina-Pushkina collection, St. Petersburg
References: Grabar, *Serov*, 1914, p. 287; Grabar, *Serov*, 1965, p. 334

286
Portrait of Countess Yelizaveta Vasilyevna Musina-Pushkina. 1896
Oil (?)
Present whereabouts unknown
Provenance: Ye. Musina-Pushkina collection, St. Petersburg

Yelizaveta Vasilyevna Musina-Pushkina, Kapnist by marriage (1870–?).
Exhibitions: 1914 (posthumous) St. Petersburg (No 105), Moscow (No 98, as *Mrs. Ye. V. Kapnist*); / 1896 Nizhni-Novgorod — All-Russia Exhibition (No 387); 1896–97 Moscow — 16th Periodical Exhibition of the Moscow Society of Art Lovers (No 61); 1897 St. Petersburg — 25th Exhibition of the Itinerant Society (No 191)
References: Grabar, *Serov*, 1965, p. 334; *Serov in the Reminiscences of His Contemporaries*, 1971, 1, p. 502

287
The River Nymph. ⟨1896⟩
Oil on canvas. 132×144 cm
The Tretyakov Gallery (since 1929).
Inv. No 11188
Provenance: I. Ostroukhov collection, Moscow; The Ostroukhov Museum of Icons and Painting, Moscow
Exhibitions: 1914 (posthumous) St. Petersburg (No 110), Moscow (No 103); 1935 The Tretyakov Gallery (No 97), The Russian Museum (No 90)
Reproductions: *Apollon*, 1911, No 10, between pp. 8 and 9; Zotov, *Serov*, 1964, No 16
References: Grabar, *Serov*, 1914, p. 288; Grabar, *Serov*, 1965, p. 410; *Serov in the Reminiscences of His Contemporaries*, 1971, 1, p. 207; 2, p. 247; Simonovich-Yefimova 1964, pp. 38, 39

Sketches and studies
for the painting *The River Nymph*
(Nos 288–292)

288
The River Nymph. ⟨1896⟩
Oil on canvas. 23×18.5 cm (exposed area)
Present whereabouts unknown
Provenance: O. Serova collection, Moscow; P. Krylov collection, Moscow; N. Bolshakov collection, Moscow
The first life study.
Exhibitions: 1952 Moscow (No 156)
References: Grabar, *Serov*, 1965, p. 410

289
The River Nymph. ⟨1896⟩
Oil on canvas. 54×72 cm
Present whereabouts unknown
Provenance: E. Helzer and T. Helzer collection, Moscow
Exhibitions: 1935 The Tretyakov Gallery (No 99), The Russian Museum (No 92); 1952 Moscow (No 154); 1958–59 The Tretyakov Gallery
References: Grabar, *Serov*, 1965, p. 410

290
The River Nymph. ⟨1896⟩
Oil on canvas, mounted on cardboard. 22×33.5 cm
Present whereabouts unknown
Provenance: A. Bedniakov collection, Moscow
Exhibitions: 1952 Moscow (No 157)
References: Grabar, *Serov*, 1965, p. 411

291
The River Nymph. ⟨1896?⟩
Oil on canvas. 54.5×72.5 cm
The Abramtsevo Museum, Moscow region (since 1964). Inv. No Ж-244

84. The River Nymph.
Cat. No 287

85. Thistle. Cat. No 293

DRAWINGS, WATERCOLORS AND ETCHINGS

Provenance: I. Kraitor collection, Moscow;
N. Vlasov collection, Moscow; I. Kachurin
collection, Moscow
A sketch of the composition.
Exhibitions: 1952 Moscow (No 155)
References: Grabar, *Serov*, 1965, p. 410
(as *The River Nymph. 1896. The Over-
grown Pond*)

292
The River Nymph. ⟨1896⟩
Oil on panel. 37×46 cm
Present whereabouts unknown
Provenance: I. Moskvin collection, Mos-
cow; L. Moskvina collection, Moscow;
R. Preobrazhenskaya collection, Moscow
A complete sketch of the composition.
Exhibitions: 1935 The Tretyakov Gallery
(No 98), The Russian Museum (No 91);
1946 Central House of Art Workers, Mos-
cow (No 53); 1952 Moscow (No 158); /
1947 Central House of Art Workers, Mos-
cow — Landscape in Russian Painting:
Second Half of the 19th Century (No 106)
References: Grabar, *Serov*, 1965, p. 411

293
Thistle. 1896
Oil on canvas. 30.5×15.8 cm
Dated by the artist, top left: *1896*
V. Petrov collection, Leningrad
References: Grabar, *Serov*, 1965, p. 410

294
The Crow and the Canary. Illustration
for Mamin-Sibiriak's
tale *The Black-headed Crow and
the Yellow Canary.* ⟨1896⟩
Gouache, watercolors and graphite, coated
with varnish, on yellow paper. 23×19 cm
Signed in pencil, top right: Съровъ (Serov)
The Tretyakov Gallery (since 1914).
Inv. No 3647
Provenance: O. Serova collection,
Moscow
Exhibitions: 1914 (posthumous) St. Petersburg (No 115c — 3rd and 4th ed.); 1935
The Tretyakov Gallery (No 348), The Russian Museum (No 408); 1958–59 The Tretyakov Gallery; 1965 The Tretyakov Gallery (p. 57), The Russian Museum; / 1949
The Pushkin Museum of Fine Arts, Mos-
cow — Russian Graphic Art: 18th to Early
20th Century; 1963 The Tretyakov Gallery
— Pencil Drawings, Watercolors, Pastels,
and Gouaches (p. 69)
Reproductions: Grabar, *Serov*, 1914,
p. 109; *Drawings and Watercolors. Catalogue*, 1956; Grabar, *Serov*, 1980, pl. 34
References: Grabar, *Serov*, 1914, pp. 254,
288; Grabar, *Serov*, 1965, p. 413

295
The Crow and the Canary.
Version. ⟨1896⟩
Black watercolor and white. 21×35 cm
On the reverse, a pencil portrait of Surikov
(sketch of the painting housed in the
Tretyakov Gallery — see No 360)
The Russian Museum (since 1912).
Inv. No P-3130
Exhibitions: 1935 The Tretyakov Gallery
(No 350), The Russian Museum (No 410);
1965 The Russian Museum
Reproductions: Grabar, *Serov*, 1914,
p. 108
References: Grabar, *Serov*, 1914, pp. 254,
288; Grabar, *Serov*, 1965, p. 413

296 (Plate 51)
In the Tundra. Reindeer Ride.
Illustration for *Pictures of Russian
Nature and Daily Life* published
by A. Mamontov, Moscow, 1898. ⟨1896⟩
India ink, gouache and graphite.
21.8×33.8 cm

Signed in pencil, bottom left: Съровъ
(Serov)
The Tretyakov Gallery (since 1926).
Inv. No 9901
Provenance: M. Riabushinsky collection,
Moscow
Exhibitions: 1914 (posthumous) St. Peters-
burg (No 111), Moscow (No 105); 1935
The Tretyakov Gallery (No 340), The Rus-
sian Museum (No 396); 1958—59 The
Tretyakov Gallery; 1965 The Tretyakov
Gallery (p. 57), The Russian Museum
Reproductions: *Pictures of Russian Nature
and Daily Life*, 1898, between pp. 4 and 5;
Grabar, *Serov*, 1914, p. 107; Grabar,
Serov, 1980, p. 97
References: Grabar, *Serov*, 1914, p. 288;
Grabar, *Serov*, 1965, p. 413

297
Portrait of a Woman. 1896
Watercolors and graphite. 38.2×28.8 cm
Signed and dated, bottom right:
Съровъ 96 (Serov, 1896)
The Russian Museum (since 1945).
Inv. No P-6557
Provenance: The Golubkina Museum,
Moscow
Exhibitions: 1965 The Russian Museum
Reproductions: *Essays on the History of
Russian Portraiture*, 1964, p. 404
Rferences: Grabar, *Serov*, 1965, p. 353

298
Recumbent Lion. 1896
Etching. 16×12 cm (plate). First state
Etched signature and date, top right:
BC 96 (VS, 1896)
Present whereabouts unknown
Provenance: S. Yaremich collection,
Leningrad
Reproductions: Yaremich, *Serov: Draw-
ings*, 1936
References: Grabar, *Serov*, 1914, p. 289;
Grabar, *Serov*, 1965, p. 411; Yaremich,
Serov: Drawings, 1936, p. 20 (No 3a)

299
Recumbent Lion. 1896
Etching. 16×12 cm (plate). Second state.
Impression on Japanese paper
Etched signature and date, top right:
BC 96 (VS, 1896)
The Russian Museum. Inv. No Гр-28214
Exhibitions: 1935 The Russian Museum
(No 1053); 1965 The Russian Museum; /

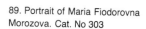

1967 The Russian Museum — Russian
Prints: Late 19th and Early 20th Centuries
(p. 65)
NOTE: Other impressions of the etching
Recumbent Lion were also displayed at
the 1898 exhibition in St. Petersburg
(Works by Russian and Finnish Artists,
No 272) and at one-man shows: 1914
(posthumous) St. Petersburg (No 140),
Moscow (No 147a).
Reproductions: Russian Prints, 1967, p. 8
References: Yaremich, Serov: Drawings,
1936, p. 20 (No 36)

1897
PAINTINGS

300
**Portrait of Antonina Sergeyevna
Sychinskaya.** ⟨1897⟩
Oil on canvas
Signed, bottom right: *Съровъ* (Serov)
Present whereabouts unknown
Provenance: A. Sychinskaya collection,
St. Petersburg
Antonina Sergeyevna Sychinskaya, née
Karzinkina.
Exhibitions: 1897 St. Petersburg —
25th Exhibition of the Itinerant Society
(No 192, as *Portrait of Mrs. A. S. K.*),
Moscow (No 192, under the same title)
References: Grabar, *Serov*, 1914, p. 288;
Grabar, *Serov*, 1965, p. 334

301 (Plate 59)
**Portrait of Grand Duke
Pavel Alexandrovich.** ⟨1897⟩
Oil on canvas. 168×151 cm
Signed and dated, bottom right:
Съровъ 97 г. (Serov, 1897)
The Tretyakov Gallery (since 1933).
Inv. No 15697
Provenance: Cavalry Regiment of Life
Guards, Petrograd; The Russian Museum

Pavel Alexandrovich (1860–1920), Grand
Duke, uncle of Nicholas II (see No 281).
Exhibitions: 1914 (posthumous) St. Peters-
burg (No 114), Moscow (No 108); 1935
The Tretyakov Gallery (No 100), The Rus-
sian Museum; 1958–59 The Tretyakov
Gallery; 1959 Museum of Russian Art,
Kiev; 1965 The Tretyakov Gallery; / 1898
St. Petersburg (No 258), Munich, Cologne,
Düsseldorf, Berlin — Works by Russian
and Finnish Artists; 1900 Paris — World
Exhibition (p. 71)
Reproductions: *Mir Iskusstva*, 1900,
No 1/2, p. 5; Grabar, *Serov*, 1914, p. 113;
Grabar, *Serov*, 1980, pl. 37
References: Grabar, *Serov*, 1914, pp. 134,
288; Grabar, *Serov*, 1965, pp. 180, 334;
*Serov in the Reminiscences of His Con-
temporaries*, 1971, 1, p. 36; Leniashin
1980, pp. 34–40

302
**Portrait of Grand Princess
Maria Pavlovna.** 1897
Oil on canvas. 24.5×19.5 cm
Inscribed, right: *Съровъ 97 Царское
Село* (Serov, 1897, Tsarskoye Selo)
M. Sokolova collection, Moscow
Provenance: Grand Duke Pavel Alexan-
drovich collection, Tsarskoye Selo; V. Pav-
lov collection, Leningrad; N. Sokolov col-
lection, Moscow
Maria Pavlovna (1890–?), daughter of
Grand Duke Pavel Alexandrovich (see
No 301).
Exhibitions: 1935 The Russian Museum
(No 1087, as *Portrait of a Girl with a Dog*);
1952 Moscow (No 162, as *Girl with a Bull-
dog*); 1965 The Tretyakov Gallery
(pp. 36, 37, under the same title); / 1951
Leningrad — Paintings by Russian Artists
from Private Collections in Leningrad: Second Half of the 19th Century (p. 16, as *Girl
with a Bulldog*)

Reproductions: Grabar, *Serov*, 1980,
pl. 38 (as *Girl with a Bulldog*)
References: Grabar, *Serov*, 1965, p. 334

303
**Portrait of Maria Fiodorovna
Morozova.** 1897
Oil on canvas. 108×87.5 cm
Signed and dated, bottom left: *Съровъ 97*
(Serov, 1897)
The Russian Museum (since 1934).
Inv. No Ж-4313
Provenance: Z. Morozova-Reinbot collec-
tion, Moscow Province; The Tretyakov
Gallery
Maria Fiodorovna Morozova (1829–1911),
mother of Savva Morozov (see No 691).
Exhibitions: 1914 (posthumous) St. Peters-
burg (No 113), Moscow (No 107); 1935
The Tretyakov Gallery (No 101), The Rus-
sian Museum (No 94); 1958–59 The
Tretyakov Gallery; 1959 Museum of Rus-
sian Art, Kiev; 1959–60 The Russian
Museum; 1965 The Tretyakov Gallery
(p. 36), The Russian Museum; / 1897–98
Moscow — 17th Periodical Exhibition of
the Moscow Society of Art Lovers (No 55);
1898 St. Petersburg — 26th Exhibition of
the Itinerant Society (No 111)
Reproductions: Grabar, *Serov*, 1914,
p. 111; Grabar, *Serov*, 1980, pl. 39
References: Grabar, *Serov*, 1914, pp. 131,
134, 288; Grabar, *Serov*, 1965, pp. 150,
334

304
**Herd of Cattle with a Horse
in the Foreground.** ⟨1897⟩
Oil on canvas
Present whereabouts unknown
References: Grabar, *Serov*, 1965, p. 414

DRAWINGS
AND WATERCOLORS

305 (Plate 66)
Horse Grazing. 1897
Graphite. 10.1×13.5 cm
Signed and dated, bottom left: *В. Съровъ
1897 г. 8 декабр* (V. Serov, 1897, 8 De-
cember)

The Tretyakov Gallery. Inv. No 7638
Provenance: The Tsvetkov Gallery,
Moscow
Exhibitions: 1935 The Tretyakov Gallery
(No 357), The Russian Museum (No 416,
as *Pasture*); 1952 Moscow (No 165)
Reproductions: *Drawings and Watercolors.
Catalogue*, 1956 (as *Pasture*);
Simonovich-Yefimova 1964, p. 60 (under
the same title); Grabar, *Serov*, 1965,
p. 198 (under the same title)
References: Grabar, *Serov*, 1965, p. 414;
Simonovich-Yefimova 1964, pp. 60, 61

306
Caucasian Grasslands. ⟨1897⟩
Watercolors and white on paper, mounted
on cardboard. 39.8×29 cm
Signed in pencil, bottom left: *Съровъ*
(Serov)
The Russian Museum (since 1898).
Inv. No P-13428
Provenance: M. Tenisheva collection,
St. Petersburg
Exhibitions: 1935 The Tretyakov Gallery
(No 734, as *Caucasian Scene*), The Rus-
sian Museum (No 439, under the same
title); / 1898 St. Petersburg — Works by
Russian and Finnish Artists (No 269, as
A Mountaineer); 1940 Leningrad — Exhi-
bition Commemorating the 125th Anniver-
sary of Lermontov's Death (No 131,
wrongly entitled *Hadjji Abrek*)
References: Grabar, *Serov*, 1965,
pp. 413, 414

307
Spring Field (Ploughman). ⟨1897⟩
Watercolors and graphite on cardboard.
18.7×28.8 cm; 18×27.5 cm (without
margins)
The Russian Museum (since 1928).
Inv. No P-13408
Provenance: O. Serova collection,
Moscow; A. Rumanov collection,
St. Petersburg
Exhibitions: 1914 (posthumous) St. Peters-
burg (No 116, dated 1898); 1935 The Tre-
tyakov Gallery (No 351), The Russian
Museum (No 412); 1965 The Russian
Museum
Reproductions: Dmitriyev, *Serov*, 1917
(as *Ploughman*, dated 1899)
References: Grabar, *Serov*, 1914, p. 288
(as *Ploughman*, dated 1896); Grabar,
Serov, 1965, p. 413

308 (Plate 94)
Sasha Serov. ⟨1897⟩
Watercolor and white. 42×58 cm
The Serov family collection, Moscow
Alexander (Sasha) Valentinovich Serov
(1891–1959), the eldest son of the artist.
Exhibitions: 1914 (posthumous) St. Peters-
burg (No 115), Moscow (No 109); 1935
The Tretyakov Gallery (No 103), The Rus-
sian Museum (No 96); 1946 Central
House of Art Workers, Moscow (No 66);
1952 Moscow (No 163); 1958–59 The Tre-
tyakov Gallery; 1965 The Tretyakov Gal-
lery (p. 57), The Russian Museum; / 1914
Malmö (Sweden) — Baltic Art Exhibition
(No 3213); 1951–52 Central House of Art
Workers, Moscow — Russian Paintings:
Second Half of the 19th and Early
20th Centuries (No 228); 1957 Central
House of Art Workers, Moscow — Works
of Russian Art from Private Collections:
Late 19th and Early 20th Centuries (p. 13)
Reproductions: Ernst, *Serov*, 1922, be-
tween pp. 24 and 25; *Essays on the
History of Russian Portraiture*, 1964, p. 57;
Leniashin 1980, p. 115
References: Grabar, *Serov*, 1914, p. 288
(erroneously mentioned twice: see the list
of Serov's works of 1907 on p. 292);
Grabar, *Serov*, 1965, pp. 280 (dated
1907), 353

309
Yura Serov. ⟨1897⟩
Pencil. 16.8×9.8 cm
The Serov family collection, Moscow
Georgy (Yura) Valentinovich Serov
(1894–1929), second son of the artist.
Exhibitions: 1935 The Tretyakov Gallery
(No 381), The Russian Museum (No 443)
References: Grabar, *Serov*, 1965, p. 353

1898
PAINTINGS

310 (Plate 69)
**In a Village. Peasant Woman
with a Horse.** 1898
Pastel on paper, mounted on cardboard.
53×70 cm
Signed and dated, bottom right:
Съровъ 98 (Serov, 1898)
The Tretyakov Gallery (since 1907).
Inv. No 1527

Provenance: V. von Meck collection,
Moscow
Exhibitions: 1935 The Tretyakov Gallery
(No 106), The Russian Museum (No 99);
1958–59 The Tretyakov Gallery; 1965 The
Tretyakov Gallery (p. 37); / 1899 Munich,
Sezession — International Art Exhibition
(p. 25, No 210, as *Die Bäuerin*); 1899
St. Petersburg — 1st International Exhibi-
tion of Paintings Organized by the *Mir
Iskusstva* Magazine (No 269); 1901–2
Moscow — Thirty-six Painters (No 156, as
Pastel); 1906 Paris, Berlin — Russian Art
(Nos 523, 432); 1923 The Tretyakov Gal-
lery — Exhibition Commemorating the
25th Anniversary of P. Tretyakov's Death
(No 35); 1924 The Tretyakov Gallery
(Rogozhsko-Simonovsky Branch) — The
Peasant in Russian Painting (No 114);
1963 The Tretyakov Gallery — Pencil
Drawings, Watercolors, Pastels, and
Gouaches (p. 69)
Reproductions: *Mir Iskusstva*, 1900,
No 1/2, p. 2; Grabar, *Serov*, 1914, be-
tween pp. 176 and 177; Grabar, *Serov*,
1965, p. 195
References: Grabar, *Serov*, 1914, pp. 150,
151, 288; Grabar, *Serov*, 1965, pp. 196,
197, 414; Fiodorov-Davydov 1965, No 2,
pp. 35, 38

311
Wife Visits Her Husband in Exile.
⟨1898⟩
Oil on canvas. 54×80 cm
The Tretyakov Gallery (since 1911).
Inv. No 1528
Provenance: O. Serova collection,
Moscow
Exhibitions: 1935 The Tretyakov Gallery
(No 104), The Russian Museum (No 97);
1958–59 The Tretyakov Gallery; 1959
Museum of Russian Art, Kiev; 1959–60
The Russian Museum; 1965 The
Tretyakov Gallery (p. 37), The Russian
Museum
Reproductions: *Apollon*, 1912, No 10,
p. 20 (as *Departure*); Grabar, *Serov*, 1914,
p. 114
References: Grabar, *Serov*, 1914, p. 288;
Grabar, *Serov*, 1965, p. 414; Fiodorov-
Davydov 1965, No 2, p. 39

312 (Plate 72)
In Winter. 1898
Gouache and pastel on cardboard.
51×68 cm
Signed and dated, bottom right:
Съровъ 98 (Serov, 1898)
The Russian Museum (since 1902).
Inv. No Ж-4311
Provenance: M. Tenisheva collection,
St. Petersburg
This landscape was painted in Domot-
kanovo (Simonovich-Yefimova 1964,
p. 61) and not in Finland as some art
historians erroneously suggested (Grabar,
Serov, 1965, p. 414; *Serov in the Re-
miniscences of His Contemporaries*, 1971,
1, p. 463).
Exhibitions: 1935 The Tretyakov Gallery
(No 107), The Russian Museum (No 100);
1959–60 The Russian Museum; 1965 The
Tretyakov Gallery (p. 37), The Russian
Museum; / 1899 St. Petersburg — 1st In-
ternational Exhibition of Paintings Organized by the *Mir Iskusstva* Magazine
(No 270 or 271)

91. Spring Field (Ploughman).
Cat. No 307

318

**Portrait of Piotr Alexeyevich
Bakhrushin.** 1898
Oil on canvas. 106×84.7 cm
Dated by the artist, bottom left: *1898 г.*
Art Museum, Omsk (since 1925).
Inv. No Ж-342
Provenance: Moscow Town Council;
The Tretyakov Gallery
Piotr Alexeyevich Bakhrushin, brother of
Vasily Bakhrushin (see No 337).
References: Grabar, *Serov*, 1965, p. 335

319

**Portrait of Pavel Petrovich
Trubetskoi.** ⟨1898⟩
Gouache. 50×26 cm (?)
Signed, bottom left: *V. Seroff*
Present whereabouts unknown
Pavel (Paolo) Petrovich Trubetskoi
(1866–1938), Russian sculptor.
Reproductions: Grabar, *Serov*, 1914,
p. 120
References: Grabar, *Serov*, 1914, p. 288;
Grabar, *Serov*, 1965, p. 33

320

**Portrait of Pavel Petrovich
Trubetskoi.** ⟨1898⟩
Pastel
Signed, bottom left: *V. Seroff*
Present whereabouts unknown
Provenance: P. Trubetskoi collection,
St. Petersburg, Paris, USA
Pavel Petrovich Trubetskoi — see No 319.
Exhibitions: 1899 St. Petersburg —
1st International Exhibition of Paintings
Organized by the *Mir Iskusstva* Magazine
(No 267)
Reproductions: *Mir Iskusstva*, 1899,
No 3/4, p. 43
References: Grabar, *Serov*, 1914, p. 288;
Grabar, *Serov*, 1965, p. 335

321

**Icon of the Virgin of Iberia Brought
to a Tavern.** ⟨1898⟩
Gouache. 37.5×54 cm
Signed in the lower left corner: *ВС (VS)*
Art Museum, Riazan (since 1923).
Inv. No 313-p
Provenance: D. Vysotsky collection, Mos-
cow; State Museum Reserve, Moscow
Exhibitions: 1935 The Tretyakov Gallery
(No 109), The Russian Museum (No 102)
References: Grabar, *Serov*, 1965, p. 415

322

Barns. 1898
Oil on cardboard. 48×71.5 cm
Signed and dated, bottom right: *Съровъ
98* (Serov, 1898)
Art Museum, Gorky (since 1948).
Inv. No. 1102
References: Grabar, *Serov*, 1965, p. 415

WATERCOLORS,
DRAWINGS
AND ETCHINGS

323

Self-portrait. ⟨About 1898⟩
Etching. 19×13.2 cm (plate). Impression
on Japanese paper
Provenance: The Serov family collection,
Moscow (until 1954)

Reproductions: *Mir Iskusstva*, 1904, No 2,
p. 47; Grabar, *Serov*, 1914, p. 118;
Grabar, *Serov*, 1965, p. 196
References: Grabar, *Serov*, 1914, pp. 152,
288; Grabar, *Serov*, 1965, pp. 200, 414;
Fiodorov-Davydov 1965, No 2, p. 38

313

From the Manor's Window. 1898
Pastel
Signed and dated, bottom left: *Съровъ 98*
(Serov, 1898)
Present whereabouts unknown
Provenance: O. Serova collection, Moscow
(until 1924)
Exhibitions: 1914 (posthumous) St. Peters-
burg (No 122), Moscow (No 120); / 1899
St. Petersburg — 1st International Exhibi-
tion of Paintings Organized by the *Mir
Iskusstva* Magazine (No 270 or 271); 1902
Moscow — Exhibition of Paintings
Organized by the *Mir Iskusstva* Magazine
(No 214, as *Winter*); 1914 Malmö (Swe-
den) — Baltic Art Exhibition (No 3207a);
1924 New York — Russian Art
Reproductions: *Mir Iskusstva*, 1902,
No 12, p. 305 (as *Winter*); Grabar, *Serov*,
1914, p. 119; Grabar, *Serov*, 1965, p. 195
References: Grabar, *Serov*, 1914, pp. 152,
288; Grabar, *Serov*, 1965, pp. 200, 414,
415; Fiodorov-Davydov 1965, No 2, p. 38

314

Sheep. Study. 1898
Oil on cardboard. 13.8×21.5 cm
Signed and dated in pen, bottom left:
В Съровъ 6 іюня 1898 Борисоглѣбскъ
(V. Serov, 6 June 1898, Borisoglebsk)
Museum of Russian Art, Kiev.
Inv. No Ж-524
References: Grabar, *Serov*, 1965, p. 415

315

**Portrait of Maria Klavdiyevna
Tenisheva.** 1898
Oil on canvas. 100×115 cm
Signed and dated, top left: *Съровъ 98*
(Serov, 1898)
Museum of Art and Architecture,
Smolensk (since 1924). Inv. No Ж-91

Provenance: The Tenisheva History and
Ethnography Museum, Smolensk
Maria Klavdiyevna Tenisheva, née Piat-
kovskaya (1867–1928), artist and patron
of the arts.
Exhibitions: 1935 The Tretyakov Gallery
(No 108), The Russian Museum (No 101);
1958–59 The Tretyakov Gallery; 1959–60
The Russian Museum; / 1899 St. Peters-
burg — 1st International Exhibition of
Paintings Organized by the *Mir Iskusstva*
Magazine (No 265)
Reproductions: Leniashin 1980, p. 237
References: Grabar, *Serov*, 1965, p. 335;
*Serov in the Reminiscences of His Con-
temporaries*, 1971, 2, p. 272

316

Portrait of Duchess N. Meshcherskaya.
⟨1898⟩
Oil on canvas
Present whereabouts unknown
Provenance: The Duke Meshchersky col-
lection, St. Petersburg; N. Meshcherskaya
collection, St. Petersburg
N. Meshcherskaya, née Countess Musina-
Pushkina.
Exhibitions: 1914 (posthumous) St. Peters-
burg (No 119), Moscow (No 116)
References: Grabar, *Serov*, 1914, pp. 136,
288; Grabar, *Serov*, 1965, p. 335

317 (Plate 61)

**Portrait of Nikolai Andreyevich
Rimsky-Korsakov.** ⟨1898⟩
Oil on canvas. 94×111 cm
The Tretyakov Gallery. Inv. No 1526
Nikolai Andreyevich Rimsky-Korsakov
(1844–1908), celebrated Russian com-
poser, conductor and public figure.
Exhibitions: 1935 The Tretyakov Gallery
(No 105), The Russian Museum (No 98); /
1899 St. Petersburg — 27th Exhibition of
the Itinerant Society (No 146)
Reproductions: *Mir Iskusstva*, 1900,
No 1/2, p. 9; Grabar, *Serov*, 1914, p. 117;
Grabar, *Serov*, 1980, pl. 42
References: Grabar, *Serov*, 1914, pp. 136,
288; Grabar, *Serov*, 1965, pp. 150, 154,
334, 335

Exhibitions: 1952 Moscow (No 391); / 1954 Central House of Art Workers, Moscow — Portraits of Prominent Personalities in Russian Art: 18th to 20th Century (No 232)
NOTE: Other impressions of this etching were displayed at the following exhibitions: 1935 The Tretyakov Gallery (No 793), The Russian Museum (No 1056); / 1967 The Russian Museum — Russian Prints: Late 19th and Early 20th Centuries (p. 65).
Reproductions: Grabar, *Serov*, 1914, p. 114; Yaremich, *Serov: Drawings*, 1936
References: Grabar, *Serov*, 1914, p. 289; Grabar, *Serov*, 1965, p. 353; Yaremich, *Serov: Drawings*, 1936, p. 21

324 (Plate 70)
Village. 1898
Watercolors and gouache on paper, mounted on cardboard. 25.5×37.5 cm
Signed and dated in pencil, bottom right: *Сѣровъ 98* (Serov, 1898)
The Tretyakov Gallery (since 1920). Inv. No 4693
Provenance: S. Bakhrushin collection, Moscow
Exhibitions: 1935 The Tretyakov Gallery (No 358), The Russian Museum (No 418); 1952 Moscow (No 166); 1958–59 The Tretyakov Gallery; 1959–60 The Russian Museum; 1965 The Tretyakov Gallery (p. 58), The Russian Museum; / 1899 St. Petersburg — 1st International Exhibition of Paintings Organized by the *Mir Iskusstva* Magazine (No 268); 1949 The Pushkin Museum of Fine Arts, Moscow — Russian Graphic Art: 18th to Early 20th Century; 1963 Moscow — Pencil Drawings, Watercolors, Pastels, and Gouaches (p. 69)
Reproductions: *Mir Iskusstva*, 1899, No 6, p. 91; Grabar, *Serov*, 1914, p. 110 (as *Gray Day*. 1897); Grabar, *Serov*, 1980, pl. 41
References: Grabar, *Serov*, 1914, p. 288 (as *Gray Day*. 1897. Oil); Grabar, *Serov*, 1965, pp. 197, 200 (as *Gray Day*. 1897), 414; Fiodorov-Davydov 1965, No 2, pp. 38, 39

325 (Plate 67)
October. 1898
Etching. 36×53.5 cm (plate). 53.4×79.3 cm (sheet). Third state. Impression on heavy paper
Etched signature, bottom left: *Сѣровъ 98* (Serov, 1898). Inscribed by the artist, bottom right: *Василію Васильевичу Матэ В. Сѣровъ 98* (To Vasily Vasilyevich Mathé. V. Serov, 1898)
The Russian Museum (since 1935). Inv. No Гр-32098
Provenance: V. Mathé collection, St. Petersburg
In the list of Serov's works (Grabar, *Serov*, 1965, p. 416) the etching is erroneously mentioned twice: first as *October* (1898) and then as a newly registered etching *Horses* (1898).
NOTE: Other impressions of this etching were displayed at the following exhibitions: 1914 (posthumous) (No 140c — 3rd and 4th ed.); / 1898 St. Petersburg — Works by Russian and Finnish Artists (No 271, as *Horses*); 1906 Paris — Russian Art (No 524, as *Chevaux*)
Reproductions: Radlov, *Serov*, 1914; Hol-

lerbach, *Serov*, 1924; Yaremich, *Serov: Drawings*, 1936
References: Grabar, *Serov*, 1914, p. 289; Yaremich, *Serov: Drawings*, 1936, pp. 20, 21; Grabar, *Serov*, 1965, pp. 415, 416

326
Portrait of Countess Varvara Vasilyevna Musina-Pushkina. 1898
Watercolor. 54.9×37.5 cm
Signed and dated, bottom right: *Сѣровъ 98* (Serov, 1898)
The Ashmolean Museum, Oxford
Provenance: V. Musina-Pushkina collection, St. Petersburg; A. Musin-Pushkin collection, Paris

Exhibitions: 1914 (posthumous) St. Petersburg (No 118), Moscow (No 115); / 1902 St. Petersburg — 4th Exhibition of Paintings Organized by the *Mir Iskusstva* Magazine (No 176); 1935 London — Russian Art (No 439); 1960 (?) London — Russian Art and Life (No 139)
Reproductions: Grabar, *Serov*, 1914, p. 115
References: Grabar, *Serov*, 1914, p. 288; Grabar, *Serov*, 1965, p. 335

327
Down a Hill (Winter). ⟨1898⟩
Watercolor, India ink and pen. 14.2×9 cm
Signed, bottom right: *Сѣровъ* (Serov)
The Russian Museum (since 1912). Inv. No P-3078
Exhibitions: 1935 The Tretyakov Gallery (No 735), The Russian Museum (No 710)
Reproductions: *Serov: The Sun of Russia*, 1913
References: Grabar, *Serov*, 1965, p. 414

328
Gray Day. ⟨1898⟩
Watercolor and gouache. 25.5×35.4 cm
The Tretyakov Gallery (since 1898). Inv. No 3648
Exhibitions: 1935 The Tretyakov Gallery (No 356), The Russian Museum (No 415, dated 1897); 1952 Moscow (No 164, dated 1897); 1958–59 The Tretyakov Gallery; 1965 The Tretyakov Gallery (p. 58), The Russian Museum; / 1889 Moscow — Exhibition of Watercolors, Pastels and Drawings Organized by the Moscow Society of Art Lovers; 1949 The Pushkin Museum of Fine Arts, Moscow — Russian

Graphic Art: 18th to Early 20th Century;
1963 The Tretyakov Gallery — Pencil
Drawings, Watercolors, Pastels, and
Gouaches (p. 70)
Reproductions: Yaremich, *Serov: Draw-ings*, 1936; *Drawings and Watercolors.
Catalogue*, 1956; Grabar, *Serov*, 1980,
pl. 40
References: Grabar, *Serov*, 1965, p. 414

329
**The Sculptor Pavel Petrovich
Trubetskoi at Work.** ⟨1898⟩
India ink. 40.5×26.5 cm
The Tretyakov Gallery (since 1927).
Inv. No 9948
Provenance: S. Zimin collection, Moscow;
State Museum Reserve, Moscow
Pavel Petrovich Trubetskoi — see No 319.
Exhibitions: 1935 The Tretyakov Gallery
(No 362), The Russian Museum (No 422);
1952 Moscow (No 167); 1958–59 The Tre-tyakov Gallery; 1959 Museum of Russian
Art, Kiev; 1959–60 The Russian Museum;
1965 The Tretyakov Gallery (p. 58),
The Russian Museum
References: Grabar, *Serov*, 1965, p. 353

330
**By the Gate of the Virgin
of Iberia.** ⟨1898⟩
India ink, sepia, graphite and pen.
21.2×32 cm
Bottom right, an impression of the artist's
signet: *BC* (VS)
The Tretyakov Gallery (since 1940).
Inv. No 25466
Provenance: N. Shchokotov collection,
Moscow
Exhibitions: 1958–59 The Tretyakov Gal-lery; 1959 Museum of Russian Art, Kiev;
1959–60 The Russian Museum; / 1963
The Tretyakov Gallery — Pencil Drawings,
Watercolors, Pastels, and Gouaches
(p. 70)
References: Grabar, *Serov*, 1965, p. 415

1899
PAINTINGS

331 (Plates 95, 96)
The Children. Sasha and Yura Serov.
⟨1899⟩
Oil on canvas. 71×54 cm
Signed, bottom right: *BC* (VS)

The Russian Museum (since 1900).
Inv. No Ж-4283
Sasha and Yura Serov — see Nos 308,
309.
Exhibitions: 1935 The Tretyakov Gallery
(No 113), The Russian Museum (No 166);
1958–59 The Tretyakov Gallery; 1965 The
Tretyakov Gallery (p. 38), The Russian
Museum; / 1900 St. Petersburg —
2nd Exhibition of Paintings Organized by
the *Mir Iskusstva* Magazine (No 174);
1959 London — Works by Russian and
Soviet Artists (No 72); 1960 Paris — Rus-sian and Soviet Painting (No 54); 1967–68
Paris — Russian Art from the Scythians to
the Present Time. Art Treasures from
Soviet Museums; 1972 Moscow, Lenin-grad, Kiev, Minsk — Portrait Paintings by
the Itinerants
Reproductions: *Mir Iskusstva*, 1900,
No 1/2, p. 3; Grabar, *Serov*, 1914, be-tween pp. 128 and 129; Grabar, *Serov*,
1965, pp. 146 (detail), 147
References: Grabar, *Serov*, 1914, pp. 139,
140, 289; Grabar, *Serov*, 1965,
pp. 177, 335

332
Model with Her Hair Down. ⟨1899⟩
Oil on canvas. 75×125 cm
Present whereabouts unknown

Provenance: O. Serova collection, Mos-cow; E. Helzer and T. Helzer collection,
Moscow
Exhibitions: 1914 (posthumous) St. Peters-burg (No 124), Moscow (No 123); 1952
Moscow (No 170); 1958–59 The Tretyakov
Gallery; 1965 The Tretyakov Gallery
(p. 38)
Reproductions: Ernst, *Serov*, 1922,
between pp. 32 and 33
References: Grabar, *Serov*, 1965,
p. 417

333
**Portrait of Alexander III in the Red
Full-dress Uniform of the Danish Royal
Regiment of Life Guards.** 1899
Oil on canvas. 170.8×117.5 cm
Signed and dated, bottom right:
Сѣровъ 99 (Serov, 1899)
The Royal Regiment of Life Guards,
Copenhagen
Alexander III — see No 232.
Exhibitions: 1935 London — Russian Art
(No 440)
References: Grabar, *Serov*, 1914, pp. 143,
144, 289; Grabar, *Serov*, 1965, pp. 180,
335; *Serov's Correspondence*, 1937,
p. 221

96. The Sculptor Pavel
Petrovich Trubetskoi at Work.
Cat. No 329

97. By the Gate of the Virgin
of Iberia. Cat. No 330

Studies for the *Portrait
of Alexander III*
(Nos 334–336)

334

Alexander III. 〈1899〉
Oil on canvas. 72×58 cm
Bottom right, an impression of the artist's
signet: *BC* (VS)
Private collection, Moscow
Alexander III — see No 232.
Exhibitions: 1914 (posthumous) St. Peters-
burg (No 132 — 3rd and 4th ed.)
References: Grabar, *Serov*, 1965, p. 336
(as *Head of Emperor Alexander III.* 1890s)

335

Fredensborg Castle. 1899
Oil on canvas. 12.5×21 cm
Inscribed in ink, bottom right: *Александру
Бенуа В. Сѣровъ 99* (To Alexander Be-
nois. V. Serov, 1899)
Private collection, Moscow
Provenance: A. Benois collection,
St. Petersburg
Exhibitions: 1914 (posthumous) St. Peters-
burg (No 135)
References: Grabar, *Serov*, 1965, p. 418

336

Decorations. 〈1899〉
Oil on cardboard. 36×27 cm
Present whereabouts unknown
Provenance: V. Mathé collection,
St. Petersburg; M. Uspensky collection,
Moscow; A. Smolianikov collection,
Moscow
Exhibitions: 1952 Moscow (No 177)
References: Grabar, *Serov*, 1965, p. 418

337

**Portrait of Vasily Alexeyevich
Bakhrushin.** 1899
Oil on canvas. 102×71 cm
Signed, bottom right: *Сѣровъ 99* (Serov,
1899)
History Museum, Moscow. Inv. No 2123
Provenance: Moscow City Council
Vasily Alexeyevich Bakhrushin
(1833–1906), factory owner, member of
the Moscow City Council.
Exhibitions: 1952 Moscow (No 172);
1958–59 The Tretyakov Gallery; 1959–60
The Russian Museum
Reproductions: Grabar, *Serov*, 1914,
p. 127; Leniashin 1980, p. 61
References: Grabar, *Serov*, 1914, pp. 136,
288; Grabar, *Serov*, 1965, p. 335

338 (Plates 103, 104)
**Portrait of Sophia Mikhailovna
Botkina.** 1899
Oil on canvas. 189×139.5 cm
Signed and dated, bottom left: *Сѣровъ 99*
(Serov, 1899)
The Russian Museum (since 1934).
Inv. No Ж-4314
Provenance: S. Botkina collection,
Moscow
Sophia Mikhailovna Botkina, née Maliuti-
na, wife of P. Botkin, a rich Moscow
merchant.
Exhibitions: 1914 (posthumous) St. Peters-
burg (No 123), Moscow (No 122); 1935
The Tretyakov Gallery (No 110), The Rus-
sian Museum (No 103); 1958–59 The

Tretyakov Gallery; 1959 Museum of Russian Art, Kiev; 1959–60 The Russian
Museum; 1965 The Tretyakov Gallery
(p. 37), The Russian Museum; / 1900
Paris — World Exhibition (p. 71); 1901
St. Petersburg — 3rd Exhibition of Paintings Organized by the *Mir Iskusstva*
Magazine (No 194, as *Portrait of Mrs. X*);
1959 Leningrad — Russian Portrait Painting: 18th to Early 20th Century (p. 34);
1971 Tokyo, Kyoto — 100 Masterpieces
from Soviet Museums (No 87)
Reproductions: *Mir Iskusstva*, 1900,
No 1/2, p. 23; Grabar, *Serov*, 1914, p. 123;
Grabar, *Serov*, 1965, p. 151
References: Grabar, *Serov*, 1914, pp. 134,
136, 288; Grabar, *Serov*, 1965, pp. 154,
156, 335; Leniashin 1980, pp. 34–40

WATERCOLORS, PASTELS, ETCHINGS, AND LITHOGRAPHS

339 (Plate 68)
Peasant Woman with a Horse. 1899
Etching. 26.5×35.5 cm (plate). Third state
Etched signature, bottom right: *BC 99* (VS,
1899). Signed in pencil along the lower
margin, right: *В. Сѣровъ* (V. Serov)
The Russian Museum. Inv. No Гр-32095
The etching reproduces the pastel *In a
Village. Peasant Woman with a Horse*
(see No 310). There are three states of
this etching.
Exhibitions: 1935 The Russian Museum
(No 1059); / 1967 The Russian Museum
— Russian Prints: Late 19th and Early
20th Centuries (p. 65)

NOTE: Other impressions of this etching kept in different collections were displayed at the following exhibitions: 1914 (posthumous) St. Petersburg (No 140), Moscow (No 147); 1935 The Tretyakov Gallery (No 796); 1952 Moscow (No 396).
Reproductions: Yaremich, *Serov: Drawings*, 1936
References: Grabar, *Serov*, 1914, p. 289; Yaremich, *Serov: Drawings*, 1936, p. 21; Grabar, *Serov*, 1965, p. 418

100. Winter Road. Cat. No 342

340 (Plate 98)
Portrait of Vasily Vasilyevich Mathé. ⟨1899⟩
Etching. 21.8×15.2 cm (plate); 32.3×25.3 cm (sheet). Third state (out of four)
The Russian Museum (since 1958). Inv. No Гр-39908
Vasily Vasilyevich Mathé (1856–1917), Russian engraver, Professor of Engraving at the Academy of Arts, St. Petersburg. A print taken from the fourth state of the plate was published as a supplement to No 2 of the *Mir Iskusstva* magazine for 1902.
Exhibitions (prints from different museums): 1914 (posthumous) St. Petersburg (No 140), Moscow (No 147); 1935 The Tretyakov Gallery (No 800), The Russian Museum (No 1060); 1952 Moscow (Nos 397, 398); 1965 The Russian Museum; / 1902 St. Petersburg — 4th Exhibition of Paintings Organized by the *Mir Iskusstva* Magazine (No 177); 1902 Moscow — Exhibition of Paintings Organized by the *Mir Iskusstva* Magazine (No 221); 1906 Paris — Russian Art (No 525); 1967 The Russian Museum — Russian Prints: Late 19th and Early 20th Centuries (p. 67)
Reproductions: Grabar, *Serov*, 1914, p. 131
References: Grabar, *Serov*, 1914, p. 289; Grabar, *Serov*, 1965, pp. 354, 355; Yaremich, *Serov: Drawings*, 1936, pp. 21, 22

341
Horseless Peasant. 1899
Watercolor and India ink
Signed and dated, bottom left: *В. Сѣровъ 99* (V. Serov, 1899)
Present whereabouts unknown
Provenance: D. Feigin collection, Petrograd (until 1918)
Reproductions: *In Aid of the Victims of Crop Failure*, 1899, p. 11; Grabar, *Serov*, 1965, p. 194
References: *Serov in the Reminiscences of His Contemporaries*, 1971, 2, pp. 19, 20; Sokolova, *Serov*, 1935, pp. 50, 52; Fiodorov-Davydov 1965, No 2, p. 39

Illustrations for Pushkin's Works (Nos 342–344)

342
Winter Road. ⟨1899⟩
Tempera on cardboard. 30×42 cm
The All-Union Pushkin Memorial Museum, Leningrad (since 1945). Inv. No Кп-7904
Provenance: P. Konchalovsky collection, Moscow
Exhibitions: 1914 (posthumous) St. Petersburg (No 127, as *The Troika*), Moscow (No 27, under the same title); 1958–59 The Tretyakov Gallery; 1959–60 The Russian Museum; 1965 The Tretyakov Gallery (p. 59, as *The Troika*), The Russian

Museum; / 1900 St. Petersburg — 2nd Exhibition of Paintings Organized by the *Mir Iskusstva* Magazine (No 180)
Reproductions: Pushkin 1899, 1, p. 106: *Mir Iskusstva*, 1900, No 1/2, p. 12; Grabar, *Serov*, 1914, p. 122
References: Grabar, *Serov*, 1914, p. 288; Grabar, *Serov*, 1965, pp. 283, 416, 417; Fiodorov-Davydov 1965, No 2, p. 39

343 (Plate 76)
Portrait of Alexander Sergeyevich Pushkin. ⟨1899⟩
Watercolors, white and graphite. 35×29.3 cm
Signed and dated, bottom left: *Сѣровъ 99* (Serov, 1899)
The All-Union Pushkin Museum, Leningrad (since 1940). Inv. No Кп-6565
Provenance: P. Konchalovsky collection, Moscow; The Tretyakov Gallery
Alexander Sergeyevich Pushkin (1799–1837), celebrated Russian poet.
Exhibitions: 1935 The Tretyakov Gallery (No 368), The Russian Museum (No 430); 1958–59 The Tretyakov Gallery; 1959–60 The Russian Museum; 1965 The Tretyakov Gallery (p. 59, as *Pushkin in Mikhailovskoye*), The Russian Museum; / 1900 St. Petersburg — 2nd Exhibition of Paintings Organized by the *Mir Iskusstva* Magazine (No 179); 1936 The Tretyakov Gallery — Pushkin in the Tretyakov Gallery (No 9)
Reproductions: Pushkin 1899, 1, after p. XXXIV; *Mir Iskusstva*, 1900, No 1/2, p. 13; Grabar, *Serov*, 1914, p. 125; Grabar, *Serov*, 1965, between pp. 258 and 259; *Serov: Drawings, Watercolors, Lithographs*, 1972, No 1 (as *Pushkin on a Park Bench*)
References: Grabar, *Serov*, 1914, p. 288; Grabar, *Serov*, 1965, pp. 283, 416 (as *Pushkin on a Park Bench*); Liaskovskaya 1965, p. 61; Fiodorov-Davydov 1965, No 2, p. 39

344 (Plate 75)
Pushkin in the Country. ⟨1899⟩
Pastel on gray paper. 65×94.5 cm
The All-Union Pushkin Museum, Leningrad (since 1940). Inv. No Кп-7156
Provenance: O. Serova collection, Moscow; P. Suvchinsky collection, St. Petersburg; The Russian Museum

Alexander Sergeyevich Pushkin — see No 343.
Exhibitions: 1914 (posthumous) St. Petersburg (No 128), Moscow (No 128); 1935 The Tretyakov Gallery (No 122), The Russian Museum (No 105); 1958–59 The Tretyakov Gallery; 1959–60 The Russian Museum; 1965 The Tretyakov Gallery (p. 59); / 1937 History Museum, Moscow — Centenary of Pushkin's Death
Reproductions: Grabar, *Serov*, 1914, p. 124; Grabar, *Serov*, 1980, pl. 45
References: Grabar, *Serov*, 1914, p. 288; Grabar, *Serov*, 1965, pp. 183, 416; Fiodorov-Davydov 1965, No 2, p. 39

345
Model with Her Hair Down. 1899
Watercolors and white on paper, mounted on cardboard. 52.4×35.5 cm
Signed and dated, bottom left: *Сѣровъ 99* (Serov, 1899)

101. Model with Her Hair Down. Cat. No 345

The Tretyakov Gallery (since 1917).
Inv. No 5480
Provenance: V. Girshman collection,
Moscow
Exhibitions: 1914 (posthumous) Moscow
(No 124); 1935 The Tretyakov Gallery
(No 367), The Russian Museum (No 429);
1958–59 The Tretyakov Gallery; 1965 The
Tretyakov Gallery (p. 58), The Russian
Museum; / 1899 St. Petersburg — Exhibi-
tion of Watercolors, Pastels, and Drawings
Organized by the Moscow Society of Art
Lovers (No 97); 1963 The Tretyakov Gal-
lery — Pencil Drawings, Watercolors,
Pastels, and Gouaches (p. 70)
Reproductions: *Drawings and Watercolors.*
Catalogue, 1956; Grabar, *Serov*, 1965,
p. 149
References: Grabar, *Serov*, 1914, p. 288;
Grabar, *Serov*, 1965, p. 417

346
Portrait of Alexander III with the
Copenhagen Harbor
in the Background. 1899
Watercolors, gouache and white.
41.6×32 cm (exposed area)
Signed and dated, bottom left: *Съровъ 99*
(Serov, 1899)
The Russian Museum (since 1926).
Inv. No P-3226
Provenance: V. Zuikov collection,
St. Petersburg; The Hermitage, Leningrad
Alexander III — see No 232.
Exhibitions: 1914 (posthumous) St. Peters-
burg (No 133 — 2nd and 3rd ed.), Mos-
cow (No 132)
Reproductions: Ernst, *Serov*, 1922, be-
tween pp. 16 and 17
References: Grabar, *Serov*, 1914, p. 289;
Grabar, *Serov*, 1965, p. 336 (the informa-
tion on the whereabouts of the portrait is
incorrect since it refers to the watercolor
repetition of the 1899 portrait painted
in oils)

102. Portrait of Anna Petrovna
Ostroumova-Lebedeva.
Cat. No 349

347 (Plate 91)
Portrait of Alfred Pavlovich
Nurok. 1899
Lithograph. 31×21 cm; 47.8×38.7 cm
(sheet)
Signed and dated, bottom left: *BC 99*
(VS, 1899)
The Russian Museum. Inv. No Гр-20363
Alfred Pavlovich Nurok (1860–1919),
music critic, worked on the editorial staff of
the *Mir Iskusstva* magazine.
This lithograph was published by *Mir
Iskusstva* in 1900 (*Fifteen Lithographs by
Russian Artists*).
Exhibitions: 1914 (posthumous) St. Peters-
burg (No 141), Moscow (No 148c —
2nd ed.); 1935 The Russian Museum
(No 1062); 1900 St. Petersburg —
2nd Exhibition of Paintings Organized by
the *Mir Iskusstva* Magazine (No 184)
NOTE: Proof impressions of this etching
were displayed at the 1952 exhibition in
Moscow (No 402, P. Kornilov collection,
Leningrad; No 403, G. Vereisky collection,
Leningrad).
References: Grabar, *Serov*, 1914, p. 289;
Grabar, *Serov*, 1965, p. 355; Liaskovskaya
1965, p. 57; Yaremich, *Serov: Drawings*,
1936, p.15

348 (Plate 92)
Portrait of Alexander Konstantinovich
Glazunov. ⟨1899⟩
Lithograph. 29.4×22 cm; 31.5×24 cm
(sheet)
Signed, bottom right: *B. Съровъ* (V. Se-
rov); bottom center: *А. Глазуновъ*
(A. Glazunov)
The Russian Museum. Inv. No Гр-20392
Alexander Konstantinovich Glazunov
(1865–1936), composer, conductor, Pro-
fessor and Director of the St. Petersburg
Conservatory.
A print made in I. Kadushin's chromolitho-
graphic shop, St. Petersburg, was pub-

lished as a supplement to No 1/2 of the
Mir Iskusstva magazine for 1900.
Exhibitions: 1935 The Russian Museum
(No 1063)
NOTE: Several copies of this lithograph
were displayed at the following exhibitions:
1914 (posthumous) St. Petersburg
(No 141), Moscow (No 148); 1952 Moscow
(No 399, 400); 1965 The Russian
Museum; / 1900 St. Petersburg —
2nd Exhibition of
Paintings Organized by the *Mir Iskusstva*
Magazine (No 184); 1954 Central House
of Art Workers, Moscow — Portraits of
Prominent Personalities in Russian Art:
18th to 20th Century (No 29); 1967 The
Russian Museum — Russian Prints: Late
19th and Early 20th Centuries (p. 67).
Reproductions: Grabar, *Serov*, 1914,
p. 132; *Serov: Drawings, Watercolors,
Lithographs*, 1972, p. 131
References: Grabar, *Serov*, 1914, p. 289;
Grabar, *Serov*, 1965, p. 355; Liaskovskaya
1965, p. 57; Yaremich, *Serov: Drawings*,
1936, p. 15

349
Portrait of Anna Petrovna
Ostroumova-Lebedeva. ⟨1899⟩
Lithograph. 28.6×36.6 cm
Signed, bottom left: *B. Съровъ* (V. Serov)
The Russian Museum. Inv. No Гр-38565
Anna Petrovna Ostroumova-Lebedeva
(1871–1955), engraver, painter, member
of the World of Art Society. During the
Soviet period she received the title of Peo-
ple's Artist of the Russian Federation and
was a Full Member of the USSR Academy
of Arts.
This lithograph was published by the *Mir
Iskusstva* magazine in 1900 (*Fifteen Lithographs by Russian Artists*). It was also
issued as supplement to Nos 9 and 10 of
this magazine for the same year.
Exhibitions: 1914 (posthumous) St. Petersburg (No 141), Moscow (No 148a); 1952
Moscow (No 401); / 1900 St. Petersburg
— 2nd Exhibition of Paintings Organized
by the *Mir Iskusstva* Magazine (No 184)
NOTE: Other impressions of the lithograph
were displayed at the following exhibitions:
1935 The Russian Museum (No 1064);
1965 The Russian Museum; / 1967 The
Russian Museum — Russian Prints: Late
19th and Early 20th Centuries (p. 67)
Reproductions: Grabar, *Serov*, 1914,
p. 130
References: Grabar, *Serov*, 1914, p. 289;
Grabar, *Serov*, 1965, p. 355; Liaskovskaya
1965, p. 57; Yaremich, *Serov: Drawings*,
1936, p. 15

1890s
PAINTINGS

350
Balcony. ⟨1890s⟩
Oil on canvas. 111×71 cm
The Kustodiyev Picture Gallery, Astrakhan
(since 1927). Inv. No Ж-310
Provenance: A. Kasyanov collection, Mos-
cow; State Museum Reserve, Moscow
Exhibitions: 1914 (posthumous) St. Peters-
burg (No 125), Moscow (No 125); 1935
The Tretyakov Gallery (No 114), The Rus-
sian Museum (No 107)
References: Grabar, *Serov*, 1914, p. 289;
Grabar, *Serov*, 1965, p. 419

351
Crow. Study. ⟨1890s⟩
Oil on cardboard. 37.2×27.2 cm
V. Petrov collection, Leningrad
References: Grabar, *Serov*, 1965, p. 419

352
Don Juan. ⟨1890s⟩
Oil on canvas. 132×177 cm
Present whereabouts unknown
Provenance: O. Serova collection, Moscow; Art Museum, Kharkov (since 1928)
References: Grabar, *Serov*, 1965, p. 420

353
Oak Tree in Domotkanovo. Study.
⟨1890s⟩
Oil on canvas. 63×86 cm
Present whereabouts unknown
Provenance: A. Dolgopolova collection; V. Kalyanov collection, Moscow
Exhibitions: 1952 Moscow (No 182); / 1955 Central House of Art Workers, Moscow — Landscape in Russian Painting: 19th and Early 20th Centuries (No 295)
Reproductions: Simonovich-Yefimova 1964, p. 36; Kopschitzer, *Serov*, 1967 (No 23)
References: Grabar, *Serov*, 1965, p. 419; Simonovich-Yefimova 1967, pp. 37, 38

354
Forest. ⟨1890s⟩
Oil on canvas. 63×75 cm (approx.)
Present whereabouts unknown
Exhibitions: 1914 (posthumous) Moscow (No 151a — 2nd ed.)
References: Grabar, *Serov*, 1965, p. 419

355
Forest View. Study. ⟨1890s⟩
Oil on cardboard. 29×24 cm
Present whereabouts unknown
Provenance: Yu. Danziger collection, Moscow
Exhibitions: 1935 The Tretyakov Gallery (No 118), The Russian Museum (No 112); 1946 Central House of Art Workers, Moscow (No 21)
References: Grabar, *Serov*, 1965, p. 419

356
Majorenhof. ⟨1890s⟩
Oil on canvas
Present whereabouts unknown
Exhibitions: 1914 (posthumous) St. Petersburg (No 116a), Moscow (No 114)
References: Grabar, *Serov*, 1914, p. 289; Grabar, *Serov*, 1965, p. 420

357
At a Watering Place. Study. ⟨1890s⟩
Oil on canvas
Present whereabouts unknown
Provenance: O. Serova collection, Moscow; V. Musina-Pushkina collection, St. Petersburg
Exhibitions: 1914 (posthumous) St. Petersburg (No 120 — 2nd and 4th ed.); 1902 St. Petersburg — 4th Exhibition of Paintings Organized by the *Mir Iskusstva* Magazine (No 180, as *Horses*)
References: Grabar, *Serov*, 1914, p. 289; Grabar, *Serov*, 1965, p. 420

358
Model Before a Stool. ⟨1890s⟩
Oil on cardboard. 79×61 cm
Present whereabouts unknown
Provenance: B. Petukhov collection, Moscow

Exhibitions: 1935 The Tretyakov Gallery (No 121)
References: Grabar, *Serov*, 1965, p. 420

359
Park. Trees by the Pool. Study. ⟨1890s⟩
Oil on canvas. 33×42 cm (approx.)
Present whereabouts unknown
Exhibitions: 1914 (posthumous) Moscow (No 151)
References: Grabar, *Serov*, 1965, p. 419

360
Portrait of Vasily Ivanovich Surikov.
⟨Late 1890s⟩. Unfinished
Oil on canvas. 100×80 cm
The Tretyakov Gallery (since 1961).
Inv. No П-32957
Provenance: The Surikovs collection, Moscow; O. Serova collection, Moscow; N. Dobychina news agency, Petrograd; M. Braikevich collection, Odessa; The Braikevich family collection, London
Vasily Ivanovich Surikov (1848–1916), Russian history painter.
Exhibitions: 1965 The Tretyakov Gallery (p. 38, dated to the early 1900s), The Russian Museum; / 1960 (?) London — Russian Art and Life (No 101); 1962 The Tretyakov Gallery — Russian Pre-revolutionary Art: New Acquisitions
Reproductions: Simonovich-Yefimova 1964, p. 102; Leniashin 1980, p. 59
References: Zhivova 1961, pp. 40–43; Grabar, *Serov*, 1965, p. 336

361
Breakers. Study. ⟨1890s⟩
Oil on cardboard. 17.5×27 cm
Picture Gallery, Kostroma (since 1923).
Inv. No 129
Exhibitions: 1935 The Tretyakov Gallery (No 117), The Russian Museum (No 111)
References: Grabar, *Serov*, 1965, p. 419

362
River. Study. 1890s
Oil
Present whereabouts unknown
Exhibitions: 1914 (posthumous) Moscow (No 151в — 2nd ed.)
References: Grabar, *Serov*, 1965, p. 419

363
Barn. Study. ⟨1890s⟩
Oil on canvas
Present whereabouts unknown
Provenance: B. Petukhov collection, Moscow
Exhibitions: 1935 The Russian Museum (No 109)
References: Grabar, *Serov*, 1965, p. 419

364
Barn. ⟨1890s⟩
Oil on canvas. 33×43 cm (approx.)
Present whereabouts unknown
Provenance: A. Kasyanov collection, Moscow
Exhibitions: 1914 (posthumous) Moscow (No 151c — 2nd ed.)
References: Grabar, *Serov*, 1965, p. 419

365
Barn with Open Gates. Study. ⟨1890s⟩
Oil on canvas. 28×41 cm
Present whereabouts unknown
Provenance: E. Nikolai collection, Leningrad; M. Kozeletskaya collection, Leningrad

Exhibitions: 1935 The Tretyakov Gallery (No 115), The Russian Museum (No 108)
References: Grabar, *Serov*, 1965, p. 419

103. Portrait of
Vasily Ivanovich Surikov.
Cat. No 360

DRAWINGS

366
From the *Famine* series. ⟨1890s⟩
India ink, graphite and pen. 28×16 cm
Below, an impression of the artist's signet:
BC (VS)
The Russian Museum (since 1926).
Inv. No Р-13406
Provenance: Society for the Advancement of the Arts
Exhibitions: 1935 The Tretyakov Gallery (No 388), The Russian Museum (No 450)
Reproductions: *Serov's Works. Catalogue*, 1935
References: Grabar, *Serov*, 1965, p. 419

367 (Plate 71)
Herd. ⟨1890s⟩
Gouache, charcoal and chalk on cardboard. 56.5×79.5 cm
The Serov family collection, Moscow
Exhibitions: 1935 The Tretyakov Gallery (No 175), The Russian Museum (No 169); 1952 Moscow (No 185)
References: Grabar, *Serov*, 1965, p. 434 (dated to the 1900s); Simonovich-Yefimova 1964, p. 37

1900
PAINTINGS

368 (Plate 130)
**Peter II and Princess Elizabeth
Riding to Hounds.** 1900
Tempera on cardboard. 41×39 cm
Signed and dated, bottom left:
Сѣровъ 1900 (Serov, 1900)
The Russian Museum (since 1900).

104. Winter in Finland.
Cat. No 378

Inv. No Ж-4291
Peter II (1715–1730), Emperor of Russia (1727–30), grandson of Peter the Great. Elizabeth (1709–1762), Empress of Russia (1741–62), daughter of Peter the Great.
Exhibitions: 1935 The Tretyakov Gallery (No 123), The Russian Museum (No 114); / 1901 St. Petersburg — 3rd Exhibition of Paintings Organized by the *Mir Iskusstva* Magazine (No 195); 1902 Moscow — Exhibition of Paintings Organized by the *Mir Iskusstva* Magazine (No 215); 1906 Paris, Berlin — Russian Art (Nos 519, 430); 1911 Rome — International Art Exhibition (No 387); 1939 The Tretyakov Gallery — Russian History Painting (No 328)
Reproductions: *Royal Hunting in Russia*, 1902, between pp. 30 and 31; Grabar, *Serov*, 1914, p. 141 (dated 1900–1); *Apollon*, 1912, No 10, between pp. 22 and 23; Grabar, *Serov*, 1965, p. 204
References: Grabar, *Serov*, 1914, pp. 242, 289; Grabar, *Serov*, 1965, pp. 202, 205, 420; Sarabyanov, *Reforms by Valentin Serov*, 1971, p. 16

369
Nicholas II's Escort. Study. ⟨1900⟩
Oil on canvas
Present whereabouts unknown
Provenance: A. Somov collection, St. Petersburg; P. Gurevich collection, Moscow
Nicholas II — see No 281.
Exhibitions: 1914 (posthumous) St. Petersburg (No 149 — 3rd and 4th ed.)
References: Grabar, *Serov*, 1914, p. 290; Grabar, *Serov*, 1965, p. 421

370
Portrait of Alexander III Watching Manoeuvres. 1900
Oil on canvas. 160×107 cm
Signed and dated, bottom right: *Сѣровъ 1900* (Serov, 1900)
The Russian Museum. Inv. No Ж-2004
Provenance: The 12th Astrakhan Grenadier Regiment, Moscow; History Museum, Moscow
Alexander III — see No 232.
Exhibitions: 1905 St. Petersburg — Russian Portrait Painting (No 1607)
Reproductions: Grabar, *Serov*, 1914, p. 142 (dated 1901–2)
References: Grabar, *Serov*, 1914, pp. 144 (dated 1901–2), 290 (dated 1901); Grabar, *Serov*, 1965, p. 337

371
Portrait of Grand Duke Mikhail Nikolayevich in a Double-breasted Jacket. 1900
Oil on canvas. 90×75 cm
Signed, bottom right: *Сѣровъ* (Serov)
The Tretyakov Gallery. Inv. No Ж-620
Provenance: Grand Duke Georgy Mikhailovich collection, St. Petersburg; T. Bogoslovsky collection, Moscow; N. Chorny collection, Moscow; A. Miasnikov collection, Moscow
Mikhail Nikolayevich (1832–1909), Grand Duke, son of Nicholas I, Chairman of the State Council (1881–1901).
It is possible that the portrait was painted not in 1900, but in 1899 (Grabar, *Serov*, 1965, p. 185).
Exhibitions: 1914 (posthumous) St. Petersburg (No 143), Moscow (No 153); 1935 The Russian Museum (No 114a); 1958–59

The Tretyakov Gallery; 1965 The Tretyakov Gallery (pp. 38, 39); / 1900 St. Petersburg — 2nd Exhibition of Paintings Organized by the *Mir Iskusstva* Magazine (Nos 173); 1902 Moscow — Exhibition of Paintings Organized by the *Mir Iskusstva* Magazine (No 207); 1906 Paris, Berlin — Russian Art (Nos 515, 426); 1968 The Tretyakov Gallery — Russian Pre-revolutionary and Soviet Art. New Acquisitions: 1963–68
Reproductions: *Mir Iskusstva*, 1900, No 1/2, p. 53; Grabar, *Serov*, 1914, p. 135; Grabar, *Serov*, 1980, pl. 49
References: Grabar, *Serov*, 1914, pp. 142, 143, 289; Grabar, *Serov*, 1965, pp. 185 (dated 1899), 336

372
Portrait of Grand Duke Mikhail Nikolayevich in a Field Marshal's Uniform. ⟨1900⟩
Present whereabouts unknown
Provenance: The Kazan Infantry Regiment, Belostok
Grand Duke Mikhail Nikolayevich — see No 371.
Exhibitions: 1905 St. Petersburg — Russian Portrait Painting (No 1613)
Reproductions: *Serov: The Sun of Russia*, 1913 (detail?)
References: Grabar, *Serov*, 1914, p. 289; Grabar, *Serov*, 1965, pp. 185, 336; *Serov's Correspondence*, 1968, p. 138

373
Portrait of Nicholas II in a Double-breasted Jacket. ⟨1900⟩
Oil on canvas. 70×58 cm
Present whereabouts unknown
Provenance: Empress Alexandra Fiodorovna collection, St. Petersburg
Nicholas II — see No 281.
Exhibitions: 1914 (posthumous) St. Petersburg (No 142), Moscow (No 152); 1901 St. Petersburg — 3rd Exhibition of Paintings Organized by the *Mir Iskusstva* Magazine (No 193); 1902 Moscow — Exhibition of Paintings Organized by the *Mir Iskusstva* Magazine (No 206)
Reproductions: *Mir Iskusstva*, 1900, No 4, between pp. 108 and 109; Grabar, *Serov*, 1914, between pp. 160 and 161
References: Grabar, *Serov*, 1914, pp. 143, 144, 289

374
Portrait of Nicholas II in a Double-breasted Jacket. ⟨1900⟩
Oil on canvas. 70×58 cm
The Tretyakov Gallery (since 1914).
Inv. No 1529
Nicholas II — see No 281.
A replica of the portrait listed under No 373.
References: Grabar, *Serov*, 1914, p. 289

375
Portrait of Nicholas II in the Uniform of the Caucasian Regiment. ⟨1900⟩
Unfinished
Present whereabouts unknown
Provenance: private collection, London
Nicholas II — see No 281.
References: Grabar, *Serov*, 1965, p. 336

376
Portrait of Nicholas II in the Uniform of the 2nd Scottish Dragoon Regiment. 1900
Oil on canvas. 116×89 cm
Signed and dated, bottom right: *1900 Сѣровъ* (1900, Serov)
The Scottish Dragoon Regiment collection
Nicholas II — see No 281.
Exhibitions: 1903 St. Petersburg — 5th Exhibition of Paintings Organized by the *Mir Iskusstva* Magazine (No 277); 1906 Paris, Berlin — Russian Art (Nos 514, 425); 1915 London — Battle Paintings at the Guildhall Picture Gallery; 1935 London — Russian Art (No 683)
Reproductions: *Mir Iskusstva*, 1902, Nos 7–12, between pp. 320 and 321; Grabar, *Serov*, 1914, p. 137
References: Grabar, *Serov*, 1914, pp. 143, 144, 289; Grabar, *Serov*, 1965, p. 336 ("painted in . . . the class of battle painting at the Academy of Arts in April 1900")

377 (Plate 113)
Portrait of Isaac Ilyich Levitan.
⟨1900⟩
Pastel on primed cardboard. 100×64 cm
Signed, left: *Сѣровъ* (Serov)
The Tretyakov Gallery (since 1922).
Inv. No 4921
Provenance: Circle of Literature and Art, Moscow
Isaac Ilyich Levitan — see No 225.
Exhibitions: 1914 (posthumous) St. Petersburg (No 149в — 3rd and 4th ed.), Moscow (No 159); 1935 The Tretyakov Gallery (No 122), The Russian Museum (No 113); 1958–59 The Tretyakov Gallery; 1965 The Tretyakov Gallery (p. 61); / 1941 The Tretyakov Gallery — Portrait Drawings: 18th to Early 20th Century (No 122); 1963 The Tretyakov Gallery — Pencil Drawings, Watercolors, Pastels, and Gouaches (p. 64)
Reproductions: *Mir Iskusstva*, 1903, No 7/8, between pp. 40 and 41; Sarabyanov, *Serov*, 1974 (No 17)
References: Grabar, *Serov*, 1914, pp. 117, 290; Grabar, *Serov*, 1965, pp. 133, 336

DRAWINGS AND WATERCOLORS

378
Winter in Finland. ⟨1900⟩
India ink and graphite. 32.2×22 cm
Bottom right, an impression of the artist's signet: *ВС* (VS)

The Tretyakov Gallery (since 1911).
Inv. No 3659
Provenance: O. Serova collection,
Moscow
Exhibitions: 1935 The Tretyakov Gallery
(No 394), The Russian Museum (No 456);
1952 Moscow (No 188); 1958–59 The Tre-
tyakov Gallery; 1965 The Tretyakov Gal-
lery (p. 62), The Russian Museum; / 1954
The Tretyakov Gallery — Sketches and
Studies by Russian Artists from the
Tretyakov Gallery Reserve: 18th to Early
20th Century (p. 54)
References: Grabar, *Serov*, 1965, p. 414
(as *Winter*, dated 1898)

379 (Plate 109)
Nude. 1900
Charcoal and chalk on brown paper.
69.8×45.4 cm
Signed and dated, bottom right: *BC 900*
(VS, 1900)
The Russian Museum (since 1928).
Inv. No P-13445
Provenance: S. Botkin collection,
St. Petersburg; A. Botkina collection,
St. Petersburg
Exhibitions: 1935 The Tretyakov Gallery
(No 396), The Russian Museum (No 458);
1965 The Russian Museum; / 1974 The
Russian Museum — Drawings by Russian
Artists: Late 19th and Early 20th Centuries
(p. 20)
Reproductions: *Apollon*, 1912, No 10, be-
tween pp. 16 and 17; *Serov: Drawings,
Watercolors, Lithographs*, 1972, No 3
References: Grabar, *Serov*, 1965,
pp. 421, 422

380 (Plate 105)
Nude. 1900
Pencil, chalk and sanguine. 69.5×46 cm
Signed and dated, bottom right: *BC 1900*
(VS, 1900)
The I. Brodsky Memorial Museum,
Leningrad. Inv. No Бр-291
Provenance: A. Ostroumova-Lebedeva
collection, St. Petersburg/Leningrad;
I. Brodsky collection, Leningrad
Exhibitions: 1935 The Tretyakov Gallery
(No 725), The Russian Museum (No 689);
1965 The Russian Museum
Reproductions: Sternin, *Graphic Works by
Serov*, 1965, No 18
References: Grabar, *Serov*, 1965, p. 422;
*Serov in the Reminiscences of His Con-
temporaries*, 1971, 1, pp. 645, 650

381
Portrait of Sergei Botkin's Children.
1900
Graphite and crayons. 54×40 cm
Signed and dated, bottom right:
В. Съровъ 1900 (V. Serov, 1900)
The Tretyakov Gallery (since 1963).
Inv. No P-866
Provenance: S. Botkin collection,
St. Petersburg; A. Botkina collection,
St. Petersburg; A. Khokhlova collection,
Moscow
Alexandra Sergeyevna Khokhlova, née
Botkina (1891–?), and Anastasia Sergey-
evna Nothaft, née Botkina (1892–1942),
daughters of Sergei and Alexandra Botkin,
Serov's friends (see No 397).
Exhibitions: 1914 (posthumous) St. Peters-
burg (No 147), Moscow (No 157); 1946
Central House of Art Workers, Moscow
(No 186); 1952 Moscow (No 186);
1958–59 The Tretyakov Gallery; 1965 The

Tretyakov Gallery (p. 61); / 1901
St. Petersburg — 3rd Exhibition of Paint-
ings Organized by the *Mir Iskusstva*
Magazine (No 196, as *Portrait of Chil-
dren*); 1902 Moscow — Exhibition of
Paintings Organized by the *Mir Iskusstva*
Magazine (No 213); 1906 Paris, Berlin —
Russian Art (Nos 527, 433); 1946 Central
House of Art Workers, Moscow — Portraits by Russian Artists: 18th to Early
20th Century (No 74); 1949 The Pushkin
Museum of Fine Arts, Moscow — Russian
Graphic Art: 18th to Early 20th Century
Reproductions: *Mir Iskusstva*, 1901, No 4,
p. 110 (as *Children*); Grabar, *Serov*, 1914,
p. 138 (as *Botkin's Children*); Bernstein
1940, fig. 85; Grabar, *Serov the Draftsman*, 1961; Grabar, *Serov*, 1980, between
pp. 256 and 257
References: Grabar, *Serov*, 1914, pp. 143,
290 (as *Botkin's Children*); Bernstein
1940, p. 45; Grabar, *Serov*, 1965, pp. 278,
357 (as *Botkin's Children*); Liaskovskaya
1965, pp. 58, 59

382 (Plate 101)
Portrait of Sergei Botkin's Children.
1900
Black lead and watercolors on paper.
49.8×40.3 cm
Signed and dated, right: *В. Съровъ 1900*
(V. Serov, 1900)
The Russian Museum (since 1928).
Inv. No P-13439
Provenance: S. Botkin collection,
St. Petersburg; A. Botkina collection,
St. Petersburg
Sergei Botkin's children — see No 381.
Exhibitions: 1935 The Tretyakov Gallery
(No 399), The Russian Museum (No 462);
1958–59 The Tretyakov Gallery; 1959–60
The Russian Museum; 1965 The
Tretyakov Gallery (p. 61), The Russian
Museum; / 1974 The Russian Museum —
Drawings by Russian Artists: Late
19th and Early 20th Centuries (p. 20)
Reproductions: Sternin, *Graphic Works by
Serov*, 1965, No 20
References: Grabar, *Serov*, 1965, p. 357

383 (Plate 110)
**Portrait of Sophia Mikhailovna
Lukomskaya.** 1900
Watercolors and white on paper, mounted
on cardboard. 43×41 cm
Signed and dated, bottom right:
Съровъ 900 (Serov, 1900)
The Tretyakov Gallery (since 1918).
Inv. No 5664
Provenance: Z. Ratkova-Rozhnova collec-
tion, St. Petersburg
Sophia Mikhailovna Lukomskaya, née
Dragomirova — see No 149.
Exhibitions: 1914 (posthumous) St. Peters-
burg (No 144), Moscow (No 154); 1935
The Tretyakov Gallery (No 391), The Rus-
sian Museum (No 454); 1958–59 The Tre-
tyakov Gallery; 1965 The Tretyakov Gal-
lery (p. 61), The Russian Museum; / 1963
The Tretyakov Gallery — Pencil Drawings,
Watercolors, Pastels, and Gouaches
(p. 70)
Reproductions: Grabar, *Serov*, 1914, be-
tween pp. 152 and 153; Grabar, *Serov*,
1965, p. 156
References: Grabar, *Serov*, 1914, pp. 140,
189; Grabar, *Serov*, 1965, pp. 177, 336;
Liaskovskaya 1965, p. 58; Sarabyanov,
Reforms by Valentin Serov, 1971, p. 12

1901
PAINTINGS

384 (Plate 99)
**Mika Morozov. Portrait of
Mikhail Mikhailovich Morozov.** 1901
Oil on canvas. 62.3×70.6 cm
Signed and dated, top left: *Съровъ 1901*
(Serov, 1901)
The Tretyakov Gallery (since 1917).
Inv. No 5325
Provenance: M. Morozov collection, Mos-
cow; M. Morozova collection, Moscow
Mikhail (Mika) Mikhailovich Morozov
(1897–1952), son of Mikhail Abramovich
Morozov (see No 405), Soviet specialist
on Shakespeare, translator and art critic.
Exhibitions: 1914 (posthumous) St. Peters-
burg (No 153), Moscow (No 162); 1935
The Tretyakov Gallery (No 124a), The
Russian Museum (No 116); 1958–59 The
Tretyakov Gallery; 1959–60 The Russian
Museum; 1965 The Tretyakov Gallery
(p. 39), The Russian Museum; / 1902
St. Petersburg — 4th Exhibition of Paintings Organized by the *Mir Iskusstva*
Magazine (No 175, as *Portrait of a Child*);
1957 Warsaw — Russian Painting: 14th to
20th Century (No 87)
Reproductions: Grabar, *Serov*, 1914,
p. 147; Grabar, *Serov*, 1965, pp. 152
(detail), 154
References: Grabar, *Serov*, 1914, pp. 143,
290; Grabar, *Serov*, 1965, pp. 177, 337

385 (Plate 73)
Rinsing Linen. Study. ⟨1901⟩
Oil on cardboard. 47.5×66 cm
Signed, center left: *Съровъ* (Serov)
Present whereabouts unknown
Provenance: M. Riabushinsky collection,
Moscow; E. Helzer and T. Helzer collec-
tion, Moscow
Exhibitions: 1914 (posthumous) St. Peters-
burg (No 150), Moscow (No 160); 1946
Central House of Art Workers, Moscow
(No 11); 1952 Moscow (No 190); 1958–59
The Tretyakov Gallery; 1965 The
Tretyakov Gallery (p. 39); / 1901
St. Petersburg — 3rd Exhibition of Paint-
ings Organized by the *Mir Iskusstva*
Magazine (No 197, as *By the River*);
1901–2 Moscow — Thirty-six Painters
(No 154, as *Washerwoman by the River*);
1951–52 Central House of Art Workers,
Moscow — Russian Painting: Second Half
of the 19th and Early 20th Centuries
(No 229a); 1961–62 Art Museum, Minsk
— Works of Russian Art from Private Col-
lections (p. 25)
Reproductions: *Mir Iskusstva*, 1901, No 4,
p. 107 (as *By the River*); Grabar, *Serov*,
1914, p. 143; Sokolova, Vlasov 1959,
p. 49; Grabar, *Serov*, 1965, p. 197
References: Grabar, *Serov*, 1914, pp. 152,
290; Grabar, *Serov*, 1965, pp. 200, 422;
Fiodorov-Davydov 1965, No 2, p. 35

386
**Portrait of Alexander Vladimirovich
Sapozhnikov.** ⟨1900–1⟩
Oil on canvas. 69.5×53 cm
Signed, top right: *Съровъ* (Serov)
Present whereabouts unknown
Provenance: E. Sapozhnikova collection,
Moscow; P. Pokarzhevsky collection,
Moscow
Alexander Vladimirovich Sapozhnikov,
nephew of Natalia Polenova, wife of the

painter Vasily Polenov. The portrait was
executed from a photograph after Sapozh-
nikov's death.
Exhibitions: 1946 Central House of Art
Workers, Moscow (No 59); 1952 Moscow
(No 189); / 1951–52 Central House of Art
Workers, Moscow — Russian Painting:
Second Half of the 19th and Early
20th Centuries (No 229)
References: Grabar, *Serov*, 1965, p. 337

387
Portrait of A. M. Goriainov. 1901
Oil on canvas
Present whereabouts unknown
Provenance: M. Goriainova collection,
St. Petersburg
Exhibitions: 1902 Moscow — Exhibition of
Paintings Organized by the *Mir Iskusstva*
Magazine (No 212); 1902 St. Petersburg
— 4th Exhibition of Paintings Organized
by the *Mir Iskusstva* Magazine (No 172)
References: Grabar, *Serov*, 1914, p. 290;
Grabar, *Serov*, 1965, p. 337

388
**Portrait of Grand Duke
Georgy Mikhailovich.** 1901
Oil on canvas. 107×107 cm
Signed and dated, bottom left:
Съровъ 901 (Serov, 1901)
The Radishchev Art Museum, Saratov.
Inv. No 843
Georgy Mikhailovich (1863–1919), Grand
Duke, Curator of the Russian Museum
since 1897.
Exhibitions: 1905 St. Petersburg —
Russian Portrait Painting (No 1614)
Reproductions: Grabar, *Serov*, 1914,
p. 145; Leniashin 1980, p. 66
References: Grabar, *Serov*, 1914, pp. 143,
290; Grabar, *Serov*, 1965, pp. 185, 337

389
**Portrait of Pavel Ivanovich
Kharitonenko.** 1901
Oil on canvas. 57×55 cm
Signed and dated, left: *Съровъ 901*
(Serov, 1901)
The Tretyakov Gallery. Inv. No 15696
Pavel Ivanovich Kharitonenko
(1852–1914), a sugar mill owner and art
collector.
Exhibitions: 1935 The Tretyakov Gallery
(No 1246), The Russian Museum
(No 117); 1958–59 The Tretyakov Gallery
Reproductions: Leniashin 1980, p. 240
References: Grabar, *Serov*, 1965, pp. 174,
337

390
**Portrait of Piotr Mikhailovich
Romanov.** ⟨1901⟩
Oil on canvas. 70×60 cm (approx.)
The Malmö Museum, Sweden
Provenance: P. Romanov collection,
St. Petersburg; A. Romanova collection,
St. Petersburg
Piotr Mikhailovich Romanov (1851–1911),
official of the Ministry of Finance, collector
of works by Russian artists.
Exhibitions: 1914 (posthumous) St. Peters-
burg (No 154), Moscow (No 163); / 1902
St. Petersburg — 4th Exhibition of Paint-
ings Organized by the *Mir Iskusstva*
Magazine (No 173, as *Portrait of Mr. R.*);
1914 Malmö (Sweden) — Baltic
Art Exhibition (No 3224)
Reproductions: Grabar, *Serov*, 1914,
p. 149

References: Grabar, *Serov*, 1914, p. 290;
Grabar, *Serov*, 1965, p. 337

391
Barns. Study. ⟨1901⟩
Oil on canvas. 50×65 cm
Signed, bottom right: *BC* (VS)
Art Museum, Kirov (since 1927).
Inv. No Ж-310
Exhibitions: 1935 The Tretyakov Gallery
(No 116), The Russian Museum (No 110);
1958—59 The Tretyakov Gallery;
1959—60 The Russian Museum
Reproductions: *Art Museum, Kirov. Cata-
logue*, 1964 (undated)
References: Grabar, *Serov*, 1965, p. 448
(undated works); Simonovich-Yefimova
1964, pp. 75, 76

392
Haystack. 1901
Oil on canvas. 71×135 cm
Signed, bottom left: *Съровъ 901*
(Serov, 1901)
The Radishchev Art Museum, Saratov
(since 1927). Inv. No 841
Provenance: V. Girshman collection, Mos-
cow; State Museum Reserve, Moscow
Exhibitions: 1914 (posthumous) St. Peters-
burg (No 151), Moscow (No 161); 1935
The Tretyakov Gallery (No 124), The Rus-
sian Museum (No 115); 1959–60 The Rus-
sian Museum; / 1902 St. Petersburg —
4th Exhibition of Paintings Organized by
the *Mir Iskusstva* Magazine (No 178, as
Barn); 1902 Moscow — Exhibition Or-
ganized by the *Mir Iskusstva* Magazine
(No 216, under the same title); 1906 Paris
— Russian Art (No 522, as *Paysage*)
Reproductions: *Mir Iskusstva*, 1902,
Nos 1–6, p. 292; Grabar, *Serov*, 1914,
p. 144
References: Grabar, *Serov*, 1914, pp. 152,
290; Grabar, *Serov*, 1965, pp. 200, 422;
Fiodorov-Davydov 1965, No 2, pp. 35, 39

393 (Plate 64)
Haystack. ⟨1901⟩
Oil on canvas. 50×61 cm
Picture Gallery, Yerevan (since 1939).
Inv. No Ж-1525

Provenance: N. Smirnov collection,
St. Petersburg; N. Dobychina collection,
St. Petersburg
A study for the similarly titled picture of
1901, now at the Radishchev Art Museum,
Saratov (see No 392).
Exhibitions: 1914 (posthumous) St. Peters-
burg (No 152 — 3rd and 4th ed.), Moscow
(No 161); 1935 The Tretyakov Gallery
(No 197), The Russian Museum (No 115a
— 2nd ed.); 1959–60 The Russian
Museum; 1965 The Russian Museum
Reproductions: Grabar, *Serov*, 1914,
p. 290; Grabar, *Serov*, 1965, p. 422
(as *Haystack near a Barn*)

**DRAWINGS,
WATERCOLORS,
GOUACHES,
AND LITHOGRAPHS**

394 (Plate 97)
Self-portrait. ⟨1901⟩
Watercolors. 49.5×36 cm
Picture Gallery, Odessa (since 1926).
Inv. No Г-1013
Provenance: V. Mathé collection,
St. Petersburg; M. Braikevich collection,
Odessa
Exhibitions: 1914 (posthumous) St. Peters-
burg (No 258, dated 1909), Moscow
(No 284, the same wrong date); 1935 The
Tretyakov Gallery (not listed in the cata-
logue), The Russian Museum (No 470);
1958–59 The Tretyakov Gallery; 1959
Museum of Russian Art, Kiev; 1959–60
The Russian Museum; 1965 The
Tretyakov Gallery (p. 62); / 1926 Odessa
— Paintings from the Odessa Art Museum
Reserve (No 110)
Reproductions: Grabar, *Serov*, 1914,
p. 269 (dated 1909); *Apollon*, 1914,
Nos 6/7, between pp. 4 and 5 (the same
wrong date); Dmitriyev, *Serov*, 1917 (the
same wrong date)
References: Grabar, *Serov*, 1914, p. 293
(dated 1909); Grabar, *Serov*, 1965, p. 357;
Liaskovskaya 1965, p. 58

395 (Plate 128)
The Tsar's Borzois. ⟨1900–1⟩
Pencil, colored pencil and chalk on gray
paper. 22.5×29.6 cm
Right, the artist's inscription: *Царская
охота борзыя Гатчина* (Royal Hunt. Bor-
zois. Gatchina)
Present whereabouts unknown
Provenance: M. Riabushinsky collection,
Moscow
Exhibitions: 1914 (posthumous) St. Peters-
burg (No 145), Moscow (No 155)
Reproductions: Grabar, *Serov*, 1914,
p. 140
References: Grabar, *Serov*, 1914, p. 290;
Grabar, *Serov*, 1965, p. 421

396 (Plate 132)
**Portrait of Vladimir Vladimirovich
von Meck.** 1901
Charcoal. 53.5×36 cm
Signed and dated, bottom right:
В. Съровъ 1901 (V. Serov, 1901)
The Tretyakov Gallery (since 1962).
Inv. No П-33710
Provenance: V. von Meck collection, Mos-
cow; E. Helzer and T. Helzer collection,
Moscow
Vladimir Vladimirovich von Meck
(1877–1932), art collector.
Exhibitions: 1935 The Tretyakov Gallery
(No 407); 1952 Moscow; 1958–59 The
Tretyakov Gallery; 1965 The Tretyakov

Gallery (p. 62); / 1961–62 Art Museum,
Minsk — Works of Russian Art from Private Collections (p. 33); 1963 The Tretyakov Gallery — Pencil Drawings, Watercolors, Pastels, and Gouaches (p. 70)
Reproductions: Grabar, *Serov the Draftsman*, 1961
References: Grabar, *Serov*, 1965, p. 357;
Liaskovskaya 1965, pp. 60, 61

397 (Plate 93)
**Portrait of Sergei Sergeyevich
Botkin.** ⟨1900–1⟩
Watercolors. 43.6×35.3 cm
Signed, bottom right: *В Съровъ* (V. Serov)
The Russian Museum (since 1928).
Inv. No P-13430
Provenance: S. Botkin collection,
St. Petersburg; A. Botkina collection,
St. Petersburg
Sergei Sergeyevich Botkin (1859–1910),
physician, Professor of the Military Medical
Academy, member of the Academy of Arts
Board (since 1905).
The date of the portrait is unknown. In the
manner of execution it is close to Serov's
watercolors of 1900–2, such as the portrait
of Botkin's children (see No 382) and the
portrait of Ilya Repin (see No 398). The
dating of the portrait to 1906 in some
sources (*Serov's Works. The Tretyakov
Gallery. Catalogue*, 1935, No 723; *Serov's
Works. The Russian Museum. Catalogue*,

1935, No 690; Grabar, *Serov*, 1965,
p. 363) disagrees with the stylistic features
of the portrait and is undoubtedly erroneous. An earlier dating is corroborated by a
comparison of the portrait with the drawing
*Anton Arensky, Sergei Botkin and Alexan-
der Glazunov Playing Cards* dated 1902
(see No 410).
Exhibitions: 1935 The Tretyakov Gallery
(No 723), The Russian Museum (No 690);
1965 The Russian Museum
Reproductions: *Essays on the History of
Russian Portraiture*, 1964, p. 58
References: *Essays on the History of Russian Portraiture*, 1964, pp. 57, 59, 60, 413;
Grabar, *Serov*, 1965, p. 363 (dated 1906);
Liaskovskaya 1965, p. 58 (described incor-
rectly as executed in India ink)

398 (Plate 111)
**Portrait of Ilya Yefimovich
Repin.** 1901
Watercolors and white. 34.6×35 cm
Signed and dated, bottom left:
Съровъ 1901 (Serov, 1901)
The Russian Museum (since 1928).
Inv. No P-13443
Provenance: S. Botkin collection,
St. Petersburg; A. Botkina collection,
St. Petersburg
Ilya Yefimovich Repin — see No 21.
Exhibitions: 1935 The Tretyakov Gallery
(No 406), The Russian Museum (No 469);
1965 The Russian Museum
Reproductions: Grabar, *Serov*, 1914,
p. 146; Grabar, *Serov*, 1965, p. 155
References: Grabar, *Serov*, 1914, pp. 140,
290; Yaremich, *Serov: Drawings*, 1936,
p. 15; Grabar, *Serov*, 1965, pp. 177, 337;
Liaskovskaya 1965, p. 58

399
**Portrait of Ilya Yefimovich
Repin.** 1901
Lithograph. 33.3×25.4 cm
Signed and dated, bottom left: *1901 г.
В. Съровъ* (1901, V. Serov)
The Russian Museum. Inv. No Гр-40330
Ilya Yefimovich Repin — see No 21.
A print was made in I. Kadushin's
chromolithographic shop, St. Petersburg,
as a supplement to No 10 of the *Mir
Iskusstva* magazine for 1901 (between
pp. 88, 89)
Exhibitions: 1935 The Russian Museum
(No 1068); 1965 The Russian Museum
NOTE: A print from the P. Kornilov collec-
tion, Leningrad, was exhibited at Serov's
one-man show of 1952 in Moscow
(No 410).
Reproductions: Yaremich, *Serov: Draw-
ings*, 1936; *Serov: Drawings, Watercolors,
Lithographs*, 1972, No 14
References: Grabar, *Serov*, 1914, p. 298
(erroneously listed as an etching dated
1899): Grabar, *Serov*, 1965, p. 356
(as *The Artist Ilya Yefimovich Repin*)

1902
PAINTINGS

400 (Plate 129)
**Catherine II Setting Out to Hunt
with Falcons.** ⟨1902⟩
Tempera on cardboard. 23×40 cm
Signed, top right: *Съровъ* (Serov)
The Russian Museum (since 1912).
Inv. No Ж-4292

106. Barns. Study. Cat. No 391

107. Haystack. Cat. No 392

108. Portrait of
Zinaida Nikolayevna Yusupova.
Cat. No 404

Provenance: M. Kutepov collection,
Gatchina
Catherine II (1729–1796), Empress of
Russia (1762–96).
Exhibitions: 1935 The Tretyakov Gallery
(No 130), The Russian Museum (No 123);
1958–59 The Tretyakov Gallery; 1965 The
Tretyakov Gallery (p. 40), The Russian
Museum; / 1903 St. Petersburg —
5th Exhibition of Paintings Organized by
the *Mir Iskusstva* Magazine (No 287);
1906 Paris, Berlin — Russian Art
(Nos 518, 429); 1911 Rome — Inter-
national Art Exhibition (No 388); 1939
The Tretyakov Gallery — Russian History
Painting (No 330)
Reproductions: *Royal Hunting in Russia*,
1902, between pp. 126 and 127; *Apollon*,
1912, No 10, between pp. 22 and 23;
Grabar, *Serov*, 1914, between pp. 256
and 257; Grabar, *Serov*, 1965, p. 207
References: Grabar, *Serov*, 1914, pp. 242,
246, 290; Grabar, *Serov*, 1965, pp. 207,
423; Sarabyanov, *Reforms by Valentin
Serov*, 1971, p. 16

401
A Shepherd Boy. Study. 1902
Oil on mahogany. 16×22 cm
Signed and dated, bottom right:
В. Съровъ 1902 (V. Serov, 1902)
N. Sokolov collection, Moscow
(since 1952)
Provenance: V. Pavlov collection,
Leningrad
Exhibitions: 1935 The Russian Museum
(No 122); 1952 Moscow (No 196)
References: Grabar, *Serov*, 1965, p. 423

402 (Plate 131)
Peter the Great Riding to Hounds. 1902
Tempera on cardboard. 29×50 cm
Signed and dated, bottom right:
Съровъ 1902 (Serov, 1902)
The Russian Museum (since 1912).
Inv. No Ж-4290

109. Tsarskoye Selo. Avenue
near the Catherine Palace.
Study. Cat. No 409

328

Provenance: M. Kutepov collection,
Gatchina
Peter the Great (1672–1725), Tsar of
Russia (1682–1725).
Exhibitions: 1935 The Tretyakov Gallery
(No 131), The Russian Museum (No 124);
1965 The Tretyakov Gallery (p. 40), The
Russian Museum; / 1903 St. Petersburg —
5th Exhibition of Paintings Organized by
the *Mir Iskusstva* Magazine (No 286, as
Peter the Great Hunting); 1906 Paris, Ber-
lin — Russian Art (Nos 517, 428); 1911
Rome — International Art Exhibition
(No 386); 1939 The Tretyakov Gallery —
Russian History Painting (No 329)
Reproductions: *Royal Hunting in Russia*,
1902, between pp. 174 and 175; *Apollon*,
1912, No 10, between pp. 22 and 23 (as
Young Peter the Great Hunting); Grabar,
Serov, 1914, between pp. 248 and 249 (as
Young Peter the Great Riding to Hounds);
Grabar, *Serov*, 1965, p. 203 (under the
same title)
References: Grabar, *Serov*, 1914, pp. 242,
246, 290; Grabar, *Serov*, 1965, pp. 205,
206, 422; Sarabyanov, *Reforms by Valen-
tin Serov*, 1971, p. 16

403 (Plates 118, 119)
**Portrait of Zinaida Nikolayevna
Yusupova.** ⟨1900–2⟩
Oil on canvas. 181.5×133 cm
The Russian Museum (since 1925).
Inv. No Ж-4307
Provenance: F. Sumarokov-Elstone
collection, St. Petersburg
Zinaida Nikolayevna Yusupova
(1861–1939), Princess, member of one of
the wealthiest aristocratic families in pre-

revolutionary Russia, was the last of the
Yusupov line. When she married Count
Felix Felixovich Sumarokov-Elstone (see
No 425), her husband was allowed, on the
Tsar's special decree, to add to his name
the title and maiden name of his wife.
Exhibitions: 1935 The Tretyakov Gallery
(No 132), The Russian Museum (No 125);
1959–60 The Russian Museum; 1965 The
Tretyakov Gallery (p. 40), The Russian
Museum; / 1902 Moscow — Exhibition of
Paintings Organized by the *Mir Iskusstva*
Magazine (No 208); 1902 St. Petersburg
— 4th Exhibition of Paintings Organized
by the *Mir Iskusstva* Magazine (No 171)
Reproductions: *Mir Iskusstva*, 1902,
Nos 1–6, p. 299; Grabar, *Serov*, 1914,
p. 151; Grabar, *Serov*, 1965, p. 189;
Grabar, *Serov*, 1980, pl. 50
References: Grabar, *Serov*, 1914,
pp. 144, 145, 290; Grabar, *Serov*, 1965,
pp. 185, 336, 337; Leniashin 1980,
pp. 73–105

404
**Portrait of Zinaida Nikolayevna
Yusupova.** ⟨1900–2⟩
Oil on canvas. 97.5×66 cm
Art Museum, Gorky (since 1927).
Inv. No 621
Provenance: The Russian Museum
Zinaida Nikolayevna Yusupova — see
No 403.
Exhibitions: 1935 The Tretyakov Gallery
(No 133), The Russian Museum (No 126)
Reproductions: *Serov's Works. The Tret-
yakov Gallery. Catalogue*, 1935; *The Gor-
ky Art Museum: Picture Gallery*, Lenin-
grad, Aurora Art Publishers, 1973, No 54
References: Grabar, *Serov*, 1965, p. 338

405 (Plate 102)
Portrait of Mikhail Abramovich Morozov. 1902
Oil on canvas. 215.5×80.8 cm
Signed and dated, bottom left:
Съровъ 1902 (Serov, 1902)
The Tretyakov Gallery (since 1917).
Inv. No 5337
Provenance: M. Morozov collection, Moscow; M. Morozova collection, Moscow
Mikhail Abramovich Morozov (1870–1903), Moscow millionaire, one of the owners of the Tver Textile Mill, collector of modern Russian and French paintings.
Exhibitions: 1914 (posthumous) St. Petersburg (No 156), Moscow (No 165); 1935 The Tretyakov Gallery (No 125), The Russian Museum (No 118); 1952 Moscow (No 197); 1958–59 The Tretyakov Gallery; 1959 Museum of Russian Art, Kiev; 1959–60 The Russian Museum; 1965 The Tretyakov Gallery (p. 39), The Russian Museum; / 1902 Moscow — Exhibition of Paintings Organized by the *Mir Iskusstva* Magazine (No 210); 1903 St. Petersburg — 5th Exhibition of Paintings Organized by the *Mir Iskusstva* Magazine (No 280); 1906 Paris — Russian Art (No 513); 1911 Rome — International Art Exhibition (No 393)
Reproductions: *Mir Iskusstva*, 1903, No 9, between pp. 140 and 141; Grabar, *Serov*, 1914, between pp. 168 and 169; Grabar, *Serov*, 1965, p. 153
References: Grabar, *Serov*, 1914, pp. 146–148, 150, 290; Grabar, *Serov*, 1965, pp. 157, 160, 168, 169, 337; Sarabyanov, *Reforms by Valentin Serov*, 1971, pp. 23, 24; Leniashin 1980, pp. 41–72

406 (Plate 125)
Portrait of Ilya Semionovich Ostroukhov. 1902
Oil on canvas. 82×76 cm
Signed and dated, top left: *Съровъ 1902* (Serov, 1902)
The Tretyakov Gallery (since 1929).
Inv. No 11185
Provenance: I. Ostroukhov collection, Moscow; The Ostroukhov Museum of Icons and Painting, Moscow
Ilya Semionovich Ostroukhov — see No 108.
Exhibitions: 1914 (posthumous) St. Petersburg (No 157), Moscow (No 166); 1935 The Tretyakov Gallery (No 126), The Russian Museum (No 119); 1958–59 The Tretyakov Gallery; 1959 Museum of Russian Art, Kiev; 1959–60 The Russian Museum; 1965 The Tretyakov Gallery (pp. 39, 40), The Russian Museum; / 1903 St. Petersburg — 5th Exhibition of Paintings Organized by the *Mir Iskusstva* Magazine (No 279)
Reproductions: *Mir Iskusstva*, 1903, No 7/8, p. 9; *Apollon*, 1911, No 10, between pp. 4 and 5; Grabar, *Serov*, 1914, p. 153; Grabar, *Serov*, 1965, p. 159
References: Grabar, *Serov*, 1914, pp. 140, 290; Grabar, *Serov*, 1965, pp. 177, 337

407 (Plate 117)
A Finnish Yard. 1902
Oil on cardboard. 75×99.5 cm
Signed and dated, bottom right:
Съровъ 1902 (Serov, 1902)
The Tretyakov Gallery (since 1913).
Inv. No 1530

Provenance: A. Golenishchev-Kutuzov collection, St. Petersburg
Exhibitions: 1935 The Tretyakov Gallery (No 127), The Russian Museum (No 120); 1965 The Russian Museum; / 1903 St. Petersburg — 5th Exhibition of Paintings Organized by the *Mir Iskusstva* Magazine (No 282, as *A Cow*); 1911 Rome — International Art Exhibition (No 404); 1925 The Tretyakov Gallery — Women in Russian Painting (No 48)
Reproductions: Grabar, *Serov*, 1914, p. 157; Zotov, *Serov*, 1964, No 20
References: Grabar, *Serov*, 1914, pp. 154, 290; Grabar, *Serov*, 1965, p. 423

408 (Plate 116)
A Mill in Finland. 1902
Oil on cardboard. 43.5×64.9 cm
Signed and dated, bottom right:
Съровъ 1902 (Serov, 1902)
The Tretyakov Gallery.
Inv. No 4704
Provenance: S. Bakhrushin collection, Moscow; State Museum Reserve, Moscow
Exhibitions: 1935 The Tretyakov Gallery (No 128), The Russian Museum (No 121); 1958–59 The Tretyakov Gallery; 1959 Museum of Russian Art, Kiev; 1959–60 The Russian Museum; 1965 The Tretyakov Gallery (p. 40), The Russian Museum; / 1903 St. Petersburg — 5th Exhibition of Paintings Organized by the *Mir Iskusstva* Magazine (No 285)
Reproductions: *Mir Iskusstva*, 1903, No 7/8, p. 14; *Khudozhnik*, 1965, No 2, p. 39
References: Grabar, *Serov*, 1914, p. 290 (as *A Mill*. A study painted on the Chornaya River, near Terijoki; erroneously dated 1903); Grabar, *Serov*, 1965, p. 423; Fiodorov-Davydov 1965, No 2, p. 39

409
Tsarskoye Selo. Avenue near the Catherine Palace. Study. ⟨1900–2⟩
Oil on mahogany. 40.5×20.5 cm
M. Kupriyanov collection, Moscow
Provenance: The Serov family collection, Moscow
Exhibitions: 1935 The Tretyakov Gallery (No 134), The Russian Museum (No 127); 1946 Central House of Art Workers, Moscow (No 46); 1952 Moscow (No 193);

1958–59 The Tretyakov Gallery; 1965 The Tretyakov Gallery (p. 40)
References: Grabar, *Serov*, 1965, p. 422

DRAWINGS AND WATERCOLORS

410
Anton Arensky, Sergei Botkin and Alexander Glazunov Playing Cards. 1902
Graphite on yellow paper. 34.9×51.1 cm
Signed and dated, bottom right:
В. Съровъ 1902 (V. Serov, 1902)
The Russian Museum (since 1926).
Inv. No P-13450
Provenance: A. Ziloti collection, St. Petersburg
Anton Stepanovich Arensky (1861–1906), composer; Sergei Sergeyevich Botkin — see No 397; Alexander Konstantinovich Glazunov — see No 348.
Exhibitions: 1914 (posthumous) St. Petersburg (No 159), Moscow (No 169); 1935 The Tretyakov Gallery (No 413), The Russian Museum (No 476); / 1974 The Russian Museum — Drawings by Russian Artists: Late 19th and Early 20th Centuries (p. 20)
Reproductions: Grabar, *Serov*, 1914, p. 152
References: Grabar, *Serov*, 1914, pp. 143, 290; Grabar, *Serov*, 1965, p. 358

411
The Tsar's Borzoi. ⟨1902⟩
Graphite, crayons and chalk on brown paper. 22.4×23.6 cm
The artist's inscription in pencil, top right: *Царск борзая Гатчина* (The Tsar's Borzoi, Gatchina); bottom left, an impression of the artist's signet: *ВС* (VS)
The Tretyakov Gallery (since 1911).
Inv. No 3658
A preparatory drawing for the painting *Peter the Great Riding to Hounds* of 1902, now in the Russian Museum (see No 402).
Exhibitions: 1914 (posthumous) St. Petersburg (No 146 — 3rd and 4th ed.), Moscow (No 156); 1935 The Tretyakov Gallery (No 405), The Russian Museum (No 468); 1958–59 The Tretyakov Gallery; 1965 The Tretyakov Gallery (p. 63),

111. The Tsar's Borzoi.
Cat. No 411

The Russian Museum
Reproductions: *Apollon*, 1912, No 10,
p. 19; *Drawings and Watercolors. Cata-*
logue, 1956; *Serov: Drawings, Water-*
colors, Lithographs, 1972, No 5 (as
A Borzoi)
References: Grabar, *Serov*, 1965, pp. 422,
423 (as *The Tsar's Borzoi*)

112. Catherine II Setting Out
to Hunt with Falcons.
Cat. No 413

412
Playing Duets. Portrait of
Ilya Ostroukhov and Sergei Diaghilev.
⟨1902⟩
Pencil. 10.4×16.5 cm
The Tretyakov Gallery (since 1960).
Inv. No P-617
Provenance: N. Ostroukhova collection,
Moscow; F. Toskin collection, Moscow;
B. Chernogubov collection, Moscow;
V. Chernogubova collection, Moscow
Sergei Pavlovich Diaghilev (1872–1929),
Russian ballet producer, art critic, and pro-
moter of Russian fine arts, music,
and theater abroad; Ilya Semionovich
Ostroukhov — see No 108.
Exhibitions: 1935 The Tretyakov Gallery
(No 409), The Russian Museum (No 472);
1952 Moscow (No 201); 1965 The
Tretyakov Gallery (p. 63); / 1954 Central
House of Art Workers, Moscow — Por-
traits of Prominent Personalities in Rus-
sian Art: 18th to 20th Century (No 209)
References: Grabar, *Serov*, 1965, p. 358

413
Catherine II Setting Out to Hunt
with Falcons. ⟨1900–2⟩
Graphite on paper, heightened with cray-
ons. 31.5×57.2 cm
Bottom right, an impression of the artist's
signet: *BC* (VS)
The Russian Museum (since 1928).
Inv. No P-3224
Catherine II — see No 400.
Provenance: S. Botkin collection,
St. Petersburg; A. Botkina collection,
St. Petersburg
A sketch for the painting of the same
name, now in the Russian Museum
(see No. 400).
Exhibitions: 1935 The Tretyakov Gallery
(No 417), The Russian Museum (No 485)
References: Grabar, *Serov*, 1965, p. 423

113. Catherine II Setting Out
to Hunt with Falcons.
Cat. No 414

414
Catherine II Setting Out to Hunt
with Falcons. 1900–2
Pencil. 17.8×21.9 cm
The Russian Museum (since 1928).
Inv. No P-3164
Provenance: A. Rumanov collection,
St. Petersburg

A sketch for the painting of the same
name, now in the Russian Museum
(see No 400).
Catherine II — see No 400.
Exhibitions: 1935 The Russian Museum
(No 486)
References: Grabar, *Serov*, 1965, p. 423

415
Portrait of Alexei Petrovich
Langovoi. 1902
Watercolor and white. 29×23 cm
Signed and dated, bottom right:
Съровъ 1902 (Serov, 1902)
The Tretyakov Gallery (since 1944).
Inv. No 26553
Provenance: A. Langovoi collection,
Moscow
Alexei Petrovich Langovoi (1857–1939),
physician, public figure and art collector.
Exhibitions: 1914 (posthumous) St. Peters-
burg (No 161), Moscow (No 171); 1935
The Russian Museum (No 483a); / 1914
Malmö (Sweden) — Baltic Art Exhibition
(No 3215); 1963 The Tretyakov Gallery —
Pencil Drawings, Watercolors, Pastels,
and Gouaches (p. 70)
Reproductions: Grabar, *Serov*, 1914,
p. 158; *Essays on the History of the Rus-*
sian Portrait, 1964, p. 63
References: Grabar, *Serov*, 1914, pp. 143,
290; Grabar, *Serov*, 1965, pp. 337, 338

416 (Plate 112)
Portrait of Vera Pavlovna Ziloti. 1902
Charcoal and chalk on yellow paper.
76×94 cm
Signed and dated, bottom left: *В. Съ-*
ровъ 1902 (V. Serov, 1902). The Russian
Museum (since 1926). Inv. No P-13444
Provenance: A. and V. Ziloti collection,
St. Petersburg; A. Bobrinsky collection
Vera Pavlovna Ziloti (1866–1939), eldest
daughter of Pavel Mikhailovich Tretyakov,
wife of the pianist and conductor A. Ziloti.
Exhibitions: 1914 (posthumous) St. Peters-
burg (No 158), Moscow (No 168); 1935
The Tretyakov Gallery (No 414), The Rus-
sian Museum (No 477); 1958–59 The Tretyakov Gallery; 1959 Museum of Russian
Art, Kiev; 1959–60 The Russian Museum;
1965 The Tretyakov Gallery (p. 62), The
Russian Museum; / 1903 St. Petersburg —
5th Exhibition of Paintings Organized by
the *Mir Iskusstva* Magazine (No 278)
Reproductions: Grabar, *Serov*, 1914,
p. 148; Grabar, *Serov*, 1980, pl. 61
References: Grabar, *Serov*, 1914, pp. 143,
290; Grabar, *Serov*, 1965, pp. 357, 358;
Liaskovskaya 1965, p. 59

417
Portrait of Zinaida Nikolayevna
Yusupova. ⟨1902⟩
Graphite, sanguine and crayons.
39.3×47.3 cm

The Russian Museum (since 1928).
Inv. No P-13437
Provenance: S. Botkin collection,
St. Petersburg; A. Botkina collection,
St. Petersburg
Zinaida Nikolayevna Yusupova — see
No 403.
Exhibitions: 1935 The Tretyakov Gallery
(No 415), The Russian Museum (No 478);
1958–59 The Russian Museum; 1965 The
Tretyakov Gallery (p. 62), The Russian
Museum
References: Grabar, *Serov*, 1965, p. 359
(dated 1903)

418 (Plate 114)
**Portrait of Konstantin Petrovich
Pobedonostsev.** 1902
Charcoal, crayons and sanguine.
56×43 cm
Signed and dated, bottom right:
В. Сѣровъ 1902 СПБ (V. Serov, 1902,
St. P[etersburg])
The Russian Museum (since 1918).
Inv. No P-13429
Provenance: A. Naryshkina collection,
St. Petersburg
Konstantin Petrovich Pobedonostsev
(1827–1907), reactionary government ad-
ministrator, Ober-Procurator of the Holy
Synod.
Exhibitions: 1935 The Tretyakov Gallery
(No 412), The Russian Museum
(No 475); / 1974 The Russian Museum —
Drawings by Russian Artists: Late
19th and Early 20th Centuries (p. 20)
Reproductions: Grabar, *Serov*, 1914,
p. 159; Grabar, *Serov*, 1965, p. 262
References: Grabar, *Serov*, 1914, pp. 143,
164, 290 (described incorrectly as a pas-
tel); Grabar, *Serov*, 1965, p. 357; Liaskovskaya 1965, p. 55

1903
PAINTINGS

419
**Peter the Great in the Palace
of Monplaisir.** ⟨1903⟩
Oil on canvas
Present whereabouts unknown
Provenance: S. Bykhovsky collection,
St. Petersburg
The first version of the painting at which
Serov worked between 1903 and 1911
(see No 402).

Exhibitions: 1914 (posthumous) St. Peters-
burg (No 177, dated 1904), Moscow
(No 187, the same wrong date)
References: Grabar, *Serov*, 1914, p. 294;
Grabar, *Serov*, 1965, pp. 440, 441

420 (Plate 122)
Terrace with a Balustrade. ⟨1903⟩
Oil on canvas. 49.5×63 cm
The Russian Museum (since 1958).
Inv. No Ж-6773
Provenance: O. Serova collection,
Moscow; A. Rimsky-Korsakov collection,
St. Petersburg; E. Nikolai collection, Lenin-
grad; B. Podvysotsky collection, Leningrad
A study for the portrait of Prince Felix
Yusupov, Count Sumarokov-Elstone
(see No 425).
Exhibitions: 1914 (posthumous) St. Peters-
burg (No 171); 1935 The Tretyakov Gal-
lery (No 139), The Russian Museum
(No 129)
References: Grabar, *Serov*, 1965, p. 424

421
**Portrait of Boris Nikolayevich
Chicherin.** 1903
Oil on canvas. 128×89 cm
Signed and dated, bottom right:
Сѣровъ 903 (Serov, 1903)
Picture Gallery, Tambov (since 1961).
Inv. No Ж-158
Provenance: A. Chicherina collection,
Tambov province
Boris Nikolayevich Chicherin (1828–1904),
Russian historian and philosopher, Profes-
sor of Moscow University, eminent public
figure.
Exhibitions: 1914 (posthumous) St. Peters-
burg (No 166a — 3rd and 4th ed.), Mos-
cow (No 176); 1935 The Tretyakov Gallery
(No 138), The Russian Museum (No 128)
Reproductions: Grabar, *Serov*, 1914,
p. 154 (dated 1902)
References: Grabar, *Serov*, 1914, pp. 143,
290 (dated 1902); Grabar, *Serov*, 1965,
p. 338

422 (Plate 126)
**Portrait of Yevdokia Ivanovna
Loseva.** 1903
Oil on canvas. 97×112 cm
Signed and dated, bottom right:
Сѣровъ 1903 (Serov, 1903)
The Tretyakov Gallery (since 1946).
Inv. No 27314

Provenance: Ye. Loseva collection,
Moscow
Yevdokia Ivanovna Loseva, née Chizhova
(1881–1936), artist, Serov's pupil.
Exhibitions: 1914 (posthumous) St. Peters-
burg (No 167), Moscow (No 177); 1935
The Tretyakov Gallery (No 140), The Rus-
sian Museum (No 130); 1952 Moscow
(No 202); 1958–59 The Tretyakov Gallery;
1959 Museum of Russian Art, Kiev;
1959–60 The Russian Museum; / 1903
St. Petersburg — 5th Exhibition of Paint-
ings Organized by the *Mir Iskusstva*
Magazine (No 281); 1962 Budapest —
Russian and Soviet Art: 18th to 20th
Century
Reproductions: *Mir Iskusstva*, 1903,
No 7/8, p. 17; Grabar, *Serov*, 1914, p. 162;
Grabar, *Serov*, 1980, pl. 64
References: Grabar, *Serov*, 1914, p. 290;
Grabar, *Serov*, 1965, p. 338

423 (Plate 120)
**Portrait of Nikolai Felixovich
Sumarokov-Elstone.** 1903
Oil on canvas. 89×68 cm
Signed and dated, bottom left: *B.C. 903*
(V. S., 1903)
The Russian Museum (since 1921).
Inv. No Ж-4305
Provenance: F. Sumarokov-Elstone
collection, St. Petersburg
Count Nikolai Felixovich Sumarokov-
Elstone (1882–1908), son of Felix Felix-
ovich (see No 425) and Zinaida Nikolayev-
na (see No 403) Yusupov.
Exhibitions: 1935 The Russian Museum
(No 133); 1959–60 The Russian Museum;
1965 The Russian Museum; / 1959 Lenin-
grad — Russian Portrait Painting: 18th to
Early 20th Century
Reproductions: *Khudozhnik*, 1978, No 2,
p. 47 (as *Portrait of Nikolai Yusupov*)
References: Grabar, *Serov*, 1965, pp. 188,
190, 338; Leniashin 1980, pp. 73–105

424 (Plate 121)
**Portrait of Felix Felixovich
Sumarokov-Elstone with a Dog.** 1903
Oil on canvas. 89×71.5 cm
Signed and dated, bottom right:
B. Сѣровъ 903 (V. Serov, 1903)
The Russian Museum (since 1921).
Inv. No Ж-4304
Provenance: F. Sumarokov-Elstone collec-
tion, St. Petersburg
Count Felix Felixovich Sumarokov-Elstone
(1887–1967), later Prince Yusupov, son of

114. Portrait of
Zinaida Nikolayevna Yusupova.
Cat. No 417

115. Portrait of
Alexei Petrovich Langovoi.
Cat. No 415

331

116. Yura and Sasha,
Serov's Children. Cat. No 431

117. Portrait of Eugène Ysaïe.
Cat. No 426

Felix Felixovich (see No 425) and Zinaida
Nikolayevna (see No 403) Yusupov.
Exhibitions: 1935 The Tretyakov Gallery
(No 145), The Russian Museum (No 132);
1958–59 The Tretyakov Gallery; 1959–60
The Russian Museum; 1965 The Tret-
yakov Gallery (p. 41), The Russian
Museum; / 1905 St. Petersburg — Russian
Portrait Painting (No 1615); 1906 Paris,
Berlin — Russian Art (Nos 510, 422);
1975 The Russian Museum — Russian
Portrait Painting: Late 19th and Early
20th Centuries (No 195); 1976–77 Frank-
fort on the Main, Munich, Hamburg —
Russian Painting: 1890 to 1917 (No 11)
Reproductions: Grabar, *Serov*, 1914,
p. 165; Grabar, *Serov*, 1980, pl. 62, 63
References: Grabar, *Serov*, 1914, pp. 143,
290 (as *Portrait of Felix Sumarokov-Elstone with a Bulldog*); Grabar, *Serov*,
1965, pp. 186, 188, 190, 338; Leniashin
1980, pp. 73–105

425 (Plates 123, 124)
**Portrait of Felix Felixovich
Yusupov.** 1903
Oil on canvas. 89×71.5 cm
Signed, bottom left: *B. C. (V. S.).* Dated,
bottom right: *903*
The Russian Museum (since 1921).
Inv. No Ж-4303
Provenance: F. Sumarokov-Elstone collec-
tion, St. Petersburg
Felix Felixovich Yusupov, Count
Sumarokov-Elstone (1856–1928), Moscow
Governor-General (1914–15), husband of
Princess Zinaida Nikolayevna Yusupova
(see No 403).
Exhibitions: 1935 The Russian Museum
(No 131); 1959–60 The Russian Museum;
1965 The Tretyakov Gallery (p. 41), The
Russian Museum
Reproductions: Grabar, *Serov*, 1980, be-
tween pp. 184 and 185
References: Grabar, *Serov*, 1914, pp. 145,
146, 191; Grabar, *Serov*, 1965, pp. 188,
338 (erroneously mentioned to have been
displayed at the Exhibition of Russian Portraits, St. Petersburg, in 1905); Leniashin
1980, pp. 73–105

DRAWINGS
426
Portrait of Eugène Ysaïe. 1903
Pencil
Signed and dated, bottom right: *BC 903*
(VS, 1903); left, an autograph: *E. Isaij*
I. Silberstein collection, Moscow
Provenance: O. Serova collection, Mos-
cow; A. Ziloti collection, St. Petersburg
Eugène Auguste Ysaïe (1858–1931),
Belgian violinist and composer, Professor
at the Conservatory of Music in Brussels.
Exhibitions: 1914 (posthumous) St. Peters-
burg (No 168), Moscow (No 179); / 1904–5
St. Petersburg, 1905 Moscow —
2nd Exhibition of the Union of Russian
Artists (Nos 312, 297); 1914 Malmö (Swe-
den) — Baltic Art Exhibition (No 3204)
Reproductions: Grabar, *Serov*, 1914,
p. 163; *Serov: Drawings, Watercolors,
Lithographs*, 1972, pl. 8
References: Grabar, *Serov*, 1914, pp. 143,
164, 290; Grabar, *Serov*, 1965, pp. 278,
360; Liaskovskaya 1965, p. 55

427 (Plate 100)
Misha Serov. ⟨1902–3⟩
Pencil. 63×48 cm
The Serov family collection, Moscow
Mikhail (Misha) Valentinovich Serov
(1896–1938), the artist's third son.
Exhibitions: 1914 (posthumous) St. Peters-
burg (No 172), Moscow (No 182); 1935
The Tretyakov Gallery (No 377, dated
1890s), The Russian Museum (No 438,
the same wrong date)
Reproductions: Grabar, *Serov*, 1965,
p. 255 (dated to the late 1890s)
References: Grabar, *Serov*, 1914, p. 290
(as *Portrait of a Child*. Drawing. 1902,

whereabouts omitted); Grabar, *Serov*,
1965, pp. 354 (dated to the late 1890s),
358 (as *Portrait of a Child*, dated 1902)

428
Phelia Litvin as Brünnhilde. Caricature.
1903
Pencil. 21×12.9 cm
The Russian Museum (since 1920).
Inv. No P-3117
Provenance: A. Benois collection,
St. Petersburg; Society for the Ad-
vancement of the Arts, Petrograd
Phelia Vasilyevna Litvin (real name
Litvinova, 1861–1936), opera singer, per-
former of heroic parts (Judith in Alexander
Serov's opera).
Exhibitions: 1914 (posthumous) St. Peters-
burg (No 226), Moscow (No 239); 1935
The Tretyakov Gallery (No 422), The Rus-
sian Museum (No 493); 1965 The Russian
Museum; / 1921 Petrograd — Works of Art
Acquired by the Society for the Ad-
vancement of the Arts and Donated to
State Museums (p. 12)
Reproductions: Grabar, *Serov*, 1914,
p. 276 (dated 1907)
References: Grabar, *Serov*, 1914, p. 291;
Grabar, *Serov*, 1965, p. 359

1904
PAINTINGS
429
Birch Tree. ⟨1904⟩
Present whereabouts unknown
Exhibitions: 1904–5 St. Petersburg — 2nd
Exhibition of the Union of Russian Artists
(No 309)
References: Grabar, *Serov*, 1965, p. 425

430

Branch of an Alder Tree. Domotkanovo. ⟨1904⟩
Pastel
Present whereabouts unknown
References: Simonovich-Yefimova 1964, p. 56

431

Yura and Sasha, Serov's Children. ⟨1902–4⟩
Tempera and gouache on cardboard. 74.8×56.5 cm
V. Petrov collection, Leningrad
Serov's children — see Nos 309, 308.
Exhibitions: 1965 The Russian Museum
References: Grabar, *Serov*, 1965, p. 338

432

Road in Domotkanovo in Winter. 1904
Pastel. 49×64 cm
Signed and dated, bottom right: *BC 904 (VS, 1904)*
Art Museum, Riazan (since 1924).
Inv. No P-443
Provenance: B. Perlei collection, Zaraisk; Museum of Local Lore, Zaraisk
Exhibitions: 1914 (posthumous) St. Petersburg (No 175), Moscow (No 185); 1935 The Tretyakov Gallery (No 143), The Russian Museum (No 136); 1965 The Tretyakov Gallery (p. 65)
Reproductions: *Apollon*, 1914, No 6/7, between pp. 20 and 21; Dmitriyev, *Serov*, 1917 (as *Road in Domotkanovo*); *Khudozhnik*, 1965, No 2, p. 39 (as *Winter Road in Domotkanovo*)
References: Grabar, *Serov*, 1914, p. 291; Grabar, *Serov*, 1965, p. 425; Simonovich-Yefimova 1964, p. 56 (as *Landscape with a Road*)

433

Reception Room in an Old Manor House. The Belkino Estate. Study. ⟨1904⟩
Oil on canvas. 88.6×67.7 cm
Signed, bottom left: *B.C. (V.S.)*

The Tretyakov Gallery (since 1927).
Inv. No 9130
Provenance: I. Morozov collection, Moscow
Exhibitions: 1935 The Tretyakov Gallery (No 141), The Russian Museum (No 134); 1904–5 St. Petersburg, 1905 Moscow — 2nd Exhibition of the Union of Russian Artists (Nos 313, 298, as *Reception Room in a Manor House*)
References: Grabar, *Serov*, 1914, pp. 158, 291 (as *Manor House*); Grabar, *Serov*, 1965, p. 425

434

Reception Room in an Old Manor House. The Belkino Estate. Study. ⟨1904⟩
Present whereabouts unknown
Provenance: O. Serova collection, Moscow
A version of the study of the same title (see No 433).
References: Grabar, *Serov*, 1914, p. 291; Grabar, *Serov*, 1965, p. 425

435

Shrovetide Merrymaking. ⟨1904⟩
Gouache and pastel on cardboard. 49.3×31.3 cm
Signed, top right: *BC (VS)*
Art Gallery, Perm (since 1928).
Inv. No Ж-372
Provenance: A. Rumanov collection, St. Petersburg; Zh. Rumanova collection, Petrograd; The Russian Museum
"About 1904 Serov worked briefly on the subject of Shrovetide merrymaking in Domotkanovo" (Simonovich-Yefimova 1964, p. 79). This record, as well as the stylistic features of the painting, make one doubt its traditional dating to 1908 and suggest that the group of works on the subject of Shrovetide was done in 1904.
Exhibitions: 1935 The Russian Museum (No 584a — 2nd ed.)
Reproductions: Dmitriyev, *Serov*, 1917 (as *Shrovetide in a Village*; described incorrectly as an oil painting and dated 1901)

References: Simonovich-Yefimova 1964, pp. 79, 166; Grabar, *Serov*, 1965, p. 433 (dated 1908)

436

Shrovetide Merrymaking. ⟨1904⟩
Pastel
Present whereabouts unknown
Provenance: O. Serova collection, Moscow
References: Grabar, *Serov*, 1914, p. 293 (dated 1908); Grabar, *Serov*, 1965, p. 433 (dated 1908)

437

Shrovetide Merrymaking. ⟨1904⟩.
Unfinished
Pastel
Present whereabouts unknown
Provenance: I. Yefimov collection, Moscow
First version.

119. Reception Room in an Old Manor House. The Belkino Estate. Study. Cat. No 433

References: Grabar, *Serov*, 1914, p. 293
(dated 1908); Grabar, *Serov*, 1965, p. 433
(dated 1908)

438
Shrovetide Merrymaking. ⟨1904⟩.
Unfinished
Pastel
Present whereabouts unknown
Provenance: O. Serova collection,
Moscow; M. Frank collection, Moscow
Second version.
Exhibitions: 1914 (posthumous) St. Petersburg (No 253), Moscow (No 272)
References: Grabar, *Serov*, 1914, p. 293
(dated 1908); Grabar, *Serov*, 1965, p. 433
(dated 1908)

439
Room in the Palace of Monplaisir.
⟨1904⟩
Oils. 30×26 cm (approx.)
Present whereabouts unknown
A study for the painting *Peter the Great
in the Palace of Monplaisir* (versions of
1910–11; see Nos 576–579).
Exhibitions: 1914 (posthumous) St. Petersburg (No 178), Moscow (No 188)
References: Grabar, *Serov*, 1965, p. 441

120. General Toptygin.
Cat. No 449

121. The Madonna. Cat. No 451

440
Stable in Domotkanovo. ⟨1904⟩
Pastel. 62×47.5 cm
Signed, bottom left: *B.C.* (V.S.)
Art Gallery, Perm (since 1947).
Inv. No P-1215
Provenance: L. Kamenskaya collection,
St. Petersburg; V. Bazhanova collection,
Perm
Reproductions: *Art Gallery, Perm*,
1976, pl. 66
References: Simonovich-Yefimova 1964,
p. 56; Grabar, *Serov*, 1965, p. 424

441
Moonlit Night. 1904
Oil on canvas. 89×71 cm
Signed and dated, bottom left: *B.C. 904*
(V.S., 1904)
Art Gallery, Perm (since 1947).
Inv. No Ж-844
Provenance: L. Kamenskaya collection,
St. Petersburg; V. Bazhanova collection,
Perm
Exhibitions: 1904–5 St. Petersburg, 1905
Moscow — 2nd Exhibition of the Union of
Russian Artists (Nos 308, 295)
References: Grabar, *Serov*, 1965, p. 425

442 (Plate 60)
**Portrait of Sergei Pavlovich
Diaghilev.** ⟨1904⟩. Unfinished
Oil on canvas. 97×83 cm

The Russian Museum, Leningrad (since
1930). Inv. No Ж-1922
Provenance: Yu. Diaghilev collection,
St. Petersburg
Sergei Pavlovich Diaghilev — see No 412.
Exhibitions: 1914 (posthumous) St. Petersburg (No 182), Moscow (No 191); 1935
The Tretyakov Gallery (No 142), The Russian Museum (No 135); 1965 The Russian
Museum
Reproductions: Grabar, *Serov*, 1914,
p. 164; Grabar, *Serov*, 1980, pl. 68
References: Grabar, *Serov*, 1914, p. 291;
Grabar, *Serov*, 1965, pp. 338, 339

443
**Portrait of Sergei Yulyevich
Witte.** 1904
Oil on canvas. 137×97 cm (approx.)
Signed and dated, top left: *Съровъ 904*
(Serov, 1904)
Present whereabouts unknown
Provenance: Tsarevich Nikolai Vocational
School, St. Petersburg
Sergei Yulyevich Witte (1849–1915),
Russian statesman.
Exhibitions: 1914 (posthumous) St. Petersburg (No 189), Moscow (No 200); / 1905
St. Petersburg — Russian Portrait Painting
(No 1608); 1914 Malmö (Sweden) —
Baltic Art Exhibition (No 3231a)
Reproductions: Grabar, *Serov*, 1914,
p. 169
References: Grabar, *Serov*, 1914, pp. 158,
160, 291; Grabar, *Serov*, 1965, pp. 174,
338

444
**Portrait of Fiodor Ivanovich
Shaliapin.** 1904
Oil on canvas
Double signature, left: *Писали Коровинъ
Конст Съровъ 1904* (Painted by
Konst[antin] Korovin and Serov, 1904).
The outline was done by Korovin, the
painting by Serov.
The Shaliapin family collection, Paris
Fiodor Ivanovich Shaliapin (1873–1938),
Russian operatic basso.
Exhibitions: 1915 Museum of Fine Arts,
Moscow — Paintings by Russian Artists,
Old and New
Reproductions: *Korovin Recollects*, 1971,
between pp. 288 and 289
References: Grabar, *Serov*, 1914, p. 292
(dated 1907); Grabar, *Serov*, 1965, p. 338

445
Portrait of Hjalmar Krussell. ⟨1904⟩
Oil on canvas. 92×70 cm (approx.)
Present whereabouts unknown
Provenance: H. Krussell collection,
St. Petersburg
Hjalmar Gustav Krussell, mechanical
engineer.
Exhibitions: 1914 (posthumous) St. Petersburg (No 188), Moscow (No 189); / 1914
Malmö (Sweden) — Baltic Art Exhibition
(No 3233)
Reproductions: Grabar, *Serov*, 1914,
p. 168
References: Grabar, *Serov*, 1914, pp. 158,
291

446 (Plate 134)
Colts at a Watering Place.
Domotkanovo. 1904
Pastel on paper, mounted on cardboard.
40×63.8 cm

Signed and dated, bottom left: *Съровъ
904* (Serov, 1904)
The Tretyakov Gallery (since 1917).
Inv. No 5655
Provenance: I. Troyanovsky collection,
Moscow
Exhibitions: 1914 (posthumous) St. Petersburg (No 174), Moscow (No 184); 1935
The Tretyakov Gallery (No 129, dated
1902), The Russian Museum (No 139);
1958–59 The Tretyakov Gallery; 1965
The Tretyakov Gallery (p. 41); / 1904–5
St. Petersburg, 1905 Moscow — 2nd Exhibition of the Union of Russian Artists
(Nos 306, 293, as *Horses at a Watering
Place in Winter*); 1906 Paris, Berlin —
Russian Art (Nos 516, 427); 1907 Venice
— 7th International Art Exhibition (No 47);
1963 The Tretyakov Gallery — Pencil
Drawings, Watercolors, Pastels, and
Gouaches (p. 71)
Reproductions: Grabar, *Serov*, 1914,
pp. 184, 185; Grabar, *Serov*, 1965, p. 201
References: Grabar, *Serov*, 1914, pp. 157,
291; Simonovich-Yefimova 1964, p. 78;
Fiodorov-Davydov 1965, No 2, p. 40;
Grabar, *Serov*, 1965, pp. 202, 424;
Sarabyanov, *Reforms by Valentin Serov*,
1971, p. 19

447
Colts. ⟨1904⟩
Pastel. 59×46 cm (approx.)
Present whereabouts unknown
Provenance: I. Yefimov collection, Moscow
A version of the pastel *Colts at a Watering
Place* (see No 446).
Exhibitions: 1914 (posthumous) Moscow
(No 184a)
References: Grabar, *Serov*, 1914, p. 291;
Simonovich-Yefimova 1964, p. 78

DRAWINGS, WATERCOLORS, PASTELS, AND GOUACHES

448 (Plate 155)
Wife Visits Her Husband in Exile.
⟨1904⟩
Watercolors and graphite. 25×36.2 cm
The Tretyakov Gallery. Inv. No 5416

Provenance: V. Girshman collection, Moscow

A version of the oil painting of the same title (see No 311).

Exhibitions: 1914 (posthumous) St. Petersburg (No 186), Moscow (No 195); 1935 The Tretyakov Gallery (No 435), The Russian Museum (No 513a — 2nd ed.); 1958–59 The Tretyakov Gallery; 1965 The Tretyakov Gallery (p. 65); / 1954 The Tretyakov Gallery — Sketches and Studies by Russian Artists from the Tretyakov Gallery Reserve: 18th to Early 20th Century (p. 54); 1963 The Tretyakov Gallery — Pencil Drawings, Watercolors, Pastels, and Gouaches (p. 71)

Reproductions: *Drawings and Watercolors. Catalogue*, 1956; Grabar, *Serov*, 1980, p. 149

References: Grabar, *Serov*, 1914, p. 291; Grabar, *Serov*, 1965, pp. 283, 425

449

General Toptygin. 1904. Illustration for Nekrasov's poem of the same title Watercolors and gouache on paper, mounted on cardboard. 22.2×33.6 cm Signed and dated, bottom right: *BC 904* (VS, 1904)

The Tretyakov Gallery (since 1935). Inv. No 21250

Provenance: A. Langovoi collection, Moscow

Exhibitions: 1914 (posthumous) St. Petersburg (No 155, dated 1902), Moscow (No 164, the same date); 1935 The Tretyakov Gallery (No 461), The Russian Museum (No 501); 1958–59 The Tretyakov Gallery; 1965 The Tretyakov Gallery (p. 64), The Russian Museum; / 1963 The Tretyakov Gallery — Pencil Drawings, Watercolors, Pastels, and Gouaches (p. 71)

Reproductions: Grabar, *Serov*, 1914, p. 268; Grabar, *Serov*, 1980, p. 167 References: Grabar, *Serov*, 1965, p. 425

450 (Plate 63)

Barns. ⟨1904⟩

Oil on cardboard. 49.5×64 cm The Brodsky Memorial Museum, Leningrad. Inv. No Ж-125 References: Grabar, *Serov*, 1965, p. 435

451

The Madonna. ⟨1904⟩

Watercolors. 51×33 cm Signed, bottom right: *BC* (VS) The Serov family collection, Moscow A watercolor of Michelangelo's sculpture in the Medici Chapel, Florence.

Exhibitions: 1914 (posthumous) St. Petersburg (No 181), Moscow (No 190); 1935 The Tretyakov Gallery (No 429), The Russian Museum (No 503); 1952 Moscow (No 208); 1958–59 The Tretyakov Gallery; 1959 Museum of Russian Art, Kiev; 1959–60 The Russian Museum; 1965 The Tretyakov Gallery (p. 64), The Russian Museum

Reproductions: Ernst, *Serov*, 1922, between pp. 48 and 49 References: Grabar, *Serov*, 1914, p. 291; Yaremich, *Serov: Drawings*, 1936, p. 7; Grabar, *Serov*, 1965, pp. 424, 425

452

The Madonna. ⟨1904⟩

Graphite on brown paper. 49.7×32.8 cm The Tretyakov Gallery. Inv. No 26477

A drawing of Michelangelo's sculpture in the Medici Chapel, Florence.

Exhibitions: 1935 The Russian Museum

References: Grabar, *Serov*, 1965, p. 425

453 (Plate 158)

Portrait of Henrietta Leopoldovna Girshman. ⟨1904⟩

Tempera on cardboard. 99.2×68.2 cm The Tretyakov Gallery. Inv. No 5585 Provenance: V. Girshman collection, Moscow

The traditional dating of the portrait to 1906 (Grabar, *Serov*, 1914, pp. 179, 292; *Drawings and Watercolors. Catalogue*, 1956, p. 70; Grabar, *Serov*, 1965, p. 363) is erroneous. Begun in the spring of 1904 (April–May), the portrait was completed at the end of the same year (*Serov in the Reminiscences of His Contemporaries*, 1917, 2, pp. 327, 328).

Henrietta Leopoldovna Girshman, née Leon (1885–1970), wife of the Moscow art collector Vladimir Osipovich Girshman (see No 629).

Exhibitions: 1914 (posthumous) St. Petersburg (No 234), Moscow (No 246); 1935 The Tretyakov Gallery (No 485), The Russian Museum (No 567); 1958–59 The Tretyakov Gallery; 1965 The Tretyakov Gallery (p. 69, dated 1906)

Reproductions: Grabar, *Serov*, 1914, p. 190 (dated 1906); Grabar, *Serov*, 1965, p. 216 (the same wrong date) References: Grabar, *Serov*, 1914, pp. 179, 180, 182, 292 (described incorrectly as a gouache and dated 1906); Grabar, *Serov*, 1965, pp. 214 (dated 1906/7), 280, 363 (dated 1905); *Serov in the Reminiscences of His Contemporaries*, 1971, 2, pp. 327, 328

454 (Plate 133)

Portrait of Cleopatra Alexandrovna Obninskaya with a Hare. ⟨1904⟩

Pastel and charcoal on cardboard. 54.5×46 cm (exposed area) Signed and dated, bottom right: *BC 904* (VS, 1904)

Art Museum, Gorky (since 1972). Inv. No 684-Га

Provenance: V. and K. Obninsky collection, Moscow; D. Cherkes collection, Moscow

Cleopatra Alexandrovna Obninskaya, née Salova (1880–1928), wife of Victor Petrovich Obninsky (see No 503)

Exhibitions: 1914 (posthumous) St. Petersburg (No 184), Moscow (No 193); 1946 Central House of Art Workers, Moscow (No 96); 1952 Moscow (No 206); 1958–59 The Tretyakov Gallery; 1965 The Tretyakov Gallery (pp. 63, 64); / 1905 St. Petersburg — Russian Portrait Painting (No 1612); 1949 The Pushkin Museum of Fine Arts, Moscow — Russian Graphic Art: 18th to Early 20th Century; 1957 Central House of Art Workers, Moscow — Works of Russian Art from Private Collections: Late 19th and Early 20th Centuries (p. 13)

Reproductions: Grabar, *Serov*, 1914, p. 167; Grabar, *Serov*, 1980, pl. 80 References: Grabar, *Serov*, 1914, pp. 158, 291; Grabar, *Serov*, 1965, pp. 278, 361; Liaskovskaya 1965, pp. 55, 59

455

Portrait of Fiodor Ivanovich Shaliapin. 1904

Black watercolor (varnished). 47.9×34.1 cm Signed and dated, right: *904 BC* (1904, VS)

The Russian Museum (since 1905). Inv. No P-13440

Fiodor Ivanovich Shaliapin — see No 444. Exhibitions: 1935 The Tretyakov Gallery (No 434), The Russian Museum (No 509); 1965 The Russian Museum; / 1904–5 St. Petersburg, 1905 Moscow — 2nd Exhibition of the Union of Russian Artists (Nos 307, 294)

Reproductions: Grabar, *Serov*, 1914, p. 166 References: Grabar, *Serov*, 1914, p. 291; Grabar, *Serov*, 1965, p. 361

122. Portrait of Fiodor Ivanovich Shaliapin. Cat. No 455

456

Tornabuoni Street in Florence. ⟨1904⟩

Watercolors on paper, mounted on cardboard. 50.6×33.7 cm Signed, bottom right: *B.C.* (V.S.) The Tretyakov Gallery (since 1929). Inv. No 11301

Provenance: I. Ostroukhov collection, Moscow; The Ostroukhov Museum of Icons and Painting, Moscow

Exhibitions: 1935 The Tretyakov Gallery (No 460), The Russian Museum (No 513); 1958–59 The Tretyakov Gallery; 1965 The Tretyakov Gallery (p. 64), The Russian Museum; / 1904–5 St. Petersburg, 1905 Moscow — 2nd Exhibition of the Union of Russian Artists (Nos 311, 296); 1963 The Tretyakov Gallery — Pencil Drawings, Watercolors, Pastels, and Gouaches (p. 71)

Reproductions: *Apollon*, 1911, No 10, between pp. 8 and 9 (as *Florence*; described incorrectly as an oil painting) References: Grabar, *Serov*, 1914, pp. 158, 291; Grabar, *Serov*, 1965, p. 424

457
Igor Emmanuilovich Grabar. Caricature.
⟨1904⟩
Pencil. 13.2×10.3 cm
The Russian Museum (since 1920).
Inv. No P-3114
Provenance: A. Benois collection,
St. Petersburg; Society for the Advance-
ment of the Arts, St. Petersburg
Igor Emmanuilovich Grabar (1871–1960),
Russian painter, art critic and eminent fig-
ure in the preservation and restoration of
art monuments; author of two major mono-
graphs on Serov.
Exhibitions: 1914 (posthumous) St. Peters-
burg (No 183), Moscow (No 192); 1935
The Tretyakov Gallery (No 431), The Russian Museum (No 506); / 1921 Petrograd
— Works of Art Acquired by the Society
for the Advancement of the Arts and Donated to State Museums (p. 12)
Reproductions: Grabar, *Serov*, 1914,
p. 277
References: Grabar, *Serov*, 1914,
pp. 275, 276, 291; Grabar, *Serov*, 1965,
p. 360

1905
PAINTINGS

458
**Konstantin Korovin on the Bank
of the Kliazma.** Study. ⟨1905⟩
Oil on cardboard. 36×51 cm
The Russian Museum (since 1923).
Inv. No Ж-1750
Provenance: Academy of Arts,
St. Petersburg
Konstantin Korovin — see No 180.
Exhibitions: 1914 (posthumous) St. Peters-
burg (No 207); 1935 The Tretyakov Gal-
lery (No 146), The Russian Museum
(No 139); 1958–59 The Tretyakov Gallery;
1965 The Tretyakov Gallery (p. 42, as
*Konstantin Korovin on the Bank of a
River*), The Russian Museum
Reproductions: Serova 1968, between
pp. 252 and 253
References: Grabar, *Serov*, 1914, p. 291
(as *Konstantin Korovin on the Bank of a
Pond*); Grabar, *Serov*, 1965, p. 339

459
**Konstantin Korovin and His Man Ser-
vant (A Discourse on the Fish, etc.).**
⟨1905⟩
Oil on canvas
Inscribed and signed, top right:
*Разсужденіе о рыбѣ и о прочемъ
посвящаю Ѳ. Шаляпину. ВС*
(A Discourse on the Fish, etc.
To F. Shaliapin. VS)
The Shaliapin family collection, Paris
Provenance: F. Shaliapin collection,
St. Petersburg
Konstantin Alexeyevich Korovin — see
No 180.
Exhibitions: 1914 (posthumous) St. Peters-
burg (No 215a), Moscow (No 228); / 1928
Brussels — Old and New Russian Art
(No 843, as *Dissertation sur le poisson*)
Reproductions: Grabar, *Serov*, 1914,
p. 283
References: Grabar, *Serov*, 1914, p. 276;
Konstantin Korovin, 1963, pp. 336, 337,
341; Grabar, *Serov*, 1965, p. 339

460
Cow. Study ⟨1905⟩
Oil on canvas. 17×26 cm
Signed and dated, bottom right: *ВС 905*
(VS, 1905)
Present whereabouts unknown
Provenance: I. Pengu collection, Leningrad
Exhibitions: 1935 The Russian Museum
(No 148a — 2nd ed.)
References: Grabar, *Serov*, 1965, p. 427
(as *A Cow in Profile to the Right*)

461 (Plate 137)
Bathing a Horse. 1905
Oil on canvas. 72×99 cm
Signed and dated, bottom right: *ВС 905*
(VS, 1905)
The Russian Museum (since 1906).
Inv. No Ж-4285
Exhibitions: 1935 The Tretyakov Gallery
(No 147), The Russian Museum (No 140);
1965 The Tretyakov Gallery (p. 42), The
Russian Museum; / 1906 St. Petersburg —
Exhibition of Paintings Organized by
Sergei Diaghilev (No 301, as *Bathing*);
1969 Warsaw — Fine Arts in Russia: 13th
Century to the Present Time; 1977 Japan
— Master Paintings from the Russian
Museum (No 9)
Reproductions: *Apollon*, 1912, No 10, be-
tween pp. 16 and 17 (as *Bathing*); Grabar,
Serov, 1914, p. 173; Grabar, *Serov*, 1965,
p. 215
References: Grabar, *Serov*, 1914, pp. 152,
154, 291; Grabar, *Serov*, 1965, p. 426;
Fiodorov-Davydov 1965, No 2, p. 40

462 (Plate 135)
Horses by the Seashore. 1905
Oil on canvas. 48.5×64 cm
The Russian Museum (since 1928).
Inv. No Ж-4309
Provenance: D. Tolstoi collection,
St. Petersburg; The Hermitage, Leningrad
Exhibitions: 1914 (posthumous) St. Peters-
burg (No 272), Moscow (No 299); 1935
The Tretyakov Gallery (No 157), The Rus-
sian Museum (No 141); 1958–59 The Tre-
tyakov Gallery; 1959 Museum of Russian
Art, Kiev; 1959–60 The Russian Museum;
1965 The Tretyakov Gallery (p. 42), The
Russian Museum; / 1911 Rome — Interna-
tional Art Exhibition (No 403); 1976 Helsin-
ki — Russian Painting and Drawing: Late
1700s to Early 1900s (No 97)
Reproductions: Simonovich-Yefimova
1964, between pp. 104 and 105
References: Grabar, *Serov*, 1914, p. 291;
Grabar, *Serov*, 1965, p. 426 (erroneously
mentioned to have been displayed at the
1902 Exhibition of Paintings Organized by
the *Mir Iskusstva* Magazine — No 180 in
St. Petersburg, No 218 in Moscow)

463 (Plate 106)
Model. ⟨1905⟩
Tempera on cardboard. 68×63 cm
(octagonal)
Signed, bottom right: *ВС* (VS)
The Tretyakov Gallery (since 1917).
Inv. No 5583
Provenance: V. Girshman collection,
Moscow
Exhibitions: 1914 (posthumous) St. Peters-
burg (No 196), Moscow (No 209); 1935
The Tretyakov Gallery (No 164), The Rus-
sian Museum (No 147); 1958–59 The Tre-
tyakov Gallery; 1965 The Tretyakov Gal-
lery (p. 67); / 1907–8 Moscow, 1908
St. Petersburg — 5th Exhibition of the
Union of Russian Artists (Nos 191, 224);
1963 The Tretyakov Gallery — Pencil
Drawings, Watercolors, Pastels, and
Gouaches (p. 71)
Reproductions: Grabar, *Serov*, 1914,
p. 172; Sarabyanov, *Serov*, 1974, No 27
References: Grabar, *Serov*, 1914, p. 291;
Grabar, *Serov*, 1965, p. 426

464
Reclining Model. Study. ⟨1905⟩
Oil on canvas. 68×104 cm
The Tretyakov Gallery (since 1963).
Inv. No Ж-481
Provenance: O. Serova collection, Mos-
cow; N. Smirnov collection, St. Petersburg;

V. Vorobyov collection, Moscow; E. Helzer and T. Helzer collection, Moscow
Exhibitions: 1914 (posthumous) St. Petersburg (No 107, dated 1896–97), Moscow (No 100, the same date); 1952 Moscow (No 161); 1958–59 The Tretyakov Gallery; 1965 The Tretyakov Gallery (p. 36, dated 1896–97)
References: Grabar, *Serov*, 1914, p. 291; Grabar, *Serov*, 1965, p. 426 (as "a reclining model, with her left leg bent and her arms behind her head")

465 (Plate 143)
Portrait of Glikeria Nikolayevna Fedotova. ⟨1905⟩
Oil on canvas. 123×95 cm (top rounded)
The Tretyakov Gallery (since 1935). Inv. No 28080
Provenance: Circle of Literature and Art, Moscow; Maly Theater, Moscow
Glikeria Nikolayevna Fedotova (1846–1925), comic actress.
Exhibitions: 1914 (posthumous) St. Petersburg (not listed in the Catalogue), Moscow (No 205); 1935 The Tretyakov Gallery (No 150), The Russian Museum (No 143); 1958–59 The Tretyakov Gallery; 1959 Museum of Russian Art, Kiev; 1959–60 The Russian Museum; 1965 The Tretyakov Gallery (p. 42); / 1906 Moscow — 3rd Exhibition of the Union of Russian Artists (No 269); 1906 St. Petersburg — Exhibition of Paintings Organized by Sergei Diaghilev (No 300); 1906 Paris, Berlin — Russian Art (Nos 512, 424)
Reproductions: *Zolotoye Runo*, 1906, No 6, p. 9; Grabar, *Serov*, 1914, p. 178; Grabar, *Serov*, 1965, p. 167
References: Grabar, *Serov*, 1914, pp. 158, 291; Grabar, *Serov*, 1965, pp. 166, 169, 339; Sarabyanov, *Reforms by Valentin Serov*, 1971, p. 20

466 (Plates 141, 142)
Portrait of Maria Nikolayevna Yermolova. 1905
Oil on canvas. 224×120 cm
Signed and dated, bottom left: *Съровъ 905* (Serov, 1905)
The Tretyakov Gallery (since 1935). Inv. No 28079
Provenance: Circle of Literature and Art, Moscow; Maly Theater, Moscow
Maria Nikolayevna Yermolova (1853–1928), dramatic actress.
Exhibitions: 1914 (posthumous) St. Petersburg (not listed in the Catalogue), Moscow (No 207); 1935 The Tretyakov Gallery (No 152), The Russian Museum (No 145); 1958–59 The Tretyakov Gallery; 1965 The Tretyakov Gallery (pp. 42, 43), The Russian Museum; / 1905 St. Petersburg — Russian Portrait Painting (No 1606); 1906 Paris, Berlin — Russian Art (No 511, 423); 1907 Moscow — 4th Exhibition of the Union of Russian Artists (No 219); 1953 Berlin, Dresden, Halle, 1954 Budapest — Soviet and Russian Pre-revolutionary Art
Reproductions: Grabar, *Serov*, 1914, p. 179; Grabar, *Serov*, 1965, pp. 164 (detail), 165
References: Grabar, *Serov*, 1914, pp. 158, 291; Radzimovskaya 1956, pp. 209–223; Liberfort 1960, pp. 51–53; Simonovich-Yefimova 1964, p. 81; Eisenstein 1964, 2, pp. 376–392; Grabar, *Serov*, 1965, pp. 166, 168, 169, 339; Sarabyanov, *Re-*

forms by Valentin Serov*, 1971, pp. 20–25; Leniashin 1980, pp. 106–135

467 (Plates 147, 148)
Portrait of Maxim Gorky. ⟨1905⟩
Oil on canvas. 124×80 cm
The Maxim Gorky Memorial Museum, Moscow (since 1937). Inv. No 806
Provenance: M. Riabushinsky collection, Moscow; Museum of Literature, Moscow
Maxim Gorky (pen-name of Alexei Maximovich Peshkov, 1868–1936), Russian writer.
Exhibitions: 1914 (posthumous) St. Petersburg (No 191); Moscow (No 202); 1935 The Tretyakov Gallery (No 144), The Russian Museum (No 137); 1958–59 The Tretyakov Gallery; 1965 The Tretyakov Gallery (pp. 41, 42, dated 1904), The Russian Museum; / 1937 History Museum, Moscow — Centenary of Pushkin's Death; 1975 The Pushkin Museum of Fine Arts, Moscow — European Portrait Painting
Reproductions: Grabar, *Serov*, 1914, p. 171 (dated 1904); *Iskusstvo*, 1941, No 3, between pp. 2 and 3 (dated 1904); *The 1905 Revolution*, 1956, between pp. 408 and 409; Grabar, *Serov*, 1965, p. 163 (dated 1904)
References: Grabar, *Serov*, 1914, pp. 158, 291 (dated 1904); Dintses 1936, pp. 461–467 (dated 1904); Arbuzov, *Gorky and Serov*, 1960, pp. 220–231; Radzimovskaya 1962, pp. 131–149; Grabar, *Serov*, 1965, pp. 161, 338 (dated 1904); Sarabyanov, *Reforms by Valentin Serov*, 1971, pp. 20, 21

468 (Plate 146)
The Funeral of Bauman. ⟨1905⟩
Graphite, charcoal and gouache on cardboard. 50×99 cm
The USSR Museum of the Revolution, Moscow. Inv. No 17991a
Provenance: O. Serova collection, Moscow
Nikolai Ernestovich Bauman (1873–1905), leader of the Moscow Bolshevik organization (1903–5), was killed by an agent of the secret police on 18 October 1905, during a mass demonstration of workers.
Exhibitions: 1935 The Tretyakov Gallery (No 163); 1952 Moscow (No 211); 1958–59 The Tretyakov Gallery; 1965 The Tretyakov Gallery (p. 43), The Russian Museum; / 1939 The Tretyakov Gallery — Russian History Painting
Reproductions: *Iskusstvo*, 1935, No 4, p. 115
References: Bakushinsky 1935, pp. 121, 122; Sokolova, *Serov*, 1935, pp. 101, 108; Grabar, *Serov*, 1965, p. 428; Sarabyanov, *Reforms by Valentin Serov*, 1971, p. 31

469 (Plate 149)
"Soldiers, Soldiers, Heroes Every One..." ⟨1905⟩
Tempera and charcoal on cardboard. 47.5×71.5 cm
Signed, bottom right: *BC* (VS)
The Russian Museum (since 1918). Inv. No Ж-4297
Provenance: M. Gorky collection; N. Dobychina collection, Petrograd
Exhibitions: 1935 The Tretyakov Gallery (No 153); The Russian Museum (No 146); 1958–59 The Tretyakov Gallery; 1959 Museum of Russian Art, Kiev; 1959–60 The Russian Museum; 1965 The

Tretyakov Gallery (p. 43), The Russian Museum
Reproductions: *Zhupel*, 1905, No 1, p. 5; Grabar, *Serov*, 1965, p. 160; *Serov: Drawings, Watercolors, Lithographs*, 1972 (No 7, described incorrectly as executed in charcoal and gouache on brown cardboard)
References: Bakushinsky 1935, p. 121; Golubev 1941, pp. 32, 33; Grabar, *Serov*, 1965, p. 427

DRAWINGS, WATERCOLORS, PASTELS, AND GOUACHES

470
The Borzoi Filou. 1905
Watercolor and gouache on cardboard. 40×74 cm
Signed and dated, bottom right: *В. Съровъ 905* (V. Serov, 1905)
D. Peshkova collection, Moscow
Provenance: V. Mathé collection, St. Petersburg; I. Mathé collection, Petrograd; A. Kohl collection, Leningrad
Exhibitions: 1914 (posthumous) St. Petersburg (No 206a), Moscow (No 221); 1935 The Tretyakov Gallery (No 149), The Russian Museum (No 142); 1952 Moscow (No 221); 1958–59 The Tretyakov Gallery; 1965 The Tretyakov Gallery (p. 68); / 1906 St. Petersburg — Exhibition of Paintings Organized by Sergei Diaghilev (No 305, as *Greyhound*); 1911 Rome — International Art Exhibition (No 389, as *Il cane*); 1914 Malmö (Sweden) — Baltic Art Exhibition (No 3229, as *Vinthund*); 1957 Central House of Art Workers, Moscow — Works of Russian Art from Private Collections: Late 19th and Early 20th Centuries (p. 13)
Reproductions: *Apollon*, 1914, No 6/7, p. 23; Grabar, *Serov*, 1965, p. 266
References: Grabar, *Serov*, 1965, p. 427

471
Peasant with a Horse near a Barn. 1905
Watercolors and gouache on cardboard (varnished). 35.8×52.5 cm
Signed and dated, bottom right: *В. Съровъ 905* (V. Serov, 1905)
The Russian Museum (since 1928). Inv. No P-3225
Provenance: S. Botkin collection, St. Petersburg; A. Botkina collection, St. Petersburg
Exhibitions: 1914 (posthumous) St. Petersburg (No 205), Moscow (No 219); 1935 The Tretyakov Gallery (No 477), The Russian Museum (No 522); 1965 The Tretyakov Gallery (p. 66); / 1906 Moscow — 3rd Exhibition of the Union of Russian Artists (No 272, as *A Horse*); 1906 St. Petersburg — Exhibition of Paintings Organized by Sergei Diaghilev (No 303)
Reproductions: *Zolotoye Runo*, 1906, No 6, p. 9 (as *At a Barn*); *Apollon*, 1912, No 10, between pp. 16 and 17 (as *A Horse*)
References: Grabar, *Serov*, 1914, p. 291 (as *A Horse near a Barn*, described incorrectly as an oil painting); Grabar, *Serov*, 1965, p. 426; Fiodorov-Davydov 1965, No 2, pp. 37, 38 (as *A Horse*)

125. Peasant with a Horse near
a Barn. Cat. No 471

472 (Plate 136)
Horses near a Pond. 1905
Gouache and watercolor on gray paper,
mounted on cardboard.
37.2×54.2 cm
Signed and dated, bottom right:
В. Съровъ 905 (V. Serov, 1905)
The Tretyakov Gallery (since 1929).
Inv. No 11300
Provenance: I. Ostroukhov collection, Mos-
cow; The Ostroukhov Museum of Icons
and Painting, Moscow
Exhibitions: 1914 (posthumous) St. Peters-
burg (No 198), Moscow (No 210); 1935
The Tretyakov Gallery (No 445), The Rus-
sian Museum (No 521); 1958–59 The Tre-
tyakov Gallery; 1965 The Tretyakov Gal-
lery (p. 65), The Russian Museum; / 1906
Moscow — 3rd Exhibition of the Union of
Russian Artists (No 231); 1906 St. Peters-
burg — Exhibition of Paintings Organized
by Sergei Diaghilev (No 304); 1963 The
Tretyakov Gallery — Pencil Drawings,
Watercolors, Pastels, and Gouaches
(p. 71)
Reproductions: *Apollon*, 1911, No 10, between pp. 8 and 9 (as *At a Watering
Place*); Grabar, *Serov*, 1914, p. 173;
Drawings and Watercolors. Catalogue,
1956; Grabar, *Serov*, 1965, p. 198
References: Grabar, *Serov*, 1914, pp. 152,
291; Grabar, *Serov*, 1965, pp. 202, 426;
Fiodorov-Davydov 1965, No 2, pp. 37, 38

126. Portrait of
Maria Nikolayevna Yermolova.
Cat. No 474

473 (Plate 154)
Pereyaslavl-Zalessky. Backyards.
⟨1904–5⟩
Watercolor. 37.5×54.2 cm
Signed, bottom right: *BC* (VS)
The Russian Museum (since 1926).
Inv. No P-13441
Provenance: A. Korovin collection,
St. Petersburg
Exhibitions: 1935 The Tretyakov Gallery
(No 747, as *A Moscow Courtyard*), The
Russian Museum (No 767, under the
same title); 1965 The Tretyakov Gallery
(p. 60, as *A Moscow Courtyard*, errone-
ously dated 1890s), The Russian
Museum; / 1906 Moscow — 3rd Exhibition
of the Union of Russian Artists (No 273,
as *A Provincial Scene*); 1906 St. Peters-
burg — Exhibition of Paintings Organized
by Sergei Diaghilev (No 302, under the
same title)

Reproductions: Grabar, *Serov*, 1980,
pl. 74
References: Grabar, *Serov*, 1914, p. 291
(as *Backyards*, dated 1904); Grabar,
Serov, 1965, pp. 425, 426

474
**Portrait of Maria Nikolayevna
Yermolova.** ⟨1905⟩
Watercolors and graphite. 20.3×11.8 cm
The artist's inscription, bottom right:
Ермолова (Yermolova)
The Tretyakov Gallery (since 1929).
Inv. No 11310
Provenance: I. Ostroukhov collection, Mos-
cow; The Ostroukhov Museum of Icons
and Painting, Moscow
A study for the portrait of 1905, now in the
Tretyakov Gallery (see No 466).
Exhibitions: 1914 (posthumous) St. Peters-
burg (No 194), Moscow (No 206); 1935
The Tretyakov Gallery (No 440), The Rus-
sian Museum (No 516); 1958–59 The Tre-
tyakov Gallery; 1965 The Tretyakov Gal-
lery (p. 67), The Russian Museum; / 1954
The Tretyakov Gallery — Sketches and
Studies by Russian Artists from the
Tretyakov Gallery Reserve: 18th to

Early 20th Century (p. 54); 1963 The
Tretyakov Gallery — Pencil Drawings,
Watercolors, Pastels, and Gouaches
(p. 72)
Reproductions: *Serov: Portrait Painting*,
1968, p. 23
References: Grabar, *Serov*, 1965, p. 361

475
**Portrait of Anna Petrovna
Troyanovskaya.** 1905
Pencil. 50×35 cm
Signed and dated, bottom right: *BC 905*
(VS, 1905)
I. Silberstein collection, Moscow
Provenance: I. Troyanovsky collection,
Moscow; A. Troyanovskaya collection,
Moscow
Anna Petrovna Troyanovskaya, née Ob-
ninskaya, wife of I. Troyanovsky, art lover
and collector of modern Russian paintings.
Exhibitions: 1914 (posthumous) St. Peters-
burg (No 204), Moscow (No 218); 1935
The Tretyakov Gallery (No 458), The Rus-
sian Museum (No 536); 1946 Central
House of Art Workers, Moscow (No 37); /
1946 Central House of Art Workers,
Moscow — Portraits by Russian Artists:
18th to Early 20th Century (No 75)
Reproductions: Grabar, *Serov*, 1914,
p. 177
References: Grabar, *Serov*, 1914, p. 291;
Grabar, *Serov*, 1965, pp. 278, 362;
Yaremich, *Serov: Drawings*, 1936, p. 15

476 (Plate 138)
**Portrait of Fiodor Ivanovich
Shaliapin.** 1905
Charcoal and chalk on canvas.
235×133 cm
Signed and dated, bottom right: *B.C. 905*
(V.S., 1905)
The Tretyakov Gallery. Inv. No 27807
Provenance: Circle of Literature and Art,
Moscow; Bolshoi Theater, Moscow
Fiodor Ivanovich Shaliapin — see No 444.
Exhibitions: 1914 (posthumous) St. Peters-
burg (No 201), Moscow (No 214); 1935
The Tretyakov Gallery (No 453), The Rus-
sian Museum (No 529); 1958–59 The Tre-
tyakov Gallery; 1965 The Tretyakov Gal-
lery (p. 66), The Russian Museum; / 1906
St. Petersburg — Exhibition of Paintings
Organized by Sergei Diaghilev (No 299);
1906 Moscow — 3rd Exhibition of the
Union of Russian Artists (No 268); 1963
The Tretyakov Gallery — Pencil Drawings,
Watercolors, Pastels, and Gouaches
(p. 72)
Reproductions: *Zolotoye Runo*, 1906,
No 6, p. 10; Grabar, *Serov*, 1914, p. 176
(detail); Grabar, *Serov*, 1965, between
pp. 168 and 169
References: Grabar, *Serov*, 1914, pp. 164,
291; Yaremich, *Serov: Drawings*, 1936,
p. 15; Grabar, *Serov*, 1965, pp. 280, 362;
Liaskovskaya 1965, p. 59; Sarabyanov,
Reforms by Valentin Serov, 1971, p. 21

477 (Plate 171)
**Portrait of Yelizaveta Sergeyevna
Karzinkina.** ⟨1905⟩
Charcoal and white. 89×58 cm
The Nesterov Art Museum, Ufa (since
1940). Inv. No Г-589
Provenance: M. Karzinkina collection,
Moscow
Yelizaveta Sergeyevna Karzinkina, née
Yachmeniova (1886–1921), ballet dancer.
Exhibitions: 1914 (posthumous) St. Peters-

burg (No 209), Moscow (No 223); 1935
The Tretyakov Gallery (No 457)
References: Grabar, *Serov*, 1914, p. 292;
Grabar, *Serov*, 1965, p. 363

478
**Portrait of Henrietta Leopoldovna
Girshman.** ⟨1904–5⟩
Pressed charcoal, sanguine and graphite
on paper, mounted on canvas.
132.2×98 cm
The Tretyakov Gallery, Moscow.
Inv. No 5584
Provenance: V. Girshman collection,
Moscow
Henrietta Leopoldovna Girshman — see
No 452.
The traditional dating to 1907 (Grabar,
Serov, 1914, p. 292) is erroneous. The
portrait was actually executed in the winter
of 1904/5 (*Serov in the Reminiscences of
His Contemporaries*, 1971, 2, p. 338).
Exhibitions: 1914 (posthumous) St. Peters-
burg (No 234), Moscow (No 247); 1935
The Tretyakov Gallery (No 484), The Rus-
sian Museum (No 566)
Reproductions: Grabar, *Serov*, 1914,
pp. 191, 192 (detail)
References: *Serov in the Reminiscences
of His Contemporaries*, 1971, 2, p. 328;
Grabar, *Serov*, 1914, pp. 180, 182, 292
(dated 1907); Grabar, *Serov*, 1965,
pp. 214, 280, 364 (dated 1907)

479
Portrait of Maxim Gorky. ⟨1905⟩
Graphite. 20.3×11.8 cm
The artist's inscription, bottom right: *Гор*
(Gor[ky])
The Tretyakov Gallery (since 1914).
Inv. No 3660
Provenance: O. Serova collection, Moscow
A sketch for the oil portrait of 1905, which
is now in the Maxim Gorky Memorial
Museum in Moscow (see No 467).
Exhibitions: 1914 (posthumous) St. Peters-
burg (No 190), Moscow (No 201); 1935
The Tretyakov Gallery (No 428), The Rus-
sian Museum (No 502); 1952 Moscow
(No 205); 1958–59 The Tretyakov Gallery;
1959–60 The Russian Museum; 1965 The
Tretyakov Gallery (p. 65), The Russian
Museum; / 1954 Central House of Art
Workers, Moscow — Portraits of Promi-
nent Personalities in Russian Art: 18th to
20th Century; 1955 The Tretyakov Gallery
— Sketches and Studies by Russian Artists from the Tretyakov Gallery Reserve:
18th to Early 20th Century (p. 54); 1963
The Tretyakov Gallery — Pencil Drawings,
Watercolors, Pastels, and Gouaches
(p. 71)
Reproductions: Grabar, *Serov*, 1914,
p. 170 (dated 1904); *Drawings and Watercolors. Catalogue*, 1956; *Serov: Portrait
Painting*, 1968, p. 24
References: Grabar, *Serov*, 1914, p. 291
(dated 1904); Arbuzov, *Gorky and Serov*,
1964, pp. 226, 227; Grabar, *Serov*, 1965,
pp. 282, 361 (dated 1904)

480 (Plate 157)
**Portrait of Maria Pavlovna
Botkina.** 1905
Black and white chalk and sanguine on
gray paper. 97×71.5 cm
Signed and dated, bottom right: *ВС 905*
(VS, 1905)
The Russian Museum (since 1926).
Inv. No P-13433

Provenance: M. Botkina collection,
St. Petersburg
Maria Pavlovna Botkina, née Tretyakova
(1875–1952), daughter of Pavel Tretyakov,
founder of the Tretyakov Gallery.
Exhibitions: 1914 (posthumous) St. Peters-
burg (No 199), Moscow (No 211); 1935
The Tretyakov Gallery (No 455), The Rus-
sian Museum (No 534); 1965 The
Tretyakov Gallery (p. 66), The Russian
Museum; / 1974 The Russian Museum —
Drawings by Russian Artists: Late 19th
and Early 20th Centuries (p. 20)
Reproductions: Grabar, *Serov*, 1914,
p. 174
References: Grabar, *Serov*, 1914, pp. 164,
291; Grabar, *Serov*, 1965, pp. 280, 362

481 (Plate 115)
**Portrait of Piotr Petrovich
Semionov-Tien-Shansky.** 1905
Charcoal, crayons and chalk on yellowish
paper. 67×51 cm
Signed and dated, bottom left: *ВС 1905*
(VS, 1905)
The Russian Museum (since 1918).
Inv. No. P-13431
Provenance: A. Naryshkina collection,
St. Petersburg
Piotr Petrovich Semionov-Tien-Shansky
(1827–1914), geographer, statistician,
botanist and entomologist, statesman,
Honorary Member of the St. Petersburg
Academy of Sciences (since 1873), collec-
tor of old Dutch painting.
Exhibitions: 1935 The Tretyakov Gallery
(No 449), The Russian Museum (No 525);
1965 The Tretyakov Gallery (p. 66), The
Russian Museum; / 1909 St. Petersburg —
Salon (No 365, as *Portrait of Semionov*);
1974 The Russian Museum — Drawings
by Russian Artists: Late 19th and Early
20th Centuries (p. 20)
Reproductions: Grabar, *Serov*, 1914,
p. 183; Grabar, *Serov*, 1980, pl. 72
References: Grabar, *Serov*, 1914, pp. 164,
292; Grabar, *Serov*, 1965, pp. 278, 363

482 (Plate 140)
**Portrait of Konstantin Dmitriyevich
Balmont.** 1905
Pastel on gray paper, mounted on card-
board. 72.5×41.5 cm

Signed and dated, bottom right: *В Сѣровъ
905* (V. Serov, 1905)
The Tretyakov Gallery. Inv. No. 9133
Provenance: M. Riabushinsky collection,
Moscow
Konstantin Dmitriyevich Balmont
(1867–1942), Russian poet and translator.
Exhibitions: 1914 (posthumous) St. Peters-
burg (No 206), Moscow (No 220); 1935
The Tretyakov Gallery (No 441), The Rus-
sian Museum (No 517); 1958–59 The
Tretyakov Gallery; 1965 The Tretyakov
Gallery (p. 66), The Russian Museum; /
1906 Paris — Russian Art (No 528); 1907
Moscow — 4th Exhibition of the Union of
Russian Artists (No 222a); 1963 The Tre-
tyakov Gallery — Pencil Drawings, Water-
colors, Pastels, and Gouaches (p. 72)
Reproductions: *Zolotoye Runo*, 1906,
No 1, between pp. 40 and 41; Grabar,
Serov, 1914, p. 181
References: Grabar, *Serov*, 1914, pp. 164,
291; Grabar, *Serov*, 1965, pp. 174, 282,
363

483
**Portrait of Fiodor Ivanovich
Shaliapin.** Sketch. ⟨1905⟩
Pencil. 20.3×12 cm
The Russian Museum (since 1926).
Inv. No. P-3163
Provenance: P. Suvchinsky collection,
St. Petersburg
Fiodor Ivanovich Shaliapin — see No 444.
Exhibitions: 1935 The Tretyakov Gallery
(No 456), The Russian Museum (No 535);
1965 The Russian Museum
References: Grabar, *Serov*, 1965, pp. 280,
362

484
**Portrait of Yury Mikhailovich
Morozov.** 1905
Sanguine and pressed charcoal on paper,
mounted on cardboard. 62.2×47.8 cm
Signed and dated, bottom right: *ВС 905*
(VS, 1905)
The Tretyakov Gallery. Inv. No. 5327
Provenance: M. Morozov collection, Mos-
cow; M. Morozova collection, Moscow
Yury Mikhailovich Morozov, son of Mikhail
Abramovich Morozov (see No 405).

127. Portrait of Maxim Gorky.
Cat. No 479

128. Portrait of
Fiodor Ivanovich Shaliapin.
Sketch. Cat. No 483

339

Exhibitions: 1914 (posthumous) St. Petersburg (No 200), Moscow (No 212); 1935 The Tretyakov Gallery (No 443), The Russian Museum (No 519); / 1909 St. Petersburg — Salon (No 367, No 474 — another edition); 1963 The Tretyakov Gallery — Pencil Drawings, Watercolors, Pastels, and Gouaches (p. 71)
Reproductions: Grabar, *Serov*, 1914, p. 175; *Apollon*, 1914, No 6/7, between pp. 18 and 19; Grabar, *Serov*, 1980, pl. 73
References: Grabar, *Serov*, 1914, pp. 164, 291; Grabar, *Serov*, 1965, p. 267

485
The Dispersal of a Demonstration by Cossacks in 1905. ⟨1905⟩
Gouache and white on cardboard.
26.8×37.8 cm
Signed, top right: *В. Сѣровъ* (V. Serov)
The Tretyakov Gallery (since 1960).
Inv. No. P-478
Provenance: Z. Berchansky collection, Paris
Exhibitions: 1965 The Tretyakov Gallery (p. 68), The Russian Museum; / 1962 The Tretyakov Gallery — Russian Pre-revolutionary Art: New Acquisitions (p. 46); 1963 The Tretyakov Gallery — Pencil Drawings, Watercolors, Pastels, and Gouaches (p. 72)
References: Grabar, *Serov*, 1965, p. 428 (as *The Year 1905*)

486 (Plate 151)
The Sumy Regiment. Sketch. 1905
Watercolors, chalk and graphite.
32.2×49.7 cm
Inscribed by the artist in the right part of the sheet: *Сумской полкъ 905 г. 14-е Декабря (14-е)* (The Sumy Regiment, 1905, 14 December)
The USSR Museum of the Revolution, Moscow (since 1931). Inv. No. 6664
Exhibitions: 1935 The Tretyakov Gallery (No 468); 1952 Moscow (No 212); 1958–59 The Tretyakov Gallery; 1965 The Tretyakov Gallery (p. 68)
Reproductions: Sokolova, Vlasov 1959, p. 100; Grabar, *Serov*, 1965, p. 162
References: Grabar, *Serov*, 1965, p. 428; Sokolova, Vlasov 1959, pp. 98, 100

487 (Plate 150)
The Year 1905. ⟨1905⟩
Watercolors and pencil on cardboard.
22.5×32 cm
Picture Gallery, Yerevan (since 1932).
Inv. No. p-531
Provenance: The Serov family collection, Moscow
A version of the composition *The Dispersal of a Demonstration by the Cossacks in 1905* (1905), now in the Tretyakov Gallery (see No 485).
Exhibitions: 1935 The Tretyakov Gallery

(No 454), The Russian Museum (No 530); 1965 The Russian Museum
Reproductions: Grabar, *Serov*, 1980, p. 155
References: Grabar, *Serov*, 1965, p. 428

488
The Year 1905.
The Revolt Is Suppressed. Caricature of Nicholas II. ⟨1905⟩
Graphite. 25×36.6 cm
On the reverse, an ink drawing *Harvest* (sketch for the *Prospects for the 1906 Harvest* — see No 499); this drawing is reproduced on Plate 145.
The Tretyakov Gallery (since 1940).
Inv. No. 25404
Provenance: State Purchasing Commission, Moscow
Nicholas II — see No 281.
Exhibitions: 1935 The Russian Museum (No 533); 1952 Moscow (No 213); 1956 The Tretyakov Gallery (p. 67), The Russian Museum; 1958–59 The Tretyakov Gallery; 1959 Museum of Russian Art, Kiev; 1959–60 The Russian Museum; / 1939 The Tretyakov Gallery — Russian History Painting (No 333); 1949 The Pushkin Museum of Fine Arts, Moscow — Russian Graphic Art: 18th to Early 20th Century; 1963 The Tretyakov Gallery — Pencil Drawings, Watercolors, Pastels, and Gouaches (p. 72)
Reproductions: *Iskusstvo i Massy*, 1930, No 1; *Drawings and Watercolors. Catalogue*, 1956; Grabar, *Serov the Draftsman*, 1961
References: Grabar, *Serov*, 1965, p. 428

489 (Plate 152)
The Year 1905.
The Revolt Is Suppressed.
Caricature of Nicholas II. ⟨1905⟩
Crayons and graphite. 29.8×25 cm
The Tretyakov Gallery (since 1935).
Inv. No. 21245
Provenance: A. Guchkov collection
Nicholas II — see No 281.
Exhibitions: 1965 The Tretyakov Gallery (p. 67); / 1939 The Tretyakov Gallery — Russian History Painting (No 332)
References: Grabar, *Serov*, 1965, p. 428 (with an incorrect Inv. No 21425)

490
At the Ferry. 1905
Watercolors. 21.5×27.3 cm
Signed and dated, bottom left: *BC 905* (VS, 1905)

The Tretyakov Gallery. Inv. No. 7639
Provenance: I. Tsvetkov collection, Moscow; The Tsvetkov Gallery, Moscow
Exhibitions: 1935 The Tretyakov Gallery (No 447), The Russian Museum (No 523); 1958–59 The Tretyakov Gallery; 1959–60 The Russian Museum; 1965 The Tretyakov Gallery (p. 65), The Russian Museum; / 1963 The Tretyakov Gallery — Pencil Drawings, Watercolors, Pastels, and Gouaches (p. 71)
Reproductions: Grabar, *Serov*, 1914, p. 182; *Drawings and Watercolors. Catalogue*, 1956; Grabar, *Serov*, 1965, p. 266; *Serov: Drawings, Watercolors, Lithographs*, 1972, pl. 6
References: Grabar, *Serov*, 1914, p. 291; Grabar, *Serov*, 1965, p. 426

491

A Church. ⟨1904–5⟩
Gouache. 38×53 cm
Signed, bottom right: *BC* (VS)
Picture Gallery, Yerevan (since 1932). Inv. No. P-540
Provenance: S. Kusevitsky collection, Moscow; The Tretyakov Gallery
Exhibitions: 1914 (posthumous) Moscow (No 303); 1935 The Tretyakov Gallery (No 196, as *A Landscape*), The Russian Museum (No 190, under the same title); 1958–59 The Tretyakov Gallery; 1959–60 The Russian Museum; 1965 The Russian Museum
References: Grabar, *Serov*, 1965, p. 426

1906
PAINTINGS

492 (Plate 127)
Catherine II Driving Out. 1906
Pastel and tempera on paper, mounted on cardboard. 47×76 cm
Signed and dated, bottom left: *Съровъ 906* (Serov, 1906)
The Russian Museum (since 1918).

Inv. No. Ж-4299
Provenance: N. Yermakov collection, St. Petersburg
Catherine II — see No 400.
Exhibitions: 1914 (posthumous) St. Petersburg (No 224); 1935 The Tretyakov Gallery (No 155), The Russian Museum (No 148); 1965 The Tretyakov Gallery (p. 43); / 1909 St. Petersburg — Salon (No 361; No 469 — another edition)
Reproductions: *Apollon*, 1912, No 10, between pp. 22 and 23; Grabar, *Serov*, 1914, p. 186
References: Grabar, *Serov*, 1914, p. 292; Grabar, *Serov*, 1965, pp. 207 (as *Catherine II Departing for Tsarskoye Selo*, erroneousy dated 1904), 316, 429

493 (Plate 144)
Portrait of Alexander Nikolayevich Turchaninov. ⟨1906⟩
Oil on canvas. 87.5×97.5 cm
Signed, top left: *В. Съровъ* (V. Serov)
The Russian Museum (not later than 1923). Inv. No. Ж-4306
Provenance: District Court, Petrograd
There is a photograph of the portrait with Turchaninov's inscription: *Д. В. Стасову на память о долголътней совмъстной дъятельности и въ знакъ глубокаго уваженія. 17 апръля 1906 г. А. Турчаниновъ* (To D. V. Stasov as a sign of deep respect and as a token of our collaboration. 17 April 1906. A. Turchaninov). This photograph is preserved in the Museum of the Institute of Russian Literature (called Pushkin's House) of the USSR Academy of Sciences (Inv. No. 86091), Leningrad. The autograph refutes the traditional dating, 1907, which was suggested by Igor Grabar (*Serov*, 1914, pp. 189, 292), and I. Silberstein and V. Samkov's dating of the portrait to October—November 1906 (*Serov in the Reminiscences of His Contemporaries*, 1971, 1, p. 476). It should be noted that the date

of the autograph coincides with the 40th anniversary of Turchaninov's work as a lawyer (he was called to the Bar on 17 April 1866). It is thus possible to consider that the portrait was completed by the middle of April 1906.
Alexander Nikolayevich Turchaninov (1836–1907), lawyer, President of the St. Petersburg Association of Barristers (1903–7).
Exhibitions: 1914 (posthumous) St. Petersburg (No 224a), Moscow (No 237); 1935 The Tretyakov Gallery (No 158), The Russian Museum (No 150); 1965 The Tretyakov Gallery (p. 44), The Russian Museum; / 1908 St. Petersburg — 5th Exhibition of the Union of Russian Artists (No 225); 1911 Rome — International Art Exhibition (No 396); 1957–58 Peking, Shanghai — Russian Art (p. 28); 1972–73 Baden-Baden, Prague, Dortmund, Bratislava — Russian Realism: 1850–1900 (p. 143); 1976 Helsinki — Russian Painting and Drawing: Late 1700s to Early 1900s (No 98)
Reproductions: Grabar, *Serov*, 1914, p. 189 (dated 1907); Grabar, *Serov*, 1965, (p. 168, the same date)
References: Grabar, *Serov*, 1914, pp. 174, 292 (dated 1907); Radlov, *Serov*, 1914, p. 36; Grabar, *Serov*, 1965, pp. 174, 339 (the same date)

494 (Plate 156)
Portrait of Vladimir Mikhailovich Golitsyn. 1906
Oil on canvas. 115×92 cm
Signed and dated, top left: *Съровъ 906* (Serov, 1906)
History Museum, Moscow. Inv. No. 2114
Provenance: Town Council, Moscow
Vladimir Mikhailovich Golitsyn (1847–1932), Prince, Governor of Moscow (1887–91), Mayor of Moscow (1897–1905).
Exhibitions: 1914 (posthumous) St. Petersburg (No 216), Moscow (No 230); 1952

133. Portrait of Yelizaveta
Sergeyevna Karzinkina.
Cat. No 495

134. Portrait of Yelizaveta
Alexeyevna Krasilshchikova.
Cat. No 496

Moscow (No 222); 1958–59 The Tretyakov
Gallery; 1959 Museum of Russian Art,
Kiev; 1959–60 The Russian Museum;
1965 The Tretyakov Gallery (p. 43), The
Russian Museum; / 1911 Moscow —
1st Exhibition of the World of Art Society
(No 305)
Reproductions: Apollon, 1912, No 10, be-
tween pp. 12 and 13 (dated 1910);
Grabar, Serov, 1914, p. 185; Leniashin
1980, p. 137
References: Grabar, Serov, 1914, pp. 174,
292; Grabar, Serov, 1965, pp. 174, 339;
Leniashin 1980, pp. 140–150

495
**Portrait of Yelizaveta Sergeyevna
Karzinkina.** 1906
Oil on canvas. 104×73.7 cm (oval)
Signed and dated, bottom left: В. Съровъ
1906 (V. Serov, 1906)
Picture Gallery, Taganrog. Inv. No. Ж-130
Provenance: M. Karzinkin collection, Mos-
cow; Ye. Karzinkina collection, Moscow;
L. Ruslanova collection, Moscow; The Tre-
tyakov Gallery
Yelizaveta Sergeyevna Karzinkina — see
No 477.
Exhibitions: 1914 (posthumous) St. Peters-
burg (No 208), Moscow (No 222); 1935
The Tretyakov Gallery (No 151), The Russian Museum (No 144, as Ye. A. Karzinkina); / 1906 Moscow — 3rd Exhibition of
the Union of Russian Artists (No 270);
1908 St. Petersburg — 5th Exhibition of
the Union of Russian Artists (No 225a);
1957 Central House of Art Workers, Moscow — Works of Russian Art from Private
Collections: Late 19th and Early 20th Centuries (p. 13)
Reproductions: Grabar, Serov, 1914,
p. 180 (as Portrait of Ye. A. Karzinkina);
Leniashin 1980, p. 179
References: Grabar, Serov, 1914, pp. 168,
170, 174, 189, 205, 292; Essays on the
History of Russian Portraiture, 1964,
pp. 52, 404; Grabar, Serov, 1965, pp. 213,
214, 339

342

496
**Portrait of Yelizaveta Alexeyevna
Krasilshchikova.** 1906
Oil on canvas. 125×71 cm
Signed and dated near the sleeve, right:
ВС 906 (VS, 1906)
Museum of Russian Art, Kiev (since
1946). Inv. No. Ж-226
Provenance: O. Serova collection, Moscow
Yelizaveta Alexeyevna Krasilshchikova be-
longed to one of the richest merchant
families of Moscow (the cotton mill of An-
na Krasilshchikova and Sons was in the
Kostroma province).
Exhibitions: 1914 (posthumous) St. Peters-
burg (No 219), Moscow (No 233)
References: Grabar, Serov, 1914, p. 292;
Grabar, Serov, 1965, p. 339 (described in-
correctly as unfinished); Serov in the Reminiscences of His Contemporaries, 1971,
1, p. 528

497
**Portrait of Yelizaveta Alexeyevna
Krasilshchikova.** 1906
Pastel on canvas. 223×100 cm
Signed and dated, bottom right:
В. Съровъ 906 (V. Serov, 1906)
Art Museum, Krasnodar. Inv. No. 294
Provenance: A. Krasilshchikova collection,
Moscow

Yelizaveta Alexeyevna Krasilshchikova —
see No 496.
Exhibitions: 1914 (posthumous) St. Petersburg (No 218), Moscow (No 232)
Reproductions: Grabar, Serov the Draftsman, 1961 (detail); Leniashin 1980, p. 244
References: Grabar, Serov, 1914, p. 292
(described incorrectly as an oil painting);
Grabar, Serov, 1965, p. 363 (described
incorrectly as unfinished)

DRAWINGS, WATERCOLORS, PASTELS, AND GOUACHES

498
Teachers Taken into Exile. 1906
Pen
Signed and dated, bottom right: Съровъ
906 (Serov, 1906)
Present whereabouts unknown
Provenance: T. Staal collection, Paris;
A. F. and A. M. Staal collection, Paris
The drawing was executed at the request
of A. F. Staal (see No. 580) for an
illustrated program to be sold during the
festival organized for the benefit of the

Peasant Union in St. Petersburg (never reproduced). A drawing, similar in composition, *An Exile Taken Away on a Cart* (1905), was reproduced in Sokolova, *Serov*, 1935, p. 102.
References: *Serov in the Reminiscences of His Contemporaries*, 1971, 2, p. 351

499
Prospects for the 1906 Harvest.
⟨1905–6⟩
India ink, watercolors and pencil.
27×33 cm
Signed, bottom right: *C (S)*
The USSR Museum of the Revolution, Moscow (since 1925). Inv. No 779
Provenance: O. Serova collection, Moscow
Reproductions: Sokolova, *Serov*, 1935, p. 105
References: Sokolova, *Serov*, 1935, p. 101; Grabar, *Serov*, 1965, p. 428

500
The Artist's Children:
Olga and Antosha Serov. ⟨1906⟩
Charcoal, chalk, sanguine and crayons on cardboard. 67×97 cm
The Serov family collection, Moscow
Olga Valentinovna Serova (1891–1946); Anton (Antosha) Valentinovich Serov (1901–1942).
Exhibitions: 1914 (posthumous) St. Petersburg (No 221), Moscow (No 235); 1935 The Tretyakov Gallery (No 465), The Russian Museum (No 544); 1946 Central House of Art Workers, Moscow (No 67); 1952 Moscow (No 223); 1965 The Russian Museum
References: Grabar, *Serov*, 1914, p. 292; Grabar, *Serov*, 1965, pp. 280, 363

501 (Plate 153)
A Recruit. ⟨1906⟩
Pastel. 37×25 cm
Signed and dated, bottom right: *Сѣровъ 906* (Serov, 1906)
The Russian Museum (since 1926).
Inv. No. P-13449
Provenance: S. Krachkovsky collection, St. Petersburg; State Museum Reserve, Moscow
Exhibitions: 1914 (posthumous) St. Petersburg (No 222); 1935 The Russian Museum (No 541); 1965 The Russian Museum

Reproductions: Grabar, *Serov*, 1914, p. 184; Grabar, *Serov*, 1980, pl. 78
References: Grabar, *Serov*, 1914, p. 292; Grabar, *Serov*, 1965, p. 429

502
A Hunt with Borzois. ⟨1906⟩
Gouache
Signed, bottom right: *BC (VS)*
Present whereabouts unknown
Provenance: Marquis Palavicini collection, London
Reproductions: *Apollon*, No 4, between pp. 48 and 49 (as *A Hunt*); Grabar, *Serov*, 1914, p. 187
References: Grabar, *Serov*, 1914, p. 187; Grabar, *Serov*, 1965, p. 429

503
Portrait of Victor Petrovich
Obninsky. 1906
Pastel
Signed and dated, bottom right: *BC 906* (VS, 1906)
Present whereabouts unknown
Provenance: V. Obninsky collection, Moscow
Victor Petrovich Obninsky (1867–1916), Russian journalist.
Exhibitions: 1914 (posthumous) St. Petersburg (No 217), Moscow (No 231)
Reproductions: Grabar, *Serov*, 1914, p. 188
References: Grabar, *Serov*, 1914, p. 292; Grabar, *Serov*, 1965, p. 363

504
Portrait of Henrietta Leopoldovna
Girshman. ⟨1906⟩
Watercolors and white on yellow paper, mounted on cardboard. 39×38.5 cm
The Tretyakov Gallery (since 1922).
Inv. No. 4913
Provenance: M. Karpova collection, Moscow
Henrietta Leopoldovna Girshman — see No 452.

135. Teachers Taken into Exile. Cat. No 498

136. The Artist's Children: Olga and Antosha Serov. Cat. No 500

137. Portrait of
Victor Petrovich Obninsky.
Cat. No 503

138. Portrait of
Henrietta Leopoldovna
Girshman. Cat. No 504

A sketch for the portrait of 1907, now in
the Tretyakov Gallery (see No 509). The
traditional dating of this sketch to 1907
(Grabar, *Serov*, 1914, p. 293; *Drawings
and Watercolors. Catalogue*, 1956, p. 70;
Grabar, *Serov*, 1965, p. 365) is erroneous.
It was actually executed in 1906 (*Serov
in the Reminiscences of His Contem-
poraries*, 1971, 2, p. 329).
Exhibitions: 1914 (posthumous) St. Peters-
burg (No 235a — 2nd ed.), Moscow
(No 249); 1935 The Tretyakov Gallery
(No 482), The Russian Museum (No 564);
1958–59 The Tretyakov Gallery; 1965 The
Tretyakov Gallery (p. 69), The Russian
Museum; / 1954 The Tretyakov Gallery —
Sketches and Studies by Russian Artists
from the Tretyakov Gallery Reserve: 18th
to Early 20th Century (p. 55); 1963 The
Tretyakov Gallery — Pencil Drawings,
Watercolors, Pastels, and Gouaches
(p. 73)
Reproductions: *Drawings and Watercolors.
Catalogue*, 1956; *Serov: Drawings, Water-
colors, Lithographs*, 1972 (pl. 9, dated
1907)
References: *Serov in the Reminiscences
of His Contemporaries*, 1971, 2, p. 329;
Grabar, *Serov*, 1914, p. 293; Grabar,
Serov, 1965, p. 365 (dated 1907)

505
**Portrait of Alexander Konstantinovich
Glazunov.** 1906
Charcoal and chalk on cardboard.
89×64.5 cm
Signed and dated, bottom right: *BC 906*
(VS, 1906)
The Tretyakov Gallery (since 1912).
Inv. No. 3661
Provenance: Kudriavaya collection,
St. Petersburg
Alexander Konstantinovich Glazunov —
see No 348.
Exhibitions: 1935 The Tretyakov Gallery

(No 463), The Russian Museum (No 542);
1958–59 The Tretyakov Gallery; 1965 The
Tretyakov Gallery (p. 69), The Russian
Museum; / 1941 The Tretyakov Gallery —
Portrait Drawings: 18th to Early 20th Cen-
tury (No 123); 1949 The Pushkin
Museum of Fine Arts, Moscow — Russian
Graphic Art: 18th to Early 20th Century;
1963 The Tretyakov Gallery — Pencil
Drawings, Watercolors, Pastels, and
Gouaches (p. 72)
Reproductions: Yaremich, *Serov: Draw-
ings*, 1936; *Drawings and Watercolors.
Catalogue*, 1956; Grabar, *Serov*, 1980,
pl. 79
References: Grabar, *Serov*, 1965, p. 363;
Yaremich, *Serov: Drawings*, 1936, p. 15

1907
PAINTINGS

506 (Plate 166)
Peter the Great. From the
Pictorial History of Russia series. ⟨1907⟩
Tempera on cardboard. 68.5×88 cm
The Tretyakov Gallery (since 1908).
Inv. No. 1531
Peter the Great — see No 402.
Exhibitions: 1935 The Tretyakov Gallery
(No 174), The Russian Museum (No 158);
1958–59 The Tretyakov Gallery; 1959
Museum of Russian Art, Kiev; 1959–60
The Russian Museum; 1965 The
Tretyakov Gallery (p. 45), The Russian
Museum; / 1907–8 Moscow, 1908
St. Petersburg — 5th Exhibition of the
Union of Russian Artists (Nos 189, 222);
1939 The Tretyakov Gallery — Russian
History Painting (No 334)
Reproductions: *Pictorial History of Russia*,
1908; Grabar, *Serov*, 1914, between
pp. 264 and 265; Grabar, *Serov*, 1980,
pl. 81, 82

References: Grabar, *Serov*, 1914,
pp. 247–251, 293; Grabar, *Serov*, 1965,
pp. 208, 210, 211, 432; Sarabyanov, *Reforms by Valentin Serov*, 1971, pp. 17, 31

507
**Portrait of Alexander Pavlovich Lensky
and Alexander Ivanovich Yuzhin,
Actors of the Maly Theater in Moscow.**
⟨1907⟩
Tempera on canvas. 149×143 cm
The Tretyakov Gallery. Inv. No. 28081
Provenance: Circle of Literature and Art,
Moscow; Maly Theater, Moscow
According to the entry of 23 November,
1907, in V. Teliakovsky's diary (*Serov in
the Reminiscences of His Contemporaries*,
1971, 2, p. 504), the portrait should be
dated to the late 1907.
Alexander Pavlovich Lensky (stage name
of Verviciotti, 1847–1908), Russian actor,
stage director and teacher of dramatic art.
Alexander Ivanovich Yuzhin (stage name
of Sumbatashvili, 1857–1927), Russian
actor and playwright, People's Artist of the
RSFSR (since 1922).
Exhibitions: 1914 (posthumous) St. Petersburg (not listed in the Catalogue), Moscow
(No 256); 1935 The Tretyakov Gallery
(No 170); / 1908–9 Moscow, 1909
St. Petersburg — 6th Exhibition of the
Union of Russian Artists (Nos 296, 383);
1911 Rome — International Art Exhibition
(No 398); 1954 Central House of Art
Workers, Moscow — Portraits of Promi-
nent Personalities in Russian Art: 18th to
20th Century (No 77)
Reproductions: Grabar, *Serov*, 1914,
p. 206; Grabar, *Serov*, 1980, pl. 89
References: Grabar, *Serov*, 1914, pp. 178,
199, 200, 293; Grabar, *Serov*, 1965,
pp. 172, 174, 340, 488 (described incorrectly as an oil painting); *Serov in the
Reminiscences of His Contemporaries*,
1971, 2, pp. 512–514

508
Portrait of Alexander Vasilyevich Kasyanov. 1907
Oil on canvas. 95×75 cm
Signed and dated, bottom left: *Съровъ 907* (Serov, 1907)
Picture Gallery of the Museum of Local Lore, Tomsk
Provenance: A. Kasyanov collection, Moscow
Alexander Vasilyevich Kasyanov, Siberian businessman.
Exhibitions: 1914 (posthumous) St. Petersburg (No 238), Moscow (No 251); 1965 The Tretyakov Gallery (p. 44), The Russian Museum
Reproductions: Grabar, *Serov*, 1914, p. 197; Grabar, *Serov*, 1965, p. 169
References: Grabar, *Serov*, 1914, pp. 174, 293; Grabar, *Serov*, 1965, pp. 174, 177, 339, 340; Leniashin 1980, pp. 150, 154, 156

509 (Plates 159, 160)
Portrait of Henrietta Leopoldovna Girshman. 1907
Tempera on canvas. 140×140 cm
Signed and dated, bottom left: *Съровъ 907* (Serov, 1907)
The Tretyakov Gallery (since 1917).
Inv. No 5586
Provenance: V. Girshman collection, Moscow
Henrietta Leopoldovna Girshman — see No 452.
Exhibitions: 1914 (posthumous) St. Petersburg (No 235), Moscow (No 248); 1935 The Tretyakov Gallery (No 157), The Russian Museum (No 149); 1958–59 The Tretyakov Gallery; 1965 The Tretyakov Gallery (p. 44), The Russian Museum; / 1907–8 Moscow, 1908 St. Petersburg — 5th Exhibition of the Union of Russian Artists (No 188, 221)

Reproductions: *Zolotoye Runo*, 1908, No 1, between pp. 12 and 13; Grabar, *Serov*, 1914, between pp. 192 and 193; Grabar, *Serov*, 1965, pp. 223, 225 (detail)
References: Grabar, *Serov*, 1914, pp. 184, 186, 188, 189, 194, 198, 293; Grabar, *Serov*, 1965, pp. 214, 217, 339; *Serov in the Reminiscences of His Contemporaries*, 1971, 2, pp. 327–330; Sarabyanov, *Reforms by Valentin Serov*, 1971, p. 24

Scenery designs for Serov's opera *Judith*, staged at the Mariinsky Theater, St. Petersburg, in 1907 (Nos 510–515)

510 (Plate 197)
Acts I and V: Square in Besieged Bethul, an Ancient Judaean Town.
⟨1907⟩
Tempera on paper, mounted on cardboard. 55.5×71.2 cm
Signed, top right: *Съров* (Serov)
The Russian Museum (since 1912).
Inv. No Ж-4294
Provenance: Directorate of the Imperial Theaters, St. Petersburg
Exhibitions: 1935 The Tretyakov Gallery (No 159), The Russian Museum (No 153); 1965 The Russian Museums; / 1909 St. Petersburg — Salon
Reproductions: Grabar, *Serov*, 1914, p. 194; Radlov, *Serov*, 1914, between pp. 16 and 17; Sokolova, Vlasov 1959, p. 62; Grabar, *Serov*, 1965, p. 299
References: Grabar, *Serov*, 1914, p. 292; Grabar, *Serov*, 1965, pp. 298 (described incorrectly as a watercolor), 430

511
Act II: Judith's House at Bethul.
⟨1907⟩
Tempera on paper, mounted on cardboard. 55×71.5 cm
Signed, top left: *Съровъ* (Serov)
The Russian Museum (since 1912).
Inv. No Ж-4295
Provenance: Directorate of the Imperial Theaters, St. Petersburg
Exhibitions: 1935 The Tretyakov Gallery (No 160), The Russian Museum (No 152, described incorrectly as an oil painting); 1958–59 The Russian Museum; 1965 The Tretyakov Gallery (p. 44), The Russian Museum; / 1909 St. Petersburg — Salon
References: Grabar, *Serov*, 1914, p. 292; Grabar, *Serov*, 1965, pp. 298 (described incorrectly as a watercolor), 430

512
Act II: Judith's House at Bethul.
⟨1907⟩
Tempera on cardboard. 47.6×73 cm
Signed, bottom left: *Съровъ* (Serov)
Inscribed by the artist, below: *Опера „Юдиѳь" 2 актъ* (Opera *Judith*, Act 2)
The Tretyakov Gallery (since 1914).
Inv. No 1532
Exhibitions: 1914 (posthumous) St. Petersburg (No 247), Moscow (No 261); 1935 The Tretyakov Gallery (No 156), The Russian Museum (No 151); 1952 Moscow (No 239); 1958–59 The Tretyakov Gallery; 1959–60 The Russian Museum; 1965 The Tretyakov Gallery (pp. 43, 44)
Reproductions: Zotov, *Serov*, 1964, No 31
References: Grabar, *Serov*, 1914, p. 292; Grabar, *Serov*, 1965, p. 430

139. Portrait of Alexander Vasilyevich Kasyanov. Cat. No 508

140. Act II: Judith's House at Bethul. Cat. No 511

345

141. Act II: Judith's House at Bethul. Cat. No 513

142. Act IV: Feast in the Tent of Holofernes. Cat. No 515

513

Act II: Judith's House at Bethul. ⟨1907⟩
Tempera on paper, mounted on cardboard. 55.7×71.5 cm
The Russian Museum (since 1941).
Inv. No Ж-8738
Provenance: G. Ehrlich collection, Leningrad
References: Grabar, *Serov*, 1965, p. 430

143. A Mule. Cat. No 516

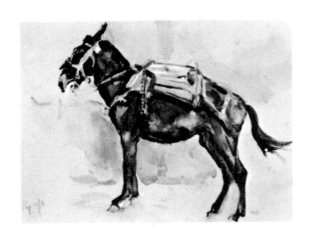

514 (Plate 196)

Act III: Holofernes's Tent. 1907
Tempera on paper, mounted on cardboard. 55×71.5 cm
Signed and dated, top right: *Съровъ 907*
(Serov, 1907)
The Russian Museum (since 1912).
Inv. No Ж-4293
Provenance: Directorate of the Imperial Theaters, St. Petersburg
Exhibitions: 1935 The Tretyakov Gallery (No 161), The Russian Museum (No 154); 1958–59 The Tretyakov Gallery; 1965 The Tretyakov Gallery (p. 44), The Russian Museum
References: Grabar, *Serov*, 1914, p. 292; Grabar, *Serov*, 1965, pp. 298 (described incorrectly as a watercolor), 430

515

Act IV: Feast in the Tent of Holofernes. 1907
Tempera on paper, mounted on cardboard. 55×73 cm
Signed and dated, top right: *Съровъ 907*

(Serov, 1907)
The Russian Museum (since 1912).
Inv. No Ж-4296
Provenance: Directorate of the Imperial Theaters, St. Petersburg
Exhibitions: 1935 The Tretyakov Gallery (No 162), The Russian Museum (No 155); 1965 The Russian Museum; / 1909 St. Petersburg — Salon
References: Grabar, *Serov*, 1914, p. 292; Grabar, *Serov*, 1965, pp. 298 (described incorrectly as a watercolor), 430

DRAWINGS, WATERCOLORS, GOUACHES, PASTELS, AND LITHOGRAPHS

516

A Mule. ⟨1907⟩
Watercolor. 23×35.3 cm
Inscribed by the artist, bottom left: *Критъ*
(Crete)
The Russian Museum (since 1912).
Inv. No P-13421
A study for the 1910 painting *Odysseus and Nausicaä* (see Nos 572–575).
Exhibitions: 1935 The Tretyakov Gallery (No 474), The Russian Museum (No 553)
Reproductions: *Serov: The Sun of Russia*, 1913
References: Grabar, *Serov*, 1914, p. 292; Grabar, *Serov*, 1965, p. 431

517

Peter the Great. ⟨1907⟩
Black chalk and pastel. 47.2×59.8 cm; 38.5×56 cm (in a frame)
The Russian Museum (since 1926).
Inv. No P-3223
Provenance: Z. Rumanova collection, Petrograd
A sketch for the 1907 picture *Peter the Great* (see No 506).
Peter the Great — see No 402.
Exhibitions: 1935 The Tretyakov Gallery (No 473), The Russian Museum (No 552)
References: Grabar, *Serov*, 1965, p. 432

518 (Plate 179)

Portrait of the Kasyanov Children.
1907
Pressed charcoal, sanguine and chalk on gray paper, mounted on cardboard. 86.5×68 cm
Signed and dated, top left: *Съровъ 907*
(Serov, 1907)
The Tretyakov Gallery. Inv. No 10029
Provenance: A. Kasyanov collection, Moscow
N. A. and T. A. Kasyanova, daughters of the Siberian businessman Alexander Vasilyevich Kasyanov (see No 508).
Exhibitions: 1914 (posthumous) St. Petersburg (No 236), Moscow (No 250); 1935 The Tretyakov Gallery (No 470), The Russian Museum (No 549); / 1907–8 Moscow — 5th Exhibition of the Union of Russian Artists (No 192)
Reproductions: Grabar, *Serov*, 1914, p. 196 (as *N. A. and T. A. Kasyanova*); Grabar, *Serov*, 1965, p. 270
References: Grabar, *Serov*, 1914, pp. 166, 293; Grabar, *Serov*, 1965, pp. 278, 365 (as *The Kasyanov Girls*)

519 (Plate 175)
Portrait of Wanda Landowska. ⟨1907⟩
Black chalk, watercolors, white and pastel on primed gray paper, mounted on cardboard. 55.5×37.5 cm
The Tretyakov Gallery (since 1929).
Inv. No 11306
Provenance: I. Ostroukhov collection, Moscow; The Ostroukhov Museum of Icons and Painting, Moscow
Wanda Landowska (1877–1959), Polish harpsichord player.
Exhibitions: 1914 (posthumous) St. Petersburg (No 228), Moscow (No 241); 1935 The Tretyakov Gallery (No 466), The Russian Museum (No 545); 1958–59 The Tretyakov Gallery; 1965 The Tretyakov Gallery (p. 70), The Russian Museum; / 1941 The Tretyakov Gallery — Portrait Drawings: 18th to Early 20th Century (No 125); 1963 The Tretyakov Gallery — Pencil Drawings, Watercolors, Pastels, and Gouaches (p. 73)
Reproductions: Grabar, *Serov*, 1914, p. 193; *Apollon*, 1914, No 6/7, between pp. 18 and 19 (dated 1906/7); Grabar, *Serov*, 1980, pl. 86
References: Grabar, *Serov*, 1965, p. 364

520 (Plate 162)
Portrait of Leonid Nikolayevich Andreyev. 1907
Watercolors and tempera on cardboad. 73.3×56.4 cm
Signed and dated, bottom left: *BC 907* (VS, 1907)
State Museum of Literature, Moscow (since 1927). Inv. No X-214
Provenance: N. Riabushinsky collection, Moscow; M. Riabushinsky collection, Moscow; State Museum Reserve, Moscow
Leonid Nikolayevich Andreyev (1871–1919), Russian novelist and playwright.
Exhibitions: 1914 (posthumous) St. Petersburg (No 230), Moscow (No 244); 1935 The Tretyakov Gallery (No 163), The Russian Museum (No 156); 1952 Moscow (No 227); 1958–59 The Tretyakov Gallery; 1965 The Tretyakov Gallery (p. 69); / 1907–8 Moscow, 1908 St. Petersburg — 5th Exhibition of the Union of Russian Artists (Nos 190, 223)
Reproductions: *Zolotoye Runo*, 1908, No 7–9, between pp. 4 and 5; Grabar, *Serov*, 1914, p. 195; Grabar, *Serov*, 1965, p. 173
References: Grabar, *Serov*, 1914, p. 292; Grabar, *Serov*, 1965, p. 364; *Serov's Correspondence*, 1937, p. 368

521
Portrait of Leonid Nikolayevich Andreyev. ⟨1907⟩
Lithograph. 23.7×18.3 cm
State Musem of Literature, Moscow (since 1934). Inv. No Б-1622
Provenance: O. Serova collection, Moscow; A. Mironov collection, Moscow
Leonid Nikolayevich Andreyev — see No 520.
Exhibitions: 1914 (posthumous) Moscow (No 148); 1952 Moscow (No 411)
NOTE: Other impressions of the lithograph from the collections of the Tretyakov Gallery and the Institute of Russian Literature (known as the Pushkin House) of the USSR Academy of Sciences, Leningrad, were shown at the following

exhibitions: 1935 The Tretyakov Gallery (No 799), The Russian Museum (No 1069); 1965 The Russian Museum.
Reproductions: Arbuzov, *Serov*, 1960, No 23
References: Grabar, *Serov*, 1914, p. 292; Grabar, *Serov*, 1965, p. 356

522 (Plate 161)
Portrait of Leonid Nikolayevich Andreyev. ⟨1907⟩
Lithograph. 25×20 cm
The Pushkin Museum of Fine Arts, Print Room (since 1920), Moscow.
Inv. No 14607
Provenance: S. Vinogradov collection, Moscow
Leonid Nikolayevich Andreyev — see No 520.
Exhibitions: 1952 Moscow (No 412)
Reproductions: *Maski*, 1912, No 1; Grabar, *Serov*, 1965, p. 172; *Serov: Drawings, Watercolors, Lithographs*, 1972, pl. 12
References: Grabar, *Serov*, 1914, p. 292; Grabar, *Serov*, 1965, p. 356

523 (Plate 169)
Portrait of Mikhail Alexandrovich Vrubel. ⟨1907⟩
Pressed charcoal, sanguine and chalk. 39.7×29.8 cm
The Tretyakov Gallery (since 1917).
Inv. No 5415
Provenance: N. Riabushinsky collection, Moscow; V. Girshman collection, Moscow
Mikhail Alexandrovich Vrubel — see No 65.
Exhibitions: 1914 (posthumous) Moscow (No 167, dated 1902); 1935 The Tretyakov Gallery (No 467), The Russian Museum (No 546); 1958–59 The Tretyakov Gallery; 1965 The Tretyakov Gallery (p. 70), The Russian Museum; / 1949 The Pushkin Museum of Fine Arts, Moscow — Russian Graphic Art: 18th to Early 20th Century; 1954 Central House of Art Workers, Moscow — Portraits of Prominent Personalities in Russian Art: 18th to 20th Century (No 151)
Reproductions: *Zolotoye Runo*, 1909, No 11/12, between pp. 86 and 87; Yaremich, *Serov: Drawings*, 1936; Grabar, *Serov the Draftsman*, 1961; Grabar, *Serov*, 1980, pl. 83
References: Grabar, *Serov*, 1965, pp. 282, 364

524
Mikhail Alexeyevich Kuzmin.
Caricature. 1907
Pencil. 24.5×30.2 cm
Inscribed in pencil in Konstantin Somov's hand, bottom right: *В. А. Сѣровъ Сентябрь 1907 г.* (V. A. Serov, September 1907)
I. Silberstein collection, Moscow
Provenance: O. Serova collection, Moscow; K. Somov collection, St. Petersburg
Mikhail Alexeyevich Kuzmin (1875–1936), Russian poet, prose writer, playwright, translator and composer.
Exhibitions: 1946 Central House of Art Workers, Moscow (No 38)
Reproductions: Grabar, *Serov*, 1914, p. 278 (dated 1909)
References: Grabar, *Serov*, 1914, p. 293 (dated 1909); Grabar, *Serov*, 1965, p. 365;

Serov in the Reminiscences of His Contemporaries, 1971, 2, p. 342 (dated 1909)

144. The Landing Stage. Nauplion. Cat. No 525

525
The Landing Stage. Nauplion. ⟨1907⟩
Watercolors. 27.5×18.3 cm
Inscribed in pencil by the artist, top right: *Невплія Nauplia*
The Russian Museum (since 1912).
Inv. No P-6541
Exhibitions: 1935 The Tretyakov Gallery (No 477), The Russian Museum (No 556); 1965 The Russian Museum
Reproductions: *Serov: The Sun of Russia*, 1913 (as *A Study*)
References: Grabar, *Serov*, 1914, p. 292; Grabar, *Serov*, 1965, p. 431

526
The Propylaea. ⟨1907⟩
Watercolors. 35×22.5 cm
Top right, an impression of the artist's signet: *BC* (VS)
The Russian Museum (since 1926).
Inv. No P-13435

145. The Propylaea. Cat. No 526

146. Portrait of Anna Karlovna
Benois. Cat. No 530

147. Fiodor Shaliapin
as Holofernes. Costume design
for Alexander Serov's opera
Judith. Cat. No 527

527

Fiodor Shaliapin as Holofernes.
Costume design for Alexander Serov's
opera *Judith.* ⟨1907⟩
Watercolors. 22×17 cm
The Russian Museum, Leningrad (since
1912). Inv. No P-6540
Fiodor Ivanovich Shaliapin — see
No 444.

Exhibitions: 1935 The Tretyakov Gallery
(No 486), The Russian Museum (No 568);
1965 The Russian Museum
References: Grabar, *Serov*, 1914, p. 292;
Grabar, *Serov*, 1965, p. 364

1908
PAINTING

528

Jukkola, Finland. Forest View.
⟨1907–8⟩
Oil on canvas
The Malmö Museum, Sweden
(since 1924)
Provenance: O. Serova collection, Mos-
cow; A. Liapunov collection, Moscow
Exhibitions: 1914 (posthumous) St. Peters-
burg (No 240), Moscow (No 253); / 1914
Malmö (Sweden) — Baltic Art Exhibition
(No 3237); 1924 New York — Russian Art
(No 682, as *Finland*)
References: Grabar, *Serov*, 1965, pp. 432,
433

529

The Smart Moscow Cabman. 1908
Tempera on cardboard. 37.5×53.5 cm
Signed and dated, bottom right: *BC 908*
(VS, 1908)
The Russian Museum. Inv. No Ж-4300
Provenance: A. Korovin collection,
St. Petersburg
A version of the picture of the same name,
now in the Tretyakov Gallery
(see No 537).
Exhibitions: 1935 The Tretyakov Gallery
(No 165), The Russian Museum (No 160);
1965 The Tretyakov Gallery (p. 45); / 1909
St. Petersburg — Salon (No 374; No 481
— another ed.)
Reproductions: *Apollon*, 1912, No 10,
p. 18; Grabar, *Serov*, 1914, p. 204 (de-
scribed incorrectly as belonging to
M. Riabushinsky, Moscow); Simonovich-
Yefimova 1964, p. 84; Grabar, *Serov*,
1980, pl. 87
References: Simonovich-Yefimova 1964,
pp. 83, 167; Grabar, *Serov*, 1965,
p. 433

530

**Portrait of Anna Karlovna
Benois.** ⟨1908⟩
Pastel on cardboard. 48×36 cm (oval)
The Russian Museum (since 1932).
Inv. No Ж-5666
Provenance: A. Benois collection,
St. Petersburg
Anna Karlovna Benois, née King
(1869–1952), painter, wife of Alexander
Benois (1870–1960), Russian artist and
art historian, one of the organizers of the
World of Art society.
Exhibitions: 1914 (posthumous) St. Peters-
burg (No 243), Moscow (No 257); 1935
The Tretyakov Gallery (No 167), The Rus-
sian Museum (No 162); 1959–60 The Rus-
sian Museum; 1965 The Tretyakov Gallery
(p. 71); / 1909 St. Petersburg — 6th Exhi-
bition of the Union of Russian Artists
(No 385); 1914 Malmö (Sweden) — Baltic
Art Exhibition (No 3231); 1959 Leningrad
— Russian Portrait Painting: 18th to Early
20th Century (p. 35)
Reproductions: Grabar, *Serov*, 1914,
p. 198; Grabar, *Serov*, 1980, pl. 92
References: Grabar, *Serov*, 1914, pp. 266,
293; Grabar, *Serov*, 1965, pp. 270, 340;

*Serov in the Reminiscences of His Con-
temporaries*, 1971, 1, pp. 430, 431

531

**Portrait of Dmitry Vasilyevich
Stasov.** ⟨1908⟩
Oil on canvas. 66×47 cm
Signed, bottom right: *Съровъ* (Serov)
The Russian Museum (since 1923).
Inv. No Ж-4308
Provenance: District Court, Petrograd;
I. Rybakov collection, Petrograd
Dmitry Vasilyevich Stasov (1828–1918),
lawyer, member of the Association of
Barristers, music critic and public figure.
Exhibitions: 1914 (posthumous) St. Peters-
burg (No 254), Moscow (No 277); 1935
The Tretyakov Gallery (No 168), The Rus-
sian Museum (No 163); 1958–59 The Tre-
tyakov Gallery; 1959 Museum of Russian
Art, Kiev; 1959–60 The Russian Museum;
1965 The Tretyakov Gallery (p. 45),
The Russian Museum; / 1911 Moscow,
St. Petersburg — 1st Exhibition of Paintings of the World of Art Society (Nos 300,
258); 1916 St. Petersburg — In Aid of
Polish Invalid Soldiers (No 132)
Reproductions: *Apollon*, 1911, No 2,
between pp. 16 and 17; Grabar, *Serov*,
1914, p. 208; Asafyev 1966, between
pp. 136 and 137; Leniashin 1980, p. 155
References: Grabar, *Serov*, 1914,
pp. 202–204, 293; Grabar, *Serov*, 1965,
pp. 224, 340

532

Portrait of Yevgeniya Alafuzova.
⟨1907–8⟩
Oil on cardboard. 48.5×54 cm (oval)
Signed, bottom left: *Съровъ* (Serov)
Picture Gallery, Odessa (since 1926).
Inv. No Ж-549
Provenance: Ye. Alafuzova collection,
St. Petersburg; M. Braikevich collection,
Odessa
Yevgenia Leon. Alafuzova, née Dobro-
tvorskaya.
Exhibitions: 1914 (posthumous) St. Peters-
burg (No 238); 1935 The Russian Museum
(No 157); / 1926 Odessa — Paintings from
the Odessa Art Museum Reserve (No 114)
Reproductions: *Serov's Works in the
Odessa Art Gallery*
References: Grabar, *Serov*, 1914, p. 292
(dated 1907); Grabar, *Serov*, 1965, p. 340

533

**Portrait of Yevdokia Sergeyevna
Morozova.** 1908
Oil on canvas. 114×75 cm
Signed and dated, bottom left: *Съровъ
908* (Serov, 1908)
The Tretyakov Gallery. Inv. No 10871
Provenance: I. Morozov collection,
Moscow
Yevdokia Sergeyevna Morozova, wife of
the art collector Ivan Abramovich Morozov
(see No 581).
Exhibitions: 1914 (posthumous) Moscow
(No 269); 1935 The Tretyakov Gallery
(No 164), The Russian Museum (No 159);
/ 1908–9 Moscow — 6th Exhibition of the
Union of Russian Artists (No 297);
1976–77 Frankfort on the Main, Munich,
Hamburg — Russian Painting: 1890–1917
(No 13)
Reproductions: *Apollon*, 1912, No 10, be-
tween pp. 8 and 9; Grabar, *Serov*, 1914,
p. 207; Leniashin 1980, p. 165

References: Grabar, *Serov*, 1914, p. 293; Grabar, *Serov*, 1965, p. 340; *Serov in the Reminiscences of His Contemporaries*, 1971, 2, pp. 366, 370

534 (Plate 176)
Portrait of Maria Nikolayevna Akimova. ⟨1908⟩
Oil on canvas. 77×62 cm
Signed, bottom right: *Съровъ* (Serov)
Picture Gallery, Yerevan (since 1929).
Inv. No Ж-548
Provenance: M. Akimova collection, Moscow; V. Kananova (Kananian) collection, Moscow
Maria Nikolayevna Akimova (Akimian, 1869–1933), daughter of a rich Moscow philanthropist V. I. Kananova (Akimova by first marriage).
Exhibitions: 1914 (posthumous) St. Petersburg (No 255), Moscow (No 278); 1935 The Tretyakov Gallery (No 169), The Russian Museum (No 164); 1958–59 The Tretyakov Gallery; 1959 Museum of Russian Art, Kiev; 1959–60 The Russian Museum; 1965 The Tretyakov Gallery (p. 45); / 1908–9 Moscow, 1909 St. Petersburg — 6th Exhibition of the Union of Russian Artists (Nos 298, 384); 1911 Rome — International Art Exhibition (No 390); 1960 Paris — Russian and Soviet Painting (No 55)
Reproductions: Grabar, *Serov*, 1914, p. 209; Sokolova, Vlasov 1959, between pp. 68 and 69; Grabar, *Serov*, 1965, p. 218
References: Grabar, *Serov*, 1914, pp. 204–206, 208, 210, 212, 293; Grabar, *Serov*, 1965, pp. 224, 227, 309, 340; *Serov in the Reminiscences of His Contemporaries*, 1971, 2, pp. 525–527

535 (Plate 177)
Portrait of Nikolai Stepanovich Pozniakov. 1908
Oil on canvas. 83×100 cm
Signed and dated, top right: *В.С. 908* (VS, 1908)
The Tretyakov Gallery (since 1948).
Inv. No 27315
Provenance: N. Pozniakov collection, Moscow
Nikolai Stepanovich Pozniakov (1879—1941), composer, Professor of the Moscow Conservatory and ballet master of the Bolshoi Theater.
Exhibitions: 1914 (posthumous) St. Petersburg (No 245), Moscow (No 259); 1952 Moscow (No 241); / 1909 St. Petersburg — Salon (No 363; No 471 – another ed.); 1909–10 Moscow — 7th Exhibition of the Union of Russian Artists (No 338); 1910–11 Odessa, Kiev, Kharkov — Art Exhibition Organized by A. Filippov (No 181); 1914 Malmö (Sweden) — Baltic Art Exhibition (No 3214); 1954 Central House of Art Workers, Moscow — Portraits of Prominent Personalities in Russian Art: 18th to 20th Century (No 190)
Reproductions: Grabar, *Serov*, 1914, p. 199; *Apollon*, 1914, No 6/7, between pp. 14 and 15; Zotov, *Serov*, 1964, pl. 33 (detail)
References: Grabar, *Serov*, 1914, pp. 178, 212, 293; Grabar, *Serov*, 1965, p. 340; *Serov in the Reminiscences of His Contemporaries*, 1971, 1, pp. 467, 468

148. Portrait of Yevgeniya Alafuzova. Cat. No 532

149. Portrait of Dmitry Vasilyevich Stasov. Cat. No 531

DRAWINGS AND WATERCOLORS

536
A Carriage. ⟨1908⟩
Watercolors and white. 15.2×28.2 cm
Signed in pencil, bottom right: *ВС* (VS)
The Tretyakov Gallery (since 1929).
Inv. No 11304
Provenance: I. Ostroukhov collection, Moscow; The Ostroukhov Museum of Icons and Painting, Moscow
Exhibitions: 1914 (posthumous) St. Petersburg (No 250), Moscow (No 268); 1935 The Tretyakov Gallery (No 489), The Russian Museum (No 576); 1952 Moscow (No 245); 1958–59 The Tretyakov Gallery; 1965 The Tretyakov Gallery (p. 72), The Russian Museum; / 1949 The Pushkin Museum of Fine Arts, Moscow — Russian Graphic Art: 18th to Early 20th Century; 1963 The Tretyakov Gallery — Pencil Drawings, Watercolors, Pastels, and Gouaches (p. 74)
Reproductions: Grabar, *Serov*, 1914, p. 205; Yaremich, *Serov: Drawings*, 1936
References: Grabar, *Serov*, 1914, p. 293; Grabar, *Serov*, 1965, p. 433

150. A Carriage. Cat. No 536

537
The Smart Moscow Cabman. ⟨1908⟩
Tempera, pastel and white. 35×50.5 cm
Signed in pencil, bottom left: *BC* (VS).
Inscribed in pencil by the artist, top right:
Лихачъ (Cabman)
The Tretyakov Gallery. Inv. No 9902
Provenance: M. Riabushinsky collection,
Moscow
Exhibitions: 1914 (posthumous) St. Peters-
burg (No 249), Moscow (No 267); 1935
The Tretyakov Gallery (No 166), The Rus-
sian Museum (No 161)
Reproductions: Grabar, *Serov*, 1980,
p. 175
References: Grabar, *Serov*, 1914, p. 293;
Grabar, *Serov*, 1965, p. 433

538
Model. 1908
Watercolors on yellow paper. 37.5×34 cm
Signed and dated, bottom right: *BC 908*
(VS,1908)
The Russian Museum (since 1912).
Inv. No P-13446
Exhibitions: 1935 The Tretyakov Gallery
(No 374, dated 1899), The Russian
Museum (No 581)
Reproductions: Dmitriyev, *Serov*, 1914
References: Grabar, *Serov*, 1965, p. 433

539 (Plate 182)
**Portrait of Vasily Ivanovich
Kachalov.** 1908
Graphite. 31.2×23.7 cm
Signed and dated, bottom right: *BC 908*
(VS, 1908)
The Tretyakov Gallery (since 1917).
Inv. No 5417
Provenance: V. Girshman collection,
Moscow
Vasily Ivanovich Kachalov (Shverubovich)
(1875–1948), actor of the Moscow Art
Theater, People's Artist of the USSR
(since 1936).
Exhibitions: 1914 (posthumous) Moscow
(No 275); 1935 The Tretyakov Gallery
(No 492), The Russian Museum (No 579);
1958–59 The Tretyakov Gallery; 1959
Museum of Russian Art, Kiev; 1959–60
The Russian Museum; 1965 The
Tretyakov Gallery (pp. 70, 71), The Rus-
sian Museum; / 1941 The Tretyakov Gal-
lery — Portrait Drawings: 18th to Early
20th Century (No 128); 1963 The Tretyakov Gallery — Pencil Drawings, Watercolors, Pastels, and Gouaches (p. 73)
Reproductions: Grabar, *Serov*, 1914,
p. 203; Grabar, *Serov*, 1965, p. 273;
*Serov: Drawings, Watercolors, Litho-
graphs*, 1972 (pl. 10)
References: Grabar, *Serov*, 1914, pp. 166,
293; Grabar, *Serov*, 1965, pp. 277, 366;
Liaskovskaya 1965, pp. 59, 60; *Serov in
the Reminiscences of His Contemporaries*,
1971, 2, pp. 345, 346

540 (Plate 181)
**Portrait of Ivan Mikhailovich
Moskvin.** 1908
Graphite on paper, mounted on cardboard.
31.2×23.7 cm
Signed and dated, bottom right: *BC 908*
(VS, 1908)
The Tretyakov Gallery (since 1917).
Inv. No 5418
Provenance: V. Girshman collection,
Moscow
Ivan Mikhailovich Moskvin (1874–1946),
actor of the Moscow Art Theater, People's
Artist of the USSR (since 1936).
Exhibitions: 1914 (posthumous) Moscow
(No 276); 1935 The Tretyakov Gallery
(No 493), The Russian Museum (No 580);
1958–59 The Tretyakov Gallery; 1959

Museum of Russian Art, Kiev; 1959–60
The Russian Museum; 1965 The Tret-
yakov Gallery (p. 71), The Russian
Museum, / 1909 St. Petersburg — Salon
(No 366; No 473 — another ed.); 1909–10
Moscow — 7th Exhibition of the Union of
Russian Artists (No 337); 1941 The Tret-
yakov Gallery — Portrait Drawings: 18th to
Early 20th Century (No 129); 1949 The
Pushkin Museum of Fine Arts, Moscow —
Russian Graphic Art: 18th to Early 20th
Century; 1963 The Tretyakov Gallery —
Pencil Drawings, Watercolors, Pastels,
and Gouaches (p. 74)
Reproductions: Grabar, *Serov*, 1914,
p. 202; Grabar, *Serov*, 1965, p. 272;
Yaremich, *Serov: Drawings*, 1936
References: Grabar, *Serov*, 1914, pp. 166,
293; Grabar, *Serov*, 1965, pp. 365, 366;
Liaskovskaya 1965, pp. 59, 60; *Serov in
the Reminiscences of His Contemporaries*,
1971, 2, pp. 348, 349

541 (Plate 183)
**Portrait of Konstantin Sergeyevich
Stanislavsky.** 1908
Graphite. 31×24 cm
Signed and dated, bottom right: *908 BC*
(1908, VS)
The Tretyakov Gallery (since 1917).
Inv. No 5419
Provenance: V. Girshman collection,
Moscow
Konstantin Sergeyevich Stanislavsky
(Alexeyev) (1863–1938), actor, stage
director, theoretician, and founder of the
Moscow Art Theater, People's Artist of the
USSR (since 1936).
Exhibitions: 1914 (posthumous) Moscow
(No 273); 1935 The Tretyakov Gallery
(No 491), The Russian Museum (No 578);
1958–59 The Tretyakov Gallery; 1959–60
The Russian Museum; 1965 The
Tretyakov Gallery (p. 70), The Russian
Museum; / 1909 St. Petersburg — Salon
(No 369; No 476 — another ed.); 1909–10
Moscow — 7th Exhibition of the Union of
Russian Artists (No 336); 1941 The
Tretyakov Gallery — Portrait Drawings:
18th to Early 20th Century (No 126); 1963
The Tretyakov Gallery — Pencil Drawings,
Watercolors, Pastels, and Gouaches
(p. 73)
Reproductions: Grabar, *Serov*, 1914,
p. 201; Grabar, *Serov*, 1965, p. 276;
Yaremich, *Serov: Drawings*, 1936
References: Grabar, *Serov*, 1914, pp. 166,
293; Grabar, *Serov*, 1965, pp. 277, 365;
Liaskovskaya 1965, pp. 59, 60

542 (Plate 170)
**Portrait of Nikolai Andreyevich
Rimsky-Korsakov.** 1908
Pressed charcoal on paper, mounted on
cardboard. 64×45 cm
Signed and dated, bottom right: *BC 908*
(VS, 1908)
The Tretyakov Gallery (since 1920).
Inv. No 5777
Provenance: S. Kusevitsky collection,
Moscow
Nikolai Andreyevich Rimsky-Korsakov —
see No 316.
Exhibitions: 1914 (posthumous) Moscow
(No 274); 1935 The Tretyakov Gallery
(No 440), The Russian Museum (No 577);
1958–59 The Tretyakov Gallery; 1965 The
Tretyakov Gallery (p. 71), The Russian
Museum; / 1909 St. Petersburg — Salon

(No 364; No 472 — another ed., as *Rimsky-Korsakov Shortly Before His Death*); 1911 Moscow — 1st Exhibition of Paintings of the World of Art Society (No 306); 1941 The Tretyakov Gallery — Portrait Drawings: 18th to Early 20th Century (No 127); 1949 The Pushkin Museum of Fine Arts, Moscow — Russian Graphic Art: 18th to Early 20th Century; 1963 The Tretyakov Gallery — Pencil Drawings, Watercolors, Pastels, and Gouaches (p. 74)

Reproductions: *Apollon*, 1912, No 10, between pp. 14 and 15; Grabar, *Serov*, 1914, p. 200; Grabar, *Serov the Draftsman*, 1961; Yaremich, *Serov: Drawings*, 1936

References: Grabar, *Serov*, 1914, pp. 166, 293; Grabar, *Serov*, 1965, p. 365

543 (Plate 180)

Portrait of N. Z. Rappoport. 1908
Tempera on primed cardboard.
98.6×62 cm
Signed and dated, bottom left: *BC 908* (VS, 1908); date not visible at present
The Russian Museum
Provenance: Z. Rappoport collection, St. Petersburg; O. Rappoport collection, Petrograd; S. Senitsiai collection, Paris
Exhibitions: 1914 (posthumous) St. Petersburg (No 251), Moscow (No 270)
Reproductions: Radlov, *Serov*, 1914, p. 33
References: Grabar, *Serov*, 1914, p. 293 (described incorrectly as an oil painting); Dmitriyev, *Serov*, 1917, p. 62; Grabar, *Serov*, 1965, p. 366 (as *The Young N. Z. Rappoport*)

1909
PAINTINGS

544

Head of Europa. ⟨1909⟩
Egg colors on icon board. 31.5×27.5 cm
F. Khmara collection, Moscow
Provenance: The Serov family collection, Moscow; K. Lipskerov collection, Moscow; D. Sezeman collection, Moscow
A sketch for the 1910 painting *The Rape of Europa* (see No 589).
Exhibitions: 1914 (posthumous) St. Petersburg (No 287a, as *Ancient Statue*), Moscow (No 322, under the same title); 1935 The Tretyakov Gallery (No 174), The Russian Museum (No 168); 1946 Central House of Art Workers, Moscow (No 51); 1952 Moscow (No 293); 1958–59 The Tretyakov Gallery; 1965 The Tretyakov Gallery (pp. 45, 46); / 1957 Central House of Art Workers, Moscow — Works of Russian Art from Private Collections: Late 19th and Early 20th Centuries (p. 13)
References: Grabar, *Serov*, 1965, p. 437 (dated 1909–10); *Serov in the Reminiscences of His Contemporaries*, 1971, 1, pp. 213, 214

545

Autumn Night. 1909
Oil on canvas. 105.5×107.5 cm
Signed and dated, bottom right: *BC 909* (VS, 1909)
Art Museum, Gorky (since 1932).
Inv. No 982

153. Autumn Night. Cat. No 545

Provenance: The Tretyakov Gallery
Exhibitions: 1935 The Tretyakov Gallery (No 173, the size given as 135×105 cm), The Russian Museum (No 167, the same error); 1958–59 The Tretyakov Gallery
Reproductions: *The Gorky Museum: Picture Gallery*, Leningrad, Aurora Art Publishers, 1973, pl. 53
References: Grabar, *Serov*, 1965, p. 433

546

Portrait of Alexandra Petrovna Lieven. 1909
Oil on canvas. 185×130 cm
Signed and dated, bottom right: *Съровъ 909* (Serov, 1909)
Art Gallery, Vladivostok (since 1966).
Inv. No Ж-55
Provenance: A. Lieven collection, Moscow; The Tretyakov Gallery; Museum of Local Lore, Vladivostok
Princess Alexandra Petrovna Lieven, née Vasilchikova (died in 1918), philanthropist, President of the Society for the Distribution of Useful Books.
Exhibitions: 1914 (posthumous) St. Petersburg (No 267), Moscow (No 293); 1958–59 The Tretyakov Gallery; / 1909–10 Moscow, 1910 St. Petersburg, Kiev — 7th Exhibition of the Union of Russian Artists (Nos 334, 411, 230); 1909–10 Kiev, Odessa, Kharkov — 8th Exhibition of Paintings Organized by the *V Mire Iskusstv* Magazine (No 237)
Reproductions: *Apollon*, 1910, No 7, between pp. 24 and 25; *Iskusstvo i Pechatnoye Delo*, Kiev, 1910, No 5, p. 188; Grabar, *Serov*, 1914, p. 214
References: Grabar, *Serov*, 1914, p. 293; Grabar, *Serov*, 1965, p. 341; *Serov in the Reminiscences of His Contemporaries*, 1971, 1, pp. 472, 473

547 (Plate 178)

Portrait of Yelena Pavlovna Oliv. ⟨1909⟩
Gouache, watercolors and pastel on cardboard. 94×66.2 cm (oval)
Signed, bottom right: *Съровъ* (Serov)
The Russian Museum (since 1926).
Inv. No P-13426
Provenance: M. Oliv and Ye. Oliv collection, St. Petersburg
Exhibitions: 1914 (posthumous) St. Petersburg (No 256); 1935 The Tretyakov Gallery (No 171), The Russian Museum (No 165); 1965 The Tretyakov Gallery (p. 45), The Russian Museum; / 1909–10 Moscow, 1910 St. Petersburg, Kiev — 7th Exhibition of the Union of Russian Artists (Nos 332, 409, 229); 1911 Rome — International Art Exhibition (No 391)

154. Portrait of Alexandra Petrovna Lieven. Cat. No 546

Reproductions: *Apollon*, 1910, No 5, between pp. 4 and 5; Grabar, *Serov*, 1914, p. 210; Grabar, *Serov*, 1965, p. 221
References: Grabar, *Serov*, 1914, pp. 175, 200, 293; Grabar, *Serov*, 1965, pp. 220, 340, 341; *Serov in the Reminiscences of His Contemporaries*, 1971, 1, pp. 471, 472

548
Portrait of Felix Felixovich Yusupov, Count Sumarokov-Elstone Sr. 1909
Oil (?)
The Yusupovs collection, France
Provenance: F. Yusupov Jr. collection
Felix Felixovich Yusupov — see No 425.
References: *Serov in the Reminiscences of His Contemporaries*, 1971, 2, pp. 300, 305

549 (Plate 209)
Portrait of Emmanuel Nobel. 1909
Oil on canvas
Signed and dated, bottom right: *Съровъ 909* (Serov, 1909)
Present whereabouts unknown
Provenance: E. Nobel collection, St. Petersburg
Emmanuel Ludwig Nobel (1859–1932), oil-well owner, nephew of Alfred Bernhard Nobel (1833–1896) who established Nobel prizes.
Exhibitions: 1914 (posthumous) St. Petersburg (No 271), Moscow (No 297); / 1909 Munich — 10th International Art Exhibition (No 1934); 1914 Malmö (Sweden) — Baltic Art Exhibition (No 3230)
Reproductions: Grabar, *Serov*, 1914, p. 217
References: Grabar, *Serov*, 1914, pp. 217, 293; Grabar, *Serov*, 1965, p. 341; *Serov in the Reminiscences of His Contemporaries*, 1971, 1, p. 123; Leniashin 1980, p. 158

DRAWINGS, WATERCOLORS, PASTELS, AND GOUACHES

550 (Plates 188, 189)
Anna Pavlovna Pavlova in the Ballet Sylphide. 1909
Tempera on primed tinted canvas.
200×175 cm
Signed and dated, bottom right: *BC 909* (VS, 1909)
The Russian Museum (since 1924).
Inv. No P-13487
Provenance: S. Botkin collection, St. Petersburg; A. Botkina collection, St. Petersburg
A poster design for the Russian Seasons in Paris, 1909.
Anna Pavlovna (Matveyevna) Pavlova (1881–1931), world-renowned Russian ballet dancer.
Exhibitions: 1914 (posthumous) St. Petersburg (No 262), Moscow (No 288); 1935 The Tretyakov Gallery (No 501), The Russian Museum (No 593); 1959–60 The Russian Museum; 1965 The Tretyakov Gallery (p. 72), The Russian Museum; / 1909–10 Moscow, 1910 St. Petersburg — 7th Exhibition of the Union of Russian Artists (Nos 333, 410, as *Portrait of Pavlova II*)
Reproductions: Poster for the Russian Seasons (Théâtre du Châtelet, Saison Russe. Opéra et ballet. Mai—juin 1909);

Apollon, 1910, No 5, between pp. 4 and 5; *Annual of the Imperial Theaters*, 1910, issue 3; Grabar, *Serov*, 1914, p. 213; Sarabyanov, *Serov*, 1974 (No 40, as *Portrait of the Ballerina Anna Pavlova*, described incorrectly as executed in charcoal and chalk on blue paper)
References: Grabar, *Serov*, 1914, p. 293; Grabar, *Serov*, 1965, pp. 233, 336; *Serov in the Reminiscences of His Contemporaries*, 1971, 2, pp. 473, 474

551
The Virgin of Yakhroma. Copy. ⟨1909⟩
Tempera on icon board, gesso ground.
31×26.5 cm
The Tretyakov Gallery (since 1965).
Inv. No Ж-477
Provenance: O. Khortik-Serova collection, Moscow
Executed in order to master the techniques of icon painting, which influenced the artist during his work on *The Rape of Europa* (1910) — see No 589.
The Virgin of Yakhroma, a 16th-century icon, was in the Tretyakov Gallery (reproduced in: Kondakov 1911, p. 152). It should be noted that another icon of the same title painted in Northern Russia in the second quarter of the 16th century, which entered the Tretyakov Gallery in 1920, was unknown to Serov.

552
An Oprichnik. ⟨1909⟩
Tempera an cardboard. 34.5×48 cm
Museum of Art and Architecture, Smolensk (since 1930). Inv. No Г-164
Provenance: A. Kasyanov collection, Moscow; The Tretyakov Gallery
Exhibitions: 1914 (posthumous) St. Petersburg (No 303a — 2nd ed.), Moscow (No 342); 1935 The Tretyakov Gallery (No 172), The Russian Museum (No 166)
Reproductions: Ernst, *Serov*, 1922, between pp. 80 and 81
References: Grabar, *Serov*, 1914, p. 293; Grabar, *Serov*, 1965, p. 433

553
Horses in Paris. ⟨1909⟩
Black chalk on cardboard. 26×62 cm
A. Yefimov collection, Moscow
Provenance: O. Serova collection, Moscow; I. Yefimov collection, Moscow
Exhibitions: 1914 (posthumous) St. Petersburg (No 276), Moscow (No 308); 1946 Central House of Art Workers, Moscow

(No 30); 1952 Moscow (No 313); 1965 The Russian Museum
Reproductions: *Apollon*, 1914, No 6/7, p. 22; Simonovich-Yefimova 1964, p. 134
References: Grabar, *Serov*, 1914, p. 294 (dated 1910); *Serov's Correspondence*, 1937, p. 167; Simonovich-Yefimova 1964, pp. 133–136; Grabar, *Serov*, 1965, p. 440 (as *A Team of Percherons in Paris*)

554
Horses in Paris. The Percherons.
⟨1909⟩
Charcoal and chalk on gray paper.
51×100 cm
The Tretyakov Gallery (since 1941).
Inv. No 26437
Provenance: N. Smirnov-Sokolsky collection, Moscow
Exhibitions: 1958–59 The Tretyakov Gallery; 1965 The Tretyakov Gallery (pp. 72, 73, dated 1909); / 1963 The Tretyakov Gallery — Pencil Drawings, Watercolors, Pastels, and Gouaches (p. 74)
References: Grabar, *Serov*, 1965, p. 440 (as *A Team of Percherons. Paris*, 1910); *Drawings and Watercolors. Catalogue*, 1956, p. 77 (dated 1910–11)

555
Percherons. ⟨1909⟩
Black chalk. 12.9×20.6 cm
Bottom left, an impression of the artist's signet: *BC* (VS)
The Serov family collection, Moscow
Exhibitions: 1935 The Tretyakov Gallery (No 530), The Russian Museum (No 601); 1965 The Tretyakov Gallery (p. 73), The Russian Museum
References: Grabar, *Serov*, 1965, p. 440 (as *A Team of Percherons in Paris*. 1910)

556 (Plate 212)
Portrait of Alexei Vikulovich Morozov. 1909
Black watercolor, white, sanguine and crayons on paper, mounted on cardboard.
93.4×59.8 cm
Signed and dated, right: *BC 909* (VS, 1909)
Art Museum, Minsk (since 1947).
Inv. No РГ-56
Provenance: A. Morozov collection, Moscow; Ceramics Museum, Kuskovo (near Moscow)
Alexei Vikulovich Morozov (1857–1934), collector of icons, porcelain, engraved and lithographed portraits.

Exhibitions: 1914 (posthumous) St. Petersburg (No 257, as *A. V. M.*), Moscow (No 283, under the same title); 1935 The Tretyakov Gallery (No 494), The Russian Museum (No 585)
References: Grabar, *Serov*, 1914, p. 293 (as *A. V. Morozov*. Watercolor); Grabar, *Serov*, 1965, p. 366

557
Portrait of Anna Vasilyevna Zetlin. 1909
Watercolors
Signed and dated, bottom right: *Съровъ 909* (Serov, 1909)
Present whereabouts unknown
Provenance: A. Zetlin collection, Moscow
Anna Vasilyevna Zetlin (1860–1935), wife of a Moscow merchant O. S. Zetlin.
Exhibitions: 1914 (posthumous) St. Petersburg (No 268), Moscow (No 294); / 1909–10 Moscow — 7th Exhibition of the Union of Russian Artists (No 335, as *A Drawing*); 1914 Malmö (Sweden) — Baltic Art Exhibition (No 3216)
Reproductions: Grabar, *Serov*, 1914, p. 215
References: Grabar, *Serov*, 1914, p. 293; Grabar, *Serov*, 1965, p. 341; *Serov in the Reminiscences of His Contemporaries*, 1971, 2, p. 356

558 (Plate 187)
Portrait of Anna Pavlovna Pavlova. ⟨1909⟩
Graphite. 34.3×21.3 cm
Signed, bottom right: *BC* (VS)
The Tretyakov Gallery (since 1929).
Inv. No 11312
Provenance: I. Ostroukhov collection, Moscow; The Ostroukhov Museum of Icons and Painting, Moscow
Anna Pavlovna Pavlova — see No 550.
Exhibitions: 1914 (posthumous) St. Petersburg (No 263), Moscow (No 289); 1935 The Tretyakov Gallery (No 496), The Russian Museum (No 589); 1952 Moscow (No 246); 1958–59 The Tretyakov Gallery; 1959 Museum of Russian Art, Kiev; 1959–60 The Russian Museum; 1965 The Tretyakov Gallery (p. 72), The Russian Museum; / 1941 The Tretyakov Gallery — Portrait Drawings: 18th to Early 20th Century (No 130); 1949 The Pushkin Museum of Fine Arts, Moscow — Russian Graphic Art: 18th to Early 20th Century; 1954 Central House of Art Workers, Moscow — Portraits of Prominent Personalities in Russian Art: 18th to 20th Century (No 88); 1960 Paris — Russian and Soviet Painting (No 56); 1963 The Tretyakov Gallery — Pencil Drawings, Watercolors, Pastels, and Gouaches (p. 74)
Reproductions: Grabar, *Serov the Draftsman*, 1961; Grabar, *Serov*, 1965, p. 279
References: Grabar, *Serov*, 1914, p. 293; Grabar, *Serov*, 1965, p. 267; Liaskovskaya 1965, p. 60; Sarabyanov, *Reforms by Valentin Serov*, 1971, p. 20

559 (Plate 184)
Portrait of Tamara Platonovna Karsavina. ⟨1909⟩
Graphite. 42.8×26.7 cm
The Tretyakov Gallery (since 1929).
Inv. No 11311
Provenance: I. Ostroukhov collection, Moscow; The Ostroukhov Museum of Icons and Painting, Moscow

Tamara Platonovna Karsavina (1885–1977), Russian ballet dancer. Her greatest successes were with Diaghilev's Ballets Russes.
Exhibitions: 1914 (posthumous) St. Petersburg (No 270), Moscow (No 296); 1935 The Tretyakov Gallery (No 499), The Russian Museum (No 590); 1958–59 The Tretyakov Gallery; 1965 The Tretyakov Gallery (p. 72), The Russian Museum; / 1941 The Tretyakov Gallery — Portrait Drawings: 18th to Early 20th Century (No 131); 1963 The Tretyakov Gallery — Pencil Drawings, Watercolors, Pastels, and Gouaches (p. 74)
Reproductions: *Sophia*, 1914, No 3, p. 94; Yaremich, *Serov: Drawings*, 1936; Grabar, *Serov*, 1965, between pp. 280 and 281; *Serov: Drawings, Watercolors, Lithographs*, 1972 (No 11)
References: Grabar, *Serov*, 1914, p. 293; Muratov 1914, pp. 93–95; Grabar, *Serov*, 1965, pp. 280, 367; Liaskovskaya 1965, p. 60; Sarabyanov, *Reforms by Valentin Serov*, 1971, p. 20

560
Portrait of Yelena Ivanovna Roerich. 1909
Black chalk, pastel and watercolors. 64.8×46.6 cm
Signed and dated, bottom right: *BC 909* (VS, 1909)
The Ashmolean Museum, Oxford
Provenance: N. and Ye. Roerich collection, St. Petersburg; M. Braikevich collection
Yelena Ivanovna Roerich, wife of the Russian painter Nikolai Roerich (1874–1947), artist, archaeologist, traveller and public figure.
Exhibitions: 1914 (posthumous) St. Petersburg (No 269), Moscow (No 295); / 1910 St. Petersburg — The Contemporary Russian Female Portrait (4th Exhibition of Paintings Organized by the *Apollon*

Magazine) (No 31); 1914 Malmö (Sweden) — Baltic Art Exhibition (No 3221)
Reproductions: *Apollon*, 1910, No 5, between pp. 8 and 9; Grabar, *Serov*, 1914, p. 216
References: Grabar, *Serov*, 1914, p. 293; Grabar, *Serov*, 1965, pp. 366, 367; Liaskovskaya 1965, p. 60

561
Portrait of Olga Konstantinovna Orlova. ⟨1909⟩
Pencil
Present whereabouts unknown
Initial concept of the portrait (see No 632).
Olga Konstantinovna Orlova, née Beloselskaya-Belozerskaya (1872–1923), Princess.
Exhibitions: 1914 (posthumous) St. Petersburg (No 285)
References: Grabar, *Serov*, 1965, p. 370 (dated 1910); *Serov in the Reminiscences of His Contemporaries*, 1971, 2, p. 42

562 (Plate 185)
Portrait of Mikhail Mikhailovich Fokine. ⟨1909⟩
Sanguine
Signed, right: *VS*
Present whereabouts unknown
Provenance: M. Fokine collection, St. Petersburg

156. Horses in Paris.
Cat. No 553

157. Horses in Paris.
The Percherons. Cat. No 554

158. Percherons. Cat. No 555

353

159. Mother and Her Child. Cat. No 565

160. The German Linz in a Railroad Car. Cat. No 566

Mikhail Mikhailovich Fokine (1880–1942), Russian ballet dancer and ballet master, dominant figure in the world of ballet, choreographer in Diaghilev's company.
Reproductions: Svetlov 1911, after p. 14; Fokine 1962 (frontispiece)
References: Grabar, *Serov*, 1914, p. 293; Grabar, *Serov*, 1965, p. 366

563 (Plate 203)
The Rape of Europa. Sketch. ⟨1909⟩
Graphite on yellowish paper.
23.5×31.2 cm
The Russian Museum (since 1928).
Inv. No P-13422
Provenance: S. Botkin collection, St. Petersburg; A. Botkina collection, St. Petersburg
Exhibitions: 1935 The Tretyakov Gallery (No 537), The Russian Museum (No 610); 1965 The Russian Museum
References: Grabar, *Serov*, 1965, p. 437

1900s
PAINTINGS

564
**Portrait of Princess
S. Kasatkina-Rostovskaya.** ⟨1900s⟩
Oil on canvas. 65×71 cm
Signed, top right: *В. Съровъ* (V. Serov)
Art Gallery, Sevastopol (since 1926).
Inv. No Ж-256
Exhibitions: 1935 The Russian Museum (No 202)
References: Grabar, *Serov*, 1965, p. 343

161. Portrait of an Unknown Man. Cat. No 568

162. Portrait of Leon Samoilovich Bakst. Cat. No 569

DRAWINGS

565
Mother and Her Child. ⟨1900s⟩
Pencil. 42.8×26.8 cm
The Russian Museum (since 1912).
Inv. No P-3128
Exhibitions: 1935 The Tretyakov Gallery (No 522), The Russian Museum (No 752); 1965 The Russian Museum
Reproductions: *Serov: The Sun of Russia*, 1913
References: Grabar, *Serov*, 1914, p. 293; Grabar, *Serov*, 1965, p. 435

566
The German Linz in a Railroad Car.
⟨1900⟩
Pencil. 11.7×7.3 cm
Autograph in pencil, bottom left: *Linz*
The Russian Museum (since 1960).
Inv. No P-53344

Provenance: The Serov family collection, Moscow
Exhibitions: 1952 Moscow (No 376)
References: Grabar, *Serov*, 1965, p. 368 (Inv. No given incorrectly as P-53444)

567 (Plate 165)
The Sporting Amusements of the Empress Anna Ioannovna. ⟨1900s⟩
Charcoal. 56×42 cm (sheet), 44×34 cm (exposed area)
The Russian Museum. Inv. No P-3222
Provenance: The Serov family collection, Moscow
Anna Ioannovna (1693–1740), Empress of Russia (1730–40).
Exhibitions: 1914 (posthumous) St. Petersburg (No 139), Moscow (No 145); 1935 The Tretyakov Gallery (No 510), The Russian Museum (No 696)
References: Grabar, *Serov*, 1965, p. 434

568
Portrait of an Unknown Man. ⟨1900s⟩
Graphite. 10.5×16.5 cm
Inscribed, top right: *Canen* (?)
The Russian Museum (since 1960).
Inv. No P-53345
Provenance: The Serov family collection, Moscow
Exhibitions: 1952 Moscow (No 378, as *Southern Type*)

References: Grabar, *Serov*, 1965, p. 367 (as *Portrait of an Unknown Man* — Francesco Tamagno?)

569
**Portrait of Leon Samoilovich
Bakst.** ⟨1900s⟩
India ink and gouache on paper, mounted on cardboard. 47×34 cm
Signed, bottom right: *Съровъ* (Serov)
The Russian Museum (since 1923).
Inv. No P-13438
Provenance: V. Argutinsky-Dolgoruky collection, St. Petersburg
Leon Samoilovich Bakst (Rosenberg) (1866–1924), Russian painter, decorative artist, set and costume designer.
Exhibitions: 1935 The Tretyakov Gallery (No 521), The Russian Museum (No 706); 1958–59 The Tretyakov Gallery; 1959 Museum of Russian Art, Kiev; 1959–60 The Russian Museum; 1965 The Tretyakov Gallery (p. 60), The Russian Museum
Reproductions: Grabar, *Serov*, 1980, pl. 52
References: Grabar, *Serov*, 1965, p. 359 (described incorrectly as executed in Paris, in the early 1900s); Liaskovskaya 1965, p. 58

1910
PAINTINGS

570 (Plate 167)
The Grand Eagle Cup. ⟨1910⟩
Tempera on cardboard. 90.5×65 cm
Picture Gallery, Yerevan (since 1930).
Inv. No Ж-670
Provenance: O. Serova collection, Moscow; The Tretyakov Gallery
Exhibitions: 1935 The Tretyakov Gallery (No 192, the size is given as 66×91 cm), The Russian Museum (No 186, the same error); 1958–59 The Tretyakov Gallery; 1965 The Russian Museum
Reproductions: *Apollon*, 1912, No 10, between pp. 30 and 31; Grabar, *Serov*, 1914, p. 218; Kopschitzer, *Serov*, 1972, No 45; Grabar, *Serov*, 1980, pl. 101
References: Grabar, *Serov*, 1914, p. 294; Grabar, *Serov*, 1965, pp. 213, 440

571
The Grand Eagle Cup. ⟨1910⟩
Oil on cardboard. 64.5×43 cm
The Russian Museum (since 1921).
Inv. No Ж-1919
Provenance: The Hermitage, Leningrad
A sketch for the painting now in the Picture Gallery, Yerevan (see No 570).
Exhibitions: 1935 The Tretyakov Gallery (No 191), The Russian Museum (No 185); 1958–59 The Tretyakov Gallery, 1959 Museum of Russian Art, Kiev; 1959–60 The Russian Museum; 1965 The Tretyakov Gallery (p. 48); / 1939 The Tretyakov Gallery — Russian History Painting (No 335)
Reproductions: Lebedev, *Serov*, 1946; Grabar, *Serov*, 1980, p. 211
References: Grabar, *Serov*, 1914, p. 294; Grabar, *Serov*, 1965, p. 440

Versions of *Odysseus and Nausicaä* (*Odyssey*, Book VI) (Nos 572–575)

572
Odysseus and Nausicaä. ⟨1910⟩
Tempera on cardboard. 50.5×97 cm
The Tretyakov Gallery (since 1911).
Inv. No 1536
Exhibitions: 1935 The Tretyakov Gallery (No 181), The Russian Museum (No 176); 1958–59 The Tretyakov Gallery; 1965 The Tretyakov Gallery (p. 47)
Reproductions: Grabar, *Serov*, 1914, between pp. 240 and 241; Grabar, *Serov*, 1965, p. 228; Nikulina 1972, between pp. 488 and 489
References: Grabar, *Serov*, 1914, pp. 228, 294; Grabar, *Serov*, 1965, pp. 229, 286, 438; Sarabyanov, *Reforms by Valentin Serov*, 1971, pp. 9, 31; Nikulina 1972, p. 489

573 (Plate 201)
Odysseus and Nausicaä. ⟨1910⟩
Tempera on cardboard. 85.5×101.5 cm
The Tretyakov Gallery (since 1923).

Inv. No 7866
Provenance: M. Karpova collection, Moscow; Proletarian Museum, Moscow
Exhibitions: 1914 (posthumous) St. Petersburg (No 296), Moscow (No 334); 1935 The Tretyakov Gallery (No 180); 1965 The Tretyakov Gallery (p. 47)
Reproductions: *Iskusstvo*, 1959, No 8, p. 61; Zotov, *Serov*, 1964, No 39; Simonovich-Yefimova 1964, p. 121; *History of Russian Art*, 1968, between pp. 240 and 241; Nikulina 1972, between pp. 488 and 489 (dated 1909–10)
References: Grabar, *Serov*, 1914, pp. 228, 294 ("Second version. Both versions were executed before the trip to Greece. . ." There is, however, another statement on p. 228: "The idea of *Nausicaä* came to the artist during his stay in Greece"); Simonovich-Yefimova 1964, p. 121; Grabar, *Serov*, 1965, pp. 229, 286, 438; Sarabyanov, *Reforms by Valentin Serov*, 1971, pp. 9, 31, 32; Nikulina 1972, p. 489

574 (Plate 199)
Odysseus and Nausicaä. ⟨1910⟩
Tempera and pastel on paper, mounted on cardboard. 34×166.9 cm (exposed area)
The Russian Museum (since 1912).
Inv. No Ж-4288
Provenance: I. Ostroukhov collection, Moscow
Exhibitions: 1935 The Tretyakov Gallery (No 183), The Russian Museum (No 178); 1965 The Tretyakov Gallery (p. 47), The Russian Museum
Reproductions: *Apollon*, 1912, No 10, between pp. 32 and 33 (dated 1910–11); Grabar, *Serov*, 1914, p. 233 (as *Nausicaä*. Detail of a painting. 1909–10); Dmitriyev, *Serov*, 1914 (as *Nausicaä*. Detail. Tempera. 1910); Sokolova, *Serov*, 1935, p. 141; Lebedev, *Serov*, 1946
References: Grabar, *Serov*, 1914, pp. 228, 294; Grabar, *Serov*, 1965, pp. 229, 286, 438; Sarabyanov, *Reforms by Valentin*

Serov, 1971, pp. 9, 31; Nikulina 1972, p. 489

575 (Plate 200)
Odysseus and Nausicaä. ⟨1910⟩
Tempera on cardboard. 49.5×65 cm
The Russian Museum, Leningrad (since 1923). Inv. No Ж-4298
Provenance: Academy of Arts Museum, St. Petersburg
Exhibitions: 1914 (posthumous) St. Petersburg (No 293); 1935 The Tretyakov Gallery (No 182), The Russian Museum (No 177); 1958–59 The Tretyakov Gallery; 1959 Museum of Russian Art, Kiev; 1959–60 The Russian Museum; 1965 The Tretyakov Gallery (p. 47), The Russian Museum
Reproductions: *Academy of Arts Museum*, 1915, p. 254; *Works by Serov in the Russian Museum*, 1970, No 17
References: Grabar, *Serov*, 1914, p. 294 (described incorrectly as an oil painting, first version); Grabar, *Serov*, 1965, p. 438; Sarabyanov, *Reforms by Valentin Serov*, 1971, pp. 9, 31; Nikulina 1972, p. 489

576
Peter the Great in the Palace of Monplaisir. ⟨1910⟩
Gouache on paper, mounted on cardboard. 74×65.2 cm
Picture Gallery, Odessa (since 1926).
Inv. No Г-1014
Provenance: M. Braikevich collection, Odessa
Peter the Great — see No 402.
Exhibitions: 1914 (posthumous) Moscow (No 298); 1935 The Tretyakov Gallery

163. The Grand Eagle Cup. Cat. No 571

164. Peter the Great in the Palace of Monplaisir. Cat. No 576

355

165. Portrait of Natalia Konstantinovna Kusevitskaya. Cat. No 585

166. Portrait of Oscar Osipovich and Rosa Gavrilovna Grusenberg. Cat. No 587

(not listed in the Catalogue), The Russian Museum (No 170); 1958–59 The Tretyakov Gallery; 1959 Museum of Russian Art, Kiev; 1959—60 The Russian Museum; 1965 The Tretyakov Gallery (pp. 48, 49); / 1926 Art Museum, Odessa — Paintings from the Odessa Art Museum Reserve (No 119); 1939 The Tretyakov Gallery — Russian History Painting, (No 336)
Reproductions: Grabar, *Serov*, 1965, p. 210 (wrong date: 1911 in the caption, 1907–9 in the list of works)
References: Grabar, *Serov*, 1914, p. 294; Grabar, *Serov*, 1965, pp. 211, 441 (as "second version, 1907–9")

577

Peter the Great in the Palace of Monplaisir. ⟨1910⟩
Tempera
Present whereabouts unknown
Peter the Great — see No 402.
References: Grabar, *Serov*, 1914, p. 294 (as "third, unfinished version")

578 (Plate 168)

Peter the Great in the Palace of Monplaisir. ⟨1910–11⟩.
Unfinished
Tempera and graphite on paper, mounted on cardboard. 62.5×47.5 cm
The Tretyakov Gallery (since 1917).
Inv. No 5654
Provenance: I. Troyanovsky collection, Moscow
Peter the Great — see No 402.
Exhibitions: 1914 (posthumous) St. Petersburg (No 275), Moscow (No 307); 1935 The Tretyakov Gallery (No 563), The Russian Museum (No 645); 1958–59 The Tretyakov Gallery; 1965 The Tretyakov Gallery (p. 49), The Russian Museum; / 1914 Malmö (Sweden) — Baltic Art Exhibition (No 334); 1939 The Tretyakov Gallery — Russian History Painting (No 338); 1963 The Tretyakov Gallery — Pencil Drawings, Watercolors, Pastels, and Gouaches
Reproductions: Grabar, *Serov*, 1914, p. 219; Zotov, *Serov*, 1964, No 40 (dated 1911); Grabar, *Serov*, 1980, pl. 102

References: Grabar, *Serov*, 1914, p. 294; Grabar, *Serov*, 1965, pp. 211, 441 (as "third version")

579

Peter the Great in the Palace of Monplaisir. ⟨1910–11⟩
Tempera on cardboard. 77×58 cm
V. Petrov collection, Leningrad
Provenance: V. Mathé collection, St. Petersburg
Peter the Great — see No 402.
Exhibitions: 1952 Moscow (No 269); 1958–59 The Tretyakov Gallery; 1965 The Russian Museum
References: Grabar, *Serov*, 1914, p. 294; Grabar, *Serov*, 1965, p. 441 (as "fourth version")

580 (Plate 173)

Portrait of Anna Markovna Staal. 1910
Tempera. Oval
Signed and dated, bottom right: *Съровъ 910* (Serov, 1910)
T. Staal collection, Paris
Provenance: A. F. and A. M. Staal collection, Paris
Anna Markovna Staal (1875–1960), wife of A. F. Staal, a barrister.
Exhibitions: 1928 Brussels — Old and New Russian Art (No 845)
Reproductions: Grabar, *Serov*, 1914, p. 229; *Khudozhnik*, 1961, No 6, p. 42; Leniashin 1980, p. 190
References: Grabar, *Serov*, 1914, pp. 212, 213, 294; Grabar, *Serov*, 1965, pp. 220, 341; Zhivova 1961, pp. 42, 43; *Serov in the Reminiscences of His Contemporaries*, 1971, 2, pp. 350–352

581 (Plate 210)

Portrait of Ivan Abramovich Morozov. 1910
Tempera on cardboard. 63.5×77 cm
Signed and dated, bottom right: *BC 910* (VS, 1910)
The Tretyakov Gallery (since 1928).
Inv. No 10872
Provenance: I. Morozov collection, Moscow; Museum of Modern Western Art, Moscow
Ivan Abramovich Morozov (1871–1921), Moscow merchant, collector of modern French painting.
Exhibitions: 1914 (posthumous) Moscow (No 306); 1935 The Tretyakov Gallery (No 176), The Russian Museum (No 171); 1958–59 The Tretyakov Gallery; 1965 The Tretyakov Gallery (p. 46), / 1957 Warsaw — Russian Painting: 14th to 20th Century (No 88)
Reproductions: Grabar, *Serov*, 1914, between pp. 216 and 217; *Essays on the History of Russian Portraiture*, 1964, between pp. 48 and 49; *History of Russian Art*, 1968, p. 225; Sarabyanov, *Serov*, 1974, No 42
References: Grabar, *Serov*, 1914, pp. 212, 294; Grabar, *Serov*, 1965, p. 341; Sarabyanov, *Reforms by Valentin Serov*, 1971, p. 9; *Serov in the Reminiscences of His Contemporaries*, 1971, 1, pp. 300–302

582 (Plates 192, 193)

Portrait of Ida Lvovna Rubinstein. ⟨1910⟩
Tempera and charcoal on canvas. 147×233 cm
The Russian Museum (since 1911).
Inv. No Ж-1915

Ida Lvovna Rubinstein (1880–1960), Russian dancer, took part in Diaghilev's Ballets Russes in Paris.
Exhibitions: 1935 The Tretyakov Gallery (No 185), The Russian Museum (No 180); 1959–60 The Russian Museum; 1965 The Tretyakov Gallery (p. 47), The Russian Museum; / 1911 Rome — International Art Exhibition (No 392); 1912 St. Petersburg — 2nd Exhibition of Paintings of the World of Art Society (No 278); 1975 The Russian Museum — Russian Portrait Painting: Late 19th and Early 20th Centuries (No 198)
Reproductions: *Apollon*, 1912, No 10, between pp. 30 and 31; Grabar, *Serov*, 1914, p. 224 (detail), between pp. 224 and 225; Radlov, *Serov*, 1914; Grabar, *Serov*, 1980, pl. 97, 98
References: Grabar, *Serov*, 1914, pp. 214, 218–220, 294; Simonovich-Yefimova 1964, pp. 115–118; Grabar, *Serov*, 1965, pp. 233, 234, 236, 342; Serova 1968, pp. 147–150, 151–168; Sarabyanov, *Reforms by Valentin Serov*, 1971, pp. 20, 25–27; *Serov in the Reminiscences of His Contemporaries*, 1971, 1, pp. 73, 74

583 (Plate 216)
Portrait of Margarita Kirillovna Morozova. ⟨1910⟩. Unfinished
Oil on canvas. 143×84 cm
Art Museum, Dnepropetrovsk (since 1928). Inv. No Ж-115
Provenance: M. Morozova collection, Moscow; The Tretyakov Gallery
The last of the three versions of the portrait; present whereabouts of the two earlier versions unknown.
Margarita Kirillovna Morozova, née Mamontova (1873–1958), pianist, wife of Mikhail Abramovich Morozov (see No 405).
Reproductions: Leniashin 1980, p. 157
References: Grabar, *Serov*, 1965, p. 342; *Serov in the Reminiscences of His Contemporaries*, 1971, 2, pp. 263–268

584
Portrait of Maria Samoilovna Zetlin. 1910
Tempera on canvas. 109×74 cm
Signed and dated: BC 910 (VS, 1910)
Present whereabouts unknown
Provenance: M. O. Zetlin collection, Biarritz, Paris; M. S. Zetlin collection, USA
Maria Samoilovna Zetlin, née Tumarkina (1882–1976), doctor of philosophy.
Exhibitions: 1914 (posthumous) St. Petersburg (No 280), Moscow (No 313); / 1911 Rome — International Art Exhibition (No 394); 1912 St. Petersburg — 2nd Exhibition of Paintings of the World of Art Society (No 282); 1914 Malmö (Sweden) — Baltic Art Exhibition (No 3222); 1928 Brussels — Old and New Russian Art (No 841); 1935 London — Russian Art (No 385); 1935 Prague — Retrospective Exhibition of Russian Painting: 18th to 20th Century (No 151)
Reproductions: *Apollon*, 1912, No 10, between pp. 8 and 9 (described incorrectly as an oil painting); Grabar, *Serov*, 1914, p. 225; Dmitriyev, *Serov*, 1917
References: Grabar, *Serov*, 1914, pp. 201, 294 (described incorrectly as an oil painting); Simonovich-Yefimova 1964, pp. 119–121; Grabar, *Serov*, 1965, pp. 224, 341; *Serov in the Reminiscences of His Contemporaries*, 1971, 2, pp. 353–358

585
Portrait of Natalia Konstantinovna Kusevitskaya. 1910
Tempera. Tondo, diam. 87 cm (approx.)
Signed and dated, bottom right: BC 910 (VS, 1910)
Present whereabouts unknown
Provenance: S. Kusevitsky collection, Moscow
Natalia Konstantinovna Kusevitskaya, née Ushkova (1881–1942), Russian sculptress, wife of the conductor Sergei Kusevitsky (1874–1951).
Exhibitions: 1914 (posthumous) Moscow (No 325)
References: Grabar, *Serov*, 1914, pp. 214, 294; Grabar, *Serov*, 1965, pp. 220, 341

586
Portrait of Natalia Konstantinovna Kusevitskaya. ⟨1910⟩. Unfinished
Oval. 80×78.5 cm (approx.)
Present whereabouts unknown
Provenance: S. Kusevitsky collection, Moscow
Natalia Konstantinovna Kusevitskaya — see No 585.
Exhibitions: 1914 (posthumous) St. Petersburg (No 289), Moscow (No 324); / 1914 Malmö (Sweden) — Baltic Art Exhibition (No 3206)
Reproductions: Grabar, *Serov*, 1914, p. 231
References: Grabar, *Serov*, 1914, pp. 213, 214, 294 ("the first conception of the portrait"); Grabar, *Serov*, 1965, p. 341

587
Portrait of Oscar Osipovich and Rosa Gavrilovna Grusenberg. ⟨1910⟩
Tempera on canvas. 100×60 cm (approx.)
Signed, top right: Съровъ (Serov)
Present whereabouts unknown
Provenance: O. Grusenberg collection, St. Petersburg
"This double portrait was painted in September 1909 at Sestroretsk" (Grabar, *Serov*, 1965, p. 341). The traditional dating of the portrait, 1909 (Grabar, *Serov*, 1914, pp. 211, 293), is wrong. In September 1910 Serov wrote: "I decided today to finish my stay here and tomorrow I shall leave Sestroretsk (six weeks is enough and to spare)" — see *Serov's Correspondence*, 1937, pp. 165, 166. The letter was erroneously dated by the editors of this volume to 1909, although it contains mention of Serov's speech in defense of Diaghilev, published in the newspaper *Rech* on 22 September 1910 (No 260). The portrait was obviously executed not in September 1909 at Sestroretsk (as suggested in *Serov in the Reminiscences of His Contemporaries*, 1971, 2, p. 449), but in August or September 1910.
Oscar Osipovich Grusenberg (1866–1940), barrister; Rosa Gavrilovna Grusenberg (died 1942), his wife.
Exhibitions: 1914 (posthumous) St. Petersburg (No 259), Moscow (No 285); / 1914 Malmö (Sweden) — Baltic Art Exhibition (No 3225)
Reproductions: Grabar, *Serov*, 1914, p. 211; Radlov, *Serov*, 1914 (in the list of works erroneously dated 1911)
References: Grabar, *Serov*, 1914, pp. 178, 200, 201, 293; Grabar, *Serov*, 1965, p. 341; *Serov in the Reminiscences of His Contemporaries*, 1971, 2, pp. 446, 449; Leniashin 1980, p. 158

588
Portrait of Sergei Andreyevich Muromtsev. 1910
Oil on canvas. 140×107 cm
Signed and dated, bottom right: Съровъ 1910 (Serov, 1910)
Art Museum, Tbilisi (since 1927). Inv. No 243
Provenance: Association of Barristers, Moscow; E. Kandelaki collection, Tbilisi
Sergei Andreyevich Muromtsev (1850–1910), Russian lawyer, Professor of Moscow University.
Exhibitions: 1914 (posthumous) Moscow (No 323); 1958–59 The Tretyakov Gallery; / 1911 Moscow — 1st Exhibition of Paintings of the World of Art Society (No 304); 1938 The Metekhi Art Museum, Tbilisi — Russian Painting: 18th and 19th Centuries (No 116)
Reproductions: Grabar, *Serov*, 1914, p. 230
References: Grabar, *Serov*, 1914, p. 212; Grabar, *Serov*, 1965, p. 341 (described incorrectly as an oil painting); *Serov in the Reminiscences of His Contemporaries*, 1971, 1, pp. 482, 483

589 (Plate 205)
The Rape of Europa. ⟨1910⟩
Tempera on canvas. 138×178 cm
The Serov family collection, Moscow
Exhibitions: 1914 (posthumous) St. Petersburg (No 292), Moscow (No 329); 1952 Moscow (No 292); 1958–59 The Tretyakov Gallery, 1965 The Tretyakov Gallery (p. 46), The Russian Museum; / 1914 Malmö (Sweden) — Baltic Art Exhibition (No 3235a)
Reproductions: Radlov, *Serov*, 1914 (described incorrectly as the property of

167. Portrait of Sergei Andreyevich Muromtsev. Cat. No 588

168. Portrait of Anna Markovna
Staal. Cat. No 603

V. Mathé, St. Petersburg); Sokolova, Vlasov 1959 (dated 1911), p. 75
References: Grabar, *Serov*, 1914, pp. 226, 228, 294 (described incorrectly as an oil painting); Grabar, *Serov*, 1965, pp. 229, 285, 286, 436; Sarabyanov, *Reforms by Valentin Serov*, 1971, pp. 9, 31, 32; Nikulina 1972, pp. 487, 488

590

The Rape of Europa. ⟨1910⟩
Oil on canvas. 71×98 cm
The Tretyakov Gallery, Moscow (since 1911). Inv. No 1535
Provenance: O. Serova collection, Moscow
A sketch for the picture of 1910, which belongs to the artist's family (see No 589).
Exhibitions: 1914 (posthumous) St. Petersburg (No 290), Moscow (No 331); 1935 The Tretyakov Gallery (No 177, described incorrectly as executed in tempera on cardboard), The Russian Museum (No 172, the same error); 1958–59 The Tretyakov Gallery; 1959 Museum of Russian Art, Kiev; 1959–60 The Russian Museum; 1965 The Tretyakov Gallery (p. 46, described incorrectly as a tempera), The Russian Museum
Reproductions: Grabar, *Serov*, 1914, between pp. 232 and 233; Grabar, *Serov*, 1965, pp. 226 (detail), 227; *History of Russian Art*, 1968, p. 243 (described incorrectly as a tempera); Nikulina 1972, pp. 488, 489 (dated 1909–10); Sarabyanov, *Serov*, 1974 (No 47, the same wrong date)
References: Grabar, *Serov*, 1914, pp. 226, 228, 294 (described incorrectly as a tempera); Grabar, *Serov*, 1965, pp. 229, 285, 286, 436 (described incorrectly as executed in tempera on cardboard); Sarabyanov, *Reforms by Valentin Serov*, 1971, pp. 9, 31; Nikulina 1972, p. 488

591

The Rape of Europa. ⟨1910⟩
Tempera and gouache on cardboard. 40×52 cm
Bottom right, an impression of the artist's signet: *BC* (VS)
The Russian Museum (since 1918). Inv. No Ж-4310
Provenance: E. Tereshchenko collection, St. Petersburg
A variant sketch for the picture of 1910 which belongs to the artist's family (see No 589).
Exhibitions: 1935 The Tretyakov Gallery (No 178), The Russian Museum (No 173); 1958–59 The Tretyakov Gallery; 1959 Museum of Russian Art, Kiev; 1959–60 The Russian Museum; 1965 The Tretyakov Gallery (p. 46), The Russian Museum
Reproductions: Zotov, *Serov*, 1964, pl. 36; *Works by Serov in the Russian Museum*, 1970 (No 18); Nikulina 1972, pp. 488, 489
References: Grabar, *Serov*, 1914, p. 294; Grabar, *Serov*, 1965, p. 436; Sarabyanov, *Reforms by Valentin Serov*, 1971, pp. 31, 32; Nikulina 1972, p. 488

592

The Rape of Europa. ⟨1910⟩
Tempera on canvas. 80×100 cm
The Tretyakov Gallery, Moscow (since 1970). Inv. No. P-2729
Provenance: The Serov family collection, Moscow; V. Vinogradov collection, Mos-

cow; O. Vinogradova collection, Moscow
A variant sketch for the picture of 1910 which belongs to the artist's family (see No 589).
Exhibitions: 1935 The Tretyakov Gallery (No 179), The Russian Museum (No 174)
References: Grabar, *Serov*, 1965, p. 436; Sarabyanov, *Reforms by Valentin Serov*, 1971, pp. 31, 32; Nikulina 1972, p. 488

593

The Rape of Europa. ⟨1910⟩
Gouache on cardboard. 57.3×83.2 cm
Present whereabouts unknown
Provenance: V. Braikevich collection, Odessa; Picture Gallery, Odessa (until 1941)
A variant sketch for the picture of 1910 which belongs to the artist's family (see No 589).
Exhibitions: 1914 (posthumous) Moscow (No 332); 1935 The Russian Museum (No 175); / 1926 Odessa — Paintings from the Odessa Art Museum Reserve (No 121)
References: Grabar, *Serov*, 1965, pp. 436, 437

SCULPTURE

594

The Rape of Europa. ⟨1910⟩
Plaster. 28×43×25.5 cm
Picture Gallery, Novosibirsk (since 1960). Inv. No C-57
Provenance: O. Serova collection, Moscow; The Tretyakov Gallery
The original sculpture executed in the course of painting the picture of the same name (see No 589).
Exhibitions: 1914 (posthumous) St. Petersburg (No 295); 1935 The Tretyakov Gallery (No 205, height given wrongly as 43 cm), The Russian Museum (No 1073, the same error); 1958–59 The Tretyakov Gallery

Reproductions: Grabar, *Serov*, 1914, p. 232
References: Grabar, *Serov*, 1914, p. 294; *Catalogue*, 1917; Grabar, *Serov*, 1965, p. 472; *Tretyakov Gallery: Sculptures. Catalogue*, 1977, p. 560

595

The Rape of Europa. ⟨1910⟩
Bronze. 28×45×23.5 cm
The founder's mark: *E. Robecch Fondeur Moscau*
The Tretyakov Gallery (since 1916). Inv. No 4041
Provenance: O. Serova collection, Moscow
The sculpture was cast from the plaster original of 1910, which is now at the Picture Gallery, Novosibirsk (see No 594).
Exhibitions: 1935 The Tretyakov Gallery (No 206, height given wrongly as 45 cm), The Russian Museum (No 1074, the same error); 1958–59 The Tretyakov Gallery
Reproductions: *Tretyakov Gallery: Sculptures. Catalogue*, 1977, p. 560
References: *Catalogue*, 1917; Grabar, *Serov*, 1965, p. 472; *Tretyakov Gallery: Sculptures. Catalogue*, 1977, p. 560

596

The Rape of Europa. ⟨1910⟩
Bronze. 28×44×29 cm
On the base, the founder's mark: *Robecchi Fondeur Moscau*
The Russian Museum (since 1937). Inv. No CK.1046
References: *Tretyakov Gallery: Sculptures. Catalogue*, 1977, p. 560

597

The Rape of Europa. ⟨1910⟩
Plaster
The Serov family collection, Moscow

598 (Plate 206)
The Rape of Europa ⟨1910⟩
Terra-cotta
A. Yefimov collection, Moscow
Provenance: I. Yefimov collection, Moscow

599 (Plate 207)
The Rape of Europa
Porcelain. 24×25×40.2 cm
The Russian Museum.
Inv. No Сф-278
Executed in porcelain in 1915
References: *Tretyakov Gallery: Sculptures.*
Catalogue, 1977, p. 560

DRAWINGS, WATERCOLORS AND GOUACHES

600 (Plate 198)
Nausicaä. ⟨1910⟩
Watercolors and graphite. 19.9×27.7 cm
Bottom right, an impression of the artist's
signet: *BC* (VS)
The Tretyakov Gallery (since 1929).
Inv. No 15787
Provenance: I. Ostroukhov collection, Mos-
cow; The Ostroukhov Museum of Icons
and Painting, Moscow
Exhibitions: 1935 The Tretyakov Gallery
(No 540), The Russian Museum (No 613);
1958–59 The Tretyakov Gallery; 1965 The
Tretyakov Gallery (p. 74), The Russian
Museum
Reproductions: *Drawings and Watercolors.*
Catalogue, 1956; Nikulina 1972, between
pp. 488 and 489
References: Grabar, *Serov*, 1965, pp. 438,
439 (as *Odysseus and Nausicaä*. Variant
sketch. 1909–10, described incorrectly as
belonging to M. Karpova)

601
Odysseus and Nausicaä. ⟨1910⟩
India ink and pencil on cardboard.
70.5×120 cm
The Tretyakov Gallery (since 1958).
Inv. No P-393
Provenance: The Serov family collection,
Moscow
Exhibitions: 1935 The Tretyakov Gallery
(No 541), The Russian Museum (No 614)
Reproductions: Nikulina 1972, between
pp. 488 and 489 (dated 1911)
References: Grabar, *Serov*, 1965, p. 438;
Nikulina 1972, p. 489

602
Odysseus and Nausicaä. ⟨1910⟩
Watercolors and gouache on cardboard.
33×99 cm
The Serov family collection, Moscow
A variant sketch.
Exhibitions: 1914 (posthumous) Moscow
(No 333); 1935 The Tretyakov Gallery
(No 184), The Russian Museum (No 179);
1946 Central House of Art Workers, Mos-
cow (No 87); 1952 Moscow (No 311);
1958–59 The Tretyakov Gallery; 1959
Museum of Russian Art, Kiev; 1959–60
The Russian Museum; 1965 The
Tretyakov Gallery (p. 47), The Russian
Museum; / 1957 Central House of Art
Workers, Moscow — Works of Russian Art
from Private Collections: Late 19th and
Early 20th Centuries (p. 13)
References: Grabar, *Serov*, 1965, p. 438;
Sarabyanov, *Reforms by Valentin Serov*,
1971, pp. 9, 31; Nikulina 1972, p. 488

603
Portrait of Anna Markovna Staal. 1910
Charcoal and chalk (?)
Signed and dated, bottom right: *BC 910*
(VS, 1910)

T. Staal collection, Paris
Provenance: A. F. and A. M. Staal collection, Paris
Anna Markovna Staal — see No 580.
Reproductions: *Khudozhnik*, 1961, No 6,
p. 43
References: Grabar, *Serov*, 1914, p. 294;
Zhivova 1961, pp. 42, 43; Grabar, *Serov*,
1965, p. 369; *Serov in the Reminiscences
of His Contemporaries*, 1971, 2,
pp. 350–352

604
**Portrait of Ida Lvovna
Rubinstein.** 1910
Graphite. 26.6×42.5 cm
The Tretyakov Gallery, Moscow (since
1929). Inv. No 11313
Provenance: I. Ostroukhov collection, Mos-
cow; The Ostroukhov Museum of Icons
and Painting, Moscow
A sketch for the 1910 portrait, now in the
Russian Museum (see No 582).
Exhibitions: 1914 (posthumous) St. Peters-
burg (No 279), Moscow (No 312); 1935
The Tretyakov Gallery (No 534), The Rus-
sian Museum (No 607); 1958–59 The Tre-
tyakov Gallery; 1959 Museum of Russian
Art, Kiev; 1959–60 The Russian Museum;
1965 The Tretyakov Gallery (p. 73), The
Russian Museum; / 1941 The Tretyakov
Gallery — Portrait Drawings: 18th to Early
20th Century (No 132); 1954 The Tret-
yakov Gallery — Sketches and Studies by
Russian Artists from the Tretyakov Gallery
Reserve: 18th to Early 20th Century
(p. 55); 1963 The Tretyakov Gallery —
Pencil Drawings, Watercolors, Pastels,
and Gouaches (p. 74)
Reproductions: Sokolova, *Serov*, 1935,
p. 145; *Essays on the History of Russian
Portraiture*, 1964, p. 89; Grabar, *Serov*,
1965, p. 230
References: Grabar, *Serov*, 1914, p. 294;
Grabar, *Serov*, 1965, p. 369

ter of Diaghilev's company. Revived the
art of male dance and was an innovator
as a ballet master.
Exhibitions: 1965 The Russian Museum
Reproductions: *Essays on the History of
Russian Portraiture*, 1964, p. 84 (dated
1909); *Theatrical Portraiture*, 1973, pl. 14
References: Grabar, *Serov*, 1965, p. 369

606 (Plate 172)
**Portrait of Isabella Yulyevna
Grünberg.** 1910
Pencil, watercolors and white. 66×42.5 cm
Signed and dated, bottom right: *B.C. 910*
(VS, 1910)
Present whereabouts unknown
Provenance: A. Gindus collection,
St. Petersburg; The Grünberg-Kamenets-
kaya family collection, Moscow
Isabella Yulyevna Grünberg, Kamenets-
kaya by marriage, daughter of Yuly
Osipovich and Maria Grigoryevna Grün-
berg (see No 145).
Exhibitions: 1914 (posthumous) St. Peters-
burg (No 278), Moscow (No 310); 1935
The Tretyakov Gallery (No 542), The Rus-
sian Museum (No 615); 1946 Central
House of Art Workers, Moscow (No 18);
1952 Moscow (No 307); 1958–59 The Tre-
tyakov Gallery; 1965 The Tretyakov Gal-
lery (p. 73), The Russian Museum; / 1911
St. Petersburg, Moscow — 1st Exhibition
of Paintings of the World of Art Society
(Nos 259, 301); 1914 Malmö (Sweden) —
Baltic Art Exhibition (No 3226); 1949 The
Pushkin Museum of Fine Arts, Moscow —
Russian Graphic Art: 18th to Early 20th
Century; 1957 Central House of Art
Workers, Moscow — Works of Russian Art
from Private Collections: Late 19th and
Early 20th Centuries (p. 13)
Reproductions: *Apollon*, 1911, No 2, be-
tween pp. 16 and 17; Grabar, *Serov*,
1914, p. 223; Grabar, *Serov*, 1965, p. 275
References: Grabar, *Serov*, 1914, pp. 166,
294; Grabar, *Serov*, 1965, p. 369

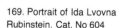

169. Portrait of Ida Lvovna
Rubinstein. Cat. No 604

605 (Plate 186)
Portrait of Vaslav Nijinsky. ⟨1910⟩
Pencil on paper, mounted on cardboard.
15.5×9.5 cm
Signed, bottom right: *VS*
Theatrical Museum, Leningrad (since
1921). Inv. No КП-2477/3
Vaslav Nijinsky (1890–1950), Russian bal-
let dancer, leading dancer and ballet mas-

607
**Portrait of Olga Konstantinovna
Orlova.** ⟨1909–10⟩
Graphite. 34.5×21 cm
The Tretyakov Gallery. Inv. No 11314
Provenance: I. Ostroukhov collection,
Moscow
Olga Konstantinovna Orlova — see
No 561.

170. Portrait of
Olga Konstantinovna Orlova.
Cat. No 607

171. Portrait of
Olga Konstantinovna Orlova.
Cat. No 608

(p. 75, dated 1911), The Russian
Museum; / 1974 The Russian Museum —
Drawings by Russian Artists: Late 19th
and Early 20th Centuries (p. 30)
Reproductions: Grabar, *Serov the Drafts-
man*, 1961 (dated 1911)
References: Grabar, *Serov*, 1914, p. 294;
Grabar, *Serov*, 1965, p. 370

610
**Portrait of Olga Konstantinovna
Orlova.** ⟨1910⟩
Graphite. 36.3×20 cm
A. Yefimov collection, Moscow
Provenance: I. Yefimov collection, Moscow
Olga Konstantinovna Orlova — see
No 561.
A cursory sketch from memory executed
by Serov in 1910 in Paris to give an idea
of the portrait of Orlova, not finished at the
time (see No 632).
References: Simonovich-Yefimova 1964,
p. 91; Grabar, *Serov*, 1965, p. 370

611
**Portrait of Sophia Vladimirovna
Olsufyeva.** ⟨1910⟩
Charcoal, gouache and chalk. 107×82 cm
Signed, bottom right: *ВС 911* (VS, 1911)
Private collection, Moscow
Provenance: Yu. Olsufyev collection,
Moscow
Sophia Vladimirovna Olsufyeva
(1886–1943), Countess, wife of the art his-
torian Yu. Olsufyev (1879–?).
Exhibitions: 1935 The Tretyakov Gallery
(No 548); 1965 The Tretyakov Gallery
(p. 75, dated 1911); / 1911 Moscow — 1st
Exhibition of Paintings of the World of Art
Society (No 303)

A sketch for the 1911 portrait, now in the
Russian Museum (see No 632).
Exhibitions: 1914 (posthumous) St. Petersburg (No 283), Moscow (No 317); 1935
The Tretyakov Gallery (No 497), The Russian Museum (No 602); 1958–59 The Tretyakov Gallery; 1965 The Tretyakov Gallery (p. 74, described incorrectly as the
initial concept of the portrait, dated
1910–11), The Russian Museum; / 1954
The Tretyakov Gallery — Sketches and
Studies by Russian Artists from the
Tretyakov Gallery Reserve: 18th to Early
20th Century (p. 55); 1963 The Tretyakov Gallery — Pencil Drawings, Watercolors, Pastels, and Gouaches (p. 74)
Reproductions: Grabar, *Serov*, 1914,
p. 226 (described incorrectly as the initial
concept of the portrait)
References: Grabar, *Serov*, 1914, p. 294;
Grabar, *Serov*, 1965, p. 370

172. Portrait of
Olga Konstantinovna Orlova.
Cat. No 609

608
**Portrait of Olga Konstantinovna
Orlova.** ⟨1909–10⟩
Graphite. 34.3×21 cm
The Tretyakov Gallery, Moscow.
Inv. No 15778
Olga Konstantinovna Orlova — see
No 561.
A sketch for the 1911 portrait, now in the
Russian Museum (see No 632).
Exhibitions: 1935 The Tretyakov Gallery
(No 531), The Russian Museum (No 588);
1965 The Tretyakov Gallery (p. 74, dated
1910–11); / 1954 The Tretyakov Gallery —
Sketches and Studies by Russian Artists
from the Tretyakov Gallery Reserve: 18th
to Early 20th Century (p. 55); 1963 The
Tretyakov Gallery — Pencil Drawings,
Watercolors, Pastels, and Gouaches
(p. 75)
Reproductions: Grabar, *Serov*, 1980,
p. 228
References: Grabar, *Serov*, 1965, p. 370;
*Serov in the Reminiscences of His Con-
temporaries*, 1971, 2, p. 42

609
**Portrait of Olga Konstantinovna
Orlova.** ⟨1910⟩
Graphite, crayons and sanguine.
65.5×43.4 cm

The Russian Museum (since 1926).
Inv. No P-13442
Provenance: O. Orlova collection,
St. Petersburg
Olga Konstantinovna Orlova — see
No 561.
A sketch for the 1911 portrait, now in
the Russian Museum (see No 632).
Exhibitions: 1914 (posthumous) St. Peters-
burg (No 284), Moscow (No 318); 1935
The Tretyakov Gallery (No 566), The Rus-
sian Museum (No 648); 1958–59 The Tre-
tyakov Gallery; 1959–60 The Russian
Museum; 1965 The Tretyakov Gallery

Reproductions: *Apollon*, 1912, No 10, between pp. 8 and 9 (described incorrectly as an oil painting dated 1911); Grabar, *Serov*, 1914, p. 222; *Ogoniok*, 1959, No 51, p. 9
References: Grabar, *Serov*, 1914, pp. 166, 294; Grabar, *Serov*, 1965, pp. 220, 369; *Serov in the Reminiscences of His Contemporaries*, 1971, 2, pp. 35, 36, 41, 42

612
Serov in a Dull Mood.
Caricature. ⟨1910⟩
Graphite. 17.5×10.7 cm
The Tretyakov Gallery (since 1926).
Inv. No 8726
Provenance: O. Serova collection, Moscow
Exhibitions: 1914 (posthumous) St. Petersburg (No 315), Moscow (No 359); 1935 The Tretyakov Gallery (No 527), The Russian Museum (No 597); 1952 Moscow (No 308); 1958–59 The Tretyakov Gallery; 1965 The Tretyakov Gallery (p. 74, dated 1910–11), The Russian Museum; / 1963 The Tretyakov Gallery — Pencil Drawings, Watercolors, Pastels, and Gouaches (p. 75)
Reproductions: Grabar, *Serov*, 1914, p. 285; Grabar, *Serov*, 1965, p. 300
References: Grabar, *Serov*, 1965, p. 369

Studies and sketches for the painting *The Rape of Europa* (1910), property of the artist's family (Nos 613–616)

613
Head of a Bullock. ⟨1910⟩
Graphite. 16×11 cm
Inscribed by the artist, bottom right: *Римъ* (Rome)
Present whereabouts unknown
Provenance: The Serov family collection, Moscow
Exhibitions: 1935 The Russian Museum (No 621); 1952 Moscow (No 296)
Reproductions: Yaremich, *Serov: Drawings*, 1936
References: Grabar, *Serov*, 1965, p. 438

614
Nude. ⟨1910⟩
Graphite on yellow paper. 26×20.4 cm
Bottom right, an impression of the artist's signet: *BC* (VS)
The Russian Museum (since 1945).
Inv. No P-6554
Exhibitions: 1935 The Tretyakov Gallery (No 779), The Russian Museum (No 718?)
References: Grabar, *Serov*, 1965, p. 439

615 (Plate 204)
Nude. ⟨1910⟩
Sanguine. 42.5×26.8 cm
The Russian Museum (since 1912).
Inv. No P-13423
Provenance: O. Serova collection, Moscow
Exhibitions: 1935 The Tretyakov Gallery (No 536), The Russian Museum (No 609); 1965 The Russian Museum; / 1974 The Russian Museum — Drawings by Russian Artists: Late 19th and Early 20th Centuries (p. 20)
Reproductions: *Serov: the Sun of Russia*, 1913; Dmitriyev, *Serov*, 1917
References: Grabar, *Serov*, 1914, p. 294; Grabar, *Serov*, 1965, p. 437

616 (Plate 202)
The Rape of Europa. Sketch. 1910
Watercolor. 25.3×31.5 cm
The Russian Museum (since 1912).
Inv. No P-13448
Exhibitions: 1935 The Tretyakov Gallery (No 539), The Russian Museum (No 612); 1958–59 The Tretyakov Gallery; 1965 The Tretyakov Gallery (p. 74), The Russian Museum
Reproductions: *Apollon*, 1912, No 10, between pp. 32 and 33
References: Grabar, *Serov*, 1965, p. 437

1911
PAINTINGS

617
Curtain for the ballet *Sheherazade*.
⟨1911⟩
Distemper on canvas. 1138×1707 cm (approx.)
Present whereabouts unknown
Provenance: S. Diaghilev collection; in 1968 the curtain was on sale at Sotheby's in London (*Catalogue of Costumes and Curtains from Diaghilev and De Basil Ballets*, London and Brandford, 1968, p. 21)
The curtain was painted by Serov in collaboration with I. Yefimov and N. Simonovich-Yefimova.
References: Grabar, *Serov*, 1914, p. 294 (dated 1910); Serov, *Correspondence*, 1937, pp. 265, 322; Simonovich-Yefimova 1964, pp. 123–125, 172, 173; Grabar, *Serov*, 1965, p. 439 (dated 1910); Kopschitzer, *Serov*, 1967, pp. 427–430; *Serov in the Reminiscences of His Contemporaries*, 1971, 1, pp. 396, 456

Designs of the curtain for the ballet *Sheherazade* (a symphonic suite based on the *Arabian Nights*, music by N. Rimsky-Korsakov).
The Russian Seasons in Paris, 1911, Théâtre du Châtelet (Nos 618–624)

618 (Plate 190)
Sketch. 1910
Tempera on cardboard. 56×72 cm
Bottom right, an impression of the artist's signet: *BC* (VS)

173. Portrait of Sophia Vladimirovna Olsufyeva. Cat. No 611

The Russian Museum (since 1918).
Inv. No Ж-1920
Provenance: E. Tereshchenko collection, St. Petersburg
Exhibitions: 1935 The Tretyakov Gallery (No 186), The Russian Museum (No 181); 1965 The Tretyakov Gallery (p. 48), The Russian Museum
Reproductions: Sarabyanov, *Serov*, 1974, No 45
References: Grabar, *Serov*, 1914, p. 294; Grabar, *Serov*, 1965, p. 439 (as "first version")

619
Sketch. ⟨1910⟩
Watercolors and gouache on cardboard. 86.5×106 cm
The Bakhrushin Theatrical Museum, Moscow. Inv. No 100198
Exhibitions: 1935 The Tretyakov Gallery (No 187), The Russian Museum (No 182); 1958–59 The Tretyakov Gallery
References: Grabar, *Serov*, 1965, p. 439 (as "second version")

174. Nude. Cat. No 614

620
Sketch. ⟨1910⟩
Watercolors and gouache on cardboard. 42×59.5 cm
The Bakhrushin Theatrical Museum, Moscow (since 1925). Inv. No 5226
Provenance: M. Karpova collection, Moscow (?)
Exhibitions: 1958–59 The Tretyakov Gallery
References: Grabar, *Serov*, 1914, p. 295 (as "fourth version?"); Grabar, *Serov*, 1965, p. 439

621

Sketch. ⟨1910⟩
Gouache on cardboard. 68×87 cm
The Tretyakov Gallery (since 1967).
Inv. No P-1159
Provenance: S. Diaghilev collection,
St. Petersburg; K. Lipskerov collection,
Moscow; A. Miasnikov collection, Moscow
Exhibitions: 1935 The Tretyakov Gallery
(No 190); 1946 Central House of Art
Workers, Moscow (No 49); 1952 Moscow
(No 297); 1958–59 The Tretyakov Gallery;
1965 The Tretyakov Gallery (p. 48), The
Russian Museum; / 1911 St. Petersburg,
Moscow — 1st Exhibition of Paintings of
the World of Art Society (Nos 281, 236)
Reproductions: *Apollon*, 1912, No 10,
between pp. 24 and 25; Radlov, *Serov*,
1914; Sokolova, *Serov*, 1935, p. 137 (in
the list of illustrations, p. 165, No 50, de-
scribed incorrectly as "curtain design for
the ballet *Sheherazade*. The Russian
Museum"); Grabar, *Serov*, 1965, p. 303
References: Grabar, *Serov*, 1914, p. 295
(as "the fifth, final design from the
S. Diaghilev collection"); Grabar, *Serov*,
1965, p. 439

622

Sketch. ⟨1910⟩
Tempera on cardboard. 38.5×57.5 cm
The Tretyakov Gallery (since 1958).
Inv. No P-805
Provenance: The Serov family collection,
Moscow
Part of the overall compositional scheme
of the curtain.
Exhibitions: 1914 (posthumous) Moscow
(No 335); 1935 The Tretyakov Gallery
(No 188), The Russian Museum (No 183);
1952 Moscow (No 299); 1958–59 The
Tretyakov Gallery; 1965 The Tretyakov
Gallery (p. 48); / 1914 Malmö (Sweden) —
Baltic Art Exhibition (No 3219)
References: Grabar, *Serov*, 1965, p. 439
(described incorrectly as executed in
gouache on paper)

623 (Plate 191)
Sketch. ⟨1910⟩
Tempera on cardboard. 66×48 cm
The Serov family collection, Moscow
Central part of the overall compositional
scheme of the curtain.
Exhibitions: 1914 (posthumous) Moscow
(No 315); 1935 The Tretyakov Gallery

(No 189), The Russian Museum (No 184);
1952 Moscow (No 300); 1965 The
Tretyakov Gallery (p. 48), The Russian
Museum; / 1914 Malmö (Sweden) — Baltic
Art Exhibition (No 3228)
Reproductions: Simonovich-Yefimova
1964, between pp. 124 and 125
References: Grabar, *Serov*, 1914, p. 295
(as "third version?"); Grabar, *Serov*, 1965,
p. 439

624

Sketch. ⟨1911⟩
Gouache on cardboard
Present whereabouts unknown
Provenance: V. Nouvel collection, Paris
References: Grabar, *Serov*, 1965, p. 439
("1910. The fifth, final design from which
the curtain was painted in Paris")

625

**Peter the Great at a Construction
Site.** ⟨1910–11⟩
Tempera on cardboard. 57×83.3 cm
On the reverse, a sketch on the same
theme.
The Tretyakov Gallery (since 1962).
Inv. No П-33709
Provenance: O. Serova collection, Mos-
cow; E. Helzer and T. Helzer collection,
Moscow
Peter the Great — see No 402.
Exhibitions: 1914 (posthumous) St. Peters-
burg (No 229), Moscow (No 337); 1952
Moscow (No 266, size given wrongly as
52×62 cm); 1958–59 The Tretyakov Gal-
lery; 1965 The Tretyakov Gallery (p. 49);
/ 1963 The Tretyakov Gallery — Pencil
Drawings, Watercolors, Pastels, and
Gouaches (p. 75)
References: Grabar, *Serov*, 1914, p. 295;
Grabar, *Serov*, 1965, pp. 211, 213, 441

626

**Peter the Great at a Construction
Site.** ⟨1910–11⟩
Tempera on cardboard. 63×92 cm
Bottom right, an impression of the artist's
signet: BC (VS)
The Russian Museum (since 1928).
Inv. No Ж-1921
Provenance: E. Tereshchenko collection,
St. Petersburg
Peter the Great — see No 402.
Exhibitions: 1935 The Tretyakov Gallery
(No 550, described incorrectly as a water-

color), The Russian Museum (No 629, the
same error); 1958–59 The Tretyakov Gallery; 1965 The Russian Museum
Reproductions: *Works by Serov in the
Russian Museum*, 1970 (No 15 — detail,
No 16)
References: Grabar, *Serov*, 1914, p. 295
(described incorrectly as done in charcoal); Grabar, *Serov*, 1965, pp. 211,
213, 441

627

**Portrait of Alexei Alexandrovich
Stakhovich.** 1911
Oil on canvas. 48×60 cm
Signed and dated, bottom right: *911 C*
(1911, S)
The Stanislavsky Memorial Museum,
Moscow
Provenance: A. Stakhovich collection,
Moscow; K. Stanislavsky collection,
Moscow
Alexei Alexandrovich Stakhovich
(1856–1919), shareholder, later actor of
the Moscow Art Theater.
Exhibitions: 1914 (posthumous) St. Peters-
burg (No 311), Moscow (No 351); 1952
Moscow (No 314); 1965 The Tretyakov
Gallery (p. 50), The Russian Museum; /
1911 Moscow — 1st Exhibition of Paint-
ings of the World of Art Society (No 234);
1914 Malmö (Sweden) — Baltic Art
Exhibition (No 3232)
Reproductions: Grabar, *Serov*, 1914,
p. 238; Leniashin 1980, p. 144
References: Grabar, *Serov*, 1914, pp. 212,
278, 295; Grabar, *Serov*, 1965, p. 342

628

**Portrait of Alexei Alexandrovich
Stakhovich.** 1911
Tempera on canvas (horizontal oval)
Signed and dated, top right: *BC 911*
(VS,1911)
Present whereabouts unknown
Provenance: E. Pashkova collection,
St. Petersburg
Alexei Alexandrovich Stakhovich — see
No 627.
Exhibitions: 1913 St. Petersburg —
3rd Exhibition of Paintings of the World of
Art Society (No 399)
Reproductions: Grabar, *Serov*, 1914,
p. 239
References: Grabar, *Serov*, 1914, pp. 212,
278, 295; Grabar, *Serov*, 1965, pp. 220,
342

629 (Plate 208)
**Portrait of Vladimir Osipovich
Girshman.** 1911
Oil on canvas. 96×77.5 cm
Signed and dated, bottom left: *BC 911*
(VS, 1911)
The Tretyakov Gallery (since 1917).
Inv. No 5587
Provenance: V. Girshman collection,
Moscow
Vladimir Osipovich Girshman
(1867–1936), Moscow factory owner, art
collector.
Exhibitions: 1914 (posthumous) St. Peters-
burg (No 313), Moscow (No 353); 1935
The Tretyakov Gallery (No 193), The Rus-
sian Museum (No 187); 1958–59 The
Tretyakov Gallery; 1959 Museum of Rus-
sian Art, Kiev; 1959–60 The Russian
Museum; 1965 The Tretyakov Gallery
(p. 49), The Russian Museum; / 1911 Mos-

175. Curtain design
for the ballet *Sheherazade*.
Cat. No 622

cow — 1st Exhibition of Paintings of the World of Art Society (No 302)
Reproductions: *Apollon*, 1912, No 10, between pp. 12 and 13 (dated 1910); Grabar, *Serov*, 1914, p. 241; Radlov, *Serov*, 1914 (in the list of Serov's works dated 1910); *Essays on the History of Russian Portraiture*, 1964, p. 46; Grabar, *Serov*, 1965, p. 176
References: *Serov in the Reminiscences of His Contemporaries*, 1971, 2, p. 333; Grabar, *Serov*, 1914, pp. 212, 295; Grabar, *Serov*, 1965, pp. 174, 342; Leniashin 1980, pp. 170—174

630 (Plate 211)
Portrait of Yelena Alexeyevna Balina. 1911
Oil on canvas. 106×77 cm
Signed and dated, top right: *B.C. 911*
(V.S., 1911)
Art Museum, Gorky (since 1929).
Inv. No 620
Provenance: Ye. Balina collection, Moscow; The Tretyakov Gallery
Exhibitions: 1914 (posthumous) St. Petersburg (No 310), Moscow (No 350); 1935 The Tretyakov Gallery (No 195), The Russian Museum (No 189); 1958–59 The Tretyakov Gallery; 1959 Museum of Russian Art, Kiev; 1959–60 The Russian Museum; 1965 The Tretyakov Gallery (pp. 49, 50)
Reproductions: Grabar, *Serov*, 1914, p. 237; *The Gorky Art Museum: Picture Gallery*, Leningrad, Aurora Art Publishers, 1973, No 55
References: Grabar, *Serov*, 1914, p. 295; Grabar, *Serov*, 1965, p. 343

631
Portrait of Lydia Nikolayevna Kamenskaya. ⟨1911⟩. Unfinished
Oil
Present whereabouts unknown
Provenance: L. Kamenskaya collection, St. Petersburg
Lydia Nikolayevna Kamenskaya, wife of I. G. Kamensky, member of the State Council.
References: Grabar, *Serov*, 1914, p. 295; Grabar, *Serov*, 1965, p. 343 (as *Portrait of P. L. Kamenskaya*)

632 (Plates 214, 215)
Portrait of Olga Konstantinovna Orlova. 1911
Tempera on canvas. 237.5×160 cm
Signed and dated, bottom right:
В. Сѣровъ 911 (Serov, 1911)
The Russian Museum (since 1912).
Inv. No Ж-4289
Provenance: V. N. and O. K. Orlov collection, St. Petersburg
Olga Konstantinovna Orlova — see No 561.
Exhibitions: 1935 The Tretyakov Gallery (No 194), The Russian Museum (No 188); 1959–60 The Russian Museum; 1965 The Tretyakov Gallery (p. 49), The Russian Museum; / 1911 Rome – International Art Exhibition, (No 395); 1912 St. Petersburg — 2nd Exhibition of Paintings of the World of Art Society (No 279); 1975 The Russian Museum — Russian Portrait Painting: Late 19th and Early 20th Centuries (No 199)
Reproductions: *Apollon*, 1912, No 10, between pp. 10 and 11 (described incorrectly

176. Peter the Great at a Construction Site. Cat. No 625

177. Peter the Great at a Construction Site. Cat. No 625 (reverse)

as an oil painting); Grabar, *Serov*, 1914, p. 227 (dated 1910); Radlov, *Serov*, 1914, between pp. 12 and 13 (in the lists of Serov's works dated 1910); Grabar, *Serov*, 1980, between pp. 232 and 233
References: Grabar, *Serov*, 1914, pp. 212, 294 (described incorrectly as an oil painting; dated 1910); Grabar, *Serov*, 1965, pp. 220, 222–224, 342 (described incorrectly as an oil painting); Sarabyanov, *Reforms by Valentin Serov*, 1971, pp. 9, 27; Leniashin 1980, pp. 175—204

DRAWINGS, WATERCOLORS, PASTELS, AND GOUACHES

633
Gabriele d'Annunzio, Ida Rubinstein and Natalia Golubeva. Caricature. ⟨1910–11⟩
Black chalk. 26.8×43 cm
The Tretyakov Gallery (since 1936).
Inv. No 15786
Provenance: I. Ostroukhov collection, Moscow

Gabriele d'Annunzio (1863–1938), Italian poet, dramatist and novelist; Ida Rubinstein — see No 582; Natalia Vladimirovna Golubeva, d'Annunzio's friend.
Exhibitions: 1935 The Tretyakov Gallery (No 533), The Russian Museum (No 606); 1958–59 The Tretyakov Gallery; 1959 Museum of Russian Art, Kiev; 1959–60 The Russian Museum; 1965 The Tretyakov Gallery (p. 73), The Russian Museum; / 1963 The Tretyakov Gallery — Pencil Drawings, Watercolors, Pastels, and Gouaches (p. 74)
Reproductions: Grabar, *Serov*, 1914, p. 280 (dated 1910)
References: Grabar, *Serov*, 1914, p. 294; Grabar, *Serov*, 1965, p. 369

634
Male Model. ⟨1910–11⟩
Sanguine. 43×26.6 cm
Bottom right, two impressions of the artist's signet: *BC* (VS)
The Russian Museum (since 1960).
Inv. No P-53340
Provenance: The Serov family collection, Moscow
Exhibitions: 1935 The Russian Museum (dated 1900s)
References: Grabar, *Serov*, 1965, p. 444 (as *Male Model Running*)

635

Model. ⟨1910–11⟩
Black pencil. 43×27 cm
The Russian Museum (since 1960).
Inv. No P-53337
Provenance: The Serov family collection,
Moscow
Exhibitions: 1914 (posthumous) Moscow;
1935 The Tretyakov Gallery (No 518), The
Russian Museum (No 703); 1952 Moscow
(No 263)
Reproductions: Yaremich, *Serov: Draw-
ings*, 1936 (as *Model with Her Back Bent.
1909–10. Black lead. 26×42 cm*)
References: Grabar, *Serov*, 1965, p. 445
(as *Model Picking Up a Cloth from the
Floor*)

636 (Plate 108)

Nude. ⟨1910–11⟩
Black chalk. 43×26.5 cm
The Russian Museum (since 1960).
Inv. No P-53338
Provenance: The Serov family collection,
Moscow
Exhibitions: 1935 The Russian Museum
(dated 1900s)
References: Grabar, *Serov*, 1965, p. 445
(as *Model Standing 3/4 to the Right, with
Her Left Hand Behind the Head*)

637 (Plate 107)

Nude. ⟨1910–11⟩
Black chalk. 43×26.7 cm
Bottom right, an impression of the artist's
signet: *BC* (VS)
The Russian Museum (since 1960).
Inv. No P-53342
Provenance: The Serov family collection,
Moscow
Exhibitions: 1935 The Russian Museum
(dated 1900s); 1965 The Russian Museum
References: Grabar, *Serov*, 1965, p. 445

638

Model. ⟨1910–11⟩
Pencil. 43×27 cm
Present whereabouts unknown
Provenance: The Serov family collection,
Moscow; A. Gordon collection, Moscow
Exhibitions: 1935 The Russian Museum
(dated 1900s); 1952 Moscow (No 260)
Reproductions: Yaremich, *Serov: Draw-*

ings, 1936 (as *Model. 1909–10. Black
lead. 27×42 cm*)
References: Grabar, *Serov*, 1965, p. 446
(as *Model Adjusting Her Hair*)

639

Model. ⟨1910–11⟩
Ink and pen. 20.5×12.4 cm
O. Vereisky collection, Moscow
Provenance: O. Serova collection, Mos-
cow; G. Vereisky collection, Leningrad
Exhibitions: 1952 Moscow (No 264)
Reproductions: Yaremich, *Serov: Draw-
ings*, 1936 (as *Model. 1909–10.
Pen. 12×20 cm*)
References: Grabar, *Serov*, 1965, p. 446
(as *Model with One Foot Forward*)

640 (Plate 163)

Peter the Great Riding. ⟨1910–11⟩
Pencil. 26.6×43 cm
The Russian Museum (since 1912).
Inv. No P-3080
Peter the Great — see No 402.
Exhibitions: 1935 The Tretyakov Gallery
(No 561), The Russian Museum (No 643);
1965 The Russian Museum
Reproductions: Grabar, *Serov*, 1914,
p. 221; Grabar, *Serov*, 1965, p. 211
(dated 1910)
References: Grabar, *Serov*, 1914, p. 295;
Grabar, *Serov*, 1965, p. 242

641 (Plate 164)

**Peter the Great at a Construction
Site.** ⟨1910–11⟩
Watercolors and gouache on paper,
mounted on cardboard. 48.9×64.7 cm
The Russian Museum (since 1912).
Inv. No P-13425
Peter the Great — see No 402.
Exhibitions: 1935 The Tretyakov Gallery
(No 560), The Russian Museum (No 642);
1959–60 The Russian Museum; 1965 The
Tretyakov Gallery (p. 75), The Russian
Museum; / 1939 The Tretyakov Gallery —
Russian History Painting (No 337)
Reproductions: *Apollon*, 1912, No 10,
between pp. 26 and 27; Grabar, *Serov*,
1914, p. 221 (described incorrectly as be-
longing to E. Tereshchenko); *Works by
Serov in the Russian Museum*, 1970
(No 15 — detail, No 16 — size given
wrongly as 63×92.7 cm); Grabar, *Serov*,
1980, pl. 103

References: Grabar, *Serov*, 1914, p. 295
(as a sketch housed at the Museum of
Alexander III in St. Petersburg); Grabar,
Serov, 1965, pp. 211, 213, 441

642

**Peter the Great at a Construction
Site.** ⟨1910–11⟩
Charcoal and chalk on brown paper.
52.1×63.2 cm
The Tretyakov Gallery (since 1953).
Inv. No P-51
Provenance: The Serov family collection,
Moscow
An early variant sketch of the composition.
Peter the Great — see No 402.
Exhibitions: 1935 The Tretyakov Gallery
(No 549), The Russian Museum (No 628);
1952 Moscow (No 265); 1965 The
Tretyakov Gallery (p. 75)
References: Grabar, *Serov*, 1965, p. 441

643

**Portrait of Konstantin Sergeyevich
Stanislavsky.** 1911
Pastel on brown paper, mounted on card-
board. 55.5×36.3 cm
Signed and dated, bottom right: *BC 911*
(VS, 1911)
The Tretyakov Gallery (since 1911).
Inv. No 3665
Provenance: O. Serova collection, Moscow
Konstantin Sergeyevich Stanislavsky —
see No 541.
Exhibitions: 1935 The Tretyakov Gallery
(No 564), The Russian Museum (No 646);
1958–59 The Tretyakov Gallery; 1965 The
Tretyakov Gallery (p. 75); / 1911 Moscow
— 1st Exhibition of Paintings of the World
of Art Society (No 233); 1963 The
Tretyakov Gallery — Pencil Drawings,
Watercolors, Pastels, and Gouaches
(p. 75)
Reproductions: *Apollon*, 1912, No 10, be-
tween pp. 14 and 15; Grabar, *Serov*,
1914, p. 244; Grabar, *Serov*, 1980, pl. 105
References: Grabar, *Serov*, 1914, p. 295;
Grabar, *Serov*, 1965, pp. 278, 342

644 (Plate 217)

**Portrait of Henrietta Leopoldovna
Girshman.** ⟨1911⟩
Pastel on cardboard. 94.4×76 cm (oval)
The Tretyakov Gallery (since 1917).
Inv. No 5588
Provenance: V. Girshman collection,
Moscow
Henrietta Leopoldovna Girshman — see
No 452.
Exhibitions: 1914 (posthumous) St. Peters-
burg (No 312), Moscow (No 352); 1935
The Tretyakov Gallery (No 565), The
Russian Museum (No 647); 1958–59 The
Tretyakov Gallery; 1965 The Tretyakov
Gallery (p. 75); / 1963 The Tretyakov Gal-
lery — Pencil Drawings, Watercolors, Pas-
tels, and Gouaches (p. 75)
Reproductions: Grabar, *Serov*, 1914,
p. 240; *Apollon*, 1914, Nos 6/7, between
pp. 24 and 25 (detail, dated 1910–11);
Dmitriyev, *Serov*, 1917; *Essays on the
History of Russian Portraiture*, 1964,
pp. 90, 91 (detail); Zotov, *Serov*, 1964,
p. 15
References: *Serov in the Reminiscences
of His Contemporaries*, 1971, 2, pp. 333,
334; Grabar, *Serov*, 1914, pp. 198, 199,
259; Grabar, *Serov*, 1965, pp. 217, 342;

Essays on the History of Russian Portraiture, 1964, p. 92; Liaskovskaya 1971, p. 58; Sarabyanov, *Reforms by Valentin Serov*, 1971, p. 25

645 (Plate 174)
Portrait of Nadezhda Petrovna Lamanova. ⟨1911⟩
Charcoal, chalk and sanguine on cardboard. 102×75.5 cm
V. Zamkov collection, Leningrad
Provenance: N. Kayutova-Lamanova collection, Moscow; M. Lamanova collection, Moscow; V. Mukhina collection, Moscow
Nadezhda Petrovna Lamanova, Kayutova by marriage (1861–1941), dressmaker; costume designer at the Moscow Art Theater (1932–41).
Exhibitions: 1914 (posthumous) St. Petersburg (No 315), Moscow (No 356); 1935 The Russian Museum (No 687); 1946 Central House of Art Workers, Moscow (No 48); 1952 Moscow (No 315)
Reproductions: Grabar, *Serov*, 1914, p. 245
References: Grabar, *Serov*, 1914, pp. 278, 295; Grabar, *Serov*, 1965, p. 371; *Serov in the Reminiscences of His Contemporaries*, 1971, 1, pp. 173, 174, 183

646 (Plate 213)
Portrait of Olga Konstantinovna Orlova. 1911
Crayons and charcoal. 65.3×49.2 cm
Signed and dated, right: *BC 911* (VS, 1911)
The Russian Museum (since 1926). Inv. No P-13436
Provenance: O. Orlova collection, St. Petersburg

Olga Konstantinovna Orlova — see No 561.
Exhibitions: 1914 (posthumous) St. Petersburg (No 282), Moscow (No 316); 1935 The Tretyakov Gallery (No 567), The Russian Museum (No 649); 1959–60 The Russian Museum; 1965 The Tretyakov Gallery (pp. 75, 76), The Russian Museum; / 1974 The Russian Museum — Drawings by Russian Artists: Late 19th and Early 20th Centuries (p. 20)
Reproductions: *Apollon*, 1914, No 6/7, between pp. 24 and 25; Sokolova, *Serov*, 1935, p. 154 (dated 1910); Leniashin 1980, p. 199
References: Grabar, *Serov*, 1914, p. 294 (dated 1910); Grabar, *Serov*, 1965, p. 370

647 (Plate 218)
Portrait of Polina Ivanovna Shcherbatova. ⟨1911⟩. Unfinished
Tempera, charcoal and pastel on canvas. 242×184 cm
The Tretyakov Gallery (since 1911). Inv. No 3666
Provenance: S. Shcherbatov collection, Moscow
Polina Ivanovna Shcherbatova (?–1966), wife of the artist and art collector S. A. Shcherbatov.
Exhibitions: 1935 The Tretyakov Gallery (No 571); 1958–59 The Tretyakov Gallery; 1965 The Tretyakov Gallery (p. 76); / 1963 The Tretyakov Gallery — Pencil Drawings, Watercolors, Pastels, and Gouaches (p. 75)
Reproductions: *Apollon*, 1912, No 10, between pp. 34 and 35; Grabar, *Serov*, 1914, p. 243; Radlov, *Serov*, 1914;

Grabar, *Serov*, 1965, p. 305; *History of Russian Art*, 1968, p. 223
References: Grabar, *Serov*, 1914, pp. 212, 278, 295; Sarabyanov, *Reforms by Valentin Serov*, 1971, p. 25; *Serov in the Reminiscences of His Contemporaries*, 1971, 1, pp. 661, 664–666, 671

648
Portrait of Polina Ivanovna Shcherbatova. ⟨1911⟩
Charcoal on cardboard. 108×70.6 cm
The Tretyakov Gallery (since 1927). Inv. No 19252
Provenance: State Museum Reserve, Moscow
A sketch for the portrait which is now in the Tretyakov Gallery (see No 647).
Exhibitions: 1935 The Tretyakov Gallery (No 570), The Russian Museum (No 652); / 1954 The Tretyakov Gallery — Sketches and Studies by Russian Artists from the Tretyakov Gallery Reserve: 18th to Early 20th Century (p. 55)
Reproductions: *Essays on the History of Russian Portraiture*, 1964, p. 88
References: Grabar, *Serov*, 1965, p. 371

649
Portrait of Polina Ivanovna Shcherbatova. ⟨1911⟩
Black chalk and sanguine. 107×66 cm
The Mustafayev Art Museum, Baku (since 1925). Inv. No 15/1163
Provenance: State Museum Reserve, Moscow
A sketch for the portrait which is now in the Tretyakov Gallery (see No 647).
Exhibitions: 1914 (posthumous) St. Petersburg (No 314), Moscow (No 354)
Reproductions: *Art Museum of the Azerbaijan SSR. Catalogue*, 1971, p. 126
References: Grabar, *Serov*, 1965, p. 371

180. Portrait of Konstantin Sergeyevich Stanislavsky. Cat. No 643

181. Portrait of Polina Ivanovna Shcherbatova. Cat. No 648

182. Diana and Actaeon.
Cat. No 651

Sketches for an unrealized
mural in the dining-room of
V. Nosov's house in Moscow
(Ovid's *Metamorphoses*). 1911
(Nos 650–653)

650 (Plate 194)
Apollo and Diana Killing Niobe's Sons.
⟨1911⟩
Watercolors, bronze and black chalk.
25.5×45.7 cm
Watermark: *1907*
The Tretyakov Gallery. Inv. No 11309
Provenance: I. Ostroukhov collection,
Moscow
Exhibitions: 1914 (posthumous) St. Peters-
burg (No 308a), Moscow (No 348); 1935
The Tretyakov Gallery (No 580), The Rus-
sian Museum (No 686); 1958–59 The
Tretyakov Gallery; 1965 The Tretyakov
Gallery (p. 76), The Russian Museum;
/ 1963 Moscow — Pencil Drawings,
Watercolors, Pastels, and Gouaches
(p.76)
Reproductions: Grabar, *Serov*, 1914,
p. 234 (erroneously included in the
O. Serova collection); *Iskusstvo*, 1934,
No 4, between pp. 170 and 171 (as a
"sketch for a mural"); Grabar, *Serov*,
1965, p. 285; Sarabyanov, *Serov*, 1974,
No 48
References: Bakushinsky 1935; Grabar,
Serov, 1914, pp. 228, 230, 295 (errone-
ously included in the O. Serova collection);
Grabar, *Serov*, 1965, pp. 286, 447; Lesiuk
1934, pp. 168–173; Sarabyanov, *Reforms
by Valentin Serov*, 1971, p. 30

651
Diana and Actaeon. ⟨1911⟩
Charcoal. 49.5×48.2 cm
The Tretyakov Gallery, Moscow (since
1958). Inv. No 30182
Provenance: The Serov family collection,
Moscow
Exhibitions: 1935 The Tretyakov Gallery
(No 575), The Russian Museum (No 681);
1958–59 The Tretyakov Gallery; 1965
The Tretyakov Gallery (pp. 76, 77 —
Inv. No P-811), The Russian Museum;
/ 1962 The Tretyakov Gallery — Russian
Pre-revolutionary Art: New Acquisitions
(p. 46)
References: Bakushinsky 1935; Grabar,
Serov, 1914, p. 295; Grabar, *Serov*, 1965,
p. 447; Sarabyanov, *Reforms by Valentin
Serov*, 1971, p. 30

652
**Diana; Eros, Apollo and Daphne;
Venus.** ⟨1911⟩
Graphite. 267×43 cm
The Tretyakov Gallery, Moscow
(since 1949). Inv. No 28404
Exhibitions: 1935 The Russian Museum
(No 656); 1958–59 The Tretyakov Gallery;
1965 The Tretyakov Gallery (p. 77),
The Russian Museum
References: Bakushinsky 1935; Grabar,
Serov, 1914, p. 295; Grabar, *Serov*, 1965,
p. 447; Sarabyanov, *Reforms by Valentin
Serov*, 1971, p. 30

653 (Plate 195)
Diana. ⟨1911⟩
Watercolors and gouache. 42×66.3 cm
Present whereabouts unknown
Provenance: O. Serova collection, Mos-
cow; E. Helzer and T. Helzer collection,
Moscow
Exhibitions: 1935 The Tretyakov Gallery
(No 573); 1952 Moscow (No 317);
1958–59 The Tretyakov Gallery; 1965
The Tretyakov Gallery (p. 77)
Reproductions: Grabar, *Serov*, 1914,
p. 234 (top)
References: Grabar, *Serov*, 1914, p. 295;
Grabar, *Serov*, 1965, p. 446

**Drawings for Krylov's *Fables*.
1895–1911 (Nos 654–675)**

654 (Plate 87)
The Wolf and the Crane
Graphite, pen and ink. 21.8×33 cm
The Tretyakov Gallery. Inv. No 8731
Exhibitions: 1935 The Tretyakov Gallery
(No 672), The Russian Museum (No 891);
1958–59 The Tretyakov Gallery; 1959

183. Diana; Eros, Apollo and
Daphne; Venus. Cat. No 652

184. The Daw in Peacock
Feathers. Cat. No 656

Museum of Russian Art, Kiev; 1959–60
The Russian Museum; 1965 The
Tretyakov Gallery (p. 78); / 1963 The Tret-
yakov Gallery — Pencil Drawings, Water-
colors, Pastels, and Gouaches (p. 76)
Reproductions: Gorlov 1951, pl. 6
References: Grabar, *Serov*, 1914, pp. 257,
262, 264, 296; Grabar, *Serov*, 1965,
p. 451; *Serov in the Reminiscences of His
Contemporaries*, 1971, 1, p. 206

655 (Plate 82)
The Wolf and the Shepherds. ⟨1898⟩
Etching. 16.1×23.9 cm
Etched, below left: *Съровъ* (Serov)
The Russian Museum. Inv. No Гр-28213
Published as a supplement to the *Mir
Iskusstva* magazine, 1900, No 1/2.
24.2×29.6 cm (sheet)
Exhibitions: 1914 (posthumous) St. Peters-
burg (No 140); 1935 The Russian Museum
(No 1057); 1952 Moscow (No 395, from
the A. Korostikhin collection, Moscow);
1965 The Russian Museum; / 1900
St. Petersburg — 2nd Exhibition of Paint-
ings Organized by the *Mir Iskusstva*
Magazine (No 183); 1902 Moscow — Ex-
hibitions of Paintings Organized by the *Mir
Iskusstva* Magazine (No 220); 1906 Paris
— Russian Art (No 526); 1967 The Rus-
sian Museum — Russian Prints: Late 19th
and Early 20th Centuries (p. 65)
Reproductions: Grabar, *Serov*, 1914,
p. 267; Yaremich, *Serov: Drawings*, 1936;
Gorlov 1951, pl. 30
References: Grabar, *Serov*, 1914, pp. 267,
268, 289 (dated 1899); Yaremich, *Serov:
Drawings*, 1936, p. 21; Simonovich-
Yefimova 1964, p. 46; Grabar, *Serov*,
1965, p. 452

656
The Daw in Peacock Feathers
Graphite. 26.8×42.5 cm
Signed, bottom right: *BC* (VS). Top left,
the artist's inscription: *Больш. доска*
(large plate); below: *8*
The Tretyakov Gallery (since 1914).
Inv. No 3625
Provenance: O. Serova collection, Moscow
Final version.
Exhibitions: 1914 (posthumous) St. Peters-
burg (No 341), Moscow (No 383 —
1st ed., No 367 — 2nd ed.); 1935 The
Tretyakov Gallery (No 656), The Russian
Museum (No 930); / 1963 The Tretyakov
Gallery — Pencil Drawings, Watercolors,
Pastels, and Gouaches (p. 77)
Reproductions: Grabar, *Serov*, 1914,
p. 262
References: Grabar, *Serov*, 1914, pp. 257,
296; Grabar, *Serov*, 1965, p. 453

657 (Plate 89)
The Daw in Peacock Feathers
Graphite on yellowish paper.
26.6×42.3 cm
The Russian Museum (since 1914).
Inv. No P-13409
Provenance: M. Rabinovich collection,
St. Petersburg
Exhibitions: 1935 The Russian Museum
(No 931); 1965 The Russian Museum
References: Grabar, *Serov*, 1914, p. 296

658 (Plate 77)
The Wolf in the Kennels. ⟨1896–98⟩
Graphite. 22.2×35.4 cm
The Tretyakov Gallery (since 1914).
Inv. No 3634

Provenance: O. Serova collection, Moscow
Exhibitions: 1914 (posthumous) St. Petersburg (No 322), Moscow (No 365 —
1st ed.; No 376 — 2nd ed.); 1935 The
Tretyakov Gallery (No 657), The Russian
Museum (No 933)
Reproductions: Grabar, *Serov*, 1914,
p. 251; Gorlov 1951, pl. 2
References: Grabar, *Serov*, 1914, pp. 260,
295; Grabar, *Serov*, 1965, pp. 288, 289,
452

659 (Plate 90)
The Crow and the Fox
Graphite and black pencil. 26.8×42.5 cm
Signed, bottom right: *BC* (VS).
Top left, the artist's inscription:
мал. доска (small plate); below: *2*
The Tretyakov Gallery (since 1914).
Inv. No 3619
Provenance: O. Serova collection, Moscow
Final version.
Exhibitions: 1914 (posthumous) St. Peters-
burg (No 335), Moscow (No 377 —
1st ed., No 361 — 2nd ed.); 1935 The
Tretyakov Gallery (No 666), The Russian
Museum (No 886); 1958–59 The Tret-
yakov Gallery; 1965 The Tretyakov Gallery
(p. 77); / 1963 The Tretyakov Gallery —
Pencil Drawings, Watercolors, Pastels,
and Gouaches (p. 76)
Reproductions: Grabar, *Serov*, 1914,
p. 263; Gorlov 1951, No 26; Simonovich-
Yefimova 1964, p. 46
References: Grabar, *Serov*, 1914, pp. 257,
296; Grabar, *Serov*, 1965, p. 453;
Simonovich-Yefimova 1964, p. 46; *Serov
in the Reminiscences of His Contemporaries*, 1971, 1, p. 206

660
A Young Crow. ⟨1895⟩
Watercolors and pencil. 22×33.5 cm
The Russian Museum (since 1925).
Inv. No P-13416
Provenance: Museum of the Academy
of Arts, Petrograd
Exhibitions: 1914 (posthumous) St. Peters-
burg (No 317); 1935 The Tretyakov Gal-
lery (No 587), The Russian Museum
(No 950)
Reproductions: Gorlov 1951, pl. 34
References: Grabar, *Serov*, 1914, pp. 262,
295; Grabar, *Serov*, 1965, p. 454

661 (Plate 86)
The Quartet
Graphite and black pencil. 26.7×42.5 cm
Signet, bottom right: *BC* (VS). Top left,
the artist's inscription: *больш. доска*
(large plate); below: *6*
The Tretyakov Gallery. Inv. No 3623
Exhibitions: 1914 (posthumous) St. Peters-
burg (No 339), Moscow (No 381 —1st ed.,
No 365 — 2nd ed.); 1935 The Tretyakov
Gallery (No 662), The Russian Museum
(No 864); 1958–59 The Tretyakov Gallery;
/ 1963 The Tretyakov Gallery — Pencil
Drawings, Watercolors, Pastels, and
Gouaches (p. 76)
Reproductions: Grabar, *Serov*, 1914,
p. 257 (as "latest version. 1898–1911");
Alexander and Valentin Serov, 1914,
between pp. 178 and 179; Gorlov 1951,
pl. 18; *Drawings and Watercolors. Cata-
logue*, 1956
References: Grabar, *Serov*, 1914, pp. 257,
262, 295; Grabar, *Serov*, 1965, pp. 454,
455

662
The Bear and the Contrabass.
Drawing for the fable *The Quartet*
Black chalk on yellowish paper.
26.3×19.8 cm
Bottom right, an impression of the artist's
signet: *BC* (VS)
The Russian Museum (since 1958).
Inv. No P-53126
Provenance: The Serov family collection,
Moscow; V. Petrov collection, Leningrad
Exhibitions: 1914 (posthumous) Moscow
(No 404); 1935 The Tretyakov Gallery
(No 588), The Russian Museum (No 868);
1946 Central House of Art Workers, Mos-
cow (No 69)
References: Grabar, *Serov*, 1965, p. 455

185. A Young Crow.
Cat. No 660

186. The Bear and the
Contrabass. Drawing for
Krylov's fable *The Quartet*.
Cat. No 662

663 (Plate 80)
The Lion and the Wolf
Graphite, pen and ink. 26.8×42.5 cm
Signed in pencil, bottom left: *BC* (VS).
Top, the artist's inscription: *Мал. доска*
(small plate); below: *9*
The Tretyakov Gallery (since 1914).
Inv. No 3626
Provenance: O. Serova collection, Moscow
Final version.
Exhibitions: 1914 (posthumous) St. Peters-
burg (No 342); Moscow (No 384 —
1st ed., No 368 — 2nd ed.); 1935 The
Tretyakov Gallery (No 665), The Russian
Museum (No 960); / 1963 The Tretyakov
Gallery — Pencil Drawings, Watercolors,

187. The Lion and the Wolf.
Cat. No 664

188. An Aging Lion. Cat. No 665

Pastels, and Gouaches (p. 77)
Reproductions: Grabar, *Serov*, 1914,
p. 259; Gorlov 1951, pl. 11; *Drawings and
Watercolors. Catalogue*, 1956
References: Grabar, *Serov*, 1914, pp. 257,
262, 296; Grabar, *Serov*, 1965, p. 457

664
The Lion and the Wolf
India ink, white and graphite on yellowish
paper. 22.3×35.6
Signed, bottom right: *Съровъ* (Serov).
Bottom, the artist's inscription:
Левъ и Волкъ XIV. к. 5 (The Lion and
the Wolf, XIV, book 5)
The Russian Museum. Inv. No P-3214
Provenance: M. Rabinovich collection,
St. Petersburg
Exhibitions: 1935 The Tretyakov Gallery
(No 632), The Russian Museum (No 961);
1965 The Russian Museum
Reproductions: *Mir Iskusstva*, 1900
No 1/2, p. 4; Gorlov 1951, pl. 12
References: Grabar, *Serov*, 1965, p. 457

665
An Aging Lion. ⟨1910–11⟩
Graphite, pen and ink. 26.8×42.3 cm
Signed in pen, bottom right: *BC* (VS)
The Tretyakov Gallery (since 1914).
Inv. No 3639
Exhibitions: 1914 (posthumous) St. Peters-
burg (No 329), Moscow (No 371 —
1st ed., No 381 — 2nd ed.); 1935 The
Tretyakov Gallery (No 653), The Russian
Museum (No 937); 1952 Moscow
(No 332); / 1963 The Tretyakov Gallery —
Pencil Drawings, Watercolors, Pastels,
and Gouaches (p. 77)
Reproductions: Gorlov 1951, pl. 7
References: Grabar, *Serov*, 1914, p. 295;
Grabar, *Serov*, 1965, p. 457; Simonovich-
Yefimova 1974, pp. 47, 48

666 (Plate 85)
An Aging Lion
India ink, pencil and white. 26.7×42.3 cm
The Russian Museum (since 1914).

Inv. No P-3213
Provenance: M. Rabinovich collection,
St. Petersburg
Exhibitions: 1935 The Tretyakov Gallery
(No 631, as *The Lion and the Donkey*),
The Russian Museum (No 938); 1965
The Russian Museum
Reproductions: Gorlov 1951, pl. 8
References: Grabar, *Serov*, 1914, p. 295;
Grabar, *Serov*, 1965, p. 457

667 (Plate 88)
The Fox and the Grapes
Graphite. 22.2×35.5 cm
Bottom right, the artist's inscription:
Лисица и виноград XVII кн 6 (The Fox
and the Grapes, XVII, book 6)
The Tretyakov Gallery, Moscow (since
1914). Inv. No 3644
Provenance: O. Serova collection, Moscow
Exhibitions: 1914 (posthumous) St. Peters-
burg (No 345/3), Moscow (No 386 — 2nd
ed.); 1935 The Tretyakov Gallery
(No 640), The Russian Museum (No 914);
1958–59 The Tretyakov Gallery; 1965 The
Tretyakov Gallery (p. 78), The Russian
Museum; / 1963 The Tretyakov Gallery —
Pencil Drawings, Watercolors, Pastels,
and Gouaches (p. 77)

Reproductions: Grabar, *Serov*, 1914,
p. 255; Gorlov 1951, pl. 16
References: Grabar, *Serov*, 1914, pp. 262
(omitted in the list of works), 299; Grabar,
Serov, 1965, p. 458

668 (Plate 84)
The Monkey and the Eyeglasses
Graphite and black pencil. 26.7×42.5 cm
Signed, bottom right: *BC* (VS). Top left,
the artist's inscription:
малая доска (small plate); below: *11*
The Tretyakov Gallery (since 1914).
Inv. No 3628
Provenance: O. Serova collection, Moscow
Final version.
Exhibitions: 1914 (posthumous) St. Peters-
burg (No 314), Moscow (No 386 — 1st
ed., No 370 — 2nd ed.); 1958–59 The
Tretyakov Gallery; 1959 Museum of Rus-
sian Art, Kiev; 1959–60 The Russian
Museum; 1965 The Tretyakov Gallery
(p. 79); / 1963 The Tretyakov Gallery —
Pencil Drawings, Watercolors, Pastels,
and Gouaches (p. 77)
Reproductions: Grabar, *Serov*, 1914,
p. 266; Gorlov 1951, pl. 36; Grabar, *Serov*,
1965, p. 295
References: Grabar, *Serov*, 1914, pp. 257,
266, 296; Grabar, *Serov*, 1965, p. 458

669 (Plate 79)
The Peasant and the Robber
Graphite and black pencil. 26.7×43 cm
Signed in pencil, bottom left: *BC* (VS)
The Tretyakov Gallery (since 1914).
Inv. No 3624
Provenance: O. Serova collection, Moscow
Final version.
Exhibitions: 1914 (posthumous) St. Peters-
burg (No 340), Moscow (No 382 —
1st ed., No 366 — 2nd ed.); 1935 The
Tretyakov Gallery (No 658), The Russian
Museum (No 898)
Reproductions: Grabar, *Serov*, 1914,
p. 264; Gorlov 1951, pl. 46
References: Grabar, *Serov*, 1914, p. 257,
265, 296; Grabar, *Serov*, 1965, pp. 294,
296, 455

670
The Monkey and the Eyeglasses
Pencil, scumbling. 26.5×42 cm
The Russian Museum (since 1937).
Inv. No P-13410
Provenance: G. Blokh collection,
Leningrad
Exhibitions: 1914 (posthumous) Moscow
(No 370a — 2nd ed.); The Russian
Museum (No 871a — 2nd ed.); 1965
The Russian Museum
References: Grabar, *Serov*, 1914, p. 296;
Grabar, *Serov*, 1965, p. 458

671
The Miller
Graphite and black pencil. 26.8×42.5 cm
Signed, bottom left: *BC* (VS). Top, the
artist's inscription: *Больш. доска* (large
plate); below: *3*
The Tretyakov Gallery (since 1914).
Inv. No 3620
Provenance: O. Serova collection, Moscow
Final version.
Exhibitions: 1914 (posthumous) St. Peters-
burg (No 336), Moscow (No 378 —
1st ed., No 362 — 2nd ed.); 1935 The
Tretyakov Gallery (No 664), The Russian
Museum (No 880); 1958–59 The Tret-

189. The Miller.
Cat. No 671

yakov Gallery; 1965 The Russian
Museum; / 1963 The Tretyakov Gallery —
Pencil Drawings, Watercolors, Pastels,
and Gouaches (p. 77)
Reproductions: Gorlov 1951, pl. 41
References: Grabar, *Serov*, 1914, pp. 257,
264, 296; Grabar, *Serov*, 1965, p. 459

672 (Plate 81)
The Pestilence. ⟨1896⟩
Black chalk. 26.7×42.5 cm
Signed, bottom right: *BC* (VS)
The Tretyakov Gallery. Inv. No 3630
Exhibitions: 1914 (posthumous) St. Peters-
burg (No 318), Moscow (No 360 —
1st ed., No 372 — 2nd ed.); 1935 The
Tretyakov Gallery (No 659), The Russian
Museum (No 856); / 1963 The Tretyakov
Gallery — Pencil Drawings, Watercolors,
Pastels, and Gouaches (p. 77)
Reproductions: Gorlov 1951, No 16a;
Grabar, *Serov*, 1965, p. 289; *Drawings
and Watercolors. Catalogue*, 1956
References: Grabar, *Serov*, 1914, p. 295;
Grabar, *Serov*, 1965, p. 459

190. The Monkey and the
Eyeglasses. Cat. No 670

673
Three Peasants
Graphite. 22.4×36 cm
Top left, in the margin, the artist's
inscription: *Три мужика XXIII кн 8.
передълать* (Three Peasants, XXIII,
book 8. Needs alteration); below: *Слабо*
(not satisfactory)
The Tretyakov Gallery (since 1914).
Inv. No 3632

191. Three Peasants.
Cat. No 673

192. Portrait of Vladimir Vasilyevich Yakunchikov. Cat. No 690

Provenance: O. Serova collection, Moscow
Exhibitions: 1914 (posthumous) St. Petersburg (No 320), Moscow (No 362 — 1st ed., No 374 — 2nd ed.); 1935 The Tretyakov Gallery (No 646), The Russian Museum (No 944); 1952 Moscow (No 343); 1958–59 The Tretyakov Gallery; 1965 The Tretyakov Gallery (p. 78); / 1963 The Tretyakov Gallery — Pencil Drawings, Watercolors, Pastels, and Gouaches (p. 77)
Reproductions: Grabar, *Serov*, 1914, p. 250; Gorlov 1951, pl. 67; Grabar, *Serov*, 1965, p. 293 (in the list of plates, p. 490, erroneously included in a private collection)
References: Grabar, *Serov*, 1914, pp. 260, 295; Grabar, *Serov*, 1965, p. 462

674 (Plate 78)
Trishka's Caftan
Graphite. 26.7×42.5 cm
Signed, bottom left: *BC* (VS). Top, the artist's inscription: *Мал. доска* (small plate); below: *5*
The Tretyakov Gallery (since 1914). Inv. No 3622
Final version.
Exhibitions: 1914 (posthumous) St. Petersburg (No 338), Moscow (No 380 — 1st ed., No 364 — 2nd ed.); 1935 The Tretyakov Gallery (No 660), The Russian Museum (No 859); 1965 The Tretyakov Gallery (p. 78); / 1963 The Tretyakov Gallery — Pencil Drawings, Watercolors, Pastels, and Gouaches (p. 76)
Reproductions: Grabar, *Serov*, 1914, p. 256; *Alexander and Valentin Serov*, 1914, between pp. 180 and 181; Gorlov 1951, pl. 51
References: Grabar, *Serov*, 1914, pp. 257, 265, 266, 296; Simonovich-Yefimova 1964, p. 47; Grabar, *Serov*, 1965, p. 463

675 (Plate 83)
The Pike
Pencil. 26×42.4 cm
The Russian Museum (since 1936). Inv. No P-13417
Provenance: The Serov family collection, Moscow
Exhibitions: 1914 (posthumous) Moscow (No 371a — 2nd ed.); 1935 The Russian

Museum (No 922); 1965 The Russian Museum
References: Grabar, *Serov*, 1914, pp. 257, 296; Grabar, *Serov*, 1965, p. 463

Undated Works
PAINTINGS

676
Head of an Old Man
Present whereabouts unknown
Provenance: The E. Sevier collection, England
Exhibitions: 1960 (?) London — Russian Art and Life (No 100)
References: Grabar, *Serov*, 1965, p. 450

677
A Yard
Oil on canvas. 36×37 cm
Signed, bottom left: *Съровъ* (Serov)
The Tretyakov Gallery. Inv. No 26706
References: Grabar, *Serov*, 1965, p. 448

678
A Road. Study
Oil on canvas. 18×22 cm
The Tretyakov Gallery. Inv. No 2637
Exhibitions: 1954 The Tretyakov Gallery — Sketches and Studies by Russian Artists from the Tretyakov Gallery Reserve: 18th to Early 20th Century (p. 50)
References: Grabar, *Serov*, 1965, p. 448

679
Woman's Head. Study
Oil on panel. 25×26 cm
The Kustodiev Picture Gallery, Astrakhan. Inv. No Ж-64
Provenance: P. Dogadin, Astrakhan
Exhibitions: 1935 The Russian Museum (No 198, described incorrectly as done in oil on cardboard. 34.5×26.5 cm); / 1951 Kiev — Paintings by Russian Artists, Old and New
References: Grabar, *Serov*, 1965, p. 343

680
Italian Landscape with a Campanile
Oil on canvas. 32×17.4 cm
Present whereabouts unknown
Provenance: A. Zotov collection, Moscow
Exhibitions: 1952 Moscow (No 368)
References: Grabar, *Serov*, 1965, p. 448

681
Crimean Landscape
Oil on canvas. 19.5×26.5 cm
Present whereabouts unknown
Exhibitions: 1935 The Russian Museum (No 195)
References: Grabar, *Serov*, 1965, p. 448

682
Edge of a Forest
Oil on cardboard. 61.5×78.5 cm
Present whereabouts unknown
Exhibitions: 1935 The Russian Museum (No 203)
References: Grabar, *Serov*, 1965, p. 448

683
Summer Landscape. A Fence. Study
Oil on canvas. 19×23.5 cm
Signed, bottom right: *Съровъ* (Serov)
Present whereabouts unknown

Provenance: A. Koludarov collection, Moscow
Exhibitions: 1952 Moscow (No 366)
References: Grabar, *Serov*, 1965, p. 448

684
Boy on the Beach. Study
Oil on canvas. 24.3×31.7 cm
Bottom right, an impression of the artist's signet: *BC* (VS)
The I. Brodsky Memorial Museum, Leningrad. Inv. No Ж-127
References: Grabar, *Serov*, 1965, p. 448

685
At the Cemetery
Oil on canvas. 37×17.5 cm
Present whereabouts unknown
Provenance: M. Ivanova collection, Leningrad
Exhibitions: 1935 The Russian Museum (No 191 — 2nd ed.)
References: Grabar, *Serov*, 1965, p. 448

686
A Model
Oil on canvas. 178×164 cm
Present whereabouts unknown
References: Grabar, *Serov*, 1965, p. 448

687
Still Life
Oil on canvas. 37×25 cm
Present whereabouts unknown
Provenance: State Purchasing Commission, Moscow
References: Grabar, *Serov*, 1965, p. 448

688
An Unknown Woman
Oil on cardboard. 50×39.6 cm
Signed, bottom right: *B. Съровъ* (V. Serov)
Present whereabouts unknown
Provenance: D. Sigalov collection, Kiev
Exhibitions: 1958 Kiev — Paintings by Russian Artists from Private Collections in Kiev: Second Half of the 19th and Early 20th Centuries (p. 15, as *Portrait of a Woman Wearing a Shako*)
References: Grabar, *Serov*, 1965, p. 343

689
A Boulevard in Paris. Sketch
Oil on canvas. 51.7×73 cm
Present whereabouts unknown
References: Grabar, *Serov*, 1965, p. 448 (erroneous statement that the picture is housed in the Tretyakov Gallery since 1958. Inv. No П-30174)

690
Portrait of Vladimir Vasilyevich Yakunchikov
Oil on canvas. 56×50 cm
O. Meshkova collection, Moscow
Provenance: A. Yar-Kravchenko collection, Moscow; V. Meshkova collection, Moscow
Vladimir Vasilyevich Yakunchikov (1855–1916), husband of Maria Fiodorovna Yakunchikova (see No 70).
Exhibitions: 1952 Moscow (No 365); 1958–59 The Tretyakov Gallery
References: Grabar, *Serov*, 1965, p. 343

691

Portrait of Savva Timofeyevich Morozov. Unfinished
Oil on canvas. 141×116 cm
Present whereabouts unknown
Savva Timofeyevich Morozov (1861–1905), factory-owner.
Exhibitions: 1952 Moscow (No 364)
References: Grabar, *Serov*, 1965, p. 343

692

Early Spring. A Barn. Study
Oil on canvas, mounted on cardboard. 21×33.5 cm
Present whereabouts unknown
Provenance: A. Bedniakov collection, Moscow
Exhibitions: 1952 Moscow (No 367)
References: Grabar, *Serov*, 1965, p. 478

693

A Finnish Yard
Oil on cardboard. 48.5×64 cm
Signed, bottom right: *Съровъ* (Serov)
The I. Brodsky Memorial Museum, Leningrad. Inv. No Ж-123
Exhibitions: 1935 The Tretyakov Gallery (No 198), The Russian Museum (No 192)
References: Grabar, *Serov*, 1965, p. 448

Note to the Catalogue

The illustrated Catalogue contains information about major works by Valentin Serov housed in the museums of Moscow, Leningrad and other Soviet cities, and also lists a number of works whose present whereabouts are unknown.

In the case of works housed in two principal repositories of Russian art, the Tretyakov Gallery in Moscow and the Russian Museum in Leningrad (called St. Petersburg before 1914 and Petrograd from 1914 to 1924), only the name of the museum is given.

The Catalogue is based on the most exhaustive list of Serov's works, compiled by I. Grabar and N. Vlasov (see Grabar, *Serov*, 1965). The subsections *Exhibitions*, *Reproductions* and *References* have been supplemented with new materials containing relevant information for the period up to and including 1978.

The Catalogue is arranged in chronological order. All works within each year are subdivided into *Paintings* and *Graphic Works* (*Drawings*, *Watercolors*, etc.). In some cases *Paintings* include works done in pastel, gouache or chalk because of their manner of execution. All drawings, unless otherwise specified, are executed on white paper.

The date of the work is given in angle brackets unless its authenticity can be proved by the artist's signature or recorded statement. Signatures and inscriptions are reproduced as given by the artist and if necessary translated into English (in parentheses).

Under *Provenance*, the former owners of the work are listed in succession.

In the case of portraits, brief information about the model is given.

Under *Exhibitions*, one-man shows are listed first and separated by a slash (/) from other exhibitions where Serov's works were displayed. References to exhibition catalogues (which sometimes underwent several editions) are given in parentheses.

The entry "1952 Moscow" refers to the two exhibitions held in the same year to commemorate the 40th anniversary of Serov's death, one in the Central House of Art Workers (24 May to 2 June) and the other in the Central Exhibition Hall of the USSR Union of Artists (6 June to 8 August). The second of these included some works from the Tretyakov Gallery reserve—for further details see the 1953 catalogue compiled by Vlasov.

Under *Reproductions*, references to earlier publications of the work concerned are listed. For well-known and frequently reproduced works, references are made only to popular editions or the ones noted for the high quality of their color reproductions. Page and plate numbers are not given if missing in the edition quoted.

Under *References*, literary sources are cited in an abbreviated form (see p. 380 for full titles).

All dimensions are given in centimeters.

List of Sources
Cited in the Catalogue
in Abbreviated Form

Academy of Arts Museum, 1915
> *The Academy of Arts Museum. Russian Painting. Catalogue*, St. Petersburg, 1915 [*Академия художеств. Музей. Русская живопись. Каталог*, Санкт-Петербург, 1915]

Alexander and Valentin Serov, 1914
> *Alexander and Valentin Serov in the Reminiscences of V. Serova* (with a supplement of selected articles by Alexander Serov), St. Petersburg, 1914 [*Серовы Александр Николаевич и Валентин Александрович. Воспоминания В. С. Серовой,* с приложением избранных статей А. Н. Серова, Санкт-Петербург, 1914]

Annual of the Imperial Theatres, 1910
> *Ежегодник Императорских театров*, 1910

Annual of the Institute of the History of Arts, 1952
> *Annual of the Institute of the History of Arts: 1952 (Painting, Architecture)*, Moscow, 1952 [*Ежегодник Института истории искусства. 1952 (живопись, архитектура)*, Москва, 1952]

Arbuzov, *Gorky and Serov*, 1964
> G. Arbuzov, "Gorky and Serov," in: *Gorky among the Artists: Reminiscences, Correspondence, Essays*, Moscow, 1964 [Г. Арбузов, «Горький и Серов», в сб.: *Горький и художники. Воспоминания, переписка, статьи*, Москва, 1964]

Arbuzov, *Serov*, 1960
> G. Arbuzov, *Serov*, Leningrad—Moscow, 1960 [Г. Арбузов, *Серов*, Ленинград—Москва, 1960]

Art Gallery, Perm, 1976
> *Art Gallery, Perm* (selection and text by V. Kulakov), Moscow, 1976 [*Пермская государственная художественная галерея* (автор-составитель В. Кулаков), Москва, 1976]

Art Museum, Kirov. Catalogue, 1964
> *Art Museum Named after M. Gorky, Kirov. Catalogue*, Leningrad, 1964 [*Кировский областной художественный музей имени А. М. Горького. Каталог*, Ленинград, 1964]

Art Museum of the Azerbaijan SSR. Catalogue, 1971
> *The Mustafayev Art Museum of the Azerbaijan SSR. Catalogue*, Leningrad, 1971 [*Азербайджанский государственный музей искусств имени Р. Мустафаева. Каталог*, Ленинград, 1971]

Art Museum, Omsk, 1980
> *Art Museum, Omsk. Painting* (text by L. Barantseva, selection by A. Gontarenko), Leningrad, 1980 [*Омский музей изобразительных искусств. Живопись* (вступительная статья Л. Баранцевой, составитель А. Гонтаренко), Ленинград, 1980]

Asafyev 1966
> B. Asafyev (Igor Glebov), *Russian Painting: Thoughts and Reflections*, Leningrad—Moscow, 1966 [Б. Асафьев (Игорь Глебов), *Русская живопись. Мысли и думы*, Ленинград—Москва, 1966]

Bakushinsky 1935
> A. Bakushinsky, "V. Serov's Legacy," *Iskusstvo*, 1935, No 4 [А. Бакушинский, «Наследие В. А. Серова», *Искусство*, 1935, № 4]

Benois 1902
> A. Benois, *A History of Russian Painting: 19th Century*, St. Petersburg, 1902 [А. Бенуа, *История русской живописи в XIX веке*, Петербург, 1902]

Bernstein 1940
> M. Bernstein, *Drawing: Teaching Problems*, Leningrad—Moscow, 1940 [М. Бернштейн, *Проблемы учебного рисунка*, Ленинград—Москва, 1940]

Catalogue, 1894
> *Catalogue of the 14th Periodical Exhibition of the Moscow Society of Art Lovers*, Moscow, 1894 [*Иллюстрированный каталог 14-й периодической выставки Московского Общества любителей художеств*, Москва, 1894]

Catalogue, 1917
> *Catalogue of the Works of Art Housed in the Town Gallery of Pavel and Sergei Tretyakov*, 27th ed., Moscow, 1917 [*Каталог художественных произведений городской галереи Павла и Сергея Третьяковых*, изд. 27-е, Москва, 1917]

Children's Leisure, 1899
> *Children's Leisure* (monthly illustrated magazine for children of school age), St. Petersburg, 1899 [*Детский отдых. Ежемесячный иллюстрированный журнал для детей школьного возраста*, Санкт-Петербург, 1899]

Chistiakov, 1953
> *Pavel Chistiakov: Letters, Notebooks, Reminiscences about Chistiakov. 1832—1919* (compiled by E. Beliutin and N. Moleva), Moscow, 1953 [*Павел Чистяков. Письма, записные книжки, воспоминания. 1832—1919* (материалы подготовлены к печати и примечания к ним составлены Э. Белютиным и Н. Молевой), Москва, 1953]

Dintses 1936
> L. Dintses, "Portrait of Maxim Gorky by Valentin Serov," in: *Maxim Gorky. Sources and Studies*, vol. 2, Moscow, 1936 [Л. Динцес, «Портрет М. Горького работы В. Серова», в кн.: *М. Горький. Материалы и исследования*, т. 2, Москва, 1936]

Dmitriyev, *Serov*, 1917
> V. Dmitriyev, *Valentin Serov*, Petrograd, 1917 [В. Дмитриев, *Валентин Серов*, Петроград, 1917]

Drawings and Watercolors. Catalogue, 1956
> *The Tretyakov Gallery. Drawings and Watercolors. Catalogues of the Tretyakov Gallery: V. Polenov, I. Levitan, V. Serov, M. Vrubel* (compiled by I. Razdobreyeva and A. Lesiuk), Moscow, 1956 [*Государственная Третьяковская галерея. Рисунок и акварель. Каталоги собраний Государственной Третьяковской галереи: В. Поленов, И. Левитан, В. Серов, М. Врубель* (составители И. Раздобреева, А. Лесюк), Москва, 1956]

Eisenstein 1964
> S. Eisenstein, *Selected Works in Six Volumes*, vol. 2, Moscow, 1964 [С. Эйзенштейн, *Избранные произведения*, в 6 тт., т 2, Москва, 1964]

Ernst, *Serov*, 1922

S. Ernst, *Valentin Serov*, Petrograd, 1921 [С. Эрнст, *В. А. Серов*, Петроград, 1921]

Essays on the History of Russian Portraiture, 1964

Essays on the History of Russian Portraiture in the Late 19th and Early 20th Centuries (edited by N. Mashkovtsev, Corresponding Member of the USSR Academy of Arts, and N. Sokolova, Corresponding Member of the USSR Academy of Arts), Moscow, 1964 [*Очерки по истории русского портрета конца XIX — начала XX века* (под редакцией члена-корреспондента Академии художеств СССР Н. Машковцева и члена-корреспондента Академии художеств СССР Н. Соколовой), Москва, 1964]

Fifteen Lithographs by Russian Artists, 1900

Fifteen Lithographs by Russian Artists, St. Petersburg, 1900 [*Пятнадцать литографий русских художников*, Санкт-Петербург, 1900]

Fiodorov-Davydov 1960

A. Fiodorov-Davydov, *"Girl in the Sunlight,"* *Khudozhnik*, 1960, No 3 [А. Федоров-Давыдов, *«Девушка, освещенная солнцем»*, *Художник*, 1960, № 3]

Fiodorov-Davydov 1965

A. Fiodorov-Davydov, *"A Master of the Landscape,"* *Khudozhnik*, 1965, Nos 1, 2 [А. Федоров-Давыдов, *«Мастер пейзажа»*, *Художник*, 1965, № 1, 2]

Fokine 1962

M. Fokine, *Against the Current. Reminiscences of a Ballet Master. Essays and Letters*, Leningrad–Moscow, 1962 [М. Фокин, *Против течения. Воспоминания балетмейстера. Статьи, письма*, Ленинград–Москва, 1962]

Golubev 1941

V. Golubev, "The History of a Picture: *9 January* by Valentin Serov," *Iskusstvo i Zhizn*, 1941, No 4 [В. Голубев, *«К истории одной картины»*, *Искусство и жизнь*, 1941, № 4]

Gorin 1958

I. Gorin, *"Phoebus Effulgent*: a Ceiling Painting by Valentin Serov," *Iskusstvo*, 1958, No 3 [И. Горин, *«Плафон В. А. Серова Феб лучезарный»*, *Искусство*, 1958, № 3]

Gorlov 1951

Valentin Serov: Drawings for Krylov's Fables (compiled by D. Gorlov), Moscow–Leningrad, 1951 [*Валентин Александрович Серов. Рисунки к басням И. А. Крылова* (составитель Д. Горлов), Москва–Ленинград, 1951]

Grabar, *Serov*, 1914

I. Grabar, *Valentin Serov: His Life and Work*, Moscow, 1914 [И. Грабарь, *Валентин Александрович Серов. Жизнь и творчество*, Москва, 1914]

Grabar, *Serov*, 1965

I. Grabar, *Valentin Serov: His Life and Work. 1865–1911*, Moscow, 1965 [И. Грабарь, *Валентин Александрович Серов. Жизнь и творчество. 1865–1911*, Москва, 1965]

Grabar, *Serov*, 1980

I. Grabar, *Valentin Serov: His Life and Work. 1865–1911*, 2nd ed., Moscow, 1980 [И. Грабарь, *Валентин Александрович Серов. Жизнь и творчество. 1865–1911*, 2-е изд., Москва, 1980]

Grabar, *Serov the Draftsman*, 1961

I. Grabar, *Serov the Draftsman*, Moscow, 1961 [И. Грабарь, *Серов рисовальщик*, Москва, 1961]

History of Russia

History of Russia: 19th Century, in nine volumes, vol. VI, Moscow, n.d. [*История России в XIX веке*, в 9 тт., т. VI, Москва, б.г.]

History of Russian Art, 1968

History of Russian Art (edited by Academician I. Grabar, V. Lazarev and A. Sidorov, Corresponding Members of the USSR Academy of Arts, and O. Shvidkovsky, Doctor of History), vol. 10, book 1, Moscow, 1968 [*История русского искусства* (под редакцией академика И. Грабаря, члена-корреспондента АН СССР В. Лазарева, члена-корреспондента АН СССР А. Сидорова и доктора исторических наук О. Швидковского), т. 10, кн. 1, Москва, 1968]

Hollerbach, *Serov*, 1924

E. Hollerbach, *Valentin Serov: His Life and Work*, Petrograd, 1924 [Э. Голлербах, *В. Серов. Жизнь и творчество*, Петроград, 1924]

In Aid of the Victims of Crop Failure, 1899

In Aid of the Victims of Crop Failure. A collection of articles published by the newspaper *Courier*, Moscow, 1899 [Сборник «Помощь пострадавшим от неурожая». Издание газеты «Курьер», Москва, 1899]

Kondakov 1911

N. Kondakov, *Iconography of the Virgin*, St. Petersburg, 1911 [Н. Кондаков, *Иконография богоматери*, Петербург, 1911]

Konstantin Korovin, 1963

Konstantin Korovin: His Life and Work. Letters, Documents, Reminiscences (introduction and selection by N. Moleva), Moscow, 1963 [*Константин Коровин. Жизнь и творчество. Письма, документы, воспоминания* (составитель и автор очерка Н. Молева), Москва, 1963]

Kopschitzer, *Mamontov*, 1972

M. Kopschitzer, *Savva Mamontov* (*Life in Art* series), Moscow, 1972 [М. Копшицер, *Савва Мамонтов* (серия «Жизнь в искусстве»), Москва, 1972]

Kopschitzer, *Serov*, 1967

M. Kopschitzer, *Valentin Serov* (*Life in Art* series), Moscow, 1967 [М. Копшицер, *Валентин Серов* (серия «Жизнь в искусстве»), Москва, 1967]

Korovin Recollects, 1971

Konstantin Korovin Recollects (selection, introduction and commentary by I. Silberstein and V. Samkov), Moscow, 1971 [*Константин Коровин вспоминает...* (составители, авторы вступительной статьи и комментариев И. Зильберштейн и В. Самков), Москва, 1971]

Lebedev, *Serov*, 1946

G. Lebedev, *Valentin Serov*, Moscow–Leningrad, 1946 [Г. Лебедев, *Валентин Серов*, Москва–Ленинград, 1946]

Leniashin 1980

V. Leniashin, *Serov's Portraiture of the Early 1900s. Main Problems*, Leningrad, 1980 [В. Леняшин, *Портретная живопись В. А. Серова 1900-х годов. Основные проблемы*, Ленинград, 1980]

Lermontov 1891

Mikhail Lermontov, *Collected Works*, vol. 2, Moscow, 1891 [М. Ю. Лермонтов, *Сочинения*, в 2 тт., т. 2, Москва, 1891]

Lesiuk 1934

A. Lesiuk, "Unrealized Frescoes by Valentin Serov," *Iskusstvo*, 1934, No 4 [А. Лесюк, *«Неосуществленные фрески В. Серова»*, *Искусство*, 1934, № 4]

Leskov 1954

A. Leskov, *The Life of Nikolai Leskov*, Moscow, 1954 [А. Лесков, *Жизнь Николая Лескова*, Москва, 1954]

Liaskovskaya 1965

O. Liaskovskaya, "Portrait Drawings by Valentin Serov," *Iskusstvo*, 1965, No 10 [О. Лясковская, *«Графические портреты Валентина Серова»*, *Искусство*, 1965, № 10]

Lieberfort 1960

I. Lieberfort, *"Portrait of Maria Yermolova* by Valentin Serov," *Khudozhnik*, 1960, No 9 [И. Либерфорт, *«Портрет М. Н. Ермоловой В. Серова»*, *Художник*, 1960, № 9]

Lvov 1895

E. Lvov, *A Voyage to the North... With 30 Drawings from Nature Executed by the Artists K. Korovin and V. Serov*, Moscow, 1895 [Е. Львов, *По студеному морю. Поездка на Север... С тридцатью рисунками с натуры, исполненными художниками К. А. Коровиным и В. А. Серовым*, Москва, 1895]

Mamontov 1911

S. Mamontov, "Valentin Serov. A Character Sketch," *Put*, 1911, December, No 2 [С. Мамонтов, *«В. А. Серов. Опыт характеристики»*, *Путь*, 1911, декабрь, № 2]

Muratov 1914
P. Muratov, "Serov," *Sophia*, 1914, No 3 [П. Муратов, «Серов», *София*, 1914, № 3]

Nechayeva 1957
S. Nechayeva, "The Second Birth of a Wonderful Painting (On Serov's Panel *Phoebus Effulgent*)," *Literaturnaya Tula*, book 13, 1957 [С. Нечаева, «Второе рождение замечательной картины (о панно В. А. Серова *Феб лучезарный*)», *Литературная Тула*, кн. 13, 1957]

Nikulina 1972
N. Nikulina, "The Theme of Antiquity in the Work of Serov: *Odysseus and Nausicaä*," in: *Antiquity and Modern Times*, Moscow, 1972 [Н. Никулина, «Тема античности в творчестве В. А. Серова: *Одиссей и Навзикая*», в сб.: *Античность и современность*, Москва, 1972]

Off. Cat. Sec., 1899
Offizieller Katalog der Internationalen Kunstausstellung des Vereins bildender Künstler „Münchener Sezession", 1899, im Kgl. Kunstausstellungsgebäude am Königsplatz gegenüber der Glyptothek, 1. Auflage, ausgegeben am 3. Juni 1899, Münchener Verlagsanstalt F. Bruchmann

Pictorial History of Russia, 1908
A Pictorial History of Russia, edited by S. Kniazkov, Moscow, 1908 [*Картины по русской истории*, под редакцией С. Князькова, Москва, 1908]

Pictures of Russian Nature and Daily Life, 1898
Pictures of Russian Nature and Daily Life, Moscow, 1898 [*Картины из русской природы и быта*, Москва, 1898]

Pushkin 1899
Alexander Pushkin, *Collected Works in Three Volumes*, Moscow, 1899 [А. С. Пушкин, *Сочинения*, в 3 тт., Москва, 1899]

Pushkin and His Time, 1962
G. Arbuzov, "Serov's Drawing for Pushkin's *Tale of the She-Bear*," in: *Pushkin and His Time*, issue 1, Leningrad, 1962 [Г. Арбузов, «Рисунок В. А. Серова к *Сказке о медведихе* А. С. Пушкина», в сб.: *Пушкин и его время*, вып. 1, Ленинград, 1962]

Radlov, Serov, 1914
Serov (essay by N. Radlov), St. Petersburg, 1914 [*Серов* (очерк Н. Радлова), Санкт-Петербург, 1914]

Radzimovskaya 1956
N. Radzimovskaya, "Valentin Serov. *Portrait of Maria Yermolova*," in: *The Tretyakov Gallery. Sources and Studies*, vol. 1, Moscow, 1956 [Н. Радзимовская, «В. А. Серов. *Портрет М. Н. Ермоловой*», в кн.: *Государственная Третьяковская галерея. Материалы и исследования*, т. 1, Москва, 1956]

Radzimovskaya 1962
N. Radzimovskaya, "On the History of the *Portrait of Maxim Gorky* by Valentin Serov," in: *The Tretyakov Gallery. Essays on Russian and Soviet Art*, Leningrad, 1962 [Н. Радзимовская, «К истории создания В. Серовым портрета А. М. Горького», в сб.: *Государственная Третьяковская галерея. Очерки по русскому и советскому искусству*, Ленинград, 1962]

Royal Hunting in Russia, 1902
Royal Hunting in Russia. A Historical Essay by N. Kutepov, vol. 3: *Late 17th and 18th Centuries*, Petersburg, 1902 [*Царская и императорская охота на Руси. Исторический очерк Н. Кутепова*, том 3: *Конец XVII и XVIII век*, Петербург, 1902]

Russian Prints, 1967
The Russian Museum, Leningrad. Russian Prints of the Late 19th and Early 20th Centuries. Exhibition Catalogue (by S. Sherman and E. Kovtun), Leningrad, 1967 [*Государственный Русский музей, Ленинград. Русский эстамп конца XIX — начала XX века. Каталог выставки* (составители С. Шерман и Е. Ковтун), Ленинград, 1967]

Sakharova, Polenov, 1950
E. Sakharova, *Vasily Dmitriyevich Polenov. Letters, Diaries and Reminiscences* (edited and introduced by A. Leonov), 2nd ed., Moscow–Leningrad, 1950 [Е. Сахарова, *Василий Дмитриевич Поленов. Письма, дневники, воспоминания* (общая редакция и вступительная статья А. Леонова), 2-е изд., Москва–Ленинград, 1950]

Sarabyanov, Serov, 1974
Valentin Serov. 1865–1911 (introduction and selection by D. Sarabyanov), Moscow, 1974 [*Валентин Александрович Серов. 1865–1911* (автор текста и составитель альбома Д. Сарабьянов), Москва, 1974]

Sarabyanov, Reforms by Valentin Serov, 1971
D. Sarabyanov, *Russian Painting of the Late 1900s and Early 1910s. Essays*, Moscow, 1971 [Д. Сарабьянов, *Русская живопись конца 1900-х — начала 1910-х годов. Очерки*, Москва, 1971]

Serova 1968
V. Serova, *How My Son Grew Up* (selected and edited by I. Silberstein), Leningrad, 1968 [В. Серова, *Как рос мой сын* (составитель и научный редактор И. Зильберштейн), Ленинград, 1968]

Serov: Drawings, Watercolors, Lithographs, 1972
Valentin Serov: Drawings, Watercolors, Lithographs. 14 Facsimile Reproductions (introduced by D. Shmarinov, selected and designed by M. Flekel), Leningrad, 1972 [*Валентин Серов. Рисунки, акварели, литографии. 14 факсимильных репродукций* (вступительная статья Д. Шмаринова; составитель М. Флекель), Ленинград, 1972]

Serov in the Reminiscences of His Contemporaries, 1971
Valentin Serov in the Reminiscences of His Contemporaries, 2 vols. (selected and edited by I. Silberstein and V. Samkov), Leningrad, 1971 [*Валентин Серов в воспоминаниях, дневниках и переписке современников*, т. 1–2 (редакторы-составители, авторы вступительной статьи, очерков о мемуаристах и комментариев И. Зильберштейн и В. Самков), Ленинград, 1971]

Serov: Portrait Painting, 1968
Valentin Serov: Portrait Painting (introduction and selection by G. Arbuzov), Leningrad, 1968 [*Валентин Серов. Портретная живопись* (составитель и автор статьи Г. Арбузов), Ленинград, 1968]

Serov: The Sun of Russia, 1913
The Sun of Russia (supplement to the 2nd edition of the *Solntse Rossii* magazine), St. Petersburg, 1913 [В. А. Серов, *Альбом «Солнце России»* (бесплатное приложение ко 2-му изданию журнала «Солнце России», Санкт-Петербург, 1913)]

Serov's Correspondence, 1937
Valentin Serov. Correspondence. 1884–1911 (introduction and notes by Natalia Sokolova), Leningrad–Moscow, 1937 [*В. Серов. Переписка. 1884–1911* (вступительная статья и примечания Наталии Соколовой), Ленинград– Москва, 1937]

Serov's Works in the Odessa Art Gallery
Serov's Works in the Odessa Art Gallery, Odessa, s.a. [*Произведения В. А. Серова в Одесской государственной картинной галерее*, Одесса, б.г.]

Serov's Works. The Russian Museum. Catalogue, 1935
The Russian Museum of Painting, Sculpture, Graphics and Drawing. Exhibition of Serov's Works. Catalogue. Introduction by L. Dintses, 2nd ed., Leningrad, 1935 [*Государственный Русский музей живописи, скульптуры, графики и рисунка. Выставка произведений В. Серова. Каталог. Автор вступительной статьи Л. Динцес*, 2-е изд., Ленинград, 1935]

Serov's Works. The Tretyakov Gallery. Catalogue, 1935
Exhibition of Serov's Works (Moscow, The Tretyakov Gallery). Catalogue, Moscow, 1935 [*Выставка произведений В. Серова. Каталог (Москва, Государственная Третьяковская галерея)*, Москва, 1935]

Simonovich-Yefimova 1964
N. Simonovich-Yefimova, *Reminiscences of Valentin Serov* (edited and commented by G. Arbuzov), Leningrad, 1964 [Н. Симонович-Ефимова, *Воспоминания о Валентине Александровиче Серове* (общая редакция Г. Арбузова), Ленинград, 1964]

Sokolova, *Serov*, 1935
N. Sokolova, *Valentin Serov*, Leningrad, 1935 [Н. Соколова, *В. А. Серов*, Ленинград, 1935]

Sokolova, Vlasov 1959
Valentin Serov (selection and introduction by N. Sokolova and N. Vlasov), Moscow, 1959 [*Валентин Александрович Серов* (авторы-составители Н. Соколова и Н. Власов), Москва, 1959]

Sternin, *Graphic Works by Serov*, 1965
Graphic Works by Valentin Serov: Drawings, Watercolors, Lithographs, and Etchings (selection and text by G. Sternin), Moscow, 1965 [*Графика Валентина Александровича Серова. Рисунки, акварели, литографии, офорты* (автор текста и составитель Г. Стернин), Москва, 1965]

Svetlov 1911
V. Svetlov, *Modern Ballet*, St. Petersburg, 1911 [В. Светлов, *Современный балет*, Санкт-Петербург, 1911]

The 1905 Revolution, 1956
The 1905 Revolution and Russian Literature, Moscow–Leningrad, 1956 [*Революция 1905 года и русская литература*, Москва–Ленинград, 1956]

Theatrical Portraiture, 1973
Theatrical Portraiture of the Late 19th and Early 20th Centuries (selection and introduction by E. Pankratova), Leningrad, 1973 [*Театральный портрет конца XIX—начала XX века* (автор-составитель Е. Панкратова), Ленинград, 1973]

Tretyakov Gallery: Sculptures. Catalogue, 1977
The Tretyakov Gallery. Sculptures and Sculptors' Drawings. Late 19th—Early 20th Centuries. Catalogue, Moscow, 1977 [*Государственная Третьяковская галерея. Скульптура и рисунки скульпторов конца XIX—начала XX века. Каталог*, Москва, 1977]

Works by Serov in the Russian Museum, 1970
Works by Valentin Serov in the Russian Museum Collection, Leningrad, 1970 [*Валентин Серов. Из собрания Русского музея*, Ленинград, 1970]

Yaremich, *Serov: Drawings*, 1936
Serov: Drawings (essay by S. Yaremich), Leningrad, 1936 [*Серов. Рисунки* (очерк С. Яремича), Ленинград, 1936]

Zhivova 1961
O. Zhivova, "Lesser Known Works by V. Serov," *Khudozhnik*, 1961, No 6 [О. Живова, «Малоизвестные работы В. Серова», *Художник*, 1961, № 6]

Zotov, *Serov*, 1964
Valentin Serov (introductory article by A. Zotov), Moscow, 1964 [*Валентин Александрович Серов* (вступительная статья А. Зотова), Москва, 1964]

Index of Works Reproduced

Numbers in italics refer to plates, while other numbers
indicate black-and-white illustrations in the Catalogue.

Index of Museums

All references are to Catalogue numbers. Figures in italics indicate that the work can be found in the plate section.

Abramtsevo Museum, Moscow region 13, 89

All-Union Pushkin Memorial Museum (the), Leningrad *343, 344*; 342

Art Gallery, Vladivostok 546

Art Museum, Ashkhabad 223

Art Museum, Dnepropetrovsk *583*

Art Museum, Gorky *454, 630*; 404, 545

Art Museum, Ivanovo *197*; 263

Art Museum, Kharkov 166

Art Museum, Kirov 391

Art Museum, Kuibyshev *99*; 234

Art Museum, Malmö (Sweden) 136

Art Museum, Minsk *97, 282, 556*; 199

Art Museum, Riazan 432

Art Museum, Sumy 80

Art Museum, Tbilisi 588

Art Museum, Tula 82

Art Museum, Ulyanovsk 190

Art Museum, Yaroslavl 174

Brodsky Memorial Museum (the), Leningrad *380, 450*; 167, 210

History Museum, Moscow *198, 494*; 214, 227, 337

Maxim Gorky Memorial Museum (the), Moscow *467*

Museum of Art and Architecture, Smolensk 315, 552

Museum of History and Architecture, Novgorod *69*; 147

Museum of Russian Art, Kiev 155, 496

Nesterov Art Museum (the), Ufa *477*; 170

Penates: The Repin Memorial Museum (the), Leningrad region 102

Picture Gallery, Kazan *149*

Picture Gallery, Odessa *122, 394*; 532, 576

Picture Gallery of the Museum of Local Lore, Tomsk 508

Picture Gallery, Sverdlovsk 185

Picture Gallery, Taganrog 495

Picture Gallery, Tiumen 134

Picture Gallery, Yerevan *393, 487, 534, 570*; 169, 491

Pushkin Museum of Fine Arts: Print Room (the), Moscow *57, 522*

Radishchev Art Museum (the), Saratov 392

Russian Museum (the), Leningrad *62, 123, 137, 142, 266, 270, 274, 280, 312, 325, 331, 338, 339, 340, 347, 348, 368, 379, 382, 397, 398, 400, 402, 403, 416, 418, 420, 423, 424, 425, 442, 461, 462, 469, 473, 480, 481, 483, 492, 493, 501, 510, 514, 547, 550, 563, 567, 574, 575, 582, 599, 615, 616, 618, 632, 636, 637, 640, 641, 646, 655, 657, 666, 675*; 2, 3, 6, 8, 19, 35, 36, 38, 47, 54, 55, 63, 64, 106, 131, 144, 163, 194, 240, 271, 279, 297,*

299, 303, 306, 307, 327, 349, 410, 413, 414, 417, 455, 457, 458, 471, 483, 511, 513, 515, 516, 525, 526, 527, 530, 531, 538, 565, 566, 568, 569, 571, 609, 614, 634, 635, 660, 662, 664, 670

Savitsky Picture Gallery (the), Penza 253

State Museum of Literature, Moscow *520*

Theatrical Museum, Leningrad *605*

Tolstoy Memorial Museum (the), Yasnaya Poliana 200

Tretyakov Gallery (the), Moscow *45, 56, 71, 73, 77, 81, 91, 96, 100, 103, 111, 116, 118, 128, 132, 133, 146, 168, 186, 187, 225, 229, 230, 239, 241, 247, 260, 267, 268, 281, 296, 301, 305, 310, 317, 324, 377, 383, 384, 396, 405, 406, 407, 408, 422, 446, 448, 453, 463, 465, 466, 472, 476, 482, 485, 488, 489, 506, 509, 518, 519, 523, 535, 539, 540, 541, 542, 558, 559, 573, 578, 581, 600, 629, 644, 647, 650, 654, 658, 659, 661, 663, 667, 668, 669, 672, 674*; 15, 17, 18, 20, 34, 40, 43, 56, 60, 105, 108, 129, 135, 188, 189, 193, 195, 201, 202, 206, 243, 252, 287, 294, 328, 329, 330, 345, 360, 378, 389, 411, 415, 433, 449, 474, 479, 485, 488, 490 (reverse), 504, 536, 537, 554, 604, 607, 608, 622, 625, 643 (reverse), 648, 651, 652, 656, 665, 671, 673

USSR Museum of the Revolution (the), Moscow *468, 486*

ВАЛЕНТИН СЕРОВ

Альбом (на английском языке)

Издательство ,,Аврора". Ленинград. 1982
Изд. № 25
Printed and bound in Austria by Globus, Vienna